Cambridge Imperial

General Editor: **Megan Vaughan**, Kings' College, Cambridge, and **Richard Drayton**, Corpus Christi College, Cambridge

This informative series covers the broad span of modern imperial history while also exploring the recent developments in former colonial states where residues of empire can still be found. The books provide in-depth examinations of empires as competing and complementary power structures encouraging the

ONE WEEK LOAN

Gerold Krozewski
MONEY AND THE END OF EMPIRE
British International Economic Policy and the Colonies, 1947–58

D1342269

Javed Majeed
AUTOBIOGRAPHY, TRAVEL AND POST-NATIONAL IDENTITY

Ged Martin
BRITAIN AND THE ORIGINS OF CANADIAN CONFEDERATION, 1837–67

W. David McIntyre
BACKGROUND TO THE ANZUS PACT
Policy-Makers, Strategy and Diplomacy, 1945–55

Francine McKenzie
REDEFINING THE BONDS OF COMMONWEALTH 1930–1948
The Politics of Preference

John Singleton and Paul Robertson
ECONOMIC RELATIONS BETWEEN BRITAIN AND AUSTRALASIA 1945–1970

Cambridge Imperial and Post-Colonial Studies Series
Series Standing Order ISBN 0-333-91908-4
(outside North America only)

You can receive future titles in this series as they are published by placing a standing order. Please contact your bookseller or, in case of difficulty, write to us at the address below with your name and address, the title of the series and the ISBN quoted above.

Customer Services Department, Macmillan Distribution Ltd, Houndmills, Basingstoke, Hampshire RG21 6XS, England

Orientalism and Race

Aryanism in the British Empire

Tony Ballantyne
Lecturer in History
University of Otago
Dunedin
New Zealand

First published in hardback 2002

First published in paperback 2006 by
PALGRAVE MACMILLAN
Houndmills, Basingstoke, Hampshire RG21 6XS and
175 Fifth Avenue, New York, N.Y. 10010
Companies and representatives throughout the world

PALGRAVE MACMILLAN is the global academic imprint of the Palgrave
Macmillan divison of St. Martin's Press, LLC and of Palgrave Macmillan Ltd.
Macmillan® is a registered trademark in the United States, United
Kingdom and other countries. Palgrave is a registered trademark in the
European Union and other countries

ISBN-13: 978–0–333–96360–9 hardback
ISBN-10: 0–333–96360–1   hardback
ISBN-13: 978–0–230–50703–6 paperback
ISBN-10: 0–230–50703–4   paperback

This book is printed on paper suitable for recycling and
made from fully managed and sustained forest sources.

A catalogue record for this book is available from the British Library.

Library of Congress Cataloging-in-Publication Data
Ballantyne, Tony, 1972–
    Orientalism and race: Aryanism in the British empire/Tony Ballantyne.
      p.cm. – (Cambridge colonial and postcolonial studies)
    Includes bibliographical references and index.
    ISBN 0–333–96360–1 (cloth) 0–230–50703–4 (pbk)
      1. Great Britain–Colonies–Race relations. 2. Racism–Great Britain–Colonies.
3. Orientalism. 4. Imperialism. 5. Aryans. 6. Race. I. Title. II. Series.

DA16 .B25 2001
305.8'009171'241–dc21

                                                               2001036893

10 9 8 7 6 5 4 3 2 1
15 14 13 12 11 10 09 08 07 06

Printed and bound in Great Britain by
Antony Rowe Ltd, Chippenham and Eastbourne

Contents

Acknowledgements ix

Map xi

Introduction: Aryanism and the Webs of Empire 1

1 The Emergence of Aryanism: Company Orientalism,
  Colonial Governance and Imperial Ethnology 18
  Trade to dominion: the birth of Company Orientalism 20
  Language and colonial power 22
  Patronage and the institutional basis of colonial knowledge 23
  Sir William Jones, Sanskrit and human origins 26
  Language and cultural comparison 27
  Colebrook and the Vedic golden age 30
  The impact of Sanskritocentrism 32
  Indocentrism: the Scottish Enlightenment in 'Further India' 33
  Orientalism, the Irish Enlightenment and settler
  self-fashioning 35
  Prichardian ethnology and the Anglo-Saxon revival 38
  Max Müller and the Aryan theory 41
  Aryans, India and 1857 44
  Aryanism as an ethnological tool 48
  Regional variation and the limits of racialization: Punjab 52
  Conclusion 54

2 Indocentrism on the New Zealand Frontier: Geographies
  of Race, Empire and Nation 56
  Pacific exploration and the question of origins 57
  The Semitic Maori? 58
  Richard Taylor and the emergence of Indocentrism 62
  Indocentrism consolidated: Edward Shortland 66
  Colonial science and philology 68
  J. T. Thomson and the 'Barata' race 70
  Tregear and the Aryan Maori 74
  Conflict, consensus and synthesis: Indocentrism
  1885–c.1930 77

The death of Indocentrism: racial origins and the rise of
   nationalism   79
   Conclusion   81

3 Systematizing Religion: from Tahiti to the Tat Khalsa   83
   'Religion'   85
   Presence and absence: Tahiti and New Zealand   87
   A discourse of negation: the search for Maori religion   89
   Missionary ethnography   90
   Affirmation: religion in India   94
   The structure of Brahmanical Hinduism: *vaidik* and *laukik*   95
   Evangelical critiques of Hinduism   97
   The 'jungle': Hinduism and ethnography   99
   Sikhism: Nanak and the Indian 'Reformation'   102
   Dissenting voices: Evangelical attacks on Sikhism   106
   Macauliffe: the dialogics of Orientalism   109
   Military recruitment and preserving Sikh identity   111
   Conclusion   116

4 'Hello Ganesha!': Indocentrism and the Interpretation of
   Maori Religion   118
   Material transformations and textualizing traditions   119
   Fixing 'tradition'   122
   Maui, evolution and comparative religion   124
   Colonial comparative mythology   127
   Hindu-centrism: Indian gods in the Pacific   129
   Religion and the crisis of imperial authority   132
   Maori phallic cults   134
   Tapu, rank and caste   138
   Religion and rationality: the Tohunga Suppression Act   142
   Conclusion   144

5 Print, Literacy and the Recasting of Maori Identities   146
   Historiographical models   147
   Pre-colonial social structure and identity   149
   Explorers and missionaries: a fatal impact?   150
   The coming of print and Christianity   152
   Literacy and social change: newspapers   154
   Literacy: a social revolution?   156
   The Bible and recasting Maori identity: Maori sectarianism   158

Christianity and unity: Kingitanga and its critics 161
Israelites not Aryans: the discourse of origins 164
Conclusion 167

6 The Politics of Language, Nation and Race: Hindu
Identities in the Late Nineteenth Century 169
Sources: 'Arya' and the Vedas 170
Arya, religion and race 172
Dayananda Sarasvati and the Arya Samaj 176
Tilak and the rewriting of the history of civilization 179
'Arya', anti-colonialism and Hindu nationalism 181
Conclusion: Arya and the definition of Hindu identity 185

Conclusion: Knowledge, Empire, Globalization 188

Notes 197

Bibliography 235

Index 256

Acknowledgements

This book, a study of the complex movements of people, ideas and identities within the British empire, has its own transnational history. Conceived in New Zealand, based on British, Indian and Australasian archival material, drafted in Cambridge and Galway, and finally reworked in Illinois, this project has been enabled by the generosity of many institutions, individuals and audiences and it is with gratitude that I acknowledge the assistance of the following.

At a personal level, I would like to thank the following for their support: my parents Joy and Garth (of course!), the Colemans, the Bells, Melissa Bell and Nigel Pacey (and now Jack), Sue and Alan Henderson, Jennie Henderson, Karen Greig, the 'Upper Hutt Hendersons', Shaun Ryan, Bryan Dunne, Rumi and Ruma Masih, Charles Schnecking and Zara Lasater, Anne and Matthew (and now Caroline) Coffey.

Historians are limited by their sources and I would to thank the staff at the following institutions for helping me to minimize my limitations: the University Library; the Royal Commonwealth Society; the Oriental Studies Library and the Cambridge South Asian Studies Centre and Archive (all in Cambridge); the Public Record Office, the British Library and the Oriental and India Office Library (London); the National Library of Scotland (Edinburgh); the National University of Ireland, Galway (especially Geraldine and the staff at inter-library loans); the Nehru Memorial Library (Delhi); the National Library (especially the Manuscripts staff) and National Archives of New Zealand (Wellington); the University of Otago Library and Dunedin Public Library. Great thanks are due to the staff of the Hocken Library and Archives in Dunedin, which I will always think of as my research 'home'. The late David McDonald, an exemplar of embodied knowledge, was an invaluable guide to the margins of the Hocken's riches: his recent death is keenly felt. My use of these archives and libraries was made possible by funding from: The New Zealand Vice Chancellor's Committee; The Cambridge Commonwealth Trust; The Smuts Memorial Fund; Wolfson College, Cambridge; and the National University of Ireland, Galway.

The arguments developed in this work have been presented in a variety of forums and I am thankful to conference and seminar audiences in Edinburgh, London, Cambridge, Dunedin, Galway, Cork, Binghamton and Urbana-Champaign. As the project neared completion in Urbana-Champaign, the thoughtful readings offered by colleagues in the History Workshop and the Socio-cultural Anthropology Seminar, in addition to my students in History 492, were greatly appreciated. I would also like to extend my sincerest thanks to the following who read or responded to various chapters, fragments, drafts and revisions: Rifa'at Abou-El-Haj, Nicholas Canny, Steve Ellis, Tagh Foley, Tim Harper, Riho Isaka, P.J. Marshall, Terry McDonough, Niall Ó Ciosáin, Andy Orta, Gearóid Ó Tuathaigh, Lachy Paterson, Norbert Peabody, Michael Reilly, Jane Samson, Anil Sethi, Pritam Singh, Robert Travers and Carey Watt.

Special acknowledgement is to due to colleagues and friends who have profoundly imprinted this work. Hew McLeod has encouraged my explorations of South Asian history and especially the history of Sikhism. My interests in colonial Christianity and the encounter between science and religion continue to be energized by my friendship with John Stenhouse. Brian Moloughney encouraged me to envisage this project as a piece of global history, while in his work and in conversation Erik Olssen has reminded me of the broader contexts of New Zealand's history. I have been fortunate to pursue that global dimension of New Zealand past and present (and much more besides) in conversation with Craig Robertson, who is a welcome slice of South Dunedin in Urbana. I am grateful for Tony Hopkins' insistence that studies of representations must be embedded in material contexts and his encouragement to explore the intersections between imperialism and globalization. I was extremely fortunate to have William O'Reilly as a friend and colleague in Galway and he explained much to me about Ireland, Celticism and the Atlantic world. In the final stages of the project, frequent conversations with Clare Crowston not only assisted me in sharpening many of my arguments, but also reminded me of the importance of the eighteenth century. Antoinette Burton's work has become indispensable for our approaches to the pasts (and presents) of empire and I am truly spoilt to have her as a senior colleague.

I am indebted to Chris Bayly who was willing to accept a student with a PhD proposal that was rather strange, especially by Cambridge standards. His enthusiastic engagement with this project and his unflagging encouragement are, like his own work, invaluable.

My greatest debt is to Sally Henderson. In so many ways, this volume bears the imprint of our ongoing discussions about language, migration, colonialism and New Zealand history. I am extremely grateful for all her thoughtfulness, support and encouragement. Our shared journey from south Dunedin to the Midwest, via many points in between, has greatly enriched the life of this Cavy boy. This book is for her.

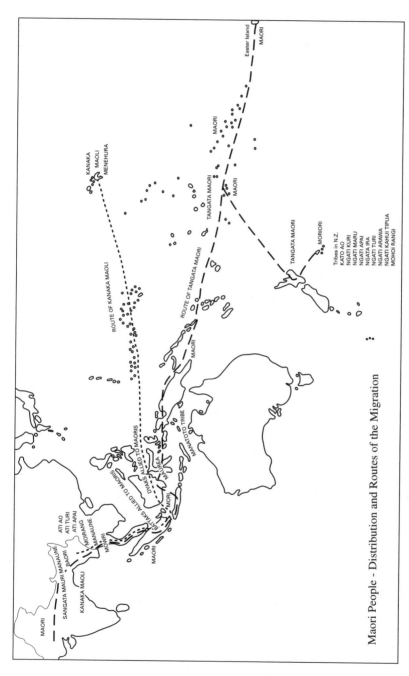

The migration of Maori from their South Asian 'homeland'. From Alfred Kingcombe Newman, *Who are the Maoris?* (n.d. [c. 1912])

Introduction: Aryanism and the Webs of Empire

Concepts like 'nation,' 'society,' and 'culture' name bits and threaten to turn names into things. Only by understanding these names as bundles of relationships, and by placing them back into the fields from which they were abstracted, can we hope to avoid misleading inferences and increase our share of understanding.[1]

Eric Wolf

Eric Wolf's insistence that historical writing should unravel the 'bundles of relationships' that constituted the past underpins this study of the complex networks that constituted the British empire. Wolf's quotation continues to resonate today as, despite increasing calls for transnational and global histories, most historical writing continues to treat nations, cultures and societies as abstract and bounded entities. Despite the work of historians on long distance trade, the integration of Eurasia (or in Marshall Hodgson's formulation Afro-Eurasia), and capitalism over the *longue durée*, most history continues to be organized on the basis of a fixed geographical referent generally congruent with a modern nation-state.[2] This study moves away from a narrow focus on one nation or civilization, instead conceiving of the British empire as a 'bundle of relationships' that brought disparate regions, communities and individuals into contact through systems of mobility and exchange. It does not dispense with the nation-state altogether, for India, New Zealand and the United Kingdom remain prominent throughout, but rather re-imagines these nations as dynamic and diverse communities constantly being remade by the migration, trade and international conflict born out of British imperialism.

1

Such an approach sets this study at odds with the established traditions of colonial history, where most historians continue to write within firmly established traditions of national, and frequently nationalistic, history. Colonial histories are often stories of the nation, as they trace the long journey from the onset of colonialism through to independence. The Bicentenary (1988) and Mabo decision (1991) have served to foreground the nation in Australian historiography while, across the Tasman, New Zealand historians have fashioned a national history that traces and legitimates the emergence of biculturalism as the foundation of government policy and national identity. South Asian historiography, more voluminous and theoretically sophisticated than its Australasian counterparts, has also exhibited a stubborn preoccupation with the nation. Even the Subaltern Studies project, which is grounded in a critique of nationalism and the power of national elites, has tended to focus on the nation or nationalism, at the expense of developments before the nineteenth century and the history of other cultural or economic spaces, such as the Islamic world or the Indian Ocean.

If nation-focused colonial histories efface the porous nature of national boundaries and erase the complex global and regional currents that shape national development, older traditions of metropolitan-focused imperial history are similarly limited. Viewing the empire and its history from London not only returns indigenous people to the margins of history while foregrounding 'gentlemanly capitalists' or Madeira merchants who saw themselves as 'Citizens of all the World', but it also identifies Britain, England or London as the nexus of empire from where capital, power and ideas flowed out to the colonies in the periphery.[3] This approach has recently been challenged by the work of historians of migration, travel and popular culture who have insisted on the manifold ways in which the experience of empire actually constituted metropolitan culture, undercutting a simple opposition between metropolitan and colonial culture.[4] Yet, in many ways, such projects have merely reinstantiated the nation as the seemingly natural unit of historical analysis, reinforcing what Kaviraj has termed the 'narrative contract' between history and the nation-state.[5] With the 'New British history' (which has returned Scotland, Wales and Ireland to a prominent place in the 'national' history), 'Britishness' itself now promises to engulf the whole empire. In Pocock's formulation, it is an analytical framework that is applicable to an 'Atlantic archipelago' that encompasses the United Kingdom, Ireland and 'British' North America, but also reaches out to the distant Australasian colonies as well.[6] While it is important to acknowledge the cultural, institutional and linguistic continuities that tied the colonies to the United Kingdom, fundamental differences in the demographic, economic and ecological frameworks of the 'new' societies prevented the simple re-creation of models inherited from Britain. The use of 'Britishness' as an analytical apparatus not only marks a return to C. W. Dilke's celebration of Britishness and empire, but also is an impoverished and reductive model for the history of multi-ethnic and polyglot colonial societies far removed from the United Kingdom.[7]

This opposition between nation-based colonial histories and metropolitan-focused imperial history has been consolidated by the recent five-volume *Oxford History of the British Empire*. Although each volume contains some valuable thematic essays, a basic division between views from the metropole and essays on specific colonies remains their main feature. While this editorial strategy, of course, merely reflects prevailing historical practice, it further legitimates the division between imperial and colonial history. This division of academic labour has been pernicious, as it has disassembled the empire into a series of discrete components, rather than conceiving of the empire as the product of the 'bundles of relationships' that Wolf identifies as being at the heart of history.

Thus, this study rejects both the metropolitan-focused project of imperial history and the tradition of colonial history that accepts the bounded and self-sufficient nation-state as its analytical frame. Instead, I attempt to foreground the relational quality of the imperial past, emphasizing the complex and shifting relationships that constituted the empire. To this end, I have adopted a mobile approach, an analysis that is not firmly rooted in one space, but rather travels between locations to take stock of the constant traffic of people, ideas and material goods. By focusing on imperial networks and patterns of cultural exchange, this volume traces both the integrative power of the empire (as it drew previously disparate communities into systems of exchange) and the indigenizing forces that worked to adapt introduced commodities, technology and ideas to local imperatives, even within the constraints of the unequal power-relations of colonialism.

This approach allows me to trace the path of one idea (in all its multiple reconfigurations), the belief that certain peoples could be understood as 'Aryan', through the archives of British imperialism. Aryanism became a crucial element within the culture of empire, providing a powerful lens for analysing the pre-colonial past of colonized societies and for the interpretation of the imperial present. At a fundamental level, the idea came to explain the very fact of empire itself. The empire could be divided into vigorous Aryans (most notably the 'energetic' British colonizers themselves), degenerate Aryan communities whose cultural vitality had been enervated by intermarriage, and backward non-Aryan peoples whose cultures might be 'leavened' through contact with Aryan rulers.[8] Within India, various commentators, not only Britons but also South Asians with a stake in the maintenance of British authority, used the Aryan theory to reconfigure British imperialism from being a series of fundamentally unequal political, social and economic relationships into a 'family reunion' between long lost Aryan cousins.

These arguments that embraced Aryanism to render colonialism anodyne, even benevolent, remind us that ideas and representations cannot be understood as autonomous constructs that are somehow free from power-relationships. In this sense, what follows is not conceived as a contribution to the 'history of ideas' – a field that struggles to break out of its narrow focus on European elites – rather it is a history of the cultural and intellectual transformations enacted by colonialism both in the colonies and in Europe itself. Historians continue to present the rise of comparative philology, the emergence of racial thought or changing theories of religion as products of the salons and studies of Europe, tracing a lineage of linguists from Locke to Saussure, narrating the rise of race from Blumenbach through to Darwin and beyond, or charting the emergence of religion as a universal analytical category from Hume to Durkheim. This study challenges the privileged place of 'Europe', at least a Europe insulated from the effects of imperialism, in shaping conceptions of race, religion and language. I locate shifting understandings of these categories within what we might term the disruptive power of empire, as the cross-cultural engagements set in train by imperialism called European beliefs and practices into question. It was the increasingly frequent encounters with societies which challenged European 'norms' that made the theoretization of race, language and religion so urgent and invested the comparative visions of the Enlightenment with cultural authority. Moreover, by insisting that 'race' or 'religion' were not simply the product of metropolitan intellectual labour, this study takes the work of British settlers, colonial administrators, indigenous leaders and intellectuals seriously. Just as we are beginning to appreciate that frontiers were contact zones where new identities and social formations were fashioned out of the unequal colonial encounters, they were also productive spaces of intellectual engagement and innovation.[9]

Aryanism and empire

Indeed, the popularity of the Aryan idea in the British empire in the long nineteenth century (not to mention twentieth-century Europe), was a product of the cultural authority of the Orientalist learning produced by the agents of the East India Company in India itself. The new ethnological and historical models arising out of Aryanism were underpinned by the ability of British scholar-administrators to access Sanskritic tradition. After all, the concept of an Aryan people, so prominent in nineteenth- and twentieth-century European nationalisms, was not European; rather it was deeply embedded in Vedic tradition. The *Rig Veda*, composed around 1500 BCE, recorded the incursion of tribes of pastoralists who identified themselves as 'Arya' (lit. noble) into India. As these settlers from Central Asia encountered the indigenous populations of north India and developed new polities and religious traditions, 'Arya' continued to function both as a marker of community and as an evaluation of cultural sophistication.

Despite the continued cultural weight of this concept within Sanskritic tradition, it remained beyond the reach of Europeans until the East India Company consolidated its position as a territorial power in South Asia. Until the 1780s, Europeans viewed Sanskrit as an enigma; the central oral and textual traditions of Brahmanical Hinduism were unattainable and leading European Orientalists doubted whether the British would ever decipher Sanskrit. But, as we shall see, the deep-seated social and cultural changes accompanying the Company's rise as a territorial power (from 1765) enabled a new generation of Company employees to learn Sanskrit and to access Brahmanical tradition. The fundamental reconfiguration of indigenous knowledge production in the wake of the Bengal famine of 1770, as well as the emergence of the East India Company as a powerful new patron of 'native learning', facilitated the work of Sir William Jones and his contemporaries. Their steady flow of dictionaries, vernacular texts and translations into a variety of European languages not only provided the linguistic apparatus that underpinned the operation of the colonial state, but also effectively textualized core Brahmanical traditions relating to history, law and religious practice. Drawing on the fruits of this process, together with his own extensive linguistic repertoire, Jones confirmed the genetic relationship between Greek, Latin and Sanskrit and mapped a new comparative vision of global history, an interpretation that insisted on the commonalities between Europe and Indian history.

In effect, Jones's ten 'Anniversary Discourses', delivered to the Asiatic Society of Bengal from 1784, mapped a new vision of global history and established a common Indo-European cultural heritage (even though the term Indo-European would not be coined until 1813). In

Jones's wake, this common heritage was welded onto a Vedic frame-work by a later generation of scholars, most notably Friedrich Max Müller. Max Müller, whose Company-sponsored translation of the Vedas (six volumes, 1849–74) marked a pivotal point in the reconfiguration of understandings of religion and ancient history, was the most influential Victorian popularizer of 'Aryanism'. His work, which reached a large popular audience in Britain and its colonies, depicted the Vedas as the foundational source for the study of 'civiliza-tion' and made the term 'Aryan' an indispensable part of the analytical vocabulary of late nineteenth- and early twentieth-century ethnology and history.

Within nineteenth-century Europe the Aryan concept was much more than a heuristic device: Aryanism was woven into the intellectual fabric of various European nationalist traditions. As Chapter 1 demon-strates, from the early nineteenth century the concept was prominent in new genealogies being fashioned for emergent nation states and it was used by various British and continental thinkers to delimit ethnic and racial boundaries within Europe. By the time Max Müller arrived in England, John Kemble and Benjamin Thorpe had elaborated a strong Anglo-Saxonist tradition, which emphasized the linguistic con-nection between English and its Germanic and Indo-European ances-tors. Within such a context, Aryanism fortified both nationalist and imperialist ideologies, either by deepening the genealogy of the national community or through its use to police the nation's bound-aries: in the British case, to delineate a series of cultural oppositions between the Saxon descendants of the Indo-Europeans and the Celtic peoples of Ireland, the Scottish highlands and Wales.[10] The 'Oriental Renaissance' engendered by the dissemination of Company Orientalism in Europe was not simply a quest for spiritual revivification through the embrace of 'Oriental learning', but was also a series of cultural and political reconfigurations as the boundaries of community were reimagined.[11]

The work of Jones, his contemporaries and his successors also had a profound impact outside of Britain and continental Europe. Rendall has demonstrated the centrality of Jones's comparative method in framing European and colonial interpretations of the cultures of South-East Asia.[12] Even in Australia, where settlers consistently asserted the fundamental 'otherness' of Aboriginal language and culture, Jones's work was influential. It was too influential for some, as J. D. Lang, the Principal of the Australian College and Senior Minister of the Church of Scotland in New South Wales, disputed the value of Jones's work and railed against the centrality of Asia in post-Jonesian work on language and migration.[13] Lang's complaints were in vain, however, as the Aryan theory became an increasingly potent, if contentious, idea within the empire. As this study makes clear, Aryanism was particularly authoritative in the Pacific where it came to provide not only an important ethnological paradigm, but also a narrative used by some white colonists to emphasize that they belonged to a long history of Aryan migrations into the region, justifying their presence in the Pacific by transmuting colonization into 'settlement'.

Although Aryanism became such an important feature of nineteenth century culture it has received uneven analytical treatment. Poliakov's *The Aryan Myth* charted Aryanism's rising influence in continental Europe to formulate a genealogy of European racial thought, constructing a narrative that led inexorably to the Holocaust. Poliakov's work, however, underemphasized the contested position of the idea in nineteenth-century European thought and neglected its remarkable influence outside Europe. Despite its recurrence in the archives of empire, historians of British imperialism have paid scant regard to Aryanism. While Leopold sketched the idea's influence among British and South Asian elites and Thapar examined the place of Aryanism in the interpretation of ancient Indian history, it was not until the publication of Trautmann's *Aryans and British India* (1997) that the Aryan idea received extended treatment.[14] In this path-breaking work, Trautmann recovered the significance of Aryanism in British India, tracing the ways in which it moulded British interpretations of Indian ethnology and history as well as its influence in Europe.

Nevertheless, Trautmann's work had three significant weaknesses. Firstly, he provided only limited discussion of the role of South Asians in making and contesting the theory. The place of Aryanism in discourses on the Hindu self or Hindu nationhood receives scant attention, being briefly sketched in an epilogue that is overly reliant upon Raychaudhuri's study of the Bengali intelligentsia in the late nineteenth century.[15] This approach glosses over divergent intellectual traditions, both within Bengal and beyond. In effect, by merely synthesizing Raychaudhuri's work Trautmann reinscribes the centrality of Bengal and *bhadralok* (Bengal's educated middle class) intellectual production, rendering other important indigenous voices silent. As a corrective to this approach, I demonstrate in Chapter 4 the very different role of Aryanism in debates over the boundaries of religious identity in late nineteenth-century Punjab, while Chapter 6 delineates important arguments about Aryanism elaborated by Indian Christians.

Secondly, in presenting what is essentially an intellectual history of Aryanism, Trautmann exhibits only limited interest in the material and political outcomes of this idea. Its pivotal influence in reshaping colonial military recruitment, in the articulation of new forms of political mobilization, and nationalist debates over the boundaries of the nation (what was the status of Muslims, south Indians and low caste people?) are only hinted at. In what follows, I insist that we must locate the history of Aryanism within colonialism's reconfiguration of power-relations. Aryanism was not simply an ideological veneer of imperialism, rather it was central to constituting colonial subjects and fashioning the very structures of colonialism (and anti-colonial nationalism). In response to both the overly literary turn of some postcolonial criticism, which has resulted in an inattention to power, and critiques of 'representation' as a purely cultural problematic, I argue that the Aryan idea is a potent reminder that representations are social and political facts.[16]

Thirdly, although *Aryans and British India* provided an important window into debates over the Aryan idea in India and Europe, Trautmann seems reluctant to cast his study as an 'imperial' story. He not only underplays important shifts in knowledge production arising from colonialism, but also neglects the impact of Aryanism beyond the drawing rooms of British India, Britain and Europe. This, taken together with his relative inattention to South Asian actors, means that he follows Poliakov to cast the Aryan theory as essentially a European story and its influence in other imperial contexts such as Malaya, Ireland, Argentina, Nigeria or the Pacific remains unspoken.[17] In contrast, this study foregrounds the hybrid nature of the Aryan idea. Extracted from its Indian context and widely transmitted within the empire, Aryanism was localized in a variety of specific cultural locations as its meaning was constantly renegotiated in debates between a variety of British, settler and indigenous groups.

The archives of empire

The increasingly global reach of Aryanism reflected the centrality of knowledge production and dissemination within the imperial project. Recent research in South Asian history has stressed the pivotal role of intelligence-gathering and the rise of the 'disciplines' (history, sociology, literary studies) in the construction of imperial authority in colonial India. Such work has typically focused on the role of knowledge in the constitution of the colonial state or regional intellectual cultures (especially Bengal); the place of the larger framework of empire remains largely unexplored. This study uses Aryanism as an analytical lens that allows us to move beyond an unproblematized focus on the local or national to examine the broader knowledge structures of the empire. It suggests that we can conceive of the empire as a series of archives, each arising out of local concerns, but braided together, however imperfectly, by institutional exchanges, webs of personal correspondence and shared bodies of knowledge.

This model for understanding the empire draws our attention to the important role of knowledge gathering in imperial contexts. Writing, collecting and circulating documents were foundations of imperial power. While the ultimate basis of imperial authority was force or the threat of force, colonial states fetishized written records and the value of documentation. J. S. Mill underlined this in 1852, as he noted 'the whole of the Government of India is carried on in writing', suggesting that 'no other [government] probably has a system of recordation so complete.'[18] Mill's observation on the superior extent and thickness of the colonial archive underlines the pivotal role of colonialism in the constitution of state practices and modernity itself. Recent scholarship has emphasized that modernity was not fashioned in Europe and then projected out to colonies in the periphery, but rather that the key enumerative and surveillance apparatuses of the modern state – from fingerprinting to the survey, from the census to the passport – were elaborated and refined in colonial contexts.[19] In light of this, the precociousness of *kaghazi raj* (rule by paper) in British India is less surprising, as it embodied the bureaucratization of modern governance, a process that Richard Drayton has recently identified as one of the most durable, if overlooked, legacies of Britain's global empire.[20]

The 'total' archive became an important imperial fantasy, best encapsulated in Borges' short story which recounts an empire that was so attached to the accuracy of its cartographic archive that it constructed a map that was the exactly the same size as the empire itself.[21] Historical empires, however, functioned not in the idealist world of Borgesian fictions, but in a real world limited by capital flows, labour supply and strict timetables: the total archive never became a reality. In addition to the finite resources of colonial regimes, the ability of indigenous groups to exploit the fissures and limits of colonial authority meant that colonial knowledge of 'native' society and politics remained imperfect. Aware of these limitations, imperial agents

worried constantly about flows of knowledge and their ability to identify 'hidden cults', unravel 'secret languages' and forestall rebellion on
the fringes of empire.[22] These 'information panics', as Bayly has termed
them, intensified as indigenous groups were 'pacified' by the state's
coercive power in the wake of uprisings against British rule and during
periods of political mobilization by indigenous groups.[23] Colonial
concern with such forms of 'rebel consciousness' (to borrow a phrase
from Guha), was an important stimulus for the study of folk religion,
local dialect and the surveillance of new religious movements on the
frontiers of empire.[24]

   Thus, in characterizing the empire as a series of interwoven archives,
this study recognizes that archives themselves were fundamentally
implicated in the processes of colonialism. For historians of colonialism the archive is deeply problematic; the manuscript collections, parliamentary papers, court records, periodicals and newspapers we use
are not simply documents that allow us to access the colonial past, but
rather were constitutive of the inequalities of that past. Within the
uneven terrains of power that characterize colonial societies, the
archive was a site of authority, a lens through which colonial subjects
were monitored and a textual framework from which discourses of
'improvement' and 'modernization' were elaborated. The archive also
could provide the basis for the formulation of colonial policy, as Prior
has shown with regard to the compilation of historical narratives that
moulded the colonial state's intervention in communal conflict. In
effect the archive constituted the 'memory of the state', as its records
of the pre-colonial past moulded the 'official mind' and guided the
policy-making process.[25]

   In light of this function of the archive, I think we need to reconcep-
tualize the place of 'native informants' and 'indigenous voices' in the
historiography of colonialism. Although historians of colonialism have
paid considerable attention to the censorship and the surveillance of
print, we know less about the ways in which colonial states solicited
and channelled indigenous opinion. This is a crucial lacuna in our
understanding of the workings of colonialism, given the ways in which
colonial officials valued indigenous 'authenticity' as they searched for
pure archives of indigenous knowledge, untainted by rebellious intent
and unembellished by inventive informants.[26] This suggests that colonial authority frequently hinged on the state's ability to induce the
subaltern to speak, rather than on its capacity to suppress indigenous
voices. Colonial governors, from Warren Hastings to Sir George Grey,
believed that a careful attention to indigenous religious idioms and an

understanding of the valences of indigenous diplomacy were the very basis for the consolidation and extension of British authority.[27] There is no better embodiment of the global aspirations of such projects than Grey's personal collection of manuscripts, ethnographic reports and printed works of ethnology that provided the intellectual foundation for his administrational crusades in South Africa, South Australia and New Zealand.[28]

Despite the prominence of indigenous voices in such archival collections, many studies of colonialism rely solely on supposedly hegemonic English-language texts, neglecting vernacular sources or the importance of indigenous thinkers. Our disciplines, as well as realities of colonialism, have prevented the subaltern from speaking. As Parry has observed – within her response to Spivak's reading of Rhys's *Wide Sargasso Sea* – postcolonialism's attribution of 'absolute power' to colonial discourses has led to a 'deliberate deafness to the native voice where it can be heard'.[29] Certainly it is important to acknowledge Spivak's analytical starting point – that the complex transformations of colonialism mean that is impossible to fully recover subaltern subjectivities – but this must be balanced by an attention to the spaces and occasions where indigenes interrogated the experience of colonialism.

In order to avoid the historical deafness that Parry warns against, this study draws extensively on Maori and Hindi sources (in addition to European language texts) in an attempt to recognize the powerful and divergent indigenous engagements with Aryanism. This linguistic breadth enables me to trace more fully the mobility of the Aryan idea, recovering the ability of South Asians to contest British appropriations of the concept, as well as tracing the efforts of Maori leaders to fashion a discourse of resistance that rejected Orientalism and invoked instead the ethnological authority of the Old Testament. Thus I use these texts to map the various strategies used by indigenous reformers, prophets and politicians to localize new ideas and to chart major shifts (and fractures) in 'native opinion'. Such an approach allows me to underline a striking but often neglected feature of anti-colonial movements: their outward looking nature and their comparative sensibility.[30] This is a crucially important point, as the literature on decolonization tends to view indigenous nationalisms as nationally bounded and self-sufficient. Yet, it seems that imperial connections arising out of print and travel led to the active cross-fertilization of anti-colonial ideologies and models; provocative evidence hints at important ties between Irish and Indian nationalists, Coptic Christianity and the Indian National Congress, the Haitian revolt and Maori proto-nationalism.[31]

Re-imagining anti-colonial movements and decolonization as the product of inter-colonial exchanges suggests that colonial intellectual life was energized by the movement of ideas and information. Although Innis and Anderson emphasized the pivotal role of print in the constitution of the nation, print also facilitated the flow of information across national boundaries.[32] We are increasingly aware that print created important transatlantic networks, where political models, evangelical sermons and travel narratives circulated freely within an enlarged public sphere.[33] In a similar vein, the proliferation of newspapers and popular journals, both in the metropole and in the colonies, also ensured the rapid circulation of a shared body of news and energized intellectual debate within the British empire. Reportage in both English-language and vernacular newspapers transcended local concerns, updating the public about developments in distant parts of the empire and beyond. Maori language newspapers, for example, carried news from Sydney to London, Delhi to Paris, New York to New Guinea.[34] The global breadth of these reports also reminds us that empires were not hermetically sealed systems and the circulation of the printed word wove states and empires together in important ways. For example, the heavy intellectual traffic between Britain and the German lands, not least in Orientalist learning, in the late eighteenth century was facilitated by swift translations and the rapid dissemination of the printed word.[35]

The authority of Orientalism in European and imperial culture had profound implications for the study of colonial cultures beyond India. As ethnology and ethnography became increasingly prominent within the nineteenth-century empire, Orientalist learning provided an important framework for the analysis of non-Christian religions and non-European languages. Antiquarians in Ireland attempted to relate the round towers of the Irish countryside to Phoenician sun worship or Hindu fertility rites, while colonial lexicographers in the Pacific attempted to find the connection between Sanskrit and various Pacific languages. These intellectual ventures reflected the disproportionate significance of Orientalist learning in a period when the second British empire was expanded and consolidated and when new institutions, including libraries on imperial frontiers, were developing. Celticists in Dublin or philologists in New Zealand could draw from the important Indological texts (such as *Asiatic Researches*, Mill's *History of British India*, or Max Müller's edition of the *Rig Veda*), that were to be found in most significant nineteenth-century athenaeums, learned societies and university libraries. Thus, at one level, we might see the global influence of Orientalism as a product of the ways in which the cultural authority of Orientalist knowledge was undergirded by the chronology of imperialism and patterns of institutional growth in the colonies.

The importance of these enmeshed archives is clear in the work of Alfred Kingcombe Newman. Newman, an important figure in the sports, politics and science of colonial New Zealand, devoted almost a decade of his life to identifying Aryan influences in the cultures of the Pacific.[36] Convinced of the Indian origins of the Polynesians, Newman's research drew upon the holdings of the Polynesian Society's library, which had assembled a significant collection of texts on Asian languages and cultures. In its early years, the Society formalized exchange relationships with the Society of Arts of Batavia (Jakarta) and two Calcutta-based journals, the *Journal of the Buddist Text Society* and the *Journal of the Asiatic Society of Bengal*, in addition to receiving works from the Bengali scholar Nobin Chandra Das.[37] But, most intriguingly, Newman fleshed out his argument from the large collection of ethnographic manuscripts and 35 volumes of dictionaries, grammars and ethnological works donated to the Society by the Assam-based ethnographer Samuel Peal.[38]

In order to confirm his Indocentric vision of Pacific history, Newman journeyed to India, retracing his footsteps back to his childhood home (he was born into an East India Company family in Madras). Newman's research focused on the Gangetic valley, 'the heart of India', as he visited Banaras and other sacred sites with the hope that he could identify cultural continuities between India and the Pacific. Still haunted by his Indian childhood and deeply interested in Polynesian culture, Newman found innumerable connections. One such link was the swastika and Newman's *Who Are the Maoris?* provided several 'secret Maori symbols' that were supposedly variations on the Hindu symbol: in Newman's eyes this was telling testament of the Indian origins of Maori (see cover illustration). The map used by Newman in the same volume to trace the migration of the Polynesians from India not only represents his vision of the region's history, but also embodies the dissemination of ethnological paradigms from South Asia to Polynesia and charts Newman's own voyage from an Indian childhood to his new home in New Zealand (see Map on p. xi).

Webs of empire

The complex history of migration and the meshing of archives that underpinned Newman's work are useful starting points for the broader reconceptualization of the British empire, and by extension imperial history, undertaken in this work. As I have already suggested, this study insists on the need for a multi-sited history of the empire that neither privileges the metropole nor accepts the nation-state as the self-evident unit for historical analysis. Recent work by Grove on colonial science, Cook on policy exchanges between India and Ireland, and Porter on missionary networks suggests that the traditional metaphor for conceptualizing the empire, the spoked wheel, is in desperate need of revision.[39] The wheel metaphor, where lines of communications, finance and personnel radiate out from London to each colony in the periphery, structures both metropolitan-focused imperial histories and the national histories of individual colonies.

To transcend the limits of the centre vs. periphery opposition and the interpretative limitations of the nation-state, this study uses webs as its organizing analytical metaphor. The exchanges traced in this volume crossed national boundaries, as ideas moved along lines of personal correspondence, through the circulation of the printed word, as a result of institutional exchanges and exhibitions and because of the mobility of travellers, missionaries and administrators. These forms of transmission did not merely transect the national boundaries of Britain or the individual colonies of its empire, but also reached out into other states, nations and imperial systems, collapsing geographical and cultural space. I emphasize, for example, the pivotal influence of both French- and German-speaking scholars on British Orientalism and Pacific studies. None of this is to deny the significance of the nation-state altogether, as this study traces both the ways in which the nation-state increasingly organized knowledge in the nineteenth century and the ways in which diverse nationalist traditions utilized the idea of Aryan origins. Rather, I am insisting that we be more sensitive to the interplay between the local, the national and the imperial: historians must adopt a more mobile approach to the imperial past to enable them to recover the transnational cultural movements which were so central in the constitution of empires.

The metaphor of the web has several advantages for the conceptualization of the imperial past. At a general level, it underscores that the empire was a *structure*, a complex fabrication fashioned out of a great number of disparate parts that were brought together into a new relationship. To my mind, the central problem with the 'cultural turn' in imperial history has not been a narrow focus on representation, but rather the inability of scholars to develop Said's insistence that Orientalism was a system of circulation. Rather than narrowly focusing on the rhetorical construction or ideological context of any given text, we need to begin to trace the transmission of ideas, ideologies and identities across space and time. The web captures the integrative nature of this cultural traffic, the ways in which imperial institutions and structures connected disparate points in space into a complex mesh of networks. Moreover, the image of the web also conveys something of the double nature of the imperial system. Empires, like webs, were both fragile, prone to crises where important threads are broken or structural nodes destroyed, yet also dynamic, being constantly remade and reconfigured through concerted thought and effort: the image of the web reminds us that the structure of empire was constantly reworked and remade.

The web metaphor also draws our attention to the crucial, but generally overlooked, horizontal linkages between colonies. The British empire, as much as a spider's web, was dependent on these intercolonial exchanges. Important flows of capital, personnel and ideas between colonies energized colonial development and the function of the larger imperial system. Such exchanges have received only limited attention in the historiography of the British empire because they transgress the analytical boundaries of both metropolitan-focused imperial history (where the empire is viewed from London out) or histories of individual colonies (where the view is from the colony towards London).

The inherently relational nature of the empire is also underlined by the image of the web. Where the spoked-wheel reduces the empire to a series of metropole–periphery binaries, the web reinforces the multiple positions that any given colony, city, community or archive might occupy. Calcutta, for example, might be seen as being in a subaltern position in relation to London, but it in turn might be a sub-imperial centre where important lines of patronage, accumulation and communication flow out into the South Asian hinterland and beyond to South-East Asia or even the Pacific.

But we might go even further than this. If we conceive of the empire not as a single web, but as a complex agglomeration of overlapping webs, it is possible to envisage that certain locations, individuals or institutions in the supposed periphery might in fact be the centre of intricate networks themselves. We will see this in the case of Samuel Peal, whose tireless correspondence from the frontiers of Assam fashioned an extensive network of intellectual exchange that reached out to Canada, the United States, the Pacific islands and Australasia, and incorporated metropolitan figures, including Max Müller himself. In turn, Elsdon Best and Percy Smith, the founding members of the

Polynesian Society and important figures in Peal's network, themselves occupied a central position in a related web of exchange. The Polynesian Society quickly became a leading centre for the study of Pacific ethnology and its membership and institutional exchange tapped considerable intellectual resources, allowing Best and Smith to assume a position of great authority in Pacific studies. This intellectual authority exercised from Wellington also reflected New Zealand's assumption of an imperial role in the Pacific: at once a colony and an imperial power, New Zealand fashioned its own webs of influence in the Pacific with limited input from Britain.

While I am suggesting that Calcutta or Wellington could function as imperial centres, I am not advocating an entirely decentred view of empire. It is crucial to recognize the disparities of power inherent within the empire and that many imperial networks, as well as economic power and imperial authority, were concentrated in Britain itself. Even at the level of intellectual production there is no doubt that Britain continued to exercise substantial power as metropolitan learned institutions, missionary and reform societies and, of course, the British government had the ability to exercise considerable influence over distant colonies. And, of course, the substantial resources available in London, Oxford or Cambridge allowed for exhibitions, museums and libraries on a scale beyond the reach of the colonies and also facilitated the work of grand theorists such as E. B. Tylor or Max Müller. It is necessary to balance this recognition of Britain's position as an imperial power that was able to fashion a global empire with an awareness of the ability of administrators, missionaries, settlers and indigenous groups in the colonies to construct bodies of knowledge and meaningful networks of exchange: metropolitan interests might have wished to dominate the empire, but they never enjoyed the hegemony they aspired to.

Thus, this study rejects a vision of Orientalism or colonial knowledge as the hegemonic imposition of metropolitan ideologies upon colonial societies: 'a mask of conquest' in Viswanathan's formulation.[40] In doing so, it moves beyond a literary focus on the static text to focus on imperial systems of circulation, recovering the transmission of ideas, information and identities across the empire. Such an approach allows us to recontextualize prominent imperial concerns that would otherwise appear marginal or even nonsensical: a correspondent to *Panjab Notes and Queries* wondering whether the nose-flute played by low caste peoples in north India indicated a cultural link with eastern Polynesia, Elsdon Best's search for remnants of Hindu phallus worship among

Maori of the rugged Urewera mountain ranges, or the important contribution of Samuel Peal to debates over Polynesian origins from his tea plantation in Naharani in Assam.[41] Like Newman's Maori 'swastikas', these are striking examples of a deep-seated concern with ethnic origins and cultural continuities within a multi-ethnic empire characterized by mobility, exchange and conflict.

1
The Emergence of Aryanism: Company Orientalism, Colonial Governance and Imperial Ethnology

Over the last decade, historians have increasingly identified the mid-eighteenth century as a period in which both the British empire and British identities underwent rapid redefinition. Popular imperialism and strident nationalism are no longer seen as the *sui generis* products of the Victorian age, as recent research has delineated increasingly aggressive imperial ideologies articulated by Britons from the conclusion of the Seven Years War through to the Age of Reform.[1] As the American crisis plunged Britain's Atlantic empire into disarray, the British state constructed new regimes of domestic surveillance and consolidated its authority on the 'Celtic fringes' (especially in the wake of the 1798 rebellion in Ireland), while commerce and conquest added a host of new territories to the empire.[2] Eager for new markets and resources, agents of empire expanded British commercial influence and political authority in Asia and the Pacific: the East India Company emerged as a South Asian territorial power in 1765 and increasingly consolidated its influence in South-East Asia following its acquisition of Penang in 1786, and James Cook led three voyages into the Pacific between 1768 and 1779, enabling the foundation of a new colony in Australia in 1788.

In his landmark *The Founding of the Second British Empire, 1763–93*, Harlow suggested that these multiple reconfigurations resulted in a 'swing to the east' in British imperial ambitions.[3] While Harlow underplayed the continuing economic importance of the Atlantic (especially the Caribbean) in the imperial system, these developments in the Asia-Pacific region were of disproportionate cultural and intellectual significance. Exploration, surveying and commerce in this region fundamentally reshaped British understandings of the world, creating a truly global system of information-gathering that underpinned a much fuller picture of geography, natural history and human variety. Chapters 1 and 2 of this work examine the place of Aryanism within the new cultural formations fashioned by this reorientation of the empire. While Chapter 2 extends the arguments developed here, by examining the transplantation of Aryanism into Pacific ethnology and history-writing, this chapter details the British 'discovery' of the Aryan concept in colonial India and its emergence as a key concept for both imperial ethnology and colonial governance. It begins by examining the rise of what I term 'Company Orientalism', a detailed and organized body of knowledge fashioned by the East India Company in the late eighteenth century. While several historians have explored changing British understandings of India in this period, insufficient attention has been paid to the profound demographic and political shifts in the 1760s and 1770s.[4] Rather than focusing narrowly on representations of Indian society, in this chapter I attempt to locate imperial ethnology more firmly within colonial political economy and changing patterns of knowledge production. By foregrounding the centrality of the Bengal famine and the subsequent reform of the Company's revenue and legal administration, I hope to deepen Thomas Trautmann's analysis of the emergence of Aryanism by embedding the work of the early Orientalists in the broader context of the material and political transformations arising from the Company's changing role in India.

From this starting point, I examine changing understandings of the relationship between language and race in British India, focusing on the impact of the linguistic research of Sir William Jones, who firmly established the genetic link between European and Indian languages. The discovery of these affinities had profound ramifications beyond India. Although Company Orientalism had limited impact in England before 1850, it was particularly influential in both the Scottish and Irish Enlightenments. In both cases, substantial material and intellectual linkages with the East India Company nourished a sustained engagement with Orientalism. Anglo-Irish antiquarians embraced Orientalism as they struggled to 'vindicate' (in the words of Charles Vallancey) the ancient history of Ireland and to fashion a Gaelicized settler identity. Conversely, Jonesian philology was harnessed by a prominent group of Scottish scholar-administrators in the Company's service in South-East Asia. Two generations of Scottish Orientalists traced the cultural connections that linked the region to India and played a central role in the extension and consolidation of British authority in the region. The chapter concludes by returning to South Asia, as I examine Aryanism's incorporation into both popular and official discourses on Indian ethnology and history. While it became an influential doctrine within the military and in intellectual projects that assembled a view of India's national past, its significance and usefulness remained disputed. Heated debates over the theory, from the time of the uprising against British rule in 1857 through to the early twentieth century, reveal the deep ideological divides and intellectual fissures that ran through the British administration and metropolitan opinion.

Trade to dominion: the birth of Company Orientalism

Although the birth of Aryanism is frequently traced back to Sir William Jones's discovery of affinities between Sanskrit, Greek and Latin, the emergence of this new paradigm should be viewed as the product of tectonic social and cultural shifts arising from the birth of British colonialism in South Asia. In 1765, in the face of the growing military prowess and economic influence of the East India Company, the Mughal emperor Shah Alam appointed the Company *diwan* (revenue manager) for Bengal, Bihar and Orissa. This appointment fundamentally transformed the Company's position in South Asia: in effect, it shifted from being primarily a trading concern (albeit an increasingly militarized one), to a territorial power. At an economic level, the position of *diwan* allowed the British to access the rich revenue base of Bengal, ending their dependence on the importation of bullion to Bengal.[5] In accepting this position, the Company implicitly recognized that it operated within a South Asian state system that had elaborate courtly traditions and highly specialized diplomatic conventions. This realization led the Company to recognize the primacy of Persian as a political language, to dispense *khilat* (gifts of incorporation) and to retain Muslim legal offices (*kotwal* and *kazi*): even the zealous Governor-General Wellesley maintained this scrupulous regard for the symbolics of Mughal authority.[6]

But the Company's entrance into Indo-Islamic traditions of administration placed new demands on its small retinue of India-based officials. In the 1760s British knowledge of South Asia was geographically limited, uneven in depth and quality and quickly outdated due to the oscillating politics of the Mughal state and its regional rivals and successors.[7] These limitations, together with a belief that an

'Englishman' was unable to 'follow the subtle native through all his arts to conceal the real value of his country and to perplex and elude the payments', meant the Court of Directors in London were doubtful of the ability of its agents in India to effectively carry out revenue collection. Instead, the Company stressed its continuity with the 'ancient form of government', relying on existing indigenous collectors under the direction of Muhammad Reza Khan.[8]

This system was abandoned in 1772 as part of the major reorganization of the Company's administration in the wake of the horrific Bengal famine of 1770. Excessive rain triggered this cataclysm which killed one-third of Bengal's population, but it seems that the rising power of the Company compounded the crisis: revenue collection actually increased during the famine and rumours concerning Company agents trading in rice and hoarding seed abounded.[9] The Company's Court of Directors was alarmed when it was informed that Muhammad Reza Khan was himself accused of pushing up the price of rice, contributing to the 'destruction of many thousands of people'. This charge, in addition to concerns about missing revenue from Dhaka (attributed to Muhammad Reza Khan's 'flagrant duplicity'), led the Court of Directors to 'stand forth as *Duan* [diwan], and by the agency of the Company's servants to take upon ourselves the entire care and management of the revenues.'[10]

This decision to 'stand forth as *Duan*' initiated a reshaping of the Company's administrational priorities. Over the following decades, great effort was devoted to composing a detailed picture of agrarian production, rural social structure and commercial relationships. Kejariwal has noted the elision of 'the exotic, the mysterious, the fantastic' in British depictions of Indian society from the 1770s, a transformation that can be attributed to the Company's changing position in the political economy of South Asia.[11] By the close of the eighteenth century, the Company had constructed a thick archive of information regarding rural life. H. T. Colebrooke and A. Lambert's *Remarks on the Present State of the Husbandry and Internal Commerce of Bengal*, for example, contained a lengthy discussion of the key commercial crops (indigo, opium and cotton), observations on village life and extensive statistics culled from official reports.[12] Similarly encyclopaedic visions of ethnology were also fashioned. In 1796 the Belgian artist Baltazard Solvyns produced a volume illustrated with 250 etchings in an attempt to organize and classify the complexity of Bengal's social structure.[13] The Company was keen to compile similarly systematized images of

communities beyond Bengal. At Governor-General Wellesley's instiga-
tion, Francis Buchanan conducted a survey of the territories acquired
by the Company in the wake of the Fourth Mysore War and surveyed
the frontiers of Bengal from 1807, producing an impressive body of statistics and ethnographic reportage.[14] Perhaps the richest and most variegated archive of topographical, ethnographic and agricultural
knowledge was fashioned over several decades by Colin Mackenzie and
his large retinue of South Indian scribes.[15]

If assuming the position of *diwan* placed higher value on knowledge
about agrarian production and ethnography, it also reshaped the institutional and linguistic basis of the Company's authority. Just as the
Company assumed full responsibility for revenue collection in 1772, it
also took full control of the justice system. Even though courts were to
continue to dispense 'indigenous law', Bengal's legal institutions were
for the first time fully incorporated into the machinery of the
Company's administration. Convinced that an efficient justice system
promoted trade and enriched revenue supplies, the Company set about
standardizing procedures, making justice quicker and more accessible,
while adapting its 'regulations to the manners and understanding of
the people, and exigencies of the country, adhering, as closely as we
were able, to their antient usages and institutions.'[16]

Language and colonial power

The expansion of the Company's responsibilities as revenue collector
and dispenser of justice meant that linguistic proficiency became the
foundation for a career in the Company's service.[17] The Company continued to have a deep investment in the 'symbolic capital' of Persian,
the dominant political language of north India, as it ensured that its
servants were proficient in the idioms required for trade and diplomacy.[18] Persianate terms continued to proliferate in Company correspondence well into the nineteenth century: Javed Majeed has
suggested that texts produced by Company administrators were written
in an 'idiom stranded between two administrative languages' (Persian
and English).[19] Indeed, in 1855 (some twenty years after the Company's
shift to English as its favoured medium), the Sanskritist H. H. Wilson
produced a manual to aid new administrators in the Company's service
to decipher the Persian terms that studded Company records.[20]

While the Company respected the administrative utility of Persian,
under Governor-General Hastings's patronage a group of young and
well-educated Company writers increasingly devoted their energies to

Sanskrit, believing that it held the key to a vast store of Indian knowledge. This was particularly pressing as the Company attempted to understand the 'classical' foundations of Hindu law. However, pandits were often reluctant to share their knowledge with the servants of the Company, because, as Hastings observed, other Europeans had used such information 'to turn their religion into derision'.[21] Moreover, initially at least, many pandits feared that accepting cash payment from 'unclean' British officials might violate the very ritual status which invested their pronouncements with authority.[22] It seems that these concerns frustrated Sir William Jones's attempts to find a Brahman willing to teach him Sanskrit, as he was eventually forced to rely on the expertise of Pandit Ramlochan, a non-Brahman *vaidya* (medicinal expert): it was only in the second half of the 1780s that Jones established sustained and cordial relationships with the Brahmans of Nadia and Calcutta.[23]

Thus non-cooperation proved to be effective strategies for the protection of Brahmanical knowledge: in this context, silence was a potent reminder of indigenous agency and the limits of British power. The leading Company Orientalist Nathaniel Brassey Halhed found that gaining a solid grounding in Sanskrit was a difficult task as the pandits 'were to a man resolute in rejecting all ... solicitations for instruction in this dialect'.[24] The compilation of Halhed's *A Code of Gentoo Laws* (1776) – the product of a complicated process of linguistic and cultural translation – made both the Company's dependence on indigenous experts and its need for a 'mastery' of key Indian languages clear. The basis for Halhed's text was a Sanskrit legal code compiled by eleven pandits who drew upon Bengali legal custom to create a new and 'definitive' vision of customary law. The Sanskrit text in turn was translated into Persian, as no European could yet read Sanskrit. This translation was in itself complicated enough, given that the pandits were illiterate in Persian and the Company's Persian translators knew no Sanskrit: in the end a Muslim scribe prepared the Persian text on the basis of one pandit's oral précis of the Sanskrit text in Bengali. When Sir William Jones later compared the Persian and Sanskrit versions, he noted the interpolations, omissions and 'dark passages' of the Persian code, concluding that this translation, 'in the third degree', was 'very erroneous'.[25]

Patronage and the institutional basis of colonial knowledge

By the mid-1780s, a decade after the publication of Halhed's *Gentoo Laws*, the Company was increasingly able to draw upon the expertise of both Hindu and Muslim learned elites. In part this reflected an increased awareness of cultural issues surrounding knowledge transmission. Hastings, for example, was finally able to enlist the renowned pandit Radhakanta Tarkavagisa by offering him a grant of land rather than cash payment.[26] But, equally importantly, the marked growth in the willingness of pandits to enter the service of the Company reflected shifts in indigenous knowledge production in the wake of the Bengal famine. The famine not only depleted the supply of students, but also dried up sources of indigenous patronage. The devastation of the famine, together with the pressure of the Company's revenue regime, eroded the ability of leading *zamindars* (large land-holders) to provide the generous patronage that they had traditionally extended to Bengali Brahmans.[27] The crisis in Calcutta's hinterland was compounded by the recurrence of famine in 1783 and broader ecological change, as abrupt shifts in the riverine system of western Bengal further undercut the vitality of many provincial commercial centres and accelerated the population drift towards Calcutta.[28] As a result of the constrained opportunities in rural centres many migratory pandits established traditional Sanskrit schools (*tols* and *chatuspathi*) in the rapidly growing city.[29] Others soon attached themselves to leading Orientalists who provided a reliable source of income. The new-found desire of some pandits to enter into European employ is suggested by H. T. Colebrooke's observation in 1797 (when, as he observed, pandits no longer 'concealed' the 'most sacred of their Vedas' from Europeans), that he could not 'conceive how it came to be ever asserted that the Brahmans were averse to instruct strangers'.[30]

While pandits from the Radh region (west of the Hughli river) were particularly prominent in the developing intellectual life of colonial Calcutta, a notable group of Shi'a Muslim scribes, members of distinguished and holy lineages, were prominent not only in British Bengal, but also in major centres of Company trade and diplomacy throughout north India. Bayly has recently traced the careers and influence of the leading members of this elite administrative clique, arguing that they shaped 'British policy in Bengal and north India for the whole period between 1756 and 1830'.[31] Bayly also notes the prominence of Muslim service families from the Allahabad and Lucknow region who served as diplomatic experts for the Company and Kashmiris who were prominent in British service in the Delhi region.[32] All of these groups were dependent on patronage, and in the complex and shifting politics of late eighteenth-century India, where traditional elites were under pressure from commercial and political change, the Company provided a reliable source of employment and payment.

Thus the devastation of rural Bengal as a result of successive famines, Calcutta's continued growth as an economic centre and the emergence of the Company as the dominant political power and influential cultural patron underpinned the emergence of a series of hybridized institutions fundamental to colonial authority. At one level, the employment of indigenous scribes and experts was simply an extension of long-established practices. Company officers relied heavily on Indian moneylenders for financing private trade and personal consumption, while the Company itself forged close links with the Jagat Seth banking family, a connection that was essential in the Company's rise to power in the 1750s and 1760s.[33] In a similar vein, European traders and administrators of consequence had long relied upon *banians*, local experts who functioned as crucial cultural intermediaries and trading partners.[34] But the Company's new responsibilities added momentum to this process, as scribal communities and learned lineages found employment in the Company's legal and revenue machinery. Most importantly, Hastings' emphasis on linguistic proficiency created new opportunities for literate South Asians, as Company recruits were sent to the *mofussil* (upcountry) to acquire languages and knowledge of the dynamics of European–Asian trade.[35]

Such systems of knowledge transmission were formalized with the establishment of the College of Fort William in Calcutta in 1800. While the college was largely the product of local administrational imperatives, Wellesley hoped that it would also be a bulwark against French ambitions in Asia and the revolutionary thought that he believed 'had reached the minds of some individuals in the civil and military service of the Company'. The discipline of language instruction and careful teaching of the 'correct principles' of government were the best methods of forestalling such global currents, as well as fortifying the moral resolve of Company functionaries in the face of the 'temptations and corruptions' of India.[36] To this end, the college employed a skilled retinue of 'native language masters', as well as large numbers of compositors, printers and other skilled workers, to assist the leading British experts appointed by the Company. Figures such as Tarinicharan Mitra, employed in the Hindustani department, or Mrtyunjay Vidyalankar, assistant to William Carey in the Bengali department, emerged as major intellectual figures: Mitra as a linguist and Mrtyunjay as a pioneer of vernacular Bengali prose.[37] While these individuals became influential in the world of Bengali letters, their structural position within the hybrid space of the college was one of subordination: they were under the supervision of British 'professors' and their salaries were markedly lower than those of their *sahibs* (masters).[38] This Calcutta model, which valued South Asian languages while simultaneously subordinating local experts to British masters, was soon replicated by the Company in colleges in Bombay and Madras.

Sir William Jones, Sanskrit and human origins

These colleges were central in shaping and transmitting the increasingly organized body of knowledge produced during the first three decades of Company Orientalism. Central to their educational programme was the research produced by Europeans and Indians attached to the learned societies that had emerged in the colonial port towns, especially the Asiatic Society of Bengal. Founded in 1784, the Society provided a crucial institutional framework for the elaboration of British studies of Indian language, religion and politics. It was a venue where Sir William Jones, the prime mover behind the establishment of the Society and its first President, reshaped the understandings of the relationship between European and Indian languages and cultures.[39]

Jones's career has been widely debated by historians, linguists and literary scholars. He has recently re-emerged as a key figure in the intellectual history of the eighteenth century and he has been recently eulogized as 'one of the first European scholars to break through European prejudices'.[40] Rather than contributing to the growing hagiographical literature surrounding Jones's career, my main concern is with delineating the new linguistic and ethnological paradigms fashioned by Jones and locating these models within shifting patterns of knowledge production and dissemination.

Jones's comparative work on Asian and European languages was the most important strand of British Indology, and perhaps European Orientalism more generally, in the eighteenth century. Although Jones is commonly identified as the parent of comparative linguistics and Indo-European studies, he initially had no interest in Sanskrit, which was not mentioned in the list of 16 subjects Jones outlined as he sailed for India.[41] The realities of the colonial justice system and Jones's concerns about the limits of colonial knowledge prompted his study of Sanskrit. He feared forgery and perjury, believing that the power of the pandits was unchecked because of their monopoly of Sanskritic knowledge.[42] With the aid of a pandit from Krishnagar, Jones began his Sanskrit studies late in 1785 and made rapid progress and he was able to describe himself as 'tolerably strong' in Sanskrit by September 1786.[43]

Jones's Sanskrit studies had a broader utility than he initially anticipated, because they reshaped his vision of language, history and ethnology. In February 1786, less than six months into his serious study of Sanskrit, Jones delivered his Third Anniversary Discourse, 'On the Hindu's [sic]' to the Asiatic Society. This paper was the first in a series of essays that explored the evidence for, and nature of, Asian ethnography and history. Because he aimed to establish a new framework of Asian history in the series, Jones was very concerned with the question of cultural origins. Indeed the final essay in the series was entitled 'On the Origin and Families of Nations'.[44]

The study of language was the essential tool for Jones's project, providing a key source for his speculations on Indian 'civil history'. He believed the careful study of etymology and grammar would demystify the 'cloud of fables' that Indians wove around the past. Fortunately the very languages used to construct Indian myths and legends were rich sources in themselves. Examining the available evidence, Jones suggested that Sanskrit 'was introduced [to north India] by conquerors from other kingdoms in some very remote age' displacing 'the pure *Hindi*' of north India.[45] He was deeply impressed by Sanskrit and his enthusiasm is seen in his famous statement that Sanskrit

> is of a wonderful structure; more perfect than the *Greek*, more copious than the *Latin*, and more exquisitely refined than either, yet bearing to both of them a stronger affinity, both in the roots of the verbs and in the forms of the grammar, than could possibly have been produced by accident; so strong indeed, that no philologer could examine them all three, without believing them to have sprung from some common source, which, perhaps, no longer exists ...[46]

Thus Jones's 'Discourse' identified a close affinity between Sanskrit and European languages, a discovery which profoundly shaped the development of linguistics, the study of early Indian history and, as we shall see, debates over Indian, British and even Polynesian identity.[47]

Language and cultural comparison

Jones's argument marks a substantial shift in the history of linguistics. His work was rigorously empirical, divorcing the study of language from broader philosophical speculations on the nature of the mind and language.[48] Instead, he argued that the study of language, like the study of nature, should be carefully inductive, adhering closely to observable facts. He attacked the speculative use of etymology as 'a medium of proof so very fallacious, that, where it elucidates one fact, it obscures a thousand, and more frequently borders on the ridiculous, than leads to any solid conclusion'.[49]

Most importantly, Jones suggested that language was a valuable source for discerning relationships between different peoples, but it was not the only source, and his discourses on Asia also examined philosophy, monumental remains, 'their *Sciences* and *Arts'* in addition to language. Nevertheless, language did bear the greatest analytical weight in Jones's reconstruction of Asian history. Etymological connections, if securely established *a posteriori*, were strong evidence of connections between peoples, but they were not enough alone to establish a link with certainty. Grammatical structure provided the key test: it could establish the relationship between languages or, just as easily, disprove it.[50] This rigorous methodology not only marked Jones's work from his more speculatively minded contemporaries but it also allowed him to identify deeply embedded grammatical and etymological affinities between Sanskrit and European languages.

These linguistic affinities moulded Jones's views of ethnology and human history. Jones reconciled his belief in the connection between Indian and European languages with the Genesis account that underpinned western understandings of language and human development: methodological innovation was not incompatible with an ethnological model derived from the Bible.[51] In his linguistic work Jones reaffirmed the essential unity of humanity, believing that even Chinese contained links to the languages of Tibet and India, further confirming the 'common origin' of language. Jones fortified Christianity by orientalizing the biblical account of Creation. He confirmed the broad outlines of Genesis: all of humanity was descended from an original couple and he was 'absolutely certain' that Iran was the post-Diluvian centre from where the 'whole race of man proceeded'.[52] He argued that after the Flood three distinct races emerged: 'Persians and Indians' (including the Greeks, Romans, Goths, Egyptians and their descendants, and probably the Chinese and Japanese), 'the Jews and Arabs', and 'the Tartars'. Not only did these three broadly defined races approximate the sons of Noah, but they were also defined primarily on a linguistic basis.[53]

It is clear that Jones's division was quite different from later nineteenth-century theories that would equate Aryans (Indians, Europeans and even Polynesians) as the sons of Japhet. In Jones's scheme the Tartars approximated the sons of Japhet, but they were uncivilized nomads who lagged well behind the other branches of the human family. The more advanced 'Jews and Arabs' were the sons of Shem. The languages of the Semites were fundamentally different from the languages of the final group, the 'Persians and Indians'. This group, the descendants of Ham, peopled Africa, India, Italy, Greece and perhaps East Asia and central America.

Jones's insistence on the Hamitic origins of what later scholars would call the Indo-European or Aryan family reflected both European and Indian sources. Thomas Trautmann has shown that Jones's theory reworked and extended Jacob Bryant's *Analysis of antient mythology* (1774–6) which argued that the Egyptians, Greeks, Romans and Indians were all the descendants of Ham.[54] This interpretation that identified Hindus as the sons of Ham was supported by Indo-Islamic sources. Muhammad Qasim Firishtah's Persian history identified the Indians as the offspring of Ham, while the *Akbar Nama* also emphasized the Hamitic origins of the Hindus, while attaching greater value to the Japhetic origins of the Mughals. The currency of these ideas among the learned Indo-Islamic elite simultaneously confirmed the ethnological framework of Genesis and supported Jones's vision of India's place in global history.[55]

Like many other eighteenth-century scholars, Jones saw the Bible as an Oriental text, suggesting that European readers should make 'all due allowances' for the 'figurative Eastern style' of Genesis.[56] His work was within a long established English tradition of ethnic theology, which used the Bible to explain cultural difference, effectively defending the Genesis account through the study of other cultures. Indeed, as we have seen, his account of post-Diluvian ethnic differences echoed the table of nations in Genesis 10. Like Lord Kames and Samuel Shuckford before him, Jones reconciled the ethnic differences confronting eighteenth-century Europeans with Biblical authority.[57]

Jones's reassertion of the accuracy of Genesis and the shared origins of Indians and Europeans established a new comparative basis for the study of cultures. Unlike some European scholars Jones did not suggest that Sanskrit was the parent of all the related Indian and European languages, or the source of all civilization.[58] Rather, Jones's emphasis on linguistic affinities created a comparative framework which combined a sensitivity to the complexity of a local (in this case Indian) culture with a desire to explain the pattern of human history at a global level. Majeed has rightly argued that 'Jones's thesis of the Indo-European family of languages ... enabled comparisons to be made between cultures on a much firmer foundation than before.'[59] Indeed, the central thrust of Jones's argument was that there was a fundamental unity in human thought, belief and action hidden under the veneer of linguistic difference. Jones noted, for example, in the First Discourse that 'the sacred poems of the *Persians and Hindus* ... seem to mean the same thing in substance, and differ only in expression.'[60]

This comparative project was further consolidated by Jones's researches on Indian chronology. He relied heavily on the aid of pandits to establish a firm basis for the chronology of Indian history. After many difficulties he was able to identify Alexander's Sandrocottas with Chandragupta and the city of Palibothra with Pataliputra (modern Patna). These identifications provided a common temporal and geographical framework for the reconstruction of Indian history from *Indian* sources and created the possibility of comparing concomitant change in Indian and European societies on the basis of a shared chronology.[61] This was a crucial moment in shaping British understandings of India's past. Where earlier Orientalists relied heavily upon classical sources for their reconstruction of Indian history, in the wake of Jones scholars were able to produce interpretations of the South Asian past drawn from local texts and traditions: the project of writing European-style histories of the Vedic period and the Aryas was possible for the first time.

Colebrooke and the Vedic golden age

Henry Thomas Colebrooke, a key figure in the Company's educational and judicial apparatus, pursued these projects. A Company writer in Madras from 1783, Colebrooke rapidly mastered Sanskrit and he was appointed the inaugural Professor of Sanskrit at Fort William College, a post he held from 1800 to 1804 before serving on the Company's Supreme Council from 1807. During this period he was especially prolific. In 1808 he completed his *Sanscrit Dictionary* for Fort William students and two years later he published *The Translation of Two Treatizes on the Hindu Law of Inheritance*, which revealed the complex regional variations in Indian legal tradition and guided the Company's judicial officers in the administration of Bengal's customary law.[62]

Colebrooke's work deepened British knowledge of Sanskrit and India's ancient history, extending and refining Jones's path-breaking research. Colebrooke, for example, revised Jones's depiction of the relationship between Indian languages, correctly arguing that Hindi did not precede Sanskrit as Jones maintained; rather it descended from it.[63] Colebrooke identified Sanskrit as the fount of Indian civilization, a very significant argument given his assertion that 'civilization had its origin in Asia'.[64] If Sanskrit embodied the precocious development of civilization in Asia, it also embodied a lost golden age: Colebrooke argued that post-Vedic Indian history was characterized by decline and degeneration. Thus Colebrooke constructed a dichotomized image of Hinduism: the beef-eating Aryas of the Vedas, whose rationality was evident in their monotheism and their village republics, were contrasted with modern Hindus who had degenerated into idolatry, polytheism and sensuality.[65] Jones himself had posited a similar argument, contrasting contemporary Hinduism with the Vedic golden age: 'how degenerate and abased so ever the Hindus may now appear ... in some early age they were splendid in arts and arms, happy in government; wise in legislation, and eminent in various knowledge'.[66]

Thus Company Orientalism, exemplified by Jones and Colebrooke, created a 'Sanskritocentric' vision of Indian culture that celebrated Sanskrit and the Vedas, but decried contemporary culture as debased and backward. This in part reflected the continuing importance of classicism in English political thought and high culture: both Jones and Colebrooke, like many eighteenth-century educated Britons, had a sound knowledge of classical languages and literature.[67] This classical sensibility encouraged them to believe that the ancient Hindus, like their Greek and Roman cousins, had created a vibrant culture that had been lost in the political fragmentation and moral turpitude of the medieval 'dark ages'. Equally importantly, their classicist vision was further encouraged by their enthusiastic engagement with Sanskritic tradition and their acceptance of the cultural authority of their own Brahmanical teachers. These Orientalists acquired their linguistic skills through the teaching of pandits who immersed their European students in the complexities of Sanskrit grammar. Jones, for example, relied heavily on the *Amarakosha* (a basic vocabulary with etymological commentary), Durgadasa's grammar plus a range of other Sanskrit linguistic works.[68] Panini, the foremost Sanskrit grammarian, who composed his works sometime before 250 BC, loomed large for European learners of Sanskrit. Panini's models, and later grammatical works such as *Siddhantakaumudi*, established the essential patterns for all Europeans who learned Sanskrit. The strength and variety of the Indian linguistic corpus greatly impressed Europeans: it was a substantial body of learning that rivaled anything produced by Greece and Rome.[69]

Although convinced of the degenerate nature of modern Indian society, these Orientalists valued India's classical past, both as the source of the traditions that were to be the basis of the Company's authority and as a store of universal knowledge.

The impact of Sanskritocentrism

This Sanskritocentric image of South Asian language and culture had a significant impact on European thought in the late eighteenth and nineteenth centuries. Its influence was uneven and took on a variety of forms, as the structure of academic institutions, the place of language in developing senses of national identity and the divergent political forces shaped the European reception of this 'discovery' of Sanskrit and the Vedas. Although its impact in England itself was both delayed and highly contested, the Aryan idea played a central role in the development of imperial ethnology, from Ireland to South-East Asia.

The work of the Calcutta-based Orientalists was widely disseminated throughout Europe. This was, to a significant degree, the product of Sir William Jones's effective marriage of letter-writing and print culture: he constructed a large web of correspondents with whom he exchanged information and texts on a range of subjects, from botany to Sanskrit, music to Hindu law. Although the first edition of *Asiatick Researches* was not printed until January 1789, by that time Jones's correspondence had whetted the appetite of learned European circles. This European audience welcomed an early-published version of his First Discourse and exhibited a voracious demand for the journal, as pirate editions of *Asiatick Researches* quickly appeared.[70] Jones's web of correspondence was impressive, including leading English intellectuals (most notably Sir Joseph Banks), important political and cultural figures in Ireland (Edmund Burke and Joseph Cooper Walker) and on the continent, where Jones's work was especially influential. Goethe observed in 1819 that the 'merits of this man [Jones] are universally known and have been emphasized and detailed on numerous occasions'.[71]

The rapid dissemination of Jones's work and influence in Europe reminds us of the porous boundaries between various empires and states (even in an age of political crisis and international conflict) and the cohesive power of correspondence and print-culture.[72] Most intriguingly, it was Georg Forster who was central in knitting together German Romanticism, Pacific studies and Orientalism: just as his account of his voyage with Cook triggered a 'Pacific craze' in Europe, his translation of Jones's Latin rendering of the Sanskrit play *Shakuntala* was central in ushering in an age of 'Indomania' in Germany.[73] Forster sent a copy of the first edition to Herder, who was stunned by its beauty and power.[74] Not only did Herder write the Preface for the second edition of Forster's work, but he was subsequently convinced that the divine origins of humanity could be firmly located in India.[75] South Asia rapidly became a key source for German Romanticism, as the importance of philology and a Romantic desire for spiritual renewal in Germany reinforced and enlarged on the 'Sanskritocentrism' of Jones and Colebrooke. Friedrich von Schlegel was convinced of the ancestral primacy of Sanskrit and India's spiritual vitality, and in September 1803 he wrote to Ludwig Tieck: 'Everything, yes, everything without exception has its origin in India.' Schwab has argued that Schlegel's conversion was the single most important factor in the rapid growth of Indological studies in continental Europe as he created a 'cultural movement out of one particular field of knowledge'.[76] More recently, Pollock has traced the emergence of an 'Indo-German' versus 'Semite' dichotomy, delineating the Nazi's deployment of a German Orientalism as an instrument of 'internal colonialism' and Aryanism's pivotal role within the 'worldview of a newly imagined [National Socialist] empire'.[77]

Indocentrism: the Scottish Enlightenment in 'Further India'

Although the English response to Jones's work was muted in comparison to its reception in Germany, it did profoundly influence models for the analysis of cultural difference within the United Kingdom and its empire. Jones's use of comparative philology as an ethnological tool was particularly influential within the context of the Scottish Enlightenment. Within the mixed-linguistic environment of their homeland, Scottish writers were less concerned with using comparative philology to buttress any claims for a precocious nationhood in the manner of German Romantics, or even a self-sufficient national identity; rather it provided a series of insights and methodologies that stimulated the writing of global history. Although there has been a recent flowering of scholarship on the Scottish Enlightenment, greater emphasis needs to be placed on the conspicuous role of Scots in the British empire as a key condition for the emergence of the Scottish traditions of moral economy, philology and 'philosophical history'.[78] A group of scholars, trained at Edinburgh University between 1784 and 1803, drew on their Company service to write histories of Asian societies that traced their rise from 'rudeness' to 'refinement' against the backdrop of the universal development of civilization. This approach, which William Robertson hoped would challenge belief in the 'natural' superiority of Europeans, prioritized language as a lens of analysis, as comparative philology allowed the level of development of any given society to be located more precisely.[79]

Alexander Hamilton, who served in India from 1783 to 1796, gained renown as an essayist and language instructor working largely within a Jonesian framework. Although Hamilton preferred a 'conjectural' account of the origin of language to Genesis, he believed that Sanskrit was of particular importance for scholars because of the linguistic affinities that Jones had demonstrated. He argued that philology was essential for historians of civilization, as language was the 'most imperishable guide' to the origin and development of nations.[80] Hamilton was an influential advocate of Jonesian philology and a popularizer of Orientalism through his writings in the leading journals such as the *Edinburgh Review* or the *Asiatic Annual Register*. A competent Sanskritist, he shared his 'embodied' knowledge of the language with Friedrich von Schlegel while he was held as a paroled prisoner in Paris following the failure of the Peace of Amiens in 1803. This encounter was a crucial vector for the introduction of Sanskrit into European learned circles and Hamilton's emphasis on comparative philology shaped the methodology of his German student. More importantly, Hamilton's understanding of language and history was communicated to budding Company men in his lectures at the Company's East India College at Haileybury until 1818.[81]

Comparative philology, with a heavy Indian focus, was particularly important in the examination of the origins and development of the peoples of 'Further India' – modern South-East Asia. British Orientalists devoted considerable efforts to delineating the peopling of South-East Asia and establishing the links between the region's languages and those of India. Francis Buchanan, for example, suggested that a common 'Tartar' stock united 'the Peninsula of India beyond the Ganges', extending through the Malay peninsula and archipelago to 'New Guinea'.[82] Texts such as William Marsden's *History of Sumatra* (1787), Stamford Raffles' *History of Java* (1817) and John Crawfurd's *History of the Indian Archipelago* (1820) were peppered with discussions of words, customs and beliefs that could be traced back to India.[83]

While the term 'Further India' suggested the profound cultural continuities linking South and South-East Asia, it also reflected the reality that the British saw both mainland and island South-East Asia as frontiers of their Indian empire. Of course, Scottish ethnologists such as Crawfurd not only had considerable experience in India but also arrived in South-East Asia in the service of the East India Company. This experience, together with the authority that Orientalist learning enjoyed during their education in Scotland, encouraged these Orientalists to fashion an imagined geography of Asia that located India as the core region, from whence cultural, religious and linguistic influences emanated outwards to societies on the 'periphery' of this Indic world. By the turn of the nineteenth century India, especially Calcutta, had become a crucial subimperial centre within Britain's commercial and colonial system.

John Leyden, who eventually became Professor of Hindustani at Fort William College, mapped the linguistic and cultural affinities within the both 'Indo-Persic' and the 'Indo-Chinese' of 'Further India'. He argued that 'examining the mutual relation of the several languages which are current [in these societies] ... is always the surest clue for developing the origin of a nation'.[84] Following Jones's path-breaking work, Leyden identified the nature and extent of Sanskrit and Arabic borrowings in Bahasa Malay. Leyden suggested that the Malays used these loan words for sophisticated legal or cultural notions following contact with Hindu and Muslim traders. Leyden believed that only such a philological approach could unravel the complexity of South-East Asian societies and history.

John Crawfurd's *History of the Indian Archipelago* shared many concerns with Leyden's work. On the basis of linguistic evidence he identified the Javanese as the most advanced of the region's peoples, but argued that their development had nonetheless arrested. Crawfurd argued the Javanese language was shallow in comparison to Indo-European languages, as it lacked the 'capacity to generalize, to make abstract or subtle distinctions'. This inadequacy fixed the Javanese as 'semi-barbarous' on the scale of civilization.[85] Linguistic affinities between the peoples of the archipelago, the Pacific and India led Crawfurd to accept William Marsden's theories of a 'Greater Polynesian' language which linked the southern Pacific rim to the rest of civilization and universal history.[86]

Orientalism, the Irish Enlightenment and settler self-fashioning

Similar debates over cultural sophistication and the boundaries of race raged much closer to home, in Ireland. While Georg Forster wove

Pacific studies and Orientalism together, Charles Vallancey laced Orientalism into the study of Irish language, culture and history. Vallancey, the English-born son of Huguenot émigrés and a leading military engineer (and later Chief Surveyor of Ireland), attempted to document Irish history and culture. Heavily influenced by both the monogenism of Genesis and studies of Oriental philology, Vallancey believed that the analysis of the Irish past was best undertaken in a comparative light. Vallancey's early work was influenced by the work of Sir William Jones's studies of Persian and drew heavily upon the work of William Marsden and J. Z. Holwell on Asian history. In his *Vindication of the Ancient History of Ireland* (1786), Vallancey argued that Irish culture exhibited profound affinities with a range of 'Eastern' traditions. Based on manuscript sources and extensive comparative vocabularies, Vallancey asserted that the Irish were in fact Pheno-Scythians who had migrated from the Caspian Sea to Ireland via Persia, Africa and Spain. In both mobilizing the growing authority of Orientalist learning and working within a well-established early modern tradition of Mosaic ethnology (where differences between peoples were explained through the ethnological and historical framework of the Bible), Vallancey was marrying the new and old to assert the antiquity and sophistication of Irish culture.[87] This argument had political implications that were made even clearer when Vallancey drew parallels between the Irish experience of English domination and the Roman destruction of Carthaginian culture.[88]

This engagement with British Orientalism grew over time, as his later *The ancient history of Ireland, proved from the Sanscrit books of the Bramins of India* (1797) was moulded by the rather speculative work of the Sanskritist Francis Wilford on Indian geography.[89] Vallancey's engagement with Orientalist learning was not unique; in fact other leading figures in Irish intellectual life had close intellectual ties with India. Edmund Burke, of course, was prominent in debates over the East India Company and was a frequent correspondent of Sir William Jones, while the leading Irish antiquarian Joseph Cooper Walker also exchanged ideas about Irish and Indian music with Jones, parallels which he examined in his *Historical Memoirs of the Irish bards*.[90] These personal connections reflected the substantial material, personal and ideological networks that linked Ireland and India within the British colonial system.[91]

What is striking about the development of Celticism in this period is the heavy interdependence between a strengthening interest in antiquarianism and philology and the political agenda of the Patriots, a group of leading Protestants resentful of the restrictions imposed by London on Irish trade (especially within the empire) and the limited opportunities for the Irish-born in British and imperial administrations. The Patriots hoped to win commercial freedom, significant constitutional concessions and cultural respect from London. Sylvester O'Halloran, a leading Patriot antiquarian and physician, stated that his *Introduction to the Study of the History and Antiquities of Ireland* was motivated by a 'natural reverence for the dignity and antiquity of my native country' which he saw as Ireland rather than Britain. He suggested his work was a response to English and Scottish authors who represented the 'Irish nation as the most brutal and savage of mankind, destitute of arts, letters, and legislation'.[92] Lawrence Parsons, an ardent defender of Vallancey's scholarship, hoped that the project pursued by Vallancey and other antiquarians would 'relieve this country from the unjust charges of ignorance and barbarism'.[93] Thus these Patriot antiquarians, who were arguing for greater constitutional rights and a share in the empire for Ireland, grounded their arguments for administrational reform in an assertion of the quality and value of Ireland's indigenous culture. These arguments were staking a particular claim to political and cultural authority: the 'native-born' Anglo-Irish were better-suited to the administration of Ireland than 'foreign' administrators born in England. In this sense we can understand the work of Celticists such as Vallancey as part of a project of settler self-fashioning, where antiquarianism and ethnology were central in the attempts of local settler elites to mark themselves off from their metropolitan counterparts through an engagement with 'indigenous' tradition: an engagement, however, that was profoundly embedded in the structures of inequality engendered by colonial domination.

These arguments were undercut by the rebellion of 1798 which checked what Colin Kidd has termed the 'latitudinarian spirit of the Irish Enlightenment'.[94] But once British authority had been reasserted, debates over Ireland's affinities with the 'East' would flare again: particularly within the lasting forum of the Royal Irish Academy (founded 1785), the institutional achievement of the Irish Enlightenment and the key space for Protestant Celticism. In October 1827, for example, L. C. Beaufort presented a paper to the Academy that suggested pre-Norman Irish architecture was shaped by Ireland's cultural origins in the 'unchanging east'.[95] Drawing particularly on the work of Jones, but also on an array of other British and continental Orientalists, Beaufort attempted to substantiate further the Oriental origins of the Irish people. Tracing similarities between Irish and 'Oriental' material culture, Beaufort identified an endless stream of analogies, affinities and resemblances: the houses of 'India and Caubul' echoed the design of the 'Irish cabin'; Irish round towers were suggestive of the pagodas of Asian temples; Irish spirituality seemed to be an offshoot of Hindu sun-veneration and Zoroastrianism. Thus, for Beaufort, the allied development of Orientalism and Celticism clearly revealed the eastern, but 'chiefly ... Persian origin' of 'many customs' found in Ireland.[96]

Arguments over the origins and development of Irish culture intensified in the early 1830s when the 'Origin and Uses of the Round Towers' was designated as the topic for the Royal Irish Academy's prize essay for 1830. Although George Petrie's winning essay, which was finally published as *The ecclesiastical architecture of Ireland* in 1845, presented a detailed critique of the diffusionist tradition and established the medieval ecclesiastical origins of the towers, it was the runner-up Henry O'Brien's essay that stimulated public debate. O'Brien's *The Round Towers of Ireland (or the mysteries of freemasonry, of sabaism, and of budhism, now for the first time unveiled)* (1834) insisted that the phallic symbolism of the round towers revealed the Oriental influence which had imprinted Ireland's culture, a heritage which could be traced back to an ancient form of fertility worship supposedly practised in Persia by Zoroastrians and Buddhists. O'Brien's argument was resurrected by Ulick Bourke's *Aryan origin of the Gaelic race and language* (1875), a work which bolstered the diffusionist argument through a heavy engagement with the works of James Cowles Prichard, Max Müller, and Henry Sumner Maine. Bourke's avowed aim was to popularize the 'Aryan' origins of the Irish and to use Aryanism to instil pride in the attainments of the Irish past. Bourke's argument was closely tied to his advocacy of the Irish language and his role as a spokesman for a 'revivalist populist nationalism'.[97]

Prichardian ethnology and the Anglo-Saxon revival

These debates over Irish origins, together with the cultural authority of Jonesian philology, provide two fruitful contexts for reading the work of the leading English ethnologist James Cowles Prichard. In England comparative philology had a less marked and less immediate impact than in Germany or Scotland and it was not until the 1840s and 1850s that linguistic research into human and national origins became popular. The English lagged well behind the rapid advances made by German philologists, and continental scholars, like Rasmus Rask, felt that English linguistic research was backward.[98] In part, this reflected the lack of institutional support for philology, for while France and Germany established university chairs in Sanskrit and Indian studies from 1812 and 1818 respectively, it was not until 1833 that the Boden chair in Sanskrit was established at Oxford.[99] Moreover, English intellectuals largely ignored the Scottish models of philologically based history. From 1808 until the 1840s James Cowles Prichard was the only scholar in England who exhibited a consistent interest in philology and its historical and ethnological applications.

Prichard, an Edinburgh-trained physician born to Quaker parents, was the foremost exponent of a linguistically driven ethnology in England.[100] In his ethnographic writings, which followed his conversion to Anglican evangelicalism in 1809, Prichard sought to reconcile his strong awareness of cultural variation with a firm belief in the primacy of Genesis.[101] In this he was influenced by British Indologists, especially Sir William Jones, seeing the flourishing of research in India as a revolution in human knowledge which mirrored advances in geology and zoology.[102] Prichard hoped that the Orientalists' philological research would throw 'much light' onto 'the history of the European nations'.[103]

Most importantly, Prichard, like Jones, used philology to defend the accuracy of Genesis and to establish relationships between apparently distinct peoples. In his landmark *Researches into the Physical History of Man* he argued that linguistic comparison could provide the 'most important' proof of the origin of nations, as the permanency of languages was 'a remarkable fact in the history of mankind'. Prichard looked to linguistic structure, rather than etymological similarity, to establish affinity. As his obituarist noted, Prichard used comparison to defend monogenism, as his comparisons inevitably found 'fixed points of coincidence or agreement, with which to form a standard of comparison for apparently discordant materials'.[104] Not surprisingly, given this methodological tendency and his religious orientation, Prichard's *Researches* affirmed the unity of humanity. Like Jones, he pushed human origins to the east and in the 1813 edition of *Researches* Prichard suggested that humanity's home was in south-west Asia between the Nile and the Ganges. On a similar linguistic basis, his *Analysis of Egyptian Mythology* (1819) asserted that Egyptian culture had developed within the universal framework of the Biblical chronology.[105] Prichard also confirmed Jones's argument that Egyptians, Indians and Europeans were the sons of Ham. But where Jones saw pigmentation as the product of climate, Prichard, at least initially, argued that colour was related to civilization, suggesting that those branches of the Hamitic family which became more civilized (such as Europeans and north Indians) were lighter in colour than those who did not advance, who, like the Africans, retained the initial dark pigmentation of Adam and Eve.[106]

In his 1831 work *The Eastern Origin of the Celtic Nations*, Prichard extended these arguments to embrace the Celts, locating the Celtic peoples of Britain and Ireland within the mainstream of the history of civilization. Drawing heavily on German philology, Prichard illustrated that sound shifts placed Celtic languages within the Indo-European family. On a rigorous empirical basis he was able to rebut those who suggested that the Celts were 'entirely distinct from the rest of mankind' showing that ancient Welsh and its derivatives were of 'cognate origin with the Sanskrit, Greek and Latin'.[107] Prichard's findings were confirmed by the well-known linguist Adolphe Pictet, whose *De l'affinité des langues celtiques avec le Sanscrit* (1837) provided lengthy discussions of phonology, word-formation and inflexion to establish the genetic relationship between Celtic languages and Sanskrit.[108] Like Vallancey's earlier work, these arguments defended the achievements of marginalized Celtic peoples by repositioning them at the heart of European and global history.

Prichard's insistence on human unity struggled against the increasing racialism of British social thought.[109] Although regional rivalries and local identities continued to dominate everyday life, many British intellectuals, politicians and religious leaders were concerned with broader levels of racial identity as they strived to define Britain's place in the world. Prichard's later works were produced during the peak of the Anglo-Saxon revival which stressed the distinct political and cultural sophistication of the English people. From the time of the Glorious Revolution on, English writers had emphasized that the constitution embodied Germanic ideals and that, as Saxons, they had always been distinguished by their love of civil liberty. David Hume's influential *History of England* (1778), for example, stressed the distinctly Germanic nature of the Saxons and contrasted them favourably with the 'abject' Britons.[110] The philologists Benjamin Thorpe and John Kemble strengthened this conception. From the early 1830s these two scholars, both of whom had strong German links, collected and published a vast range of Anglo-Saxon literature which emphasized the connection between England's Anglo-Saxon heritage and Germanic culture.[111]

Thomas Arnold, headmaster of Rugby School and Professor of History at Oxford, expressed the growing Teutonmania most forcefully. He acknowledged that English culture was a complex amalgam of

Semitic, Greek, Roman and German influences, but argued that the distinctive nature of the English was due to their German heritage.[112] Following Thomas Arnold's lead, English thinkers drew an increasingly rigid opposition between the Saxons and the Celts, between the English and the Welsh and Irish, and between Protestant and Catholic. Even those who attempted to promote Celtic Studies, like Matthew Arnold, were deeply ambivalent about the value of Celtic culture and language.[113] These views were carried over into political discourse and policy. Roberts has shown, for example, that the *Reports of the Commissioners of Inquiry into the State of Education in Wales* (1847) depicted Wales as a land sunken in superstition, crippled by a primitive language and degraded by rampant immorality.[114] These cultural stereotypes were further bolstered by the polygenist anthropology of Robert Knox and W. F. Edwards that applied rigid taxonomies to classify European populations into distinct communities.[115] The assertion of England's Germanic character continued to be a powerful force into the 1870s as English historians, such as J. R. Green and William Stubbs, used the Saxon heritage as the starting point for their nationalist narratives.[116]

However, Teutonmania was just one competing strand in the complex interplay of ideas about what constituted Englishness. Some English authors insisted that the nation's genealogy could be traced back to the Israelites, an idea which was popular both at home and in the colonies into the mid-nineteenth century.[117] For some, the Teutonic and Semitic arguments were reconcilable; Richard Brothers, for example, argued that the English were essentially Saxon, and that the Saxons themselves were Semites.[118] But another group of British historians and ethnologists dissented from both the Teutonic and Semitic arguments, upholding Daniel Defoe's characterization of the English as 'a Mongrel half-bred Race.... In whose hot Veins now Mixtures quickly ran'.[119] R. G. Latham, the leading British ethnologist of the mid-nineteenth century, supported this theory in his *Ethnology of the British Islands* (1852). Latham argued that 'Kelts, Romans, Germans, and Scandinavians ... supply us with the chief elements of our population, elements which are mixed up with each other in numerous degrees of combination'.[120] Britons, he noted, were 'more or less hybrid'.[121]

Max Müller and the Aryan theory

It was the research of Friedrich Max Müller that brought Orientalism to a large metropolitan audience and consolidated Aryanism's position at the centre of British imperial thought. After studying Sanskrit in both Germany and France, Max Müller travelled to London in 1846 to extend the research for his translation of the *Rig Veda*. Max Müller soon became close friends with Baron Bunsen, the Prussian plenipotentiary to Great Britain. Bunsen proved an influential contact, as his understandings of philology and history moulded Max Müller's work, and his influence also helped to secure Company backing for Max Müller's translation.[122] The quality of this translation won him a central role in the British academic establishment and from 1850 on he held teaching positions at Oxford, assuming the Chair of Comparative Philology created for him there in 1868.

While Max Müller's research was conducted within a very different political and intellectual framework than that of Jones and Colebrooke, in a profound sense his work was a continuation of that early Company Orientalist tradition. Although he would elaborate influential theories regarding the development of language, the movement of peoples and the evolution of religious sensibility, Max Müller consistently privileged India in his grand theories, insisting on the primacy of Sanskrit and the *Rig Veda*.[123] Towards the end of his life he reflected that 'if anything was unexpected, it was the discovery of a literature in India...of a literature more ancient than Homer, of a language less changed than Latin, of a religion more primitive than that of the Germans as described by Tacitus.'[124] But the Vedas not only provided a window on the birth of civilization itself, they also embodied a common linguistic and religious heritage to which both South Asians and Europeans were heirs. The *Rig Veda* introduced Max Müller to the Aryas, the nomadic pastoralists who migrated from central Asia into north India. While Jones's identification of the affinities between Greek, Latin and Sanskrit was an implicit starting point for much of Max Müller's research, he reworked Jones's interpretation of ethnic origins. Rejecting the notion that Europeans and Indians were the descendants of Ham, Max Müller returned to the longer established tradition of identifying Europeans (and by extension Indians) as the sons of Japhet.[125]

He was convinced that the Sanskrit-speaking Aryas had left the earliest records of the great Aryan migrations that had reshaped the demography and culture of Eurasia as a whole. This process was not a mere antiquarian curiosity, rather it profoundly imprinted Max Müller's contemporary world. As early as 1854, he suggested that when a Briton confronted 'a Greek, a German, or an Indian, we recognise him as one of ourselves'.[126] Because of this shared ancestry, the *Rig Veda* was particularly significant, as it provided the most ancient source, the 'oldest monument of Aryan speech and Aryan thought', for the reconstruction of the shared European and Indian past.[127] Like Jones and Colebrooke, Max Müller exhibited a stronger interest in India's past than in its present. Indians and Europeans shared a common heritage, but for Max Müller their contemporary position was fundamentally different. He believed that Europeans had continued to build upon the high achievements of their Aryan ancestors, while Indian culture had become stagnant, even degenerate. Certainly, the indigenous communities of South Asia had been greatly 'improved' through their contact with the incoming Aryas. This process was most marked in South India as a result of the 'peaceful' settlement by Brahmans and the inability of Muslim dynasties to establish lasting influence in the South. In the long term, however, the purity of Vedic Hinduism had been lost amid the flowering of popular Hinduism and the pernicious effects of Muslim authority.

However, because this degeneration was the product of a historical process rather than innate and essential difference, it was reversible. Max Müller hoped that by making the Vedas available in a new English edition to an educated Indian audience and by fashioning an image of the 'Vedic Golden Age' he would enable Indians to reform Hinduism and recapture the lost glory of their ancient history. This personal mission to revivify and purify Hinduism reflected the larger duty of Britain as imperial masters. Soon after his arrival in Britain, Max Müller argued that the role of Britons as fellow members of the 'Japhetic race' was to aid in the regeneration of their 'Arian brethren' in South Asia. This programme was best achieved through the use of indigenous vernaculars to communicate 'knowledge and instruction' and in this sense the British could do no better than follow the examples of the early Arya Brahmans who settled in the South and adopted local languages. The pursuit of Orientalist knowledge as the basis of colonial reform was, in Max Müller's view, both fundamental to Britain's role as an imperial power and an important quest for a nation that shared Japhetic origins with the South Asians who now were subject to British authority.

If Max Müller's work contained a curious mix of the old and the new, it was extremely influential. Not only did he cement the importance of philology as a tool for ethnology, but it was his work that popularized the Aryan concept. While the physician and Orientalist Thomas Young had coined the phrase 'Indoeuropean' to describe the related languages of Eurasia in 1813 and James Cowles Prichard pioneered 'Arian' as an ethnological term, it was Max Müller who

cemented the centrality of 'Aryan' within the lexicon of European ethnology and imperial culture. The notion of a shared Aryan heritage
that united Indians and Britons was widely disseminated through his
books, essays and lectures. The first edition of *History of Sanskrit
Literature* sold out within five months and in 1878 he had to deliver his
Hibbert lectures on the development of Indian religions in separate
morning and afternoon sessions to meet popular demand.[128]

Although Max Müller's research was widely disseminated, its authority was contested in light of Britain's imperial role. Some South Asians
immediately recognized the political and cultural potential for his
arguments for a colonized people. In 1874 a Bengali correspondent in
the *Indian Mirror* explained the impact of philological tradition which
culminated in Max Müller's work: 'We were niggers at one time. We
now become brethren.' European scholarship had elevated India: 'The
advent of scholars like Sir William Jones found us fully established in a
rank above that of every nation as that from which modern civilization
could be distinctly traced ... it is to the study of the roots and
inflexions of Sanskrit that we owe our national salvation.'[129] As the
final chapter of this book shows, Max Müller's interpretations of
Indian languages, religion and history were an important source for
the articulation of new visions of Hindu identity in the later nineteenth and early twentieth centuries.

While Max Müller's work was popular with Indians and fed into the
redefinition of Hindu identity, Britons were generally reluctant to
wholly accept Max Müller's vision of their shared origins with Indians
or his high valuation of Vedic culture.[130] The intricacies of comparative
philology were frequently glossed over or questioned, and in the
colonies race frequently became a crucial heuristic device and social
category.[131] In a context of colonial domination, racial history and
identity became highly politicized, particularly in the wake of the
crises that shook British colonial authority in the 1850s and 1860s.

Aryans, India and 1857

The revolt against British domination in 1857–58 made the question of
shared origins particularly sensitive: how could the English possibly be
related to such a 'barbaric' and 'savage' people? For many Britons 1857
convinced them that Indians were profoundly and essentially different.
Edward Byles Cowell, Professor of History at Presidency College,
Calcutta, noted this shift in British attitudes towards Indians in 1857:

'Nearly every Englishman ... now talks with haughty bitterness of the "niggers"'. Cowell also observed that 'nigger' was in general use in the newspapers following the revolt.[132] W. H. Russell reported that some Britons now felt that if 'niggers have souls, they're not the same as ours.'[133] J. W. Kaye remembered the intensity of English feeling in the wake of the revolt: 'the very sight of a dark man stimulated our national enthusiasm almost to the point of frenzy.'[134] These arguments not only insisted on the somatic differences between Indians and Europeans, but also conflated race and religion by postulating a fundamental spiritual difference between the races. Within this context, Max Müller's earlier insistence that an Englishman would recognize himself in an Indian found little support.

It is important to emphasize that the stark racial language of the post-rebellion period articulated deep-seated resentment about relations with servants and moneylenders, covert fears of miscegenation and the visceral anxieties that had long shaped the life of the small British community in India.[135] In other words, new racial ideologies were not minted in the crucible of the rebellion, rather Britons exhibited greater confidence in race as a marker of difference. This is most clear in the racialization of British Christianity, for although British Christians offered prayers and fasting as penance on 7 October 1857 (a 'day of national humiliation'), the rebellion actually fed Christian militarism in Britain. Many Christians believed the rebellion was providential, an act of a God angry at the neglect of Christianity in India.[136] This belief affirmed the view that divine dispensation guided British expansion and confirmed images of India as a land of fanatical heathens perpetually on the brink of rebellion.

But this growth in Christian militarism at home did not result in increased support for missionary activity among the administration in India. Senior government officials (except, perhaps, in the Punjab) were hostile towards missionary activity, as it was seen to exhibit the same fanaticism that supposedly characterized Islam. After the restoration of British authority many, including Disraeli and Sir Charles Wood, argued that Indians felt threatened by missionary activity and that the tampering of evangelicals in the 'private' sphere of Indian religion had in fact undermined British authority.[137] The debate over the establishment of a new church in Kanpur after the Mutiny encapsulated these tensions. As Metcalf has shown, the English community in Kanpur staunchly resisted the attempts from London, by the Society for the Propagation of the Gospel, to found a church for the Indians of Kanpur. The government of India sided with the British in Kanpur and subsequently established a memorial church, designed for the exclusive use of the cantonment's residents and dedicated to those Britons who died at Kanpur.[138] Evangelical missionaries were frustrated by this increasing identification between Christianity and British rule, believing that the spiritual needs of Indians were being sacrificed for political expediency. But for many Britons in India their religion had become identified with race: it was a cultural signifier that set them apart from Indians, not something to be shared with them.

The Mutiny also had a powerful psychological legacy, creating profound fear and distrust of Indians. Paxton has demonstrated how these anxieties were repeatedly expressed in British writing in the wake of the revolt. Indeed, she has suggested that the savage Indian rapist and the sacralized British heroine were dominant tropes in Britain's response to the revolt.[139] The figure of the wanton and rebellious sepoy, and his antithesis the indolent and effeminate Bengali *babu*, distanced Britons from their Indian subjects in the decades following 1857.[140]

Yet popular imperial ideologies grounded in the essentialized oppositions of race continued to be contested by influential figures within the British community in India: even in this moment of great crisis, the colonizing culture was riven by conflict and contestation. John Muir, a leading Sanskrit expert who taught at Banaras Sanskrit College, offered an elaborate and sophisticated summation of the connections between Britons and Indians in the wake of the rebellion. Muir's *Original Sanskrit Texts on the Origin and Progress of the Religion and Institutions of India* (3 vols, 1858–61) marshalled a huge weight of evidence from Sanskrit tradition to confirm the linguistic affinities between Sanskrit and European languages. After providing 29 pages of comparative vocabularies, comparing Sanskrit, Latin and Greek, Muir observed that 'the most primitive, the most fundamental, and the most essential parts' of these three languages were shared.[141] Muir confirmed Max Müller's earlier assessment of the value of the *Rig Veda* as a source, noting that it offered: 'the most authentic materials which we can ever obtain for our researches into the earliest history, religious and political, of the Indian people, and into their pre-historical relations with the other branches of the Indo-European family.'[142] Taken together, the *Rig Veda* and the linguistic evidence convinced Muir that Indians and Europeans were members of the same race, and he argued that on 'physiological grounds there is no reason for denying that the Indians are descended from the same stock as the nations of Europe.'[143] Muir readily accepted, unlike the later Max Müller, that linguistic affinities were a solid test of race, arguing that diet and climate produced the variation in complexion within the Aryan family.[144] Where Max Müller was afraid that a conflation of language and race would lead to the marginalization of supposedly non-Aryan groups in Europe, Muir believed that the congruence of race and language was an even more powerful proof of European and Indian fraternity.

Trautmann has suggested that by the third edition of his book Muir had retreated from this argument.[145] Certainly, as Muir himself notes, there were many attacks in the 1860s on the equation of language with race. John Crawfurd, for example, stressed that race was immutable and physical evidence, not language, was its only test.[146] But such attacks, moulded by the growing strength of Darwinian evolution, physical anthropology and pessimism regarding non-whites in the wake of the colonial conflicts of the 1850s and early 1860s, did not force Muir to uncouple race and language. In the third edition, published in 1874, Muir surveyed and dismissed these criticisms, before asserting his basic argument 'the original Sanskrit-speaking Indians were derived from the same stock as the Iranians, the Greeks, and the Romans'.[147]

Muir's willingness to make and maintain this argument is significant for two reasons. Firstly, these theories were being articulated within this general climate of heightened racial antagonism, and secondly, Muir's observations were aimed at as much an Indian as a British audience. In the first volume of the first edition, Muir noted that the collection was 'mainly for the use of Hindus who wish to become critically acquainted with the foundation on which their ancestral religion reposes.'[148] All editions noted on their title page that the works were 'chiefly for the use of students and others in India'. Indian students at the Banaras Sanskrit College were, therefore, encouraged not only to apply comparative philology to Sanskrit materials, but also to accept that linguistic and racial affinities linked India and Europe. Muir's work can thus be located within the broader traditions of Banaras Sanskrit College where Orientalists, such as J. R. Ballantyne, hoped to purify Indian knowledge and mould Indian traditions to western systems of reasoning.[149] The hybridity of Muir's texts, which drew on a range of European and Indian sources and provided extensive quotations in the *nagari* script for quotation, reflected the continued importance of this synthesizing drive well into the 1870s.

Other Britons also used a belief in shared origins to attack the growing Anglo-Indian arrogance in the public sphere. The most notable example of this was a lecture delivered to the Dalhousie Institute, Calcutta, by Samuel Laing in May 1862. Laing, a retiring Finance Member of the Viceroy's Council, addressed an audience containing Viceroy Lord Elgin and numerous other prominent members of Calcutta's administrative and clerical establishment.[150] In his lecture Laing asserted the unity of Aryan languages and cultures, but reserved particular praize for Zoroastrianism, which he identified as 'the most pure and rational of all religions'.[151] He identified intellectual capacity as the defining trait of all Aryans – after all there was 'no such thing as a stupid Arian nation'. But this intellectualism, Laing argued, made the Aryan 'more susceptible of outward influences' than either the 'stereotyped' Chinese or the 'narrow' Semite: indeed Aryan history was characterized by 'perpetual change'. The dominant direction of this change was forward, but Indian civilization had diverged from this path of progress. Fortunately, Laing suggested, Aryans had a unique 'capacity for regeneration', so India's decline was only temporary, and it could in the future lead 'the van of Arian nations'. While Laing believed that the 'Hindoo' had the same ability as other Aryans, his lecture was based on a rigid opposition he drew between Indians and other peoples under white domination. To speak of the regeneration of the 'Negro', 'Red American' or 'Australian' was 'mere moonshine' as none of these peoples could 'have written the *Ramayana* or *Mahabharata*, or composed the grammar of Panini'.[152] The Indian press enthusiastically received Laing's lecture. Maine remarked that 'I scarcely see a single native book or newspaper which does not contain some allusion to Mr. Laing's argument.' Although Laing assured his audience that linguistic science and politics were 'separate domains', his speech was significant for its timing, asserting Aryan unity and the potential of Indians when the memory of the revolt was still fresh. Maine recognized this, describing the speech as an 'act of courage, for I know how obstinate were those prejudices which he sought to overthrow'.[153] However, Laing's call for a recognition of Indo-European unity, like Muir's linguistic proofs, was frequently ignored as the social distance between the two communities continued to widen throughout the later nineteenth century: for the majority of Britons Indians had to be ruled with a firm hand, 'brothers' or not.

Aryanism as an ethnological tool

Although most Anglo-Indians attempted to distance themselves from South Asians in the second half of the nineteenth century, rejecting the possibility that they shared anything significant with the 'natives' they ruled over, Aryanism became deeply embedded within the culture of the British administration. The Aryan theory was particularly useful for British scholars and administrators who wanted to explain the broad sweep of South Asian history, as it offered a powerful framework for ethnological analysis that was seen to have legitimacy because it was itself a product of Sanskritic tradition. The rise of the Aryan concept was closely related to the growing power of the colonial state and its interest in constructing a coherent image of the boundaries and past of India as a 'nation'.[154] The Aryan 'invasion' provided the key starting point for this national narrative and many Britons imagined India's history as essentially the story of the changing fortunes of the Indo-Aryans. In a volume on Vedic India in the popular series *The Story of Nations* the prolific Victorian ethnologist Zénaïde Ragozin observed that Indian 'history *is to us* that of this race's (the Indo-Aryans) vicissitudes on the Himalayan continent, on which it has been supreme so long, materially and spiritually; that the history of Indian thought and speech is pre-eminently that of the Aryan mind'.[155]

The Aryan idea was not simply influential in the realm of representation and its popularity had marked socio-economic and political outcomes. Most importantly, Aryanism was one of the most important ideas guiding the reorganization of military recruitment in the wake of the 1857 rebellion. As imperial authority shifted from the Company to the Crown, the British reoriented military recruitment away from South India and Bengal towards northern regions of South Asia, especially Nepal, Punjab and Rajasthan, which were believed to be the home of 'martial races'. The 'martial races' policy was underpinned by a constellation of ideas about the effects of topography, climate and diet on a community's masculinity and military prowess. In short, rugged hilly landscapes, meat-eating and cooler climates were believed to produce hardy and robust men better suited to military service. For British recruiting officers, these environmental factors, however, were working within a racial matrix: an Aryan soldier from the northern hills was preferable to his non-Aryan neighbour. Aryan soldiers of 'pure' lineages could draw upon the 'warrior spirit' imprinted by a military heritage that stretched back to Vedic times, particularly soldiers of the *kshatriya varna* (warrior-ruler caste) whose *varna-dharma* (caste-based duty) was based on their ability to bear arms. By the turn of the twentieth century, the shift away from Bengal and the South as recruiting grounds was almost complete, as soldiers were overwhelmingly drawn from the 'Aryan' north, especially Punjab, the first Indian 'home' of the Aryans.[156] This shift to the north had profound long-term material consequences, as military service became fundamentally important in the region's economy, social structure and cultural values.[157]

The fundamental opposition drawn by this heavily gendered military Orientalism between manly 'Aryans' and the timid, effeminate southerners reflected the general ethnological contrast drawn between 'Aryans' and 'Dravidians'. This dichotomy was based on an awareness that the languages of central and southern India diverged in structure and etymology from the Sanskrit-derived languages of north India (such as Bengali, Punjabi and Rajasthani). Rev. Robert Caldwell used the term Dravidian (from the Sanskrit *dravida*) to designate these southern languages, creating a linguistic geography that marked off south and central India from the north. Caldwell firmly argued that the Dravidian languages, which seemed to exhibit some Scythian influences, were 'essentially different from, and independent of, Sanskrit'.[158] Although Caldwell was cautious about the direct relationship between language and race, British scholars in India generally accepted that language provided important evidence in tracing cultural affinities and the path of Indian history. The ethnologist and philologist Brian Hodgson, for example, argued that the 'immutability of language' was a stronger guide to ethnic identity and relations in India than physique, skin colour or appearance. For Hodgson, like Muir, race and language were effectively one and the same.[159] Hodgson argued that a fundamental linguistic unity linked all the aboriginal population, from the Dravidian speakers of the south to the Tibetan aborigines of the Himalayas.[160]

However unwilling, Caldwell had provided the terminology for a rigid opposition that quickly became a driving force in British interpretations of Indian history. A third linguistic grouping, Turanian (tribal speakers of a distinct group of non-Aryan languages), was often used in conjunction with or, as in Hodgson's case, coalesced with the Dravidian category. Taken together the Turanian and Dravidian peoples were a perfect foil for the definition of the characteristics of Indian Aryans. Aryans were (originally at least) tall, light complexioned, meat-eating and vigorous monotheists while the Dravidians and Turanians tended to be short, dark, vegetarian polytheists prone to idolatry and indolence.[161]

For those English commentators who accepted the philological proofs of common origin, but who were reluctant to accept the modern north Indian as an equal, this opposition provided a neat solution, as they were able to stress the hybrid nature of Indian Aryans. As the Aryans pressed south and south-east, some intermarried with the weaker Turanian and Dravidian peoples.[162] This intermarriage slowly introduced both inferior 'blood' and superstition into the Aryans, reducing the percentage of 'pure Aryan blood' until the Aryan identity of north Indians had become debased and their culture corrupted.[163] Thus racial admixture had weakened the Indian Aryans and it was this process that accounted for the differences between the European and Indian branches of the racial family. Ironically this interpretation was being forwarded in India at the same moment that many Britons proudly proclaimed that their very status as a mongrel race had elevated them to the forefront of world power. These apparently contradictory positions remind us that powerful interpretations in the metropolis were often modified or abandoned in light of the peculiar local requirements in the colonies. In post-Mutiny India, where increasing numbers of women accompanied their husbands and British social and commercial life was rigidly circumscribed within racialized patterns of town planning, few Britons were likely to argue that intermarriage was beneficial.[164]

The opposition between Aryan and Dravidian/Turanian elements in Indian culture also powerfully shaped British discourse on Indian aesthetics. James Fergusson, in his influential *History of Indian and Eastern Architecture*, reserved his highest praise for the Greek-influenced Gandharan art and the Buddhist monuments constructed between 200 BCE and 100 CE at Sanchi, Bharhut and Amrarvati. These, however, were brief moments of progress within an overall pattern of Indian artistic decline.[165] Fergusson divided the remainder of Hindu architecture into three classes: the Indo-Aryan of north India, the transitional Chalukyan style of the Deccan (which he devoted little attention to) and the Dravidian of south India.[166] These divisions were simultaneously aesthetic and racial. Indeed he argued that architecture was a more reliable guide to Indian racial history than Indian historical records. It was a 'great stone book, in which each tribe and race has written its annals and recorded its faith'.[167] Indo-Aryan architecture, for example, showed that the Aryans had rapidly intermarried with the aboriginal peoples of northern India and 'so degraded the purer religion of India [Vedic monotheism] into the monstrous system of idolatry that now prevails in this country.'[168] Fergusson reserved his harshest judgement for the 'Dravidian' architecture of south India. The elaborate decoration of these temples was distasteful: indeed the Madurai temple complex was full of the 'most barbarous' and 'the most vulgar' embellishments.[169]

The Aryan category also influenced the work of leading Anglo-Indian social theorists, most notably Henry Sumner Maine. Maine, like

Fergusson, believed that Indian Aryans had been enfeebled by their intermarriage with India's indigenous population, but Maine's attitude towards Aryan theories was more ambivalent. He never supported the philological proofs of common origins or their implications in the legal essays or lectures that he gave in India. When he did raise the possibility of common ancestry during his career in India, Maine dismissed it as politically irrelevant. In a lecture delivered before the Senate of the University of Calcutta in 1864, he expressed reservations about the linguistic proofs of affinity and suggested that even if the proofs were infallible the theory would not actually benefit Hindus.[170]

However, after his return to England, Maine drew heavily on the comparative method and made frequent use of Aryan as a category of analysis.[171] In 1871 he published *Village Communities in the East and West* in which he argued that the Indian Aryans, like their Teutonic cousins, established independent village councils that ruled over villages organized around communal land ownership. Thus Maine's later work consistently emphasized that Indians shared a common Aryan heritage with Europeans. Indeed for Maine, the very notion of civilization itself was nothing more than a synonym for 'the old order of the Aryan world'.[172] But in India, Aryan development had arrested as intermarriage with primitive indigenes curbed the progressiveness that naturally characterized other Aryan communities. India exhibited 'a whole world of Aryan institutions ... in a far earlier stage of growth' than was observable in any European branch of the Aryan family.[173] So on the one hand Maine elevated Indians to the status of Aryans, but on the other he suggested that north India effectively was an Aryan museum, where the early forms of Aryan society were frozen and on display for the European observer. Following the lead of Sir Charles Metcalfe, Maine had depicted India as a stagnant and timeless society, an enduring trope of western representations of India, and communicated this vision to thousands of young men entering the ICS.[174]

Regional variation and the limits of racialization: Punjab

These scholarly debates over Aryanism not only operated at an all-India level, but also fed into local and regional debates over history and identity.[175] This was particularly the case in the Punjab, which had been firmly identified as the first Indian home of the Aryas and the site of many of India's past glories. Max Müller noted that it was the Vedic home of the Aryas and that the Vedas contained glorious hymns 'addressed to the rivers of the Penjab'.[176] British historians, like Vincent A. Smith, depicted Alexander's incursion into the Punjab in 326 BCE as the high point of India's ancient past.[177] For Madame Blavatsky, the matriarch of Theosophy, the Punjab was also synonymous with the glories of the Aryan race. She compared the supposedly 'dwarfed and weakened' men of Bengal and the Deccan with Punjab, where 'the lethal influence of Mussulman, and later on of European, licentiousness, has hardly touched the orthodox Aryan castes, [and there] one still finds the finest men – so far as stature and physical strength go – on the whole globe'.[178] This opposition drawn between Punjabis and Bengalis was common in the nineteenth century and Blavatsky's quotation illuminates particularly the firm equation made between Aryan characteristics and manliness.[179]

While Blavatsky, Smith and Max Müller (like the army recruiting manuals that imagined ancient Aryan warrior traditions being passed from generation to generation of Punjabi peasants) celebrated the Aryan qualities of the Punjab, Aryanism actually had limited purchase among the province's British administrators. Those British officials with linguistic knowledge and first-hand experience of Punjab were hesitant to identify the region as wholly or even predominantly Aryan in character. The strong influence of Islam and the heterogeneous nature of Punjabi society meant that Punjabi culture was markedly different from the Sanskritized culture of the north Indian Hindi belt. Joseph Davey Cunningham, in the opening chapter of his *History of the Sikhs*, provided his readers with a detailed inventory of these different groups populating the Punjab.[180] Cunningham agreed that the Punjab, like the rest of north-western India and the Ganges valley, was 'colonized by a warlike sub-division of the Caucasian race' whose Vedic monotheism had eventually given way under the pressure of intermarriage with polytheistic non-Aryas.[181] But his concern with differentiation through caste, tribal and racial identities, and Sikhism's ability to counteract these centrifugal forces, meant that he had limited use for such a broad category as 'Aryan'.

His brother Alexander, the archaeological surveyor to the government of India, confirmed the heterogeneous racial history of the Punjab. Although he recognized the Punjab as the home of the Indo-Aryans, his report on his excavations conducted around Lahore and Peshawar in 1863–64 noted the waves of migration which had created the diverse population of modern Punjab. In his view the population was made up of three basic racial groups, 'Early Turanians or

Aborigines, Aryas or Brahmanical Hindus and Later Turanians or Indo-Scythians', but each of these groups contained internal divisions of language, specific place and date of origin, and social practice.[182] Richard Temple, on the other hand, argued that Punjabi fairy tales definitely were Aryan in character, like those of Bombay, Bengal and Oudh. While these tales evinced a distant north Indian ethnic unity, Temple dismissed the possibilty of a 'united India' as 'sheer nonsense': Aryan identity had rapidly diversified so that inter-regional and even intra-regional differentiation and hostility characterized modern Indian life.[183]

The divergence of the Punjab scholar-administrators from the Aryan model was most clear in Denzil Ibbetson's seminal 1883 census report, which emphasized the layering of Punjabi identities through caste, tribe, religion and language. Although Ibbetson did refer to the Aryan ethnic category, he located this category in the ancient past: it offered him little analytical power when attempting to describe and account for the diversity of modern Punjab.[184] While other ethnographers such as W.W. Hunter and H.H. Risley saw caste as essentially a racial structure, Ibbetson was a strong advocate of a historicized and functionalist interpretation of caste.[185] Caste, he argued, was primarily the product of access to economic resources and political power, rather than a racial hierarchy. As caste was largely a product of occupation (and social duties arising out of occupation), it was a fluid structure, shifting as a result of alterations in economic and political configurations.[186] And, in fact, Ibbetson suggested that 'classical' caste models were frequently undercut in Punjab by tribes of 'yeomen' who disregarded the *varna* hierarchy and organized themselves into egalitarian land-holding conglomerates.[187]

Conclusion

Thus, significant strands in scholarly discourse resisted the common stress on the primacy of race and the analytical power of the 'Aryan' category. Although British understandings of India became increasingly racialized throughout the nineteenth century, we must not be blind to the contested nature of British ethnography and historical writing. The theory of shared Aryan origins was a powerful influence in nineteenth-century India because of its generality and flexibility. As we have seen, it was used by some as the keystone in their interpretation of Indian history, languages or aesthetics. Others forwarded particular variants of the theory to serve their moral agenda, either to defend the Raj or to attack Anglo-Indian arrogance. But this generality, which allowed a belief in shared origins to serve such different ends, meant that this same theory had only limited application at a regional level, even in the case of the Punjab which was believed to the Indian home of the Aryas. British officials who actually knew the Punjab well at the district, subdistrict or village level were only too aware of the complex reality of Punjabi society. Aryan theories that had considerable appeal in Oxbridge colleges or Calcutta lecture halls provided no real assistance in settling disputed irrigation rights, modifying revenue assessments or describing Punjabi kinship.

This is an important caveat, reminding us that ideas worked in different spheres and that they had different uses and limitations. Aryan theories did little to forward British ethnography in Punjab and they did not buttress British authority within the province. Rather, they were only really applicable at the broadest levels of national or universal history, where they could be harnessed to particular understandings of religion, morality and civilization. It is also important to note that even when common origins or the sophistication of Vedic culture were accepted, modern Indian society was often depicted as static and degraded. Even Samuel Laing believed that India had degenerated rather than developed. Two historical narratives coexisted in the works of Maine, Laing and Max Müller. Despite the shared glories of the ancient Aryan past, Europeans had advanced rapidly, leaving their Indian 'brothers' slowly to degenerate into the worst excesses of idolatry, sensuality and sloth. So although these theories potentially questioned European pre-eminence and undercut the special authority attached to the Greco-Roman world, European dominance in the nineteenth century was rarely questioned by European proponents of Aryan theories. The morality of Anglo-Indian arrogance may have been challenged by a belief in British and Indian brotherhood, but British political dominance was not. Until the late nineteenth century the Sanskritocentric vision ultimately had more impact in the world of European Oriental scholarship than on colonial politics where economics, political expediency and crude racial stereotypes tended to marginalize philology.

2
Indocentrism on the New Zealand Frontier: Geographies of Race, Empire and Nation

This chapter examines a series of cultural connections and intellectual exchanges between India and the Pacific that have been elided by historians of empire as well as being neglected within the historiography of individual colonies. From the early nineteenth century, Orientalist learning played a central role in the development of Pacific studies, providing comparative evidence, analytical frameworks and methodological insights that were embraced by scholar-administrators and ethnographers in the Pacific. While at a general level, this engagement with Orientalism reflected the cultural authority that the work of Jones, Prichard or Max Müller enjoyed, more specifically, however, it was a powerful 'imagined geography' borne out of European imperialism.

From the time of Magellan, European explorers envisaged the Pacific as an extension of Asia, the furthest frontier of 'Further India'. Hugo Allard's 'India quae Orientalis dicitur' (1652), for example, depicted Australia within an Asian representational framework, not only defining it in relation to India, but also populating it with elephants and coconut palms.[1] Even as exploration progressed, Australia and the central Pacific continued to be seen as part of the conceptual geography of the 'East Indies' or the 'Orient'. Many of the new maps from the 1770s through to the early nineteenth century, although full of new detail, presented images that framed Australia and New Zealand against Asia.[2] This conceptual geography was reinforced at a linguistic level by the use of the term 'Australasia' to designate Australia, New Zealand and their outlying islands: this neologism was coined by Charles de Brosses in his 1756 discussion of the structure of the Indian Ocean world and entered English in 1766.[3]

This tendency to view the Pacific as an Asian frontier was extended and consolidated during the nineteenth century, especially in New Zealand where there was a sustained and enthusiastic engagement with Jonesian philology and Prichardian ethnology. New Zealand was charted, described and settled in a world that was fundamentally shaped by the 'Oriental renaissance' and this powerful thread in the intellectual life of the young colony moulded understandings of Maori language and history. The nature and source of Maori culture was not only a prime concern for colonial administrators and pioneering ethnologists, but was also crucial in the definition of settlers' identities and the emergence of a cultural nationalist tradition.[4] Orientalism was not simply transplanted to the Pacific from India and Europe, rather it was appropriated and woven into new and innovative discourses that actively re-imagined not only the history of British imperialism, but also the broad sweep of universal history.

Pacific exploration and the question of origins

European interest in Maori origins began with James Cook's first voyage (1768–71). The *Endeavour* journals of both James Cook and Joseph Banks reveal their attempts to relate Maori to other Pacific peoples and to the rest of humanity. Language was an important key and both men constructed basic Pacific word-lists. Banks recognized variations in vocabulary and pronunciation between 'northern' and 'southern' Maori, but he believed these dialects were closely related and exhibited a definite affinity with Tahitian. He noted that Tupaia, the Tahitian guiding the *Endeavour*, 'at the very first understood and conversd with them [Maori] with great facility.'[5] Cook concurred, arguing that the common origins of Maori and Tahitians were embedded in their languages: 'nothing is so great a proff [sic] of they all having had one Source as their Language'.[6] In keeping with traditions that viewed the Pacific as an extension of Asia, both men believed that Maori origins lay to the west of New Zealand, discounting a migration from either America or the great Southern Continent, the existence of which they increasingly doubted.[7]

What is striking within these early discussions of Maori origins is the elision of indigenous traditions that recounted the migration of tribal communities to New Zealand from the ancestral homeland of Hawaiki.[8] John Hawkesworth, who edited the journals of Banks and Cook for his popular compilation of Pacific voyages, noted that both

Maori and Tahitians suggested that their origins could be traced to 'HEAWIJE', but proceeded to emphasize the importance of linguistic evidence that suggested that Tahitians and Maori shared a common origin at the expense of the traditions of Maori themselves.[9] This marginalization of Maori knowledge in part reflected the inaccessibility of these traditions within a context of early contact, where Europeans were reliant on Polynesian cultural brokers like Tupaia to navigate a path through fraught and fleeting encounters. Moreover, narratives of origins and migrations were not only considered *tapu* (sacred, restricted) knowledge, but were also clothed in the difficult language of myth, which was well beyond the limited linguistic ability of the Europeans.

Most importantly, however, it was felt that the cultural origins and affinities that shaped Maori culture were embedded within the Maori language. Just as Jones believed that careful linguistic analysis allowed the Orientalist to undercut Hindu mythic history, Pakeha (settler) scholars believed that language was a more reliable guide to the ancient Maori past than Maori traditions. The vocabularies compiled by Cook and Banks should be read not only as an attempt to create a basic framework for cross-cultural communication, but also as initiating a long-term project to assemble a linguistic map of the Pacific, a chart that would enable the ethnologist to trace affinities between different peoples within the Pacific and beyond. Debates over Maori origins in the nineteenth century, therefore, must be contextualized within this larger concern with language and the place of non-European societies within the history of civilization.

The Semitic Maori?

Until the 1850s, the Bible remained a crucial framework for Pacific ethnology. As we have already seen, British Orientalists and ethnologists continued to use Genesis as an ethnological framework until the mid-nineteenth century. Their understanding of Genesis, however, had been reshaped by the rise of Orientalism: the Bible was understood as an Oriental text and many ethnologists had orientalized the Garden of Eden, believing that human origins could be traced back to Persia or South Asia.[10] This tradition of what Colin Kidd terms, 'ethnic theology' was transplanted to New Zealand by representatives of the Church Missionary Society (CMS) on their arrival in 1814.

This 'ethnic theology' developed very unevenly on the colonial frontier as early missionary texts, much like the fragmentary records left by the sealers, whalers and adventurers who visited New Zealand from the 1790s, were heavily anecdotal, offering little theoretical reflection or sustained analysis. Sorrenson and Elsmore have suggested missionary ethnographers elaborated a vision of the 'Semitic Maori'. Such a reading, however, is rather misleading, as it attributes greater analytical coherence to early missionary ethnography than is warranted. In reality early missionary descriptions of Maori society were far more concerned with the personalities of the great chiefs (Ruatara, Hongi Hika, Hone Heke, Kawiti, Tamati Waka Nene), inter-tribal rivalries and the cultural impact of Europeans than with the analysis of ancient Maori history.

Both Sorrenson and Elsmore identify Samuel Marsden, the patriarch of the New Zealand CMS mission, as the earliest exponent of the Semitic Maori thesis. This argument rests heavily on one short passage within Marsden's voluminous correspondence, travel accounts and journals. In 1819 he speculated that 'I am inclined to believe that they [Maori] have sprung from some dispersed Jews' and he pointed, rather vaguely, to some affinities in 'religious superstitions and customs'.[11] But neither Sorrenson nor Elsmore quote the opening of these speculations: 'With respect to the origin of the natives of these islands we are still in the dark. I could not learn that they had any traditions amongst them from whence they came.'[12] Clearly, Marsden was uncertain about the quality of his information and he was even unaware of Maori traditions of migration from the ancestral home of Hawaiki. Marsden's ignorance meant that his theory was speculative, seemingly grounded in the belief that Maori enthusiasm for commerce and new commodities suggested that they had 'like the Jews a great natural turn for traffic; they will buy and sell anything they have got.'[13] The fragmentary and tentative nature of these speculations undercuts any identification of Marsden as a serious advocate of Semitic origins.

Thomas Kendall, one of the missionaries under Marsden's supervision, explored the possibility of a Maori–Israelite connection in a fuller, if equally guarded manner. Whereas Marsden hinted at Semitic origins on the basis of Maori commercial acumen, Kendall's more sophisticated reflections were grounded in linguistic comparison. After receiving Parkhurst's *Hebrew Lexicon* as a gift, he was struck by the affinities between Maori and Hebrew: 'The prefixes and affixes are placed nearly in the same way ... Many words are set down in Hebrew in the same manner as I shall spell those of the same meaning in the New Zealand language.' But Kendall was cautious, stopping short of suggesting that Maori were direct descendants of the Israelites, stating 'I do not pretend to say that the New Zealanders are descendants of the Jews, nor do I really think they really are so.' This linguistic debt, Kendall suggested, probably arose from Maori having 'been formerly acquainted with that people.'[14] After Kendall returned from England in 1820, his views on the cultural provenance of Maori shifted abruptly. He no longer emphasized linguistic affinities; rather he placed greater store in comparisons of mythology and cosmology. These led him to repudiate any possibility of a Semitic connection, as he insisted that religious comparison demonstrated that Maori were related to the ancient Egyptians, and were thus Hamitic, not Semitic.[15]

Kendall's flirtations with a grand diffusionist theory received little support from Samuel Lee, who worked with Kendall in the preparation of the first grammar of the Maori language. Lee, the Professor of Oriental Languages at Cambridge, deduced no such affinities with Hebrew when Kendall arrived in Cambridge with the *ariki* (chiefs) Hongi and Waikato and his collection of Maori language material.[16] This is of particular significance, as Lee had a thorough knowledge of Hebrew and was at the forefront of religious translation and the systematization of previously non-literate languages. In his introductory essay to the new CMS grammar, Lee eschewed speculation on Maori origins or any attempts to trace linguistic affinities beyond the Pacific Ocean. He firmly placed Maori within the languages of the Pacific; following Jones's emphasis on grammatical comparison, he argued that it exhibited the same absence of conjugation and declension which characterized its 'Sister Dialects of Tonga and the Malayans'.[17]

George Lillie Craik, Professor of English Literature at Belfast, synthesized existing accounts of the Maori in an 1830 volume for the Library of Entertaining Knowledge. Sorrenson has suggested that Craik adhered to the Semitic Maori thesis, but this is an oversimplification of Craik's rich summation of European accounts of Maori. Craik identified a possible affinity between the Maori word for bone (*iwi*) and Eve, who of course, was created from bone.[18] However, Craik did not stress this Semitic connection; rather he insisted that Maori institutions were profoundly imprinted by an Asian heritage. He suggested that the hierarchical Maori polity was a Pacific form of Oriental despotism, as, like the hereditary leaders of 'most other Asiatic races', Maori *ariki* (chiefs) exercised their dominance over 'the great body of people'.[19] This argument reflected Craik's acceptance of an Orientalized interpretation of Genesis. In the tradition of Sir William Jones, he argued that: 'the wave of population, which has spread itself over so large a portion of the surface of the globe, has flowed from the central region which all history points to as the cradle of our race, and which may be here described generally as the southern tract of the great continent of Asia.'[20] Although Craik did not name any particular region of South Asia as the home of the English and Polynesian races, he did assert the fundamental unity of the British and Maori racial heritage in the phrase 'our race'.

Robert Maunsell, a CMS missionary in New Zealand from 1835, extended the work of Lee and Kendall. Maunsell's linguistic work on Maori, like his own training in classical languages at Trinity College, Dublin, was sophisticated and culminated in his translation of the entire Old Testament in 1858. His work was a long way removed from the earlier piecemeal observations of his poorly educated predecessors. In 1842, he completed a new Maori grammar that recognized dialectical variation and the rapid change of Maori as a result of contact with European settlers. Maunsell was not convinced of an etymological or structural affinity between Hebrew and Maori, although he noted similarities could 'occasionally' be observed. He did model his grammar, however, on Hebrew grammars, as European languages did not provide a useful model for Maori. Although Maunsell doubted any direct relationship between Maori and Hebrew, he believed that they shared an expressive and allusive quality, an argument that echoed Sir William Jones's identification of the Bible as an 'Oriental text'.[21]

Other figures who noted the similarity between Jewish customs and Maori exhibited similar caution. William Barrett Marshall, an assistant naval surgeon, observed similarities between *tapu* and the 'Levitical laws of excommunication'. He suggested such affinities were 'worthy of a fuller discussion' and tentatively posed the question whether the 'lost tribes of Israel are not to be found in New Zealand?'[22] Joel Polack, a Jewish trader based at Kororareka (Russell), suggested that Maori resembled 'the Chaldean ancestors of Abraham ... before the divine dispensation'.[23] But Polack has hinted that Maori might have descended from 'Asiatic' stock. *Moko* (tattooing), he theorized, was of Asian origin as Leviticus contained injunctions against such practices. This, he argued, was 'proof sufficient' that tattooing 'was among the abominations of the Asiatics, from whom these people are evidently descended.'[24] Polack's work constituted an important source for Alexander Marjoribanks's *Travels in New Zealand* (1845), which replicated Polack's oscillation between a Semitic and Asian homeland: Marjoribanks suggested that tattooing and Maori funerary practices 'leave but little doubt of their Asiatic origin, or that they were descended from the Jews'.[25]

It is clear therefore that settlers and missionaries did not elaborate confident or consistent visions of the Semitic Maori in the first half of the nineteenth century. Maori society was confusing; Maori appearance, language, social structure and rituals were complex and strange, yet exhibited affinities with many different 'nations'. But where exactly did they fit? Authors such as Craik, Polack and Marjoribanks noted linguistic traits and cultural patterns that paralleled both Asian and Semitic cultures. Suggestions of a Semitic connection coexisted with other equally provisional speculations: in New South Wales, J. D. Lang suggested that the Pacific was peopled from the Americas, while a growing number of scholars echoed Samuel Lee's early suggestion that Maori were related to Malays.[26] The multiplicity of potential homelands identified by these early ethnographers, together with their uncertainty, reflect the shaky basis of early ethnology on the colonial frontier. Hampered by a continued reliance on the tolerance and generosity of Maori leaders, hindered by poor resources and limited linguistic ability, travellers and missionaries alike struggled to assemble coherent analyses of Maori culture.

This project was simultaneously being pursued by European scholars who attempted to solve the question of Polynesian origins by linking the languages of the Pacific directly back to the Indo-European family. Wilhelm von Humboldt suggested that traces of an ancient form of Sanskrit, or 'pre-Sanskrit' could be discerned in the Polynesian languages.[27] Heavily influenced by Company Orientalism and elaborating an argument first posited by William Marsden, Franz Bopp argued that a Malayo-Polynesian language family united most of the Pacific and South-East Asia. These languages, Bopp believed, had emerged from a degraded form of Sanskrit and this Sanskritic influence was quite evident when Maori and Sanskrit words were compared.[28] J. R. Logan, editor of the *Journal of the Indian Archipelago*, who followed Crawfurd and Leyden to suggest that the Malays and the Polynesians owed a significant cultural and linguistic debt to India, confirmed this Indocentric vision within English language scholarship. Indeed, he termed South-East Asia and Polynesia the 'Indo-Pacific Islands'.[29]

Richard Taylor and the emergence of Indocentrism

Settler ethnographers soon fashioned Indocentric models that were underpinned by both an engagement with Orientalist traditions and close study of Maori culture. By the mid-1840s, several developments had coalesced to transform intellectual production on the colonial frontier. The influx of settlers in the wake of the signing of the Treaty of Waitangi not only necessitated a rapid process of state building, but also consolidated a number of important social institutions where knowledge was produced and circulated. Newspapers, reading rooms and post offices developed quickly in even small urban centres, providing communication networks that were utilized by both settlers and Maori. Mission stations, which remained the most significant sites of cultural transmission and cultural exchange, enjoyed greater prosperity and the generation of university educated missionaries who arrived in New Zealand from the mid-1820s had gained considerable cultural literacy and had consolidated a sound base for linguistic and ethnographic analysis. Maori converts, who engaged the missionaries in enthusiastic discussions of Scripture, translation and theology, were crucial in both the vernacularization of Christianity and the explication of Maori language and cosmology to missionaries and colonial officials. Both missionary and secular presses consolidated this knowledge through the production of the array of linguistic works, periodical articles and socio-political surveys of colonial life produced in the wake of the Treaty.[30]

Thus, in the late 1840s Taylor was working in a social and intellectual environment that was markedly different from that which had shaped early missionary and settler accounts of Maori culture. Sorrenson has suggested that Taylor was 'the most persuasive advocate of all' for the Semitic Maori theory.[31] However, this interpretation of Taylor's work neglects both its internal development from 1848 to 1870 and Taylor's engagement with Orientalism as he moved towards an Indocentric interpretation of Maori cultural development. In his *A Leaf from the Natural History of New Zealand* (1848), Taylor first broached the issue of Maori origins. He identified affinities between Maori and other peoples of the 'South Seas Islands', and tentatively identified the Sandwich Islands as the immediate origin of Maori. However, he felt that the transmission of culture stretched further back in time and space. In 1848, Taylor favoured the comparison of religions as the best method for identifying origins, emphasizing the 'remarkable resemblance of many of their [Maori] customs to those of the Jews [which] *would almost entitle us to suppose* they were connected with the lost tribes of Israel.'[32] Here again it is important to note the caution and ambivalence in this last sentence. There is no doubt that Taylor believed in the accuracy of Genesis, but he was uncertain whether he could confidently locate Maori within the tradition of ethnic theology within which he was working.

He returned to this issue in his 1855 work, *Te Ika a Maui* (the Fish of Maui – i.e. the North Island). Although the variations in Maori somatic features convinced Taylor that Maori were 'decidedly a mixed race', he was certain that Maori belonged to the Polynesian family. Taylor believed that the immediate source of Maori migration was the Easter Island region, but the question of the ultimate source of Maori was more vexing.[33] He discounted the Malay as 'the grand progenitor' of the Maori with confidence. Resemblances between Maori and Bahasa Malay, suggested by Lee, were only to be found in 'a very few words'.[34]

On the other hand, he was aware of a possible Indian connection. Where his fellow CMS missionary Octavius Hadfield privately explored connections between Maori, Sanskrit and Greek in his journal, Taylor now publicly posited a range of cultural parallels that linked Hindu India and the Maori branch of the Polynesian family. He catalogued these links, ranging over language, custom and material culture, in two short sentences:

> The affinity between Sanscrit and Maori is much closer, as well as their customs; the widow sacrificing her life at the husband's death is a remarkable agreement. The figures sculptured on the caves of Ellora and Salsette bear a singular resemblance to the Maori *hei tiki* in their form.[35]

Nevertheless, in 1855 Taylor was not convinced that Maori culture was solely or even primarily indebted to India. Physical evidence, 'the oblique eye, the yellow countenance, the remarkable depression of the space between the eyes', and house design indicated 'that some portion at least of the race is of Chinese or Japanese descent'. This, he speculated, perhaps arose from intermarriage as probably 'at least one junk, if not more, has reached New Zealand'.[36] Still there was the evidence of Maori links with the Jews. Taylor suggested that, on the basis of 'a list of a few words' which 'seem to bear affinity' to Hebrew, he was 'venturing to hint ... [we can] discover in the widely-spread Polynesian race, a remnant of the long-lost tribes of Israel'. Here again the stylistics of the passage undercut his assertion: the verbs 'seem', 'hint' and 'venturing' are weak and his caution is displayed in his use of the diminutives 'remnant' and 'few'. Taylor then suggested how this migration might have occurred. Either Maori were descendants of the lost tribes who had been scattered when they were carried to Assyria, or, perhaps, they had been part of a wave of Jewish migration following Titus's sacking of Jerusalem. Either way, a wave of Jews pushed east towards India, where some remained, while 'some would pass on thence and people the Indian Isles, as the Malays'. Others perhaps, 'followed the caravans across Central Asia, Thibet, and Tartary, until they reached the Eastern Coast' from where they peopled the Pacific moving 'from island to island'. This speculative history firmly asserted the unity of humanity: even if Taylor was somewhat uncertain about the Semitic origins of Maori, he had no doubt they were part of God's Creation. This unity was borne out in language, as he noted that 'remote and isolated' Maori also contained words that appeared similar to 'European tongues'. Indeed, his vocabulary compared Maori words to Hebrew, Greek, Latin, Sanskrit, French, Gothic, Turkish, Malay, Tongan, Scottish and Teutonic. These linguistic affinities, he argued, revealed 'a natural unity of thought' which united all humanity.[37]

Some twelve years later, in 1867, Taylor published *Our Race and its Origin*. This work was a closer examination of the peopling of the Pacific in light of debates about human origins engendered by new theories of geological and biological development. Chamber's *The Vestiges of Creation* and Darwin's *Origin of Species* challenged Taylor's predilection for the ethnic theology tradition. Taylor offered a scathing summation of their theories of 'development': that life originated in protozoa, 'a pure gelatinous substance' and 'advancing to something else in the course of myriads of ages, passing from one form to another, until at last from the monkey emerged the man; and in the gorilla we ... behold one of our grand progenitors.' Attacking this evolutionary narrative of progress, Taylor confidently asserted that Creation was 'comparatively recent' and humans were created in a 'perfect form', denying the vast temporal scope required for evolution and rejecting the possibility that species improved or transmuted over time. Moreover, in response to John Crawfurd's polygenism, he asserted that all humanity 'originated with a single pair' and the post-Diluvian world 'began with four original pairs'.[38] The importance of this defence of the Christian monogenist tradition is embodied in the 'Our Race' in Taylor's title: this phrase referred to humanity as a whole rather than to Europeans or, even more narrowly, Britons.

Although in *Our Race and its Origin* Taylor briefly discussed the contribution of the Jews to the peopling of the world, he placed even greater emphasis on Maori culture's debt to South Asia. He rehearsed the evidence he had offered in 1855: Maori language revealed a heavy debt to Sanskrit both in vocabulary and 'the character of the language' and again he asserted the *hei tiki* 'is remarkable for its Indian form', recalling the sculptures at 'the rock temples of Salsette and Elephanta'.[39] Taylor amplified this argument, noting that language provided 'strong evidence in support of the original unity of our race', stressing that the 'amount of Indian words and roots in European tongues is great' and that this debt was found in the languages of Polynesia as well. He then drew upon Max Müller to assert the unity of 'Indo-European idioms' and suggested this reflected a period of cultural unity before the 'first separation of the Northern and Southern Aryans'.[40] Taylor had firmly moved away from the Semitic Maori thesis, reorienting settler debates about Maori origins towards India and the Sanskritocentric vision created by Jones and extended by Max Müller (rather than the German tradition of Bopp and von Humboldt). Taylor's insistence on the centrality of language in affirming human unity, and his use of Max Müller and also Prichard, reflected his attempt to place his argument on a solid scholarly footing through reference to the latest metropolitan scholarship. This unity was of particular importance as Taylor, like Muir and Laing in India, hoped that a recognition of racial 'fraternity' would check 'the strong feeling of aversion which the white entertains for the coloured races', and he encouraged his fellow settlers to continue to 'equalize' and fraternize' with Maori despite the recent war which had cast them as enemies.[41]

By the second edition of *Te Ika a Maui*, published in 1870, Taylor had retreated even further from the Semitic connection. This edition retained the first's emphasis on Japanese and Chinese influences in the Pacific, with Taylor affirming that this Asian influence could be observed in the Maori physique and countenance.[42] But following his engagement with Müller and the notion of Aryanism, he placed still greater emphasis on the Indian connection, suggesting that 'India presents many points of agreement with Polynesia, both in customs and language'. He presented a full discussion of affinities between Maori and Hindus based upon recent British works on Indian ethnography and history. Maori were more directly connected with Asians as, Taylor argued, they entered the Pacific from the 'shores of Asia'. During this extended migration, Maori intermarried with the other Pacific peoples and East Asians, becoming a 'mixed' race.[43]

Indocentrism consolidated: Edward Shortland

Thus, contrary to Sorrenson's assertion that Taylor was 'the most persuasive advocate of all' of a Maori–Semitic connection, Taylor's work elaborated a new Indocentric paradigm. This approach marked two important transitions. Firstly, he was the first scholar resident in New Zealand who encouraged enthusiastically the Orientalist and ethnological tradition grounded in Jonesian philology that developed out of the British encounter with India, believing that these frameworks illuminated the mysteries surrounding Maori origins. And secondly, his work reflected the growing popularity of theories that emphasized the Indian contribution to the early development of civilization. These two frameworks, one methodological (philology) and one geocultural (Indocentrism), framed the debates about Maori origins which grew more heated and pressing over the final three decades of the nineteenth century, when it appeared that Maori were rapidly dying out.[44]

This emergent paradigm was consolidated and popularized by the ethnographer, linguist and long-serving government official Edward Shortland. In an essay published for the crowds which flocked to the 1865 New Zealand Exhibition, Shortland suggested that Maori were a mixed race, retaining many 'pure Indian' features but with distinguishable Papuan elements as well. Maori, he argued, were part of a migratory wave of a 'brown race of Indians' from Asia and had established themselves 'by force' in the Malay Peninsula. From this centre, the Pacific was peopled as different branches of the race moved from island to island, some moving on quickly while others intermarried and introduced non-Indian elements into the race.[45]

Shortland's work added great weight to the Indocentric hypothesis as he attempted to synthesize Oriental philology and ethnology with Maori narratives of migration. He argued that Maori traditions of migration from Hawaiki fitted the diffusionist framework which identified Asia as the cradle of Polynesian culture. Shortland distinguished six dialectal and physical divisions within Maoridom, which could be traced back to the various canoes that had each transplanted a particular cross-section of the migrating Indo-Pacific race.[46] In knitting these divergent learned traditions together, Shortland invested his arguments with the authority that came from both the intellectual cachet of Orientalism and the cultural value of a 'mastery' of indigenous oral tradition.

Shortland insisted that Maori were connected to the Indo-European linguistic family, identifying Maori as a branch of the Malayo-Polynesian language family, a group of languages that superficially bore little resemblance to the structure of Indo-European languages. He followed Bopp's 'careful comparison' of Indo-European and Malayo-Polynesian personal pronouns and numerals to assert 'that both owe their origin to a common source'.[47] Shortland explored this connection between Polynesians and Aryans in the early chapters of his *Maori Religion and Mythology* (1882). He began by arguing that philological research established 'that all known languages are derived from one parent original source'. Thus Maori and Aryan languages did have a common origin even if this was at 'a very remote time'.[48] Maori, like other Polynesian languages, had remained stationary in a 'very primitive form' after its separation from this original language. Maori culture and language, Shortland argued, were 'essentially conservative': they contained the 'very primitive condition of the human race'.[49] Thus, a study of Maori culture could unlock the distant past of civilization. In this later work Shortland did not exhibit the same concern with the geographic origins of the Aryans that typified his 1865 essay; rather he attempted to delineate the relationship between Maori mythology and the structures of mythology more generally. Therefore, in suggesting that Maori diverged early from the mainstream of Aryan cultural development and forever remained arrested at that 'primitive' point, Shortland simultaneously recognized Maori as Aryans and highlighted the cultural distance between Maori and Paheka.

Taken together, Taylor and Shortland elaborated a new vision of Maori history, one which located it within the grand diffusionist traditions of ethnology and Oriental philology. The significance of this body of work dated from the 1850s and 1860s reveals the limitations of the existing historiography on colonial racial thought, which marks the publication of Tregear's *The Aryan Maori* in 1885 as embodying the rise of comparative philology and Aryanism.[50] As well as offering a truncated history of Aryanism, such interpretations contain the implicit suggestion that the adoption of comparative philology could only promote a thesis of Aryan origins, which, as we shall see, was certainly not the case. Moreover, it also neglects the powerful spur that the foundation of the *Transactions and Proceedings of the New Zealand Institute* provided to ethnographic research in New Zealand from 1868. This publication was an invaluable forum for scholarly exchange and debate over Maori origins for almost two decades before the publication of Tregear's *The Aryan Maori*.

Colonial science and philology

The publication of the first volume of *Transactions and Proceedings of the New Zealand Institute* in 1868 marked the growing institutional maturity of colonial intellectual life. The New Zealand Institute Act of 1867 established the Institute for the 'promotion of art and science' through its published proceedings, library, laboratory and museum.[51] Most importantly, the Institute was a national body, which would draw upon and coordinate the intellectual efforts of provincial learned societies. Intriguingly, the Institute can be located in the long tradition of British colonial science drawing from French models, as Governor Bowen (who was also the Institute's President,) evoked the École Centrale, which functioned as the 'heart and centre of technical and scientific education', as the blueprint for the New Zealand institute.[52] Bowen argued that within colonial contexts an effective centre for synthesizing and disseminating knowledge was crucial for two reasons. Firstly, knowledge was of immense value to the colonial state in a country 'which has yet to be subdued and replenished for the use of civilized man': the 'advancement of Art and Science' would aid both the pacification and domestication of a turbulent frontier. Secondly, after a long career as a colonial administrator in the Ionian Islands and Queensland, Bowen was convinced that the diffusion of 'useful knowledge' and 'scientific education' was the most effective defence against the 'speculative manias by which the popular mind in new countries is frequently misled'.[53]

The Institute's *Proceedings*, which drew heavily upon papers presented to provincial literary and scientific societies, was a crucial forum for ethnological and ethnographic research. The very first volume of the *Transactions* revealed both the influence of comparative philology on colonial intellectual circles and a strong concern with the boundaries of race and ethnicity within the multi-ethnic colony. In the first volume C. J. Abraham, the Bishop of Wellington, contributed a philological analysis of English vowel sounds which he believed were shaped by a heavy Celtic influence, which marked English off from the languages of their '*Teutonic* kinsfolk'.[54] Abraham, who was educated at Thomas Arnold's private school at Laleham, suggested that he was following the younger Arnold 'in ascribing much more of our language and civilization than used to be conceded, to the Celtic inhabitants of Great Britain'.[55]

If we follow George Stocking to locate ethnology in its multiple contexts, the cultural utility of philology on the colonial frontier becomes clear.[56] Most obviously, by viewing Abraham's argument against the demographic and political contexts of the mid-1860s, we can see Abraham's attempts to use linguistic analysis to minimize ethnic and religious difference. Although immigration propaganda might have celebrated New Zealand as a new England, Abraham's assertion of the value of 'Celtic civilization' was attuned to the ethnic and religious mix of the settler population: Irish migrants comprised some 18.3 per cent of the total settler population in 1867.[57] Most importantly, Abraham made his assertions about the birth of Britishness to an audience gripped by mounting, if largely illusory, fears of colonial Fenianism in the wake of religious and ethnic conflict on the West Coast goldfields.[58] His vision of a hybridized and inclusive Britishness countered the ethnic exclusiveness of transplanted colonial Anglo-Saxonist, Hibernian and Orange traditions. Looking beyond the boundaries of the settler community, Abraham's argument was even more provocative within the context of colonial race relations. In suggesting that it was the engagement with the Celts that transformed Teutonic migrants into Britons, Abraham's argument implicitly suggested that the encounter with Maori would similarly transform the settlers: like Taylor, he saw language as a weapon against the racial and ethnic dichotomies that racked colonial society in the late 1860s.

Abraham's paper, with its philological orientation and social relevance, clearly marked the path ahead, and the comparative study of language would be a recurring concern in the papers presented to the provincial philosophical societies and published in the *Transactions* over the next forty years. In another essay in the first volume of the *Transactions* Charles Fraser, a liberal Presbyterian minister from Christchurch, emphasized the methodological framework for such research. Outlining a model for colonial university education, Fraser argued that classical languages remained foundational in the colonial context. However, Fraser also noted that Greek and Latin did not have 'the exclusive claims to be studied'; rather 'the Sanscrit of India' and Anglo-Saxon 'have as certain, though not as great, a claim upon our attention'. Not only should New Zealand students learn Sanskrit, but they should also study comparative philology, as 'illustrated in the works of Bopp and Max Müller'.[59]

J. T. Thomson and the 'Barata' race

Fraser's claim for the cultural authority of Orientalism and educational importance of Sanskrit reflected a growing engagement with Orientalism generally and India in particular within the colony. If Taylor's work marked a shift towards an Indocentric vision of Maori language and history, the philology of John Turnbull Thomson, the Chief Surveyor of

Otago from 1856 and the first Surveyor General of New Zealand from 1876, reconfigured the contribution of Orientalism to Pacific studies. Thomson, who gained considerable linguistic knowledge during his time as an East India Company surveyor in the Straits Settlements (where he studied with the renowned Abdullah Abdul Kadir) and Singapore, introduced a new precision into discussions of the links between Polynesia and South Asia.[60] In a series of articles published in *Transactions* from 1871 to 1878, he offered a sophisticated vision of Maori origins based on linguistic comparison and reconstruction.

Thomson firmly rejected Taylor's inclination to see Maori as transplanted 'Southern Aryans', arguing that Maori descended from an 'archaic negro race occupying the peninsula of Hindostan, anciently termed the country of Barata', an argument which drew heavily upon Indological studies of south Indian and tribal languages.[61] Thomson's Asian experience convinced him that the region was populated by a series of great waves of migration, but deep-seated differences remained between races, particularly between the Aryans of north India, the 'Turanian' tribal peoples of mountains and jungles, and the peoples of the 'Dravidian' south. In keeping with the Jonesian tradition, Thomson asserted that the best test of these affinities was, however, linguistic analysis. In his 1872 paper 'On Barata Numerals' Thomson compared Maori numerals to 34 languages from the Pacific and Asia. He suggested that this comparison established the linguistic unity of the race that had radiated out, because of Aryan and Tibetan incursions, from its Indian centre to Madagascar in the west and into the Pacific in the east. Those groups, who were now at the peripheries of the racial community like Maori in New Zealand and the peoples of Madagascar, had changed little. They had retained this Indian language in it purest form, while groups such as the Malays who remained close to their ancient homeland, had changed under the influence of 'Arian, Thibetan, and other continental races'.[62]

His 1878 paper 'Barat or Barata Fossil Words' marked the culmination of Thomson's researches into Maori origins. This paper, which drew on extensive secondary reading in the languages of South Asia, South-East Asia, Africa, the Pacific and material he collected in England, stressed the essential unity of the 'Malagas-malayo-polynesian' or Barata race. He believed that philological enquiry established this unity. Certain words, such as Saxon remnants in English or Barata remnants in Maori, were frozen like fossils, 'embedded' in the bedrock of language, and did not change under foreign cultural and political influence. Thus the philologist was akin to a geologist, having to excavate the language to identify the oldest possible stratum of words. Once identified, these fossil words would establish 'derivative, national or tribal connection with the parent region, however remote in time or distant in space'.[63] Nevertheless, Thomson noted that the philologist had to proceed with caution, as not all words that exhibited linguistic similarity proved 'affinity of race'. Loan-words in particular had to be discounted, so in fact the only safe basis for comparison were the basic terms common to all societies: body parts, geographical and astronomical features, basic instructions and widely distributed food items.[64] Thomson supplied 18 pages of comparative vocabularies to affirm his earlier conclusions of Barata racial unity and Indian origins. Traces of this negroid Indian influence were not to be found among the descendants of the 'Indo-Germanic or Aryan' peoples of north India or the mongoloid 'Turanians'. These were people foreign to India, and Thomson insisted that languages, including the Sanskrit-derived vernaculars of northern India, bore no relation to the Barata race. The Aryan and Barata, Pakeha and Maori, races were fundamentally dissimilar.

While the assiduously scientific tone of Thomson's work, peppered with linguistic terminology, comparative tables and detailed annotation, reflected his general concern with professionalizing colonial science, it also veiled the material and political implications of his argument.[65] But even a cursory examination of Thomson's popular writings allows us to contextualize his philological research within his broader understanding of race and colonial development. Thomson felt that Maori, as the most isolated members of the primitive Barata race, were doomed to die out in the face of competition from the robust and racially 'superior' settlers. However, settlers should not fall prey to 'crude sentiment' and regret 'the waning of the aboriginal race' because it was an inevitable process essential to the civilization of New Zealand. Thomson asked his readers 'is it better to have a forbidding wilderness fixed in gloomy forest ... or a lovely garden set in green fields and waving corn?'[66] Maori were simply an obstacle to 'an energetic, industrious people pressing for land'. Maori, unlike the Europeans, or the Chinese on Otago's goldfields, were doomed to die out because they lacked 'moral capital' and the settlers could not 'help him who has not the power of restraint built up and developed within himself'.[67] This argument about the absence of moral capital among 'primitive peoples' racialized the philosophical history tradition of the

Scottish Enlightenment, reducing Maori to an impediment to progress and improvement.[68]

Although Thomson asserted that the Malay and Maori were of 'cognate race' he formed a much more pessimistic image of Maori.[69] Thomson's paternalistic depiction of the Malay as 'a good-humoured, respectful, unsophisticated, little copper-coloured man' recognized the Malay as a good colonial subject who might be 'improved' under the stewardship of the British.[70] Maori, on the other hand, were paying the price for their isolation, as Thomson argued that cross-cultural contact and social change were necessary for cultural advancement. Thus the same isolation that ensured the relative purity of their Barata language destined Maori to extermination because the 'energetic, industrious people' settling the land would engulf their 'static' culture. Maori would die out: 'the rough, shaggy Maori stealthily moving through the fern thicket in search for roots' was to be replaced by a 'fair haired lassie tending her goats on the *braes*'.[71] The extinction of Maori was the necessary penultimate act in a racial drama that would culminate with New Zealand's Europeanization, or more specifically, the birth of a transplanted version of Thomson's beloved borderlands at the distant southern edge of empire.[72]

Thomson's argument shaped debates over Maori origins for the next two decades. Some immediately resisted his argument. R. C. Barstow agreed that Bahasa Malay bore little resemblance to Maori, but where Thomson found a historical argument to account for this, Barstow used this to dismiss the Asian connection altogether. His attack on previous ethnology is indicative of an imagined geography that saw the Pacific as an Asian frontier: 'I believe we are too old-world in our ideas, and have got into the habit of looking to Asia for every migration'. Barstow argued that Indocentric theories privileged the ancient civilizations of Eurasia, neglecting the cultural vitality of the Americas, and instead suggested that the Polynesians had entered the Pacific from the Peruvian coast, an argument that had been elaborated some four decades earlier by J. D. Lang.[73]

But the Indocentric paradigm drew wide support. W. H. Blyth cast himself as Thomson's defender: he not only upheld the primacy of 'comparative study', but argued that 'Mr. Thomson's discovery marks a new departure, for it concentrates the study: the rays of diffusion that mark the spread of the Maori race converge to a focal point, Bharata.'[74] Following Thomson's lead, Blyth rejected Taylor's view that Maori might be considered 'Southern Aryans', as he asserted that Maori were of 'an An-Aryan, or Turanian origin'.[75] As we shall see in Chapter 4, Blyth used this racial framework to argue that Maori religion was essentially a form of transplanted Hindu polytheism.

Tregear and the Aryan Maori

While Edward Tregear was not the progenitor of Indocentrism on the New Zealand frontier, he was one of its most enthusiastic advocates, as he devoted considerable energy to popularizing the Aryan theory in both New Zealand and Britain from the 1880s. In his *The Aryan Maori* (1885), Tregear asserted that comparative philology held the key to tracing relationships between different communities. Rather then simply dividing communities into the Hamitic, Semitic and Japhetic divisions characteristic of ethnic theology, philological analysis allowed 'the civilized world' to be divided into three 'great families': the monosyllabic languages of East Asia; the agglutinated languages of the Tartars and Lapps; and 'the inflected languages of the Semitic and Aryan races'. On the basis of etymological and mythological comparison, Tregear rejected Thomson's identification of Maori as part of the Barata race. He confidently asserted that Maori were not only Aryan, but that their language preserved the original Aryan language 'in an almost inconceivable purity'. Linguistic comparison could show that Maori probably left India four thousand years ago and migrated almost directly to New Zealand.[76]

New Zealand historians have devoted considerable attention to Tregear's work and its reception, especially the heated exchange between Tregear and A. S. Atkinson over philological methodology.[77] Howe's recent reappraisal of these debates has undermined the image of Tregear as an amateur dabbling in philological matters that were beyond his comprehension, clearly showing that Tregear was increasingly concerned with justifying his methodology and strengthening his arguments with footnotes and detailed discussions of European authorities.[78] Indeed Tregear, more than any other New Zealand scholar, enthusiastically engaged with recent European linguistic research and actively attempted to have his work published in Europe. He envisaged comparative mythology and philology as major scientific breakthroughs that opened 'endless paths of inquiry' and promised 'always new delights beyond'.[79] Although the *The Aryan Maori* was characterized by assertion rather than methodological self-reflexivity, Tregear took the methodological requirements of philology more seriously than the acerbic review by the lawyer and philologist A. S. Atkinson allowed.[80]

In many ways Atkinson, and more recent historians, have failed to recognize the importance of Tregear's intended audience: *The Aryan Maori* was published by the Government Printer and it was aimed at a broad readership. Understandably, in this popular form (unlike his essays in *Transactions*), Tregear did not enter into a detailed discussion of the complexities of philological method.[81] The *New Zealand Herald* attacked Tregear on these methodological grounds, condemning his focus on etymological rather than structural comparison. However, the central objection of the reviewer was not so much methodological as racial, as he castigated Tregear for chasing a 'will-o'-the-wisp' because the 'very primitive' Maori language bore no resemblance to the sophisticated Indo-European languages.[82] Another reviewer echoed these two concerns: Tregear's comparisons were not grounded in a solid knowledge of Grimm's law of consonantal change, but more importantly, Maori could not be compared to the Aryan languages which were at the highest stage of linguistic development.[83] However, such methodological concerns did not prevent Tregear from gaining many enthusiastic reviews, in both New Zealand and Britain, and receiving letters of praise from Lubbock, Charles Dilke, the Earl of Pembroke and even Max Müller himself.[84]

Tregear vigorously cultivated these links outside New Zealand. He established a network of correspondents throughout the Pacific, including the missionary ethnographer William Wyatt Gill in Mangaia, King Kalakaua in Hawaii and, most notably, the Hawaii-based Abraham Fornander, who also argued that Polynesian languages belonged to the Indo-European language family.[85] In Europe, Tregear corresponded with Adolf Bastian, the director of the University of Berlin's Ethnological Museum, and Max Müller.[86] He also made the most of opportunities in Britain, publishing articles on philology, mythology and British migration. Such publications could also be a vehicle for Tregear's cultural nationalism, as can be seen in the fervour of his scathing review of J. Anthony Froude's *Oceania*.[87]

This programme of extensive publication in Britain from 1888 to 1890 placed Tregear firmly at the heart of colonial science. He was a key member of the Wellington Philosophical Society (where he elaborated his Aryan Maori theories in a series of papers in the late 1880s) and he was elected President of the New Zealand Institute in 1892. His publications in Britain received high recognition with his election as a Fellow of the Royal Historical Society in 1890.[88] Obviously, then, the majority of his contemporaries held Tregear's research in higher esteem than Atkinson.

Belgrave and Belich have suggested that Tregear's *Aryan Maori* established a 'whitening' discourse which effectively transformed Maori into sun-tanned Europeans, thereby strengthening the settler's ideology of racial amalgamation. Indeed, New Zealand historians have assumed that the Aryan theories transplanted to New Zealand were Eurocentric and emphasized the Caucasian origins and nature of Maori.[89] While such interpretations remind us of the political significance of Aryanism, they offer only a partial reading of Aryanism's provenance and the cultural work of Aryanism in the New Zealand context. At the most fundamental level, New Zealand historians have excised the crucial foundations of settler Aryanism in long-established Orientalist and ethnological traditions that developed out of the British encounter with South Asia. In arguing that Aryanism worked as a 'whitening discourse' in colonial New Zealand, Belich not only suggests that Aryanism was essentially a *European* concept, but also neglects the Indocentric cultural vision that underpinned Aryanism in both nineteenth-century Europe and South Asia. Following on from this, the assumption that Aryanism naturally legitimated colonization is also misleading; as we have seen, in unsettling long-established oppositions between Europeans and non-Europeans, colonizer and colonized, Aryan theories could just as easily subvert colonial authority and racial hierarchies as reinforce them. Tregear himself argued that any European or settler who considered themselves superior to Maori had 'travelled little' and no European should 'blush' to recognize their affinity with the 'Bengalee' or the Maori 'heroes of Orakau'.[90]

Tregear's Aryanism should not be seen as a simple attempt to create a 'white New Zealand'; rather we should understand his work within a long lineage of texts that celebrated an Indocentric vision of the history of civilization: Tregear's *Aryan Maori* reminds us that Raymond Schwab's 'Oriental Renaissance' was not restricted to Europe, but flourished in the Pacific as well.[91] As the one of the colony's most prominent Theosophists, Tregear believed that western culture could be revivified by an engagement with the 'Oriental spirituality' characteristic of the ancient Aryans and that was still discernible in Maori thought as well as the Vedas.[92] In identifying Maori, South Asians and Britons as part of this Aryan family, Tregear reimagined the empire through the lens of Aryanism. This allowed him to erase the conflict and violence of colonialism to imagine British imperialism in India and Pakeha power in New Zealand as reunions of long-lost Aryan siblings. Such an argument was neither 'whitening' nor 'assimilationist' for Tregear believed that, as fellow Aryans, Maori (or South Asians) were part of the same racial stock as Britons. Thus, rather than using assimilationist arguments to legitimate colonialism, Tregear instead naturalized the settler presence by denying racial difference and viewing the British empire not as a series of highly unequal power relations but as the product of a new wave of Aryan migration.

Conflict, consensus and synthesis: Indocentrism 1885 – *c.* 1930

Despite Tregear's popularity, some scholars still doubted the Aryan connection on racial grounds. In the same year as Tregear's *Aryan Maori* appeared, Francis Dart Fenton, the first Chief Judge of the Native Land Court, published a detailed summation of the debate over Maori origins. This work marked the final attempt by settler ethnologists to deploy the ethnic theology tradition to answer the question of Maori origins, as Fenton grounded his work in a detailed reading of Genesis. A close reading of Maori ethnography against the backdrop of the Old Testament led Fenton to assert that Maori were Cushites descended from Ham, rejecting the possibility of Aryan origins or any substantial connection with India. While identifying the supposedly African character of Maori, Fenton's text resisted the growing power of racial science, as (in a vein reminiscent of Sir William Jones's earlier identification of South Asians as descendants of Ham) he celebrated the sophistication of Maori oratory and material culture.[93]

Gerald Massey, the famous English spiritualist who conducted a lecture tour of New Zealand in the 1880s, also elaborated an Afrocentric history of Maori in opposition to the prevailing Indocentrism. He argued that clues to human origins would not be found in the 'degenerated' poetry of the Vedas, but rather in the 'gesture-signs' and 'ideographic' representations of 'the original matter of human thought' which were to be located in ancient Egypt.[94] Massey depicted Africa as the 'Mother' of humanity, asserting it was 'the womb of the human race, with Egypt for the outlet into all the world'.[95] From Egypt different groups radiated outwards, preserving the particular linguistic and cultural traits of the 'Motherland' at the time of their departure. But where Fenton emphasized the sophistication of Maori cultural production, Massey offered a starkly racialized vision of Maori degeneration. He argued that Maori had departed Africa at an early point and in the course of a long migration and subsequent isolation Maori culture deteriorated rapidly: any Maori cultural achievements were a result of their early intercourse with civilization.[96] The 'primitive' nature of Maori language placed them 'next to the Negroid type' as Massey rejected any Semitic connection as a 'mirage'. This primitiveness was in contradistinction to European advancement. Echoing the branching historical narratives used to establish the 'inferiority' of Indo-Aryans, Massey argued that 'savages' such as Maori and the 'Kaffirs, Hottentots or Bushmen' showed evolution to be 'undoubtedly a descending as well as an ascending progression'.[97]

Samuel Peal, an enthusiastic ethnographer and botanist on the Assam frontier, also attacked the supposed Aryan nature of the Maori in order to emphasize differences between Maori and Europeans. Peal was a leading authority on the ethnography of India's north-east frontier and forged an extensive web of correspondents including E. B. Tylor, William Wyatt Gill and Horatio Hale, and Percy Smith and Elsdon Best in New Zealand.[98] On the basis of this extensive network of intellectual exchange, Peal elaborated an Indocentric vision of the Pacific that disputed the authority of Aryanism. Peal argued that the Maori belonged to a non-Aryan racial community that included 'Indo-Mongoloids, Dravidians, Malays, Papuans, Polynesians, Formosans, Australians, Massai of east Africa'.[99]

Thus, for Peal, both East Africa and the Pacific were extensions of Asia, a large cultural network that was peopled from the Gangetic basin. Two ancient waves of migration into India, the first being 'Nigreto' or 'Australo-Dravidian' peoples who were soon followed by the Tibetan or 'Himalic' races, produced new communities including the Kol, the Bihari and the Kasia. In India's distant pre-Aryan past these new hybrid racial communities, which Peal termed the Mon-Anam or Gangetic race, dominated Upper Burma, the Gangetic basin and much of the north Indian hinterland. A new wave of Tibetan migrants eventually displaced the Mon-Anam, forcing one branch towards Madagascar and east Africa while the larger wave of migrants moved east, settling in South-East Asia and finally in Polynesia. En route to Polynesia, the Mon-Anam were exposed to a variety of new cultural forces, most notably Aryan influences resulting from the introduction of Hinduism into Java and the incursions of Muslim traders into South-East Asia. The resulting veneer of Aryan cultural accretions could not, however, disguise the essentially pre-Aryan nature of Polynesian society.[100]

Although Peal exhibited some interest in comparative philology, his argument prioritized race, reflecting the racialization of Indian ethnology charted in Chapter 1. He believed that he could identify 'many (20) singular racial customs' shared by this racial group, particularly the separation of young or unmarried men in communal barracks.[101] Thus, for Peal, Maori were definitely non-Aryan, as he felt that Maori origins were likely to be located in the Gangetic basin, among the very tribal peoples, especially the Nagas, whom he knew so well.[102] Such 'savages' could provide clues to the early history of Europeans, but such evidence had to be collected quickly because 'the missionary and the Trader' were 'revolutionizing the savage rapidly'. Maori, like the other branches of this racial family, were destined to die out in the face of the racial superiority and cultural sophistication of Europeans.[103]

But these critiques of Aryanism delivered from afar by Peal and Massey carried limited weight in New Zealand and Fenton's work was overshadowed by the accessibility of Tregear's *Aryan Maori*. Most importantly, however, by the 1890s competing visions of Maori connections to India were beginning to be woven into an Indocentric synthesis. The attempts to locate Maori origins within Aryan, Dravidian or tribal communities were no longer of particular concern, as various aspects of Thomson's, Peal's and Tregear's research could be drawn upon and reconciled if Maori origins were depicted as more generally Indian. Elsdon Best, who corresponded with Peal on phallic worship and almost certainly used some of the 35 books gifted to the Polynesian Society on Samuel Peal's death, also affirmed the Maori's Indian origins.[104] Percy Smith, also encouraged by his correspondence with Peal, emphasized the Indian connection in a series of articles and books that spanned over twenty years.[105] This tradition lasted until the mid-century: Peter Buck, in his popular *Vikings of the Sunrise*, also accepted that his Maori ancestors 'probably did live in some part of India'.[106]

The death of Indocentrism: racial origins and the rise of nationalism

Yet, as the conflicting visions of the connections between Indian and Polynesian were synthesized into numerous popular works of Maori origins, two major transformations slowly undercut the cultural weight of Indocentrism generally and Aryanism in particular. The *coup de grâce* to the diffusionist tradition was delivered by the professionalization of anthropology and the rise of a new materialist tradition of anthropological analysis. This paradigm shift is embodied by Raymond Firth's work on economic relationships and his study of kinship patterns. Bearing the clear imprint of Malinowski's functionalism, Firth's *Primitive Economics of the New Zealand Maori* (1929) set a new agenda for the study of Maori culture. Where Tregear, Smith and Best constructed a genealogy of Polynesian culture and 'excavated' the remnants of Asian practices, Firth foregrounded the material frameworks of indigenous culture and emphasized the importance of internal structures and dynamics.[107] The *Primitive Economics of the New Zealand Maori* made it clear that the work of anthropology was unravelling the local development of culture, rather than identifying its distant roots in ancient homelands.

This intellectual rupture in the late 1920s echoed a longer and more gradual cultural transformation that also undercut the Indocentric tradition. While Tregear celebrated successive waves of Aryan migration that peopled the Pacific with Polynesian and then British settlers, many of his contemporaries militated against the reality of contemporary Asian migration. In the wake of the emergence of a sizeable community of Chinese miners in the Otago goldfields, the interests of the labour movement and settler nationalists coalesced in attempts to restrict Chinese immigration and naturalization. The Asiatic Restriction Bill of 1896 embodied this attempt to construct a legislative and bureaucratic border to protect New Zealand from the threat of 'Asiatics'.

Like its Australian neighbours, New Zealand adapted legislation from Natal as the basic framework for its exclusionary regime. During extended parliamentary debates, numerous politicians attempted to ensure that the legislation's provisions would be directed at East Asians and not South Asians. At a fundamental level, this reflected concerns about imperial citizenship as 'Hindoos', unlike the Chinese and Japanese, were 'citizens of empire'. But opposition to the Chinese also reflected distinctions drawn between different Asian peoples on the basis of racial origins.[108] C. C. Bowen, MP for Canterbury, argued that it was essential to protect the interests of the small Parsi community in New Zealand, arguing that they were a 'remarkably able race of men' that formed the 'backbone of the commerce of Bombay'. Their commercial acumen was important to the future of the colony.[109] In a similar vein, G. S. Whitmore protested: 'It is monstrous that the Sikhs – who are here in considerable numbers...and who saved India for us, should be excluded'.[110] Alfred Kingcombe Newman expressed the fears of miscegenation that troubled many settlers as he observed that 'not all Asiatics would degrade our race'. In exempting South Asians, 'this Bill would keep out the worst of the Asiatics' while recognizing the special status of Indians.[111]

These debates reveal ways in which languages of race and nationhood became blurred, as visions of colonial citizenship and national identity were defined.[112] Fundamental to colonial nationalism was what we can term a 'discourse of fixity', a series of arguments that celebrated the European or British migrant committed to their new home and the fruits of citizenship in the face of transnational movements of migrants from the Guangdong region which incorporated New Zealand into a broader network of trans-Pacific migration. William Pember Reeves, an important architect of the restrictive immigration regime and influential historian, constructed a rigid opposition between the white settler family and the male Chinese sojourner. In contrast to the settler family, which was committed to economic and social progress of the colony, Chinese migrants – 'strangers and sojourners in the land' – were self-seeking.[113]

Conclusion

In Reeves's work, we can see how colonial nationalism worked to construct the boundaries of the nation, policing its frontiers against those who threatened the vision of a homogeneous and progressive citizenry. Within this context, Aryanism slowly lost its power, as its inherent diffusionism and its focus on Asia were out of step with nationalism's celebration of the immobile and the fixed. Moreover, by the 1920s the exemption of South Asians from the immigration regime was under siege. Farming groups, newspaper editors and the newly formed White New Zealand Defence League launched a sustained attack on the morals, work discipline and intellect of the South Asian migrants, insisting that they would never be assimilated. Aryanism played a prominent role in these arguments. Holding a dim view of Gujarati migrants, the editor of the *Franklin Times* bemoaned:

> Unfortunately, we in New Zealand know but little of the Aryans of India. A few of them come here and work for a while, but they do not settle in this country. Our knowledge of India is practically confined to inhabitants of Central India, a degraded race that would be exterminated tomorrow by the war-like Northerners, who detest and despise them.[114]

Here Aryanism was reworked to insist on the debased nature of the existing Asian communities in New Zealand and to shore up the national borders against future migration from Asia.

Thus, in celebrating the fixity of the ideal settler family and in defining and policing the boundaries of the state, nationalist ideologies worked actively to mask or sever the horizontal connections that nourished the growth of the colony and, more specifically, the emergence of Indocentric visions of Maori culture. The convergence of the new materialist anthropology championed by Firth and visions of a homogeneous and self-sufficient nation undermined the authority of the diffusionist tradition. Quickly, the crucial intellectual linkages between South Asia and New Zealand atrophied and they were soon forgotten by anthropologists keen on excising diffusionism from their disciplinary genealogy and a nationalist tradition that increasingly imagined the nation as the product of the local encounter between Maori and Pakeha. An imagined (if contested) geography of Aryanism, which pictured the Pacific as being peopled by successive waves of Aryans culminating in British colonization, was replaced by a colonial nationalism intent on preserving the country's borders against the 'threat' of Asian migrants. Distant India, once imagined as the ancestral home of Maori, had no place in New Zealand's future.

3
Systematizing Religion: from Tahiti to the Tat Khalsa

So far this study has focused on the relationship between race and language within debates over Aryanism, tracing the rise of Company Orientalism, the dissemination of ethnological models from British India throughout the empire, and the ways in which Aryanism reshaped a range of colonial identities, ideologies and institutions. In this chapter, my analysis shifts to focus on 'religion', a key but often neglected problematic within histories of colonialism. Colonial governments exercised authority over communities whose cosmologies and ritual traditions were at sharp variance with the Protestant traditions that many Britons hoped to transplant to the frontiers of empire. Here I argue that the reality of cultural difference within the empire not only worked to invest the category of 'religion' with particular salience, but that it also transformed European understandings of the very meaning of 'religion'. British imperial expansion in the later eighteenth century provided vast amounts of fresh evidence about non-Christian cultures and new testing-grounds for European theories about the nature of religion. The extension of British mercantile and missionary activity into the Pacific and the hinterlands of the great South Asian port cities brought the informal and formal servants of empire into contact with a range of 'new', and often challenging, beliefs and practices.

'Religion' provided a key analytical lens for the discussion of these cultural forms, despite the fact that the very concept of religion was deeply embedded within the theological and cultural traditions of Christendom. Europeans, convinced that religion was a universal cultural phenomenon that in fact transcended the bounds of Christendom, searched for the components of religion: a founder, sacred texts, religious experts and an organized community of believers. Not only was religion universal, however, but as a category it was separable from material culture and other forms of cultural practice: religion could be distinguished from economics or politics.[1] This vision of religion as a distinct and self-contained cultural system was materialized in numerous initiatives pursued by both missionaries and colonial administrators intent on reshaping indigenous subjectivities: from identifying 'priestly' experts to military recruitment, from the publication of endless texts on indigenous 'religious' traditions to the working of colonial censuses, religion was an indispensable category within the variegated cultural terrain of empire.

Print played a central role in these attempts to identify and define religion. At a fundamental level, European understandings of 'religion' were grounded in a privileging of the written word. This textualism reflected the powerful impact of Protestant reformers who, from the sixteenth century on, insisted on the vernacularization of Christianity and identified scriptural literacy as the foundation of faith. The printed word also became a crucial vehicle for disciplining thought and action, as a bewildering array of prescriptive tracts outlined orthodoxy and orthopraxy. This disciplinary power of print was important for Evangelicals and humanitarians concerned with lawlessness and impiety among male-dominated settler populations and newly converted indigenes. In turn, indigenous urban reformers, conservative revivalists and prophetic leaders who also set about purifying the faith of their fellow believers embraced print's power as a prescriptive tool. The colonial public sphere was moulded by these debates over 'religion', as various colonized groups offered competing visions of belief, practice and the boundaries of community. As we shall see in Chapters 5 and 6, the interweaving of literacy and religion offered powerful tools to indigenous leaders who fashioned radical new visions of history, religion and the future of colonized societies. The discovery, definition and negotiation of religion was at the very heart of the colonial encounter.

This chapter examines these processes in both the Pacific and South Asia, tracing the divergent representations of 'religion' in these two regions. I begin by examining responses to the Pacific, delineating a discourse of negation that until the 1840s (developments after the 1840s in New Zealand are discussed in the next chapter) denied the existence of Maori religion. After examining the cultural, intellectual and political forces that led Europeans to doubt that Maori possessed a religion, the chapter then turns to India, where Europeans struggled to make sense of a landscape punctuated by *mandirs* (temples), mosques and *gurud-waras*. In this section I trace shifting and competing representations of Hinduism, focusing on an opposition that both Brahmans and Britons drew between 'high' and 'popular' forms of religion. Finally, the chapter concludes by examining the ways in which both the colonial state and urban Punjabi reformers manipulated images of popular Hinduism as an all-consuming 'jungle' to promulgate a newly system-atized vision of Sikhism. The efforts of Tat Khalsa ideologues to police forms of popular belief and practice and their success in fashioning a distinctive series of lifecycle rituals is a powerful example of the system-atization of 'religion' under colonialism.

'Religion'

We need to begin by briefly examining what Europeans understood by religion: what were the origins of this concept and how did it change over time? We should begin by noting that religion is a relatively recent concept born out of European culture and its encounters with traditions beyond its borders.[2] As Talal Asad has emphasized, although 'religion' is commonly understood as a 'transhistorical and transcul-tural phenomenon', it is without 'autonomous essence': rather 'its con-stituent elements and relationships are historically specific' and its very definition is 'the historical product of discursive processes'.[3]

These discursive processes have been at work over the *longue durée* of Christian history. In contrast to the pre-Christian era, where *religio* related to the maintenance of time-honoured ritual practices and the observance of the gods of one's ancestors, early Christian writers rein-scribed the meaning of *religio* by stressing belief over practice. Eager to distinguish themselves from their pagan neighbours and to claim cultural authority, Christian writers placed new emphasis on the bonds of piety that tied the worshipper to the one True God.[4] This accent on faith, on orthodox monotheism, was fundamental to the Christian tradition throughout the medieval period. The equation of religion with piety was the basis of an enlarged and consolidated vision of reli-gion in the wake of the Reformation. During the seventeenth century, as Europe was racked by disputes over Christian doctrine, the nature of the physical universe and the qualities of the indigenous peoples of the Americas, 'religion' increasingly came to be seen as a *system*. Piety was now identified as simply one component, albeit a crucial one, within a larger series of practices and structures.

Peter Harrison has recently demonstrated that heated post-Reformation doctrinal debates, which sought to define Protestant belief, underpinned this shift from 'religion' as 'faith' or 'piety', to 'religion' as a 'system of beliefs'. Seventeenth-century literature increasingly concerned itself with identifying what the Calvinist Richard Younge described as the 'fundamental principles of Christian religion'. 'Religion' was seen as a series of propositions or beliefs that could be simply summarized and even conveyed in the form of a chart or diagram.[5] In this form, religion could be identified as distinct and self-contained, something that could be separated from economics or politics, a definition that has recently been identified as an important move towards an essentialized and privatized vision of the cultural practices we denote as 'religion'.[6]

This important cultural shift was underpinned by the textualization of European culture. Protestantism's drive to vernacularize Christianity not only placed greater emphasis on what we might term 'scriptural literacy', but also stimulated a proliferation of religious almanacs, devotional texts, household guides and pamphlets ascribing new models of Christian behaviour targeted specifically at women and children.[7] If this process of textualization was central in propagating models of piety and social discipline, print and literacy also played a central role in marking the Protestant tradition off from magic, paganism and Catholicism, with its 'idols', sacramental 'magic' and priestly ritual.[8]

Thus, the seismic institutional, spiritual and social shifts of the Reformation redefined 'religion'. If this new understanding of religion as a system of beliefs, practices, and institutions was moulded by Protestant practice and propaganda, encounters with non-Christian communities were another crucial context for delineating the nature of religion. Questions of religious belief and practice were prominent in traveller's accounts, the letters and journals of explorers, missionaries and merchants and the correspondence of political envoys. These encounters in the 'contact zone' of the imperial frontier provided opportunities for the analysis of new and unfamiliar belief systems, creating analytical spaces for both the re-evaluation of Christianity and the discussion of the nature of religion at a general or theoretical level.[9] 'Religion' itself was frequently elusive in these encounters, as concepts of *dharma* (duty, obligation, virtue) in South Asia and *tapu* (in conjuncture with the supernatural, inviolate) in the Pacific were not exact synonyms for religion. The incommensurability of these cultural keywords forcibly remind us that 'religion' was never a self-evident category awaiting discovery, rather that it was the product of complex acts of translation, codification and social reform which outlined core beliefs, stipulated normative forms of practice and delineated the boundaries of the believing community.

Presence and absence: Tahiti and New Zealand

Identifying religion in the Pacific, however, proved difficult. As Chidester has observed, early modern explorers in the Pacific Ocean, like their counterparts in the Americas, often doubted that the indigenous populations they encountered had a religion. Early Catholic missionaries, for example, concluded that the people of the Caroline Islands had 'no notion of religion' and that, more generally, there was not 'the least spark of religion' to be observed in the whole Pacific.[10] While such characterizations reflected the great linguistic and cultural barriers in early contact in the Pacific, they were also an assertion of political power, of an imperial entitlement grounded in the 'backwardness' of the natives.

The intensification of cultural contact in the Pacific from the 1760s modified this pattern. In the central Pacific, Europeans established sustained relationships with a range of Polynesian societies that had developed hierarchical forms of political organization, consolidated important divisions of labour and elaborated complex sequences of ritual performances. These communities could not easily be dismissed as mere 'savages' lacking religion, rather the structured nature of their polities and their strong interest in trade suggested that they possessed a significant degree of cultural sophistication. Most importantly, it seemed that they were religious and in an Enlightenment Europe where orthodox theologians, deists and anti-Church *philosophes* were concerned with religious diversity, the 'natural' religions of the Pacific were of special interest.

The European encounter with Tahiti, which became a crucial reference point in Enlightenment thought, framed European perceptions of the rest of the Pacific. Tahitians were idealized in both pictorial and literary representation as European artists drew heavily on both classical and neoclassical conventions to depict the Tahitians as the 'Greeks of the Pacific'.[11] The French explorer Philibert de Commerson, for example, depicted Tahiti as a Pacific Arcadia, arguing that it was the 'one spot on the earth's surface which is inhabited by men without vices, prejudices, wants, or dissensions'.[12] Tahiti also served as a vehicle for Denis Diderot and Jean-Jacques Rousseau's critiques of the strong social regulation of 'civilized' life in eighteenth-century Europe. Thus, French explorers and philosophers depicted Tahiti as an idyllic land, where humans existed in a happy and free state, unfettered by the anxieties and inequalities produced by a rapacious church, private property, urbanization and mechanization.

Tahiti provided late-eighteenth century explorers with both an experiential and textual lens for the analysis of Maori society: Tahiti not only preceded New Zealand on many trajectories across the Pacific, but its symbolic importance meant that for many Europeans it was the Pacific. Maori society in the 1770s was less likely to provide evidence for 'noble savages' revelling in a state of nature. Living in a rugged landscape and a cooler climate, Maori led a more vigorous but precarious existence than the Tahitians. More importantly, fortified settlements, the prominence of weapons and tales of frequent warfare and cannibalism convinced Cook's companions that Maori were not naive innocents living in perfect harmony. In New Zealand, the *Endeavour* crew seemingly had found a hardened and experienced branch of the Polynesian family. Banks's juxtaposition of the 'Stout, Clean Limnd and active' Maori with the 'fat' and 'lazy inhabitants of the South Sea Isles', established what was to become the central comparison between Maori and other islanders.[13] Thus Maori were classified as 'hard savages', more akin to the ruthless, heroic and proud Huron and Iroquois of the Jesuit's writings than their easy-going cousins in libertine Tahiti.[14] Johann Reinhold Forster stated this position most clearly, describing Maori as a 'race of men, who amidst all of their savage roughness, their fiery temper, and cruel customs, are brave, generous, hospitable, and incapable of deceiving'.[15]

Most importantly, Tahiti was a key point of contrast for discussions of Maori religion. European observers noted significant variations in Pacific religions, especially between Tahiti and Hawaii, where important ritual performances were mass spectacles, and New Zealand, where Maori cosmological knowledge and ritual were less accessible. Tahitians might have appeared physically 'soft' but Cook's crew identified signs of cultural advancement. Although a non-literate society, lacking any religious 'books', the *Endeavour* crew found evidence of religion in Tahiti, identifying religious experts, places of worship, and important rituals. *Marae*, large spaces utilized for public worship, were prominent in early traveller's accounts of Tahiti. These spaces were dominated by *ahu*, or stepped platforms, and usually contained a large raised table on which offerings were left for the gods.[16] *Tahu'a*, or priests, oversaw the performance of these rituals and sacrifices. Thus, to observers from Enlightenment Europe, Tahitians seemed to be modern pagans with a religion constructed around priestly ritual and the importance of sacrifice: Tahitians had not yet succumbed to the stultifying pressure of zealous moralism or an all-powerful Church. In contrast to Tahiti, Maori society lacked any external features of religion. Within the harsher climate and rugged landscape of New Zealand, this Pacific paganism had never emerged.

A discourse of negation: the search for Maori religion

The importance of Tahiti as a reference point for the New Zealand accounts of the *Endeavour* crew is most marked in the heavy dependence on a Tahitian who acted as a cultural guide and translator. Tupaia, a 'priestly' *ariki* (chief), functioned as the principal intermediary between the *Endeavour's* officers and Maori. Although Banks and Parkinson learnt some basic Tahitian during their three-month stay in Tahiti, they found it difficult to communicate with Maori, whereas Tupaia soon overcame variations in vocabulary and pronunciation to become an effective translator and cross-cultural broker.

During the *Endeavour's* stay at Uawa (Tolaga Bay), between 23 and 29 October 1769, Tupaia attempted to gain some insight into Maori religious beliefs. Uawa was one of the power bases of the Te Aitanga-a-Hauiti (now known as Ngati Porou) descent-group that dominated the East Cape. The Te Aitanga-a-Hauiti *whare wananga* (school of learning), which regularly attracted learned men from other North Island tribes, was located at Uawa.[17] Banks reported that Tupaia engaged in a long exchange with one local 'priest', who was presumably associated with the *whare wananga*: 'They seemd to agree very well in their notions of religion only Tupia was much more learned than the other and all his discourse was heard with much attention.'[18] Cook hastily summarized the information Tupaia and his crew had gathered at Uawa, which was their first prolonged contact with any Maori. Cook noted that the 'Religion of the Natives bear some resemblance to the George Islanders' and that 'they have gods of war, of husbandry & c but there is one supreme god who the[y] call _____ he made the world and all that therein is _____ by Copolation'.[19] These blank spaces in Cook's text reveal the fragility of Cook's grasp of the cultural and intellectual traditions he was encountering, a world where religion was not a self-evident system awaiting analysis.

Salmond has observed that the *Endeavour's* ethnographic record was 'noticeably sparse' in its discussion of Maori religion and mythology in comparison to the rich information gathered on Maori housing, clothing, weapons, tattooing and carving.[20] This paucity of information reflects two factors. Firstly, Cook and his crew never had the time or knowledge to cement the relationships and understandings that would allow them to explore those aspects of Maori culture that were not easily observable. The encounter at Uawa was the only occasion when the *Endeavour's* crew was able to access reservoirs of Maori sacred knowledge and to engage with *tohunga* on a wide variety of subjects such as cannibalism, tattooing and social organization.

Secondly, Tupaia was the only member of the *Endeavour's* crew with sufficient linguistic ability to gain insight into Maori beliefs, but, apart from his discussions at Uawa, he exhibited little inclination to engage Maori on such topics. Tupaia, who had convinced Banks that he was 'more learned' than Maori in matters of religion, exhibited a firm belief in Tahitian superiority: he ridiculed Maori understandings of Polynesian myths and traditions.[21] Tupaia's dismissal of Maori culture left a significant gap in European knowledge of the Pacific, and, at least in part, established the framework for a discourse that questioned the very existence of Maori religion.

John Hawkesworth was immediately struck by this problem when he was preparing his compilation of the *Endeavour* journals. He observed: '[o]f the religion of these people it cannot be supposed that we could learn much; they acknowledge the influence of superior beings, one of whom is supreme, and the rest subordinate'.[22] Beyond this Hawkesworth noted that all Maori encountered by Cook and Banks shared a common account of creation, but only scanty and conflicting information regarding forms of worship and burial had been collected.[23] At the turn of the nineteenth century, Maori 'religion' was nothing more than a few short sentences, fragmentary references that provided no solid basis for the identification of a religious 'system'.

Missionary ethnography

The arrival of CMS missionaries in New Zealand in December 1814 established the first significant intellectual and religious linkages between the Maori and the European world. Missionaries, unlike the traders, sealers and escaped convicts who the Maori had occasionally dealt with since the founding of the New South Wales colony in 1788, were very interested in Maori ideas about creation, the supernatural and the human condition. But where Cook and Banks were guided by an Enlightenment agenda to collect and classify knowledge to reveal more about humanity's 'natural state', evangelical missionaries believed that a mastery of indigenous language and culture was a vital first step in vernacularizing Christianity and facilitating conversion. Daily contact with Maori at the mission stations, together with strong relations between the CMS mission and their chiefly patrons, allowed the missionaries to compile a dense archive concerning indigenous politics, Maori material culture, the distribution of resources and the rhythm of their exploitation.

Their understanding of Maori beliefs, however, grew slowly and haphazardly. While observation and daily conservation provided considerable insight into agricultural practice, craftsmanship and social organization, it still provided little insight into Maori religion. Ritual practice was protected by numerous strict protocols that maintained *tapu* and guarded against malevolent magic, while the transmission of 'religious' knowledge was embedded in kin-group relationships or controlled in the more formalized setting of a *whare wananga*: these frameworks for knowledge-transmission ensured that many key oral traditions were beyond the reach of Europeans.

These restrictions, together with the missionaries' difficulties in mastering the rich and allusive language of proverbs and mythology, restricted the flow of information to the missionaries. While the CMS catechist John Flatt acknowledged the existence of 'the native God and the native Religion' when he gave evidence to the 1837–38 House of Lords Select Committee on New Zealand, he affirmed the reality that 'we [the missionaries] are still in a great degree ignorant of the real Superstition of the New Zealanders'.[24]

Many missionaries, however, would not have accepted either Hawkesworth's or Flatt's use of the word 'religion' to describe Maori belief. Missionary texts were clearly structured by an evangelical worldview that led them to dismiss Maori cosmography, ritual and religious beliefs as primitive superstition rather than religion. Maori believed that the human world (*te ao marama* – the world of light) was in almost constant contact across a thin and permeable barrier with the supernatural realm of the dead, spirits and gods. Missionaries dismissed the omens and prophecies that linked these worlds as folk-knowledge, the superstitious beliefs of the uneducated mind. Indeed the missionaries believed that Maori, as a non-literate society, were without a coherent body of religious knowledge: this belief not only frustrated missionary attempts to grasp Maori cosmology but also inclined them to doubt the very existence of Maori religion.

Some of the leading missionary ethnographers unequivocally dismissed Maori religion. In the early 1820s Thomas Kendall explored the contours of Maori cosmology and ritual in a series of letters: these remarkable documents remained unpublished as Kendall attempted to use the 'impure' nature of Maori religion to explain his adulterous relationship with Tungaroa, the daughter of the Rakau, an influential Nga Puhi chief.[25] Earlier in his career, however, Kendall had argued in a letter reproduced in the *Missionary Register* that Maori lacked even the most rudimentary forms of worship: 'He does not, so far as I can learn, bow down to a stock [sic] or a stone; but he magnifies himself in a god.' The only elements he could discern in the Maori worldview were 'pride and ignorance, cruelty and licentiousness'.[26] A year later he reported that Maori were 'exceedingly superstitious, and what religion they profess is constituted of Rites the most horrible and offensive to an Englishman and a Christian'.[27]

These denials of 'religion' in one of the most popular evangelical journals were powerful proclamations of the superiority of Christianity and the necessity for the evangelization of Maori. Christianity would not only replace these 'horrible and offensive rites', but would also provide an ethical basis for Maori society as a whole. Equally importantly, such claims about the absence of Maori religion were not simply made to gain support for missionary activity on the frontier, but rather they were an attempt to claim political and moral authority for missionaries vis-à-vis other Europeans on the frontier. Evangelical missionaries in the Pacific consistently attacked the immorality and impiety of sealing gangs, whalers and beachcombers. Missionaries in northern New Zealand fought hard to cordon Maori off from the 'corrosive' effects of contact with these 'white savages'.[28] Vernacularized Christianity was the basis for this crusade, as they hoped that the maintenance of the Maori language would impede the formation of new relationships with white traders and seamen and that Christianity would provide a strong moral code to guide them in any contact they did have.[29] In short, missionaries used the absence of Maori religion to authorize their opposition to the New Zealand Company's programme for colonization and to fashion a vision of Maori's future based on Protestant Christianity.

Such denials of Maori religion would persist for the next four decades. In the first volume of *The Transactions and Proceedings of the Institute* in 1868, against the backdrop of continuing racial conflict,

William Colenso argued: 'Religion, according to both the true and popular meaning of the word, they had none ... They had neither doctrine nor dogma, neither cultus nor system of worship. They knew not of any Being who could properly be called God.'[30] Colenso clearly drew his criteria from a Christian framework and Maori simply failed all of his tests. William Williams, the aging patriarch of the New Zealand mission, was similarly dismissive of Maori religion. He argued that the Maori lacked Scripture, temples, priesthood and 'had no idea of a beneficent Being who might bless and prosper them'. In short the 'New Zealanders had no fixed religious system properly so called.'[31] In these comments the implicit Christian framework of missionary ethnography becomes explicit: Maori lacked Scripture, a readily recognizable religious organization and places of worship: therefore Maori had no religion.

These opinions seem characteristic of most CMS missionary ethnographers, but some were even more extreme in their portrayal of Maori religion. The Wesleyan missionary James Stack dismissed Maori tradition as 'a long round of absurdities'.[32] The Catholic Bishop Pompallier, who founded the Marist mission to New Zealand in 1838, described Maori as 'infidel' and argued that Maori cannibalism and love of warfare were clear markers of their apostasy.[33] Christian models of religion were so powerful than even the most unorthodox of European observers doubted the existence of Maori religion. The artist Augustus Earle, who enraged missionaries with his libertine morality, reflected in his New Zealand journal that he had 'never discovered any symptoms of religion in these people, except ... in a great variety of absurd and superstitious ceremonies'.[34] James Buller produced the shortest and most damning nineteenth-century summation of Maori religion as he bluntly asserted: 'the Maoris are devil worshippers.'[35]

This telling characterization of Maori belief reveals another powerful strand of evangelical thought moulding missionary depictions of Maori. Missionaries believed that they were battling no less than Satan himself in New Zealand. Although Satan's influence was discernible to Evangelicals when they surveyed their own society, and they believed Satan's power animated Catholicism and the worldly ambitions of the Pope, they nevertheless believed that Christianity was a powerful force in European society.[36] But because Maori had no religion, they were particularly susceptible to Satan's power. Richard Davis expressed this fear of Satan's worldly power in 1829: 'From my first arrival in this country to the present moment it has been and still is, my opinion that before the gospel takes effectual root in this country, there will be a considerable opposition made by Satan and his emissaries ... we must not expect Satan to give up his hold peaceably.'[37] Samuel Marsden believed that inter-tribal conflict and cannibalism were clear signs of 'the baneful influence the Prince of darkness has over the minds of these poor heathens'.[38] William Williams, Bishop of Waiapu, reflected in 1867 that in the early decades of the mission 'Satan had obtained a strong hold upon the people, and led them captive at his will' and 'the more they gave themselves up to his [Satan's] power, the stronger was the influence which he exercized over them.'[39]

Christianity was the only hope for Maori: without true religion Satan would always enslave them no matter how much they adopted the external trappings of 'civilization'. Thus the evangelical worldview, with its stress on the primacy of Scripture and the worldly power of Satan, doubted even the existence of a Maori 'religion'. This, combined with the difficulties in gaining access to Maori beliefs, prevented Europeans gaining any substantial insight into Maori cosmography and mythology until the second half of the nineteenth century.

Affirmation: religion in India

While Enlightenment and post-Enlightenment commentators such as Banks, Marsden and Earle were unable to identify a religious tradition among Maori, their counterparts in India quickly established a dense archive of texts describing a bewildering array of philosophy and practice. If finding a key to unlock Maori religion had proved extremely difficult, in India the British were able to locate a 'priesthood', 'Scripture' and places of worship quickly and easily. The study of Indian religions seemed to offer a rich store of knowledge about India's history and its current condition. Equally importantly, this knowledge was politically useful, as the East India Company was responsible for administering large regions of South Asia after 1765, and it was essential for the Company to understand the beliefs of its subjects, soldiers and rivals. The remainder of this chapter explores British interpretations of 'Hinduism', the most important of these traditions, focusing on the opposition drawn by British observers between 'popular' and 'high' Hinduism, and how these interpretations of Hinduism in turn provided a framework for the analysis of other Indian religious traditions such as Sikhism.

As we have seen, by the Enlightenment Europeans understood religion as a system, a series of distinct but interrelated components ultimately composing that religious tradition. Like Christianity, each of these traditions was believed to have a historical founder, 'sects' or 'denominations', priests and sacred texts that provided doctrine.[40] Throughout the eighteenth century, European observers understood Indian thought and practice through a Judeo-Christian framework. The immense variety of South Asian cultures provided enough evidence to satisfy Europeans when they looked for a theistic god, priests and bibles. The Jesuit Jean Bouchet, for example, found strong resemblances between Abraham and Brahma, Moses and Krishna and suggested that the Hindus believed in a 'confused' version of the Trinity.[41] In 1799 the British Unitarian Joseph Priestly argued that just as there were linguistic connections between India and Europe, the 'Hindu scriptures' provided 'testimonies in favour of the truth of Mosaic history' as they revealed an original unity of belief.[42]

Although European knowledge of the Vedas was scant at this time, given the textualism that underpinned European understandings of 'religion' they loomed large in late eighteenth-century understandings of Hinduism. Orientalists imagined the Vedas as an Indian Bible, the authoritative source for all Indian 'theology' and 'ritual'. Alexander Dow argued that they contained 'the religion and philosophy of the Hindoos ... and like the sacred writings of other nations, are said to have been penned by divinity', while Warren Hastings identified the Vedas as the 'original scriptures of the religion of Brahma'.[43] While this view of Hinduism, at least in part, reflected the primacy of scripture in the Protestant tradition, we must also remember that the Company Orientalists in late eighteenth century Bengal were seeking an Indian basis for Company rule and they believed that the ancient texts of 'classical' Hinduism would provide this foundation.

The structure of Brahmanical Hinduism: *vaidik* and *laukik*

Thus late eighteenth-century discussions of Hinduism focused largely on textual traditions, reflecting a view of Indian society coloured by their dependence on pandits as language teachers, textual commentators and cultural translators. The resulting view of Indian society accepted by the British protected Brahmanical superiority. Brahmans drew an opposition between *shastrik* or *vaidik* (based on the Shastras or Vedas) and *laukik* (popular) practice, upholding *vaidik* practice as a normative standard. The role of Brahmans as the key interpreters of *vaidik* tradition, which represented the Vedas as pure and eternal, ensured that their social vision was enshrined in the systematized visions of Hindu law adopted by the British.[44] Thus the British largely accepted the Brahmanical view of Indian society, which stressed the primacy of the Vedas, the debased nature of popular belief and the importance of the *varna* caste model, which was, of course, crowned by the Brahmans. Therefore, the 'British discovery of Hinduism' in the eighteenth century was a discovery of Sanskritic tradition that the Brahmans presided over. The power of the pandits, together with the natural tendency for British observers to look for points of agreement between Hinduism and Christianity, imposed a clear structure and doctrinal orthodoxy on the fluidity of Indian religious traditions.

The British debt to Brahmanical models is most obvious in the persistent opposition drawn between 'high' and 'low' Hinduism, which replicated the hierarchical opposition drawn between *vaidik* and *laukik* practice. Luke Scrafton, for example, suggested that the Brahman subscribed to an admirably pure monotheism. But these high truths were beyond the reaches of the simple folk who struggled to understand the subtle sophistication of monotheism. Thus, the Brahmans relied heavily on images and idols, believing 'sensible objects were necessary' for teaching 'the vulgar masses'.[45] In a similar vein, Charles Wilkins argued that the *Bhagavad-Gita* established 'the unity of the Godhead' in opposition to popular Hinduism that was based on 'idolatrous sacrifices'.[46]

Once established by eighteenth century Orientalists such as Scrafton and Wilkins this opposition between high and low Hinduism exhibited remarkable endurance. It was given its fullest scholarly expression in the works of Monier Monier-Williams, the Boden Professor of Sanskrit at Oxford. In *Indian Wisdom* (1875), his first major monograph on Hinduism, Monier-Williams suggested that Hinduism essentially operated on two levels. Firstly, there was the 'spiritual Pantheism' of Brahmanism. Brahmanism, Monier-Williams argued, held that a 'Universal Spirit' imbued the whole universe and through contemplation the individual would realize 'the mere illusion of separate existence'.[47] In this 'simple creed', there was much to admire and the Christian could discern points of agreement between Brahmanism and Christianity. However, underneath Brahmanism was a shapeless tangle of popular religion. In his 1877 work *Hinduism*, a volume he prepared for the Society for Promoting Christian Knowledge, Monier-Williams delineated the divergences between 'elite' and 'popular' Hinduism. He suggested that Brahmanism was the 'original, simple, pantheist doctrine' and constituted the 'root-dogma' of Hinduism. Brahmanism was,

however, overshadowed by the vastness of the 'all-tolerant, all-compli-
ant, all-comprehensive, all-absorbing' system of popular Hinduism,
which had a 'capacity for almost endless expansion'. This was the
result of a historical process of degeneration, as in the post-Vedic age
Hinduism had lost its doctrinal coherence, giving rise to a multiplicity
of cults and philosophical schools, most notably Shaivism,
Vaishnavism and Tantrism, the 'darkest' form of degenerate medieval
Hinduism. Only the 'strictness in the maintenance of caste' held
Hinduism together amid the modern prevalence of polytheism, idol-
worship and regional traditions such as the reverence of Kali in Bengal.
Monier-Williams's simultaneous admiration for Sanskrit literature and
support for missionary activity undoubtedly shaped these oppositions
between Brahmanism and popular Hinduism, and between the glories
of the Vedic past and the degeneration of medieval and modern
Hinduism. Regrettably, for Monier-Williams, India's classical past,
where one could find echoes of Christianity, had been obscured by the
'exuberant outgrowth' of polytheism and 'monstrous mythology'.[48]

Evangelical critiques of Hinduism

Monier-Williams's texts also reflect changes in British religious history,
particularly the rise of Evangelicalism as a force throughout the
empire. Nineteenth-century missionary accounts of India were full of
sati, Oriental licentiousness and the 'absurdities' of Hindu idolatry and
polytheism. Polytheism, superstition and idolatry were depicted as the
core of Hinduism, overshadowing the vigour of the high textual tradition of Sanskrit. Hinduism, like all other heathen creeds, was perceived
as a stronghold for Satan. This shift in understanding was signalled by
Charles Grant's 'Observations' (1796). After returning from India,
Grant wrote 'Observations' as an attack on British Orientalism and
advocated an aggressive programme of Company-sponsored
Christianization. Hinduism was a polytheistic creed whose gods were
given to sexual profligacy; worship was also tainted by signs of sexual
corruption (as seen in temple prostitutes or the adoration of the Shiva
lingam); Brahmans ('a crafty and imperious priesthood') enslaved
the masses and underwrote the despotic rule of Indian tyrants.[49]
Grant's text reflected a powerful shift in metropolitan thought, as
Evangelicalism became a political and moral force that shaped public
discourse at home and which was able to bring considerable pressure to
bear upon the East India Company.

Grant's work was also moulded by Evangelical fears of the effects of irreligion in the wake of the French Revolution and drew upon stock anti-Catholic images in his depiction of Hinduism. Just as British Protestants attacked the Catholic veneration of the Virgin Mary and the belief in the intercession of the saints as idolatrous, they dismissed Hinduism as superstitious idolatry. As the rising power of Evangelicalism coalesced with renewed fears of French expansion, Protestantism provided Britons with a common idiom for political, religious and diplomatic discourse.[50] Arguments condemning priestly power, the debauched sexuality of monasteries and Catholic ritual sharpened in anti-Catholic polemics were easily turned against popular Hinduism.[51] Evangelicals believed their brand of Christianity would bring about moral and religious regeneration in India, in the same manner that it was the perfect antidote to Catholic superstition and corruption: Evangelicalism was to be a vehicle for global reform and renewal. Claudius Buchanan, a Company chaplain and strong advocate of the evangelization of India, argued that missionary activity was central to India's future: Christianity had to replace the abominable practices of Hinduism. Buchanan believed Hinduism was characterized by 'horrid rites' which were even more offensive than the 'inhuman practices' to be found in New Zealand.[52]

Not all Evangelicals, however, supported this bleak picture of Hinduism. James Long attacked such missionary propaganda with indignation and zeal. He dismissed Evangelical propaganda as exaggerated and misleading, suggesting that his characterization of Hindu immorality was no more applicable to Hindus 'than a description of Billings Gate and the Old Bailey, in London, would be to the inhabitants of the west end of the town'.[53] Although Long maintained an opposition between high and low Hinduism (and Christianity), his text is a salutary reminder that even Evangelicals clashed in debates about Hinduism, Indian morality, and Christianization. There is no doubt that the dominant picture of Hinduism produced by Evangelicals was negative, but this interpretation was not uncontested.

It is important to note that these Evangelical critiques of Hinduism were primarily intended for a British reading public. Their aim was twofold. Firstly, by emphasizing Hindu polytheism, idolatry and licentiousness (which echoed stock images in anti-Catholic propaganda), Evangelicals attempted to secure financial, spiritual and political support from British Christians for the proselytization of India. Secondly, Evangelicals were questioning the Company's 'toleration' of Hinduism and the place of religion in the colonial public sphere.

Charles Grant argued that it 'would be too absurd and extravagant' to believe that the British administration should 'uphold errors and usages, gross and fundamental, subversive of the first principles of reason, morality, and religion'. In the eyes of Evangelicals like Grant, truth and morality were universal notions that should dictate Company policy.[54] The Company's continued toleration of Hinduism was incompatible with notions of good government and only served to further retard India's development.

The dominant picture of the decadence of popular Hinduism was not, however, solely a product of the missionary zeal of Evangelicalism. Other British intellectual and political forces drew on and nourished this hostility towards popular religious practice. The most important of these critiques was James Mill's *The History of British India*, which attempted to explode the authority attached to Orientalist learning by attacking the 'corrupt' morality and religion of India.

Mill began by attacking Brahmanical authority. The language of Brahmanical Hinduism was characterized by an 'unparalleled vagueness' and their religion consisted of a 'multiplicity of fictions' marred by 'endless discrepancies'. To the objective observer, like Mill, Hinduism had 'no coherent system' and, as such, it was not even a proper religion: any detailed discussion of Indian religions, like that offered by Jones, was purely the product of 'imagination'. Mill dismissed Sanskrit accounts of Creation as a 'gross and disgusting picture of the universe' characterized by 'disorder, caprice, passion, contest, portents, prodigies, violence, and deformity'. But Sanskrit texts, Mill argued, were not the best guide to the reality of Hinduism: what really should be examined were the 'wretched ceremonies [which] constituted almost the whole of its practical part'.[55] Hinduism revealed the degraded state of Indian society: it was a ritualistic charade concocted by Brahmans. Only a rigid policy of anglicization would free India from its shackles.

The 'jungle': Hinduism and ethnography

If metropolitan Evangelical and Utilitarian critiques attacked the virtues of Brahmanical Hinduism extolled by eighteenth-century Orientalists, the role of the 'high' Hindu tradition was also questioned by ethnographers with a closer knowledge of Indian society. As observation became increasingly important in British India's 'information order', greater weight was placed on the practice of Hinduism as opposed to the textualism of Orientalism grounded in the study of 'classical' traditions.

H. H. Wilson's work placed greater emphasis on the historical development of Hinduism than was found in the rather static interpretations crafted by Jones and Colebrooke. The history of Hinduism, for Wilson, was characterized by almost relentless growth as the Brahmans were so tolerant of new belief and practices that they were essentially 'indifferent' to religious truth. Because of this laxity, Hinduism steadily diverged from its 'dignified' Vedic roots, as 'numerous, and almost always frivolous, and insipid, and immoral legends' were spawned by the *Puranas* and the great epics.[56] As a result, the classical texts stressed by Jones and Colebrooke had been obscured by the development of modern cults based on the exclusive veneration of the *avatar*s of Vishnu and Shiva. Morality was absent from modern Hinduism, as Vaishnavism and Shaivism were based on 'the absolute sufficiency of faith alone, wholly independent of conduct'. Thus 'grotesque veneration' characterized modern popular Hinduism. This degeneration had given rise to a 'crazy and rotten' array of cults, which constituted the 'heterogeneous compound' of modern popular Hinduism.[57] Although Wilson followed the Evangelical and Utilitarian critiques in denigrating popular Hinduism as 'mischievous and disgraceful', his work marks a significant departure in its historicizing vision and in the stress he placed on the observation of contemporary religious practice.[58]

While Wilson's historicizing interpretation revised late eighteenth-century understandings of Hinduism, A. C. Lyall challenged the opposition between high and popular Hinduism. Lyall, who had supplemented a sound textual knowledge with first-hand observation of Hinduism in Berar, argued that those Orientalists who relied on the Brahmanical vision of 'elaborate scriptures and sacerdotal ordinances' could 'furnish forth a comprehensive system'. However, those who ventured out of their district offices and Calcutta libraries soon encountered a 'whole jumble of contradictory ideas and practices, a medley of popular superstitions'.[59]

The clear structures discerned by eighteenth-century Orientalists were now undermined by the weight of first-hand observation. Lyall asserted that the British encountered in India 'the extraordinary fecundity of the superstitious sentiment'. Indians were deeply concerned with spiritual matters and Hinduism was 'alive with incessant movement and change', but this religious energy was directionless.[60] The Brahmans had failed to control the 'wandering beliefs of an intensely superstitious people' and as a result modern Hinduism exhibited an 'entire absence of system': again, Hinduism lacked the coherent structures that characterized true religion.[61]

For Lyall, the formlessness of Hinduism provided the Christian observer with 'the nearest surviving representative of a half-civilized society's religious state', comparable to the state of popular piety in the Mediterranean before the advent of Christ. Indeed, Lyall suggested, in India 'we catch a reflection of classic polytheism'.[62] Modern Hinduism was the best living example of 'natural religion'. This primitive creed invested the natural world with supernatural significance, expressing, in Lyall's view, the hopes and fears of early humans. But whereas Europeans progressed beyond this rudimentary stage with the advent of the Romans and the rise of Christianity, religion progressed more slowly in India because of its physical isolation and lack of stable government. The Brahmanical system did achieve 'the intellectual climax of the evolution of Natural religion': Pantheism. But this 'intellectual Hinduism' had only limited power. As we have seen, Lyall was convinced that modern popular Hinduism had swamped the original purity of Brahmanism, which had been unable to withstand the 'luxuriant growth of religious fancies and usages'.[63]

Thomas Metcalf has noted that Lyall's work typifies the shift from a 'coherent notion' of Hinduism constructed by British Orientalists and their Brahmanical collaborators to a broader but more unstable understanding of Hinduism.[64] At the very same moment that Hinduism, as the largest of India's religious 'communities', seemed to be indispensable to the analysis of Indian society, the very same diversity that the British stressed threatened to collapse the category. Popular Hinduism seemed to be so diverse, complicated and contradictory that it almost defied analysis. Like the jungle it was so often compared to, Hinduism seemed wild, exuberant and threatening to nineteenth-century observers.

Thus a range of intellectual, political and religious forces coalesced to undermine the authority of eighteenth-century studies of Indian religions. Where affinities between Vedic religion and Christianity were once emphasized, difference came to dominate nineteenth-century discourses on popular Hinduism. Increasingly Hinduism was believed to provide a key to Indian social organization: its hosts of gods, intricate rituals and endless castes were believed to be a defining characteristic of Indian society. The increasing emphasis on racial difference identified in Chapter 1 was easily absorbed into these understandings of Hinduism. The intermarriage between Aryan and non-Aryan elements proved a fertile but disastrous union, as it had engendered innumerable, but deformed offspring. These new 'sects' and 'cults' rose and fell with frightening speed, which troubled an administration that hoped to rule on the basis of clear taxonomies.

Sikhism: Nanak and the Indian 'Reformation'

The rest of this chapter traces the emergence of one such clear taxonomy, in the attempts of the colonial state and urban reformers to systematize Sikh 'religion'. Nineteenth-century Europeans understood Sikhism against these interpretations of popular Hinduism as an unruly and all-consuming jungle. The historiography on British representations of Sikhism is largely corrective in ambition, highlighting 'distortions' borne out of British ignorance or the political requirements of colonialism.[65] But this corrective tradition fails to contextualize interpretations of Sikhism against the broader backdrop of the British engagement with Hinduism. This is an important point because British understandings of Sikhism were not the simple products of self/other, colonizer/colonized dichotomies. The textual construction of Sikhism was the product of a range of complex comparisons, where British political concerns, relationships with the Sikh elite, understandings of Hindu polytheism and British visions of Christian history informed the Indologist's reading of Sikh history and tradition.

Major James Browne wrote the first major European account of Sikhism, *The History of the Origin and Progress of the Sikhs,* which was published in 1788 by the Company as part of the India Tracts series. Between 1782 and 1785 Browne served as Personal Agent at the court of Shah Alam in Delhi. One of his duties in the court was to collect information regarding the Sikhs, whom the British saw as a potentiality destabilizing force in the Delhi and Awadh regions. Browne garnered what information he could, relying heavily on a Persian text produced for him by Buddh Singh Arora of Lahore.[66] On the basis of Buddh Singh's text, Browne suggested that Nanak's religion appeared 'to bear that kind of relation to the Hindoo religion, which the Protestant does to the Romish'.[67] Browne's description of Sikhism as a reformed Hinduism established an interpretative framework that dominated Sikh studies until the early twentieth century. Sikhism was consistently seen as an improvement on the Hindu tradition, as it seemed to break away from the polytheism, idolatry and caste-sensitivities that were believed to riddle and retard the Hindu mind.

Other British observers confirmed Browne's interpretation, most notably Charles Wilkins, whose sketch of Sikhism was also published in 1788. Just as he described Brahmanical religion through Christian terminology, Wilkins's description of Sikhism produced a religion that sounded remarkably like the outlines of Christianity. Nanak's reforming vision created a new religion grounded in a belief in 'one God, omnipotent and omnipresent'. Nanak's monotheistic teachings had a strong moral component, as 'there will be a day of retribution, when virtue will be rewarded and vice punished'.[68]

Once established, the trope of Nanak as the Hindu 'Reformer' became firmly embedded in western understandings of South Asian culture. Monier-Williams, for example, depicted Nanak's vision as a refreshing change from the 'degeneration' of medieval Hinduism. He noted that Nanak's compositions in the *Adi Granth* ('the Bible of the Sikhs') were 'promulgated about the time of our Reformation' and prohibited 'idol-worship' while 'teaching the unity of the Godhead pantheistically'.[69] Although he thought that Sikhism was likely to succumb to the power of Hindu superstition, there is no doubt that he believed Nanak's vision was a bright point in the darkness of modern Hinduism.[70]

J. D. Cunningham provided perhaps the most sympathetic nine-teenth-century account of Sikhism. Indeed many contemporaries believed that he was far too sympathetic to Sikhism and the independent kingdom of the Punjab. Cunningham argued that Nanak was the heir to a tradition of medieval Hindu reform in north India (as seen in Gorakhnath and Kabir), but Nanak's reform was more comprehensive, compelling and effective. Nanak inculcated a clear moral vision into his 'increasing body of faithful worshippers'. Thus, in short, of all the Hindu reformers Nanak alone was able to 'perceive the true principle of reform'. His success in creating a coherent religious vision counteracted the centrifugal tendencies of Hinduism, as Nanak was able to 'lay those broad foundations which enabled his successor Gobind to fire the minds of his countrymen with a new nationality'.[71]

The prolific evangelical essayist, and one time Punjab judicial commissioner, Robert Needham Cust introduced Indian and British Christian audiences to the teachings of Nanak. Cust's vision of Christianity and religious history was more universalist than many Evangelicals and he cast himself as an advocate of certain aspects of non-Christian religions. He suggested that all religions shared 'common features', and that non-Christian religions had also 'contributed to the great store' of religious knowledge which shaped Christian thought.[72] He also attacked his 'narrow-minded religionists' who had an exclusive vision of God and salvation. He reminded his readers: 'God is not the God of Christians only. Christ did not die for the Christians only, but for the whole world.' All religions, no matter how crude or sophisticated, expressed the spiritual hunger of humanity. The 'ancient simplicity of the Vedas' should be admired by 'every true heart' as they expressed 'the childhood of our race and religion'. They contained the pure essence of religion, albeit in a 'childlike' form, and expressed the essentially spiritual nature of all humans.[73]

Cust's theory of religious development, like Max Müller's, was simultaneously developmental and degenerationist. While the European branch of the Aryan family built upon Vedic monotheism, the mainstream of Hinduism declined rapidly in the post-Vedic age, as it spawned transmigration, caste and the 'gigantic abominations of Vaishnavism and Saivism'.[74] This decline resulted from the debasement of 'the simple Vedic faith and cult' by intermarriage with non-Aryans and the ever-increasing dominance of the Brahmans.[75] In short, hybridization explained the debased and unsystematic nature of modern Hinduism.

Guru Nanak broke, at least temporarily, this cycle of degeneration. Cust suggested that on the basis of his teaching Nanak 'must be considered truly Good as well as truly Great'.[76] Nanak, in fact, was an instrument of God:

> We cannot but admit, that he was one of those, on whom the Almighty has vouched safe special blessings ... he laboured unceasingly ... to reform the lives and religion of his countrymen, to break through the tyranny of Priestcraft, outward Ritual, and Caste. He taught that purity of thought, word and deed, abstinence from Lust, Anger, and Avarice, were better than feeding Brahmans, or making offerings at Temples.[77]

But Sikhism was not able to fully distance itself from the 'wild stories' and superstitions of the masses. Nanak never fully 'abandoned' the Hindu tradition and Sikhism maintained links to Hinduism. This was, Cust argued, obvious in the *janam-sakhi* literature, the accounts of Nanak's life composed by his followers in the centuries after his death. The *janam-sakhi*s were as fantastic as popular Hinduism, as they were 'full of fable, and invention, displaying such intense ignorance, that they are more calculated to deceive than instruct.'[78] Cust offered his biography of Nanak as a purified and rationalistic account: 'This is the first attempt to compose a narrative, from which all the marvellous has been excluded, and which Hindu, Mahomedan, and Christian can credit.'[79] Similarly, new translations of the *Adi Granth* and *Dasam Granth* would show modern Sikhs 'how much they have deviated from the example and precepts of their great Teacher.'[80] Cust believed that Sikhism had the potential to escape from modern Hinduism's corrupt practices and idol-worship, but this potential was not fulfilled as the Sikhs had not maintained the distinctiveness of their identity. Many Sikhs still observed caste restrictions, were still ensnared by a belief in transmigration, and maintained such close relations with Hindus that modern Sikhism was really only a 'sect' of the 'Brahmanical Religion'.[81]

Other British administrators, however, were convinced that Sikhism had achieved a cleaner break from the Hindu tradition. Lepel Henry Griffin, a leading figure in the Punjab provincial government, described Guru Nanak's goal as to 'raise Hinduism from degraded forms of superstition and polytheism into which it had fallen'. But, in Griffin's view, it was the inauguration of the Khalsa, the militarized 'brotherhood' of the pure and pious, by Guru Gobind Singh that finally demarcated a clear boundary between Sikhism and Hinduism. The Khalsa embodied Sikhism's egalitarian social vision because its emphasis on 'brotherhood' attacked caste, which Griffin believed was the very foundation of Hinduism. Sikhism's repudiation of caste meant that Hinduism and Sikhism were fundamentally incompatible: 'Hinduism has been ever hostile to Sikhism, for the latter faith attacked it in its most vital principle of caste without which the whole Brahmanical system falls to the ground.'[82] Echoing Monier-Williams, Griffin imagined Hinduism's 'vitality' as 'ivy-like', as it tried to obliterate and crush 'heterodox forms of Hinduism' like Buddhism and now Sikhism. Thus Sikhism appeared in Griffin's work as a reformed and purified Hinduism which simultaneously attacked caste and chafed against Muslim oppression.[83]

This tradition of emphasizing Sikhism's monotheism and its moral 'purity' in relation to Hinduism is of great significance. This image was generated by Orientalists in the service of the Company or the British government of India after 1858. Cust and Griffin were influential figures in the shaping and implementation of policy in British Punjab and their writings moulded British conceptions of Punjabi society. Sikhism's attack on caste and its perceived 'superior' morality elevated

Sikhs above the Hindu masses and the 'fanaticism' of Islam in the British official mind.

Dissenting voices: Evangelical attacks on Sikhism

But while this understanding was dominant, it was not unchallenged: the study of Indian religions remained a hotly contested field in British India. Although the majority of British observers praised Nanak as a reformer of 'medieval' Hinduism, some Europeans suggested Sikhism was still too close to the Hindu tradition to merit any praise. In July 1851 *The Church Missionary Intelligencer* discussed the beginnings of the CMS mission to Punjab, offering a lengthy discussion of the peoples and religions of the region. This article was a battle cry for proselytization and its starting point was an attack on the desiccating effects of Sikhism: 'The inhabitants of the Punjab are like the lands around them, which are laying waste for want of irrigation. The Sikh religion cannot benefit them. It has been tried and found worthless.' Punjab's future without 'the fertilizing stream of the gospel' was bleak. Nanak's vision was 'crude and unconnected' and he was too 'latitudinarian' to wrench Punjabis free of 'the polytheistic tendencies of the Hindu'.[84] Sikhs were rapidly being absorbed back into Hinduism and the minimal progress made by Nanak was lost. The only hope lay in the gospel, which promised great spiritual rejuvenation and renewal.

Ernest Trumpp, the most powerful nineteenth-century critic of Sikhism, extended evangelical attacks on Sikh belief. The Secretary of State for India approached Trumpp in 1869 to begin work on a translation of the Kartarpur *Granth* manuscript of the *Adi Granth* and the *Dasam Granth*. Trumpp was a skilled Tübingen-trained linguist who had been sent by the CMS to Karachi in 1854 to conduct research on Sindhi and Pushto, before illness forced him to return to a teaching position at Tübingen.[85] Initially Trumpp was enthusiastic about the translations, but he soon encountered difficulties. After an initial attempt at translating the *Adi Granth*, Trumpp discovered that he was unable to decipher 'a considerable residuum of words and grammatical forms to which I could get no clue', concluding that 'native assistance' would be required. Trumpp returned to India in late 1870 and immediately encountered further problems. The two Sikh *granthi*s he had enlisted to aid him in Lahore warned that the *Granth* could not be translated 'in the literal grammatical way' Trumpp desired and were unable to help him with many of the difficult constructions and idioms.[86] Trumpp's work progressed slowly and a period working with *granthi*s at Amritsar was similarly unproductive.

Trumpp decided that his slow progress was entirely the product of the decay of Sikhism: the Sikhs had 'lost all learning' and he believed that he was 'frequently ... misled' by the *granthi*s.[87] But these difficulties were as much a product of Trumpp's own arrogance and insensitivity as they were a product of a decline in the Sikh intelligentsia. Trumpp alienated the *granthi*s at Amritsar by blowing cigar smoke over the pages of the *Granth*, which they believed to be the embodiment of the Guru![88] Moreover, Trumpp was not interested in Sikhism per se; rather he undertook the translation because he was primarily interested in the linguistic and philological issues raised by the text. After working for eight years, largely independently with limited lexicographical support, he concluded that the language of the *Granth* was 'incoherent and shallow in the extreme, and couched at the same time in dark and perplexing language, in order to cover these defects. It is for us Occidentals a most painful and almost stupefying task, to read only a single Rag'.[89]

This hostile assessment of the language of the *Granth* (combined with Trumpp's tense relations with the *granthi*s), the difficulties he faced in translating a heterogeneous text of various dialects into his non-native English and his financial squabbles with the Indian government, did not incline Trumpp to create a positive image of Sikhism.[90] He believed that Sikhism was a 'reformatory movement' in spirit, but it had failed to achieve anything of real religious significance. Trumpp argued that his translation would attract very few readers, as 'Sikhism is a waning religion that will soon belong to history'. Moreover, he suggested that the *Adi Granth* did not actually represent or shape 'the popular notions of the masses'. While the Sikh intelligentsia only had a partial understanding of the *Granth*, the 'vulgar' Sikhs were not interested in its 'lofty metaphysical speculations' as their religion was 'concrete and adapted to their every-day wants'.[91] He noted that the 'vulgar' did not observe many of the *rahit-nama*s (codes of conduct) injunctions: for example, to recite an *ardas* before starting work and recite the *rahiras* when eating the evening meal.[92]

Such laxity, Trumpp argued, indicated that the Sikh 'Reformation' was short-lived. Nanak's followers 'soon ended up in a new bondage, which was quite as tiresome as that which they had thrown off'. This bondage was the 'martial spirit' inculcated by Guru Gobind Singh's Khalsa, a military brotherhood largely composed of 'rude and ignorant Jats'. The Khalsa was not the brotherhood of the 'pure' as its members 'surpassed their fellow-countrymen in all sorts of vices and debauchery, to which they added a rapacious and overbearing conduct'.[93]

Thus Trumpp struck at the heart of Sikh history and identity. He minimalized the impact of Nanak's teaching, ridiculed the Jats who increasingly dominated the *Panth* (community), questioned Sikh morality and dismissed the *Adi Granth* as an obtuse and juvenile work. Early in his project he rejected the possibility of working on the *Dasam Granth*. Trumpp left Lahore in early 1872, according to Lepel Griffin, the Officiating Secretary of the Punjab Government:

> unwilling to undertake the translation of the Granth of Guru Gobind Singh, which he considers a work which would not repay translation, and which would be, from its puerility and difficulties of style, so distasteful to him as to make it impossible for him to complete the translation.[94]

Nevertheless, Trumpp still cast himself as the authority on Sikhism, believing that the traditional Sikh intelligentsia had 'lost all learning'. Not only could the *Dasam Granth* be discarded as an obtuse collection of Puranic tales, but Trumpp presented only a partial translation of the *Adi Granth* (about one-third of the total *Granth*), believing it would 'be a mere waste of paper' to have translated and printed the 'minor' Rags. In reality, Trumpp suggested, the only value of the *Granth* was as a 'treasury of the old Hindui dialects': the sacred foundational text of Sikhism had been reduced to a string of quaint usages and unusual grammatical constructions.[95]

Although, as N. G. Barrier has pointed out, Trumpp's translation and introductory essays did make a substantial contribution to Punjabi linguistics, his unapologetic dismissal of Nanak and Sikhism had a more influential effect.[96] His text provided a powerful call-to-arms for a newly emerging Sikh intelligentsia, who were striving to clearly delineate Sikh identity and represent Nanak's 'Reformation' as a clean break from the Hindu tradition. Trumpp's extreme position, which put him at odds with Griffin, Cust and other leading scholar-administrators, prompted this western-educated Sikh elite to whole-heartedly engage with British Orientalist learning. The most notable outcome of this engagement was the work of Max Arthur Macauliffe.

Macauliffe: the dialogics of Orientalism

In 1893 Macauliffe resigned from the ICS after a distinguished career in the Punjab administration where he served as a Deputy Commissioner between 1882 and 1884 and as a Divisional Judge from 1884. From the mid-1870s, Macauliffe became interested in the ethnography and religious history of the Punjab. In 1875, he produced an article in the *Calcutta Review* on the shrine to *Pir* Sakhi Sarvar in the Suliman Mountains establishing Macauliffe as the most influential British interpreter of Sikh tradition.[97] Macauliffe's *The Sikh Religion* (six volumes, 1909) created a vision of Sikh scripture and history that has remained tremendously influential within the Sikh *Panth*.

In one sense Macauliffe worked within the analytical framework established within nineteenth-century Indology, as his work marks the culmination of the trope of Sikhism as 'Reformed Hinduism'. The introduction to the first volume of *The Sikh Religion* begins: 'The fifteenth century was a period of singular mental and political activity. Both in Europe and India men shook off the torpor of ages, and their minds awoke to the consciousness of intellectual responsibility.'[98] This passage echoed his earlier observation that a 'great succession of men, the Sikh Gurus' had transformed and purified the Hindu tradition.

> In them the East shook off the torpor of ages, and unburdened itself of the heavy weight of ultra-conservatism which has paralysed the genius and intelligence of its people. Only those who know India by actual experience can adequately appreciate the difficulties the Gurus encountered in their efforts to reform and awaken the sleeping nation.[99]

The rhetoric of these passages is extremely revealing. Macauliffe manipulated stock Orientalist images to emphasize the strength and significance of Sikhism. Nanak and his followers were thus represented as a group animated by a newly discovered religious enthusiasm that allowed them to break out of the spiritual solemnitude of medieval Hinduism. The weight of Hindu tradition was again conceived as the enemy of spiritual progress and Macauliffe drew on a well-established Orientalist tradition of representing India as a slothful and timeless land. These stock devices could be used to construct oppositions within Indian culture, in this case between Hinduism and Sikhism, as well as between India and Europe. The effect of these metaphors was heightened by Macauliffe's assumption of personal authority, as he reminded his audience that only 'those who know India by actual experience' could appreciate the full achievements of the Sikh Gurus. Elsewhere Macauliffe announced that 'I bring from the East what is practically an unknown religion.'[100] Through these pronouncements of experience and expertise Macauliffe attempted to give particular authority to his analysis of the Sikh past.

Indeed Macauliffe's Preface to the first volume of *The Sikh Religion* is a fascinating document that attempted to establish his credentials as the sole authoritative interpreter of Sikh scripture and history. He began by noting that because of its composite vocabulary and the lack of lexicographic support the 'Granth Sahib thus becomes probably the most difficult work, sacred or profane, that exists'.[101] But by careful consultation with the 'few' remaining *gyanis* (learned individuals) and a sensitivity to 'traditional interpretations' the translator could slowly untangle the linguistic, metaphorical and philosophical problems the *Adi Granth* presents. Macauliffe then contrasted his approach with that of Trumpp:

> A portion of the Granth Sahib was translated some years since by a German missionary at the expense and under the auspices of the India Office, but his work was highly inaccurate and unidiomatic, and furthermore gave mortal offence to the Sikhs by the odium theologicum introduced into it. Whenever he saw an opportunity of defaming the Gurus, the sacred book, and the religion of the Sikhs, he eagerly availed himself of it.[102]

This highly unfavourable portrait of Trumpp served to counterpoint and authorize Macauliffe's position. In order to further achieve this aim Macauliffe went on to explain that in addition to consulting extensively with *gyanis* concerning the meaning of particular words or phrases, he also felt it necessary to submit his work to 'native criticism'. After all there were 'few, if any, translations of Oriental works made in Europe, even by the most eminent scholars, which are accepted by the learned natives of the East.' In order to confront the full weight of Sikh learning Macauliffe submitted 'every line' of his translation to the 'most searching criticism of learned Sikhs' and even solicited such criticism by publishing 'invitations in Sikh newspapers' for those interested to consult his work.[103]

Thus, in many respects, Macauliffe's work was the product of a highly collaborative effort, fitting Irschick's model of colonial knowledge as a dialogic construct: it was the result of the meeting and mutual modification of Indian and European learned traditions.[104] In addition to the lexicographical aid he derived from learned members of the Sikh community, Bhai Sant Singh of Kapurthala and Bhai Prem Singh of Amritsar worked for a month and a half checking the accuracy of Macauliffe's translation.[105] The renowned scholar Sardar Kahn Singh Nabha assisted Macauliffe by reading the proofs produced by the Clarendon press.[106] Following this extensive consultation, the Sikh intellectual elite received Macauliffe's work with enthusiasm. Macauliffe cited *The Khalsa*'s proclamation that his 'English translation of our Scriptures' would create a new age of religious understanding and purity: 'the promiscuousness in Sikh ideas will vanish, and Tat [pure] Khalsa will begin to start on a new career.'[107]

In reality, Macauliffe's close relationship with the Sikh elite and their vision of the Sikh past undercuts his self-representation as an authority revealing the definitive interpretation of a little known religion. Despite this tension between Macauliffe as authoritative author and his reliance on Sikh *gyanis*, his preface is strikingly modern. His careful recognition of his informants, his emphasis on the value of 'actual experience' (field-work), the disclosure of his linguistic credentials and his reflections on the translation process sit comfortably with the modernist anthropological tradition. Thus in his work we have journeyed a long way from Wilkins's two-hour visit to the *gurdwara* at Patna or the piecemeal anti-Sikh information collected by James Browne at the Mughal court.

Military recruitment and preserving Sikh identity

Macauliffe's career raises the important question explored by Richard Fox in his *Lions of the Punjab: Culture in the Making*: what was the role of the colonial administration and 'western authorities', such as Macauliffe, in defining Sikh identity in the nineteenth century? Fox suggests that Sikh identity was fundamentally reshaped in the colonial period, as British administrators and Orientalists promoted 'Sikhism as a separate religion and Singh [the Khalsa] as a separate social identity'. By sponsoring the Singh identity (the 'orthodox' Sikh identity of those who had been inaugurated into the Khalsa, maintaining uncut hair and the other outward symbols of the Khalsa), the British 'domesticated' the potentially troublesome martial groups of the Punjab, creating a group of 'loyal lions' who were to serve as 'guardians of the Raj'. The main device for achieving this aim was military recruitment, where rigid tax-onomies ensured that only those Punjabis who fitted the British notion of Sikhism were enlisted.[108] Therefore the well-known modern Sikh identity was essentially the product of British 'racial determinism' and the Orientalist (in the Saidian sense) construction of Punjabi culture. Ultimately, however, Fox suggests, this colonial project backfired, as the 'loyal lions' turned on their British masters in the heated struggle over British control of Sikh *gurdwaras* during the 1920s and 1930s.

Fox is certainly correct in identifying the emergence of a more unified sense of Sikh identity in the last third of the nineteenth century. The 'Singh', or more correctly *kes-dhari* (a believer with uncut hair) identity, was increasingly promulgated, and understood by outside observers, as the 'orthodox' form of Sikhism. Oberoi's research has revealed the complex programme of ideological reformulation and socio-religious reform that underpinned the increasing dominance of this 'orthodox' Sikh identity. Although Oberoi notes that colonialism was a crucial economic and political framework for these changes, the momentum for religious reform came primarily from within the urban Sikh elite that comprised the Singh Sabha movement. Oberoi notes that his interpretation challenges Fox's claim that the 'Singh' identity was largely a product of the imperial imagination. Fox's vision of an all-powerful imperial state that was able to remake Sikhism to serve its own ideological needs completely effaces the importance of the pre-colonial Sikh tradition or the activities of the Punjabi reformers. Colonialism, Oberoi suggests, was integral in determining the eco-nomic and social milieu in which the Sikh reformers were working, but played little direct role beyond that.[109]

One question, however, that neither Oberoi nor Fox really explores is the confluence of Sikh and British interests and social imaginations. In two areas at least Sikh identities were formed out of a shared indige-nous and British understanding of the character of the Sikh tradition: its martial quality and the nature of popular Hinduism. The martial nature of the Sikh community was quickly established as an important trope in British representations of India. European travellers to the Punjab in the 1830s and 1840s commonly identified the Sikhs as a 'manly' and 'martial' community. G. T. Vigne, for example, suggested that the 'young Sikh was ... like the ancient Scythian, brought up to be a warrior.'[110] Observations on the physique and masculinity of the Sikh leaders and soldiers punctuate W. T. Osborne's account of Ranjit Singh's court: 'He is a fine-looking man,' 'Sher Sing is also a fine, manly-looking fellow' and 'Rajah Soocket Sing ... is ... one of the handsomest of the Sikh [*sic*] chiefs, who are all eminently good-looking.'[111] These depictions of Punjabis, at least in part, reflected the continuing importance of environment and diet in British notions of character: the Punjabi was superior because he ate meat, lived in a milder climate and was closer to the invigorating air of the hills.[112] This military prowess was clearly displayed in the Anglo-Sikh wars when the 'sturdy Punjab warriors' distinguished themselves by displaying a high 'degree of daring and enterprise' in resisting the British.[113] After the annexation of the Punjab, and in light of increasing doubts over the Madras Army's performance and the loyalty of Hindustani sepoys, the Punjab increasingly became the most important recruiting ground for the Indian army. The Eden Commission Report on the structure of the Indian army identified Punjab as the 'home of the most martial races of India and is the nursery of our best soldiers'.[114]

G. F. MacMunn, an officer with a distinguished record in the Indian army, neatly summarized this view which upheld the Punjabi as the most martial of Indians:

> The Punjabi generally, but especially the Sikh, has become a world wide adventurer ... tall, well-knit men, with their long hair pulled up under their head-dress, their beard and whiskers neatly curled up close to the face, and their military bearing all stamp the man ... As a fighting man, his slow wit and dogged courage gave him many of the qualities of the British soldier at his best.[115]

This example of what we might term 'military Orientalism' shows the continuing importance of notions of character, racially determined physique and intelligence in the imperial imagination: Sikh soldiers were seen as superior because their physique and character resembled that of the British soldier. What is also clear from MacMunn's summation is the crucial role of the external signifiers of the Tat Khalsa identity in constituting Sikhs' martial status.

While Fox's argument almost entirely effaces indigenous agency in suggesting that the colonial state effectively forged this Sikh identity, there is no doubt that the British did see themselves as playing an important role in 'policing' Sikh tradition.[116] This reflected British understandings of the history of Sikhism, which they saw principally in terms of a movement from the quietism and piety of Nanak to the military brotherhood of the Khalsa. The British believed that the Khalsa, which included the dagger (*kirpan*) as one of its signifiers, transformed the Sikhs into a warrior race and that the Sikhs were hardened by their ongoing battle against 'Muhammadan tyranny'. R. W. Falcon's 1896 officers' manual enshrined this official understanding, suggesting that recruitment should be aimed only at those 'Sikh tribes which supplied converts to Sikhism in the time of Guru Gobind Singh, who in fact formed the Singh people': more recent converts were to be avoided as they could not be considered 'true Sikh tribes'.[117]

The ultimate test of 'Sikh-ness' was whether an individual maintained the external symbols of Sikhism: 'Singhs, the members of the Khalsa; these are the only Sikhs who are reckoned as true Sikhs ... The best practical test of a true Sikh is to ascertain whether calling himself a Sikh he wears uncut hair and abstains from smoking tobacco.' Falcon mapped these martial qualities across the different regions of the Punjab, warning officers away from eastern and southern regions where the 'Hindustani type' was prevalent and against those regions where the Sikh identity was 'very diluted by Hinduism'.[118] Once recruited Sikh troops were placed in Sikh regiments, they were required to undergo the Khalsa's *khande ki pahul* initiation rite, to maintain the external symbols of their Sikh identity at all times and to accept the authority of the *granthi*s (reciters and interpreters of holy texts) appointed by the Army to perform Sikh rituals.[119] By encouraging this identity the British administration was able to foster a distinct but loyal community and nurture Sikh antipathies toward 'purbias', the soldiers of Hindustan and Bengal.[120]

It has been customary to see British recruitment of Sikh soldiers as the product of the power of British racial thought and the need to pacify the Punjab by absorbing demobilized soldiers of the Punjab state into the British army. But the importance of *izzat* (face, honour) and warrior values in Punjabi, but especially Jat, culture also conditioned the representation of Sikhs as a martial community.[121] Values shared by indigenous groups and the colonial state, or those values that could be understood as shared, have been largely neglected in the examination of the relationships between the Sikh elite and the British. The evidence does suggest that the articulation of a fundamentally militaristic Sikh identity arose out of a shared cultural and economic interest in military service. The imbrication of Sikh reforming values and military service is quite clear: Oberoi notes that from 1898 Sikh units started establishing their own branches of the Singh Sabha and Sikh regiments bankrolled Singh Sabha projects, funding various tracts and pamphlets and subscribing to reforming journals.[122] The supposed confluence of religious purity and military prowess meant that both the Singh Sabhas and the colonial state supported the tradition of Sikh military service. Rajiv A. Kapur, for example, has suggested that the 'Tat Khalsa emphasis on Sikh traditions of valour and militarism' was an important force in the success of First World War recruitment drives in Punjab.[123]

These common British and Sikh visions were also clear in attitudes towards 'popular Hinduism'. As the earlier section of this chapter demonstrated, the British believed that popular Hinduism was an all-consuming jungle that threatened to stifle the reforming impulses evident in more 'rationalistic' movements such as Sikhism. British scholar-administrators and Tat Khalsa leaders alike feared the decay of Sikhism. Falcon noted the 'great slackness there is at the present time in taking the *pahul* [Khalsa initiation rite], very many who call themselves Singhs ... omit to take the pahul though adopting the surname and keeping some of the observances.'[124] The missionary Henry Martyn Clark noted in *Panjab Notes and Queries* that he had encountered a group of seasonal-workers who observed the injunctions of the *rahit* at home, but would cut their hair and openly smoke when they were working away from their villages. Surely this was evidence of the decay of Sikhism?[125] These were the fears that the British were responding to when they insisted on recruiting 'pure' Sikhs and ensuring their Sikh troops maintained all the observances of their faith.

This brings us back to Macauliffe and his relationship with the Sikh elite. Macauliffe insisted that Sikhism was a distinctive religion and that its history was characterized by a constant battle against Hinduism. Popular Hinduism, he argued, was like a 'boa constrictor of the Indian forests ... it winds round its opponents, crushes it in its fold, and finally causes it to disappear in its capacious interior.' Sikhism was threatened with this same fate: 'the still comparatively young religion is making a vigorous struggle for life, but its ultimate destruction is ... inevitable without state support.'[126]

This argument dovetailed nicely with the agenda of the Sikh reformers who were proclaiming '*ham hindu nahin*' (we are not Hindus). Central to this drive was the textualization of Sikh tradition. From the early 1870s, Tat Khalsa reformers attempted to fashion a newly systematized vision of Sikh history, belief and practice. This reformist elite, which drew on complex social networks that transcended kin, place and caste, attempted to discipline Sikh faith and practice, drawing a clear and distinct boundary between their followers and the syncretistic traditions of the countryside. In addition to policing forms of belief (particularly devotion to popular saints and various forms of magic), they fashioned an elaborate series of lifecycle rituals that they hoped would prevent the assimilation of Sikhism into popular Hinduism. These new standards were propagated in pamphlets, newspaper articles and ultimately through their incorporation into the *rahit-nama* (code of religious discipline) tradition.[127] In 1909, the Imperial Legislative Council passed the Anand Marriage Act, which recognized and codified a distinctive Sikh ritual that formally marked Tat Khalsa Sikhs off from their Hindu and Muslim neighbours.[128]

This formal support of the Tat Khalsa by the colonial state, like the proclamation of a leading Sikh periodical that, as a result of Macauliffe's translation, 'the promiscuousness in Sikh ideas will vanish, and Tat [pure] Khalsa will begin to start on a new career', reveals the close interdependence of the British and Tat Khalsa programmes.[129] Such evidence of the dialogic construction of Sikh identity, where shared visions of the nature of 'popular Hinduism' and religious reform coalesced to promote the newly systematized Tat Khalsa identity, undercuts Fox's argument which constructs the colonial state as an all-powerful force capable of reformulating indigenous identity at will. The Tat Khalsa identity was not so much the product of British 'domestication' as the result of the interplay between the distinct, but often complementary, agendas and cultural values of both Tat Khalsa and British elites. Most importantly, it reflected understandings of 'religion' that both colonizer and colonized accepted: that religion was a system, a distinct series of beliefs, practices and structures that could be described and delimited by the printed word.

Conclusion

The systematization of Sikh identity is a reminder of the limitations of any Saidian approach which suggests that a simple 'self versus other' dichotomy was utilized by British Orientalists to distance themselves from Indians. This chapter has clearly demonstrated that British scholars were responding to a complex array of social, political and religious concerns, and deployed a range of representational strategies in their depictions of both Polynesian and Indian religions. Until the 1850s British and Pakeha scholars imagined Maori culture as fundamentally irreligious: Maori had no notion of the divine and lacked any religious organization. Nineteenth-century depictions of popular Hinduism were also marked by strong 'othering'. While the Maori were seen as 'other' because they lacked religion, India was depicted as 'other' because it was perceived as so fundamentally religious that religion saturated every aspect of life and moulded Indian society into distinct religious communities. But alongside, and often competing with, these 'othering' discourses, British commentators forwarded other views of non-Christian religions. Late eighteenth-century Orientalists, imbued by cosmopolitanism and convinced of the unity of humanity, found many affinities between Hindu and Christian belief. On the other hand Evangelicals, despite their conviction that both Hinduism and Maori culture were largely corrupted, insisted that indigenous peoples were not entirely 'other': all humans were created by God and were capable of salvation. Any study of British encounters with non-Christian communities must recover these deep-seated conflicts and variant agendas within the colonizing culture.

Debates over the Sikh identity also reveal the importance of multipoint comparisons in the construction of identity. 'Indian' identities were not simply constructed through a generalized opposition between Indianness and Britishness. A complex web of ideas about the nature of religion, Europe's religious history and the nature of Indian religions informed the British belief that Sikhism was perhaps the purest of all the Indian religious traditions. Sikhism was initially defined in relationship to Christian history: it was seen as the product of an 'Indian Reformation' and strong parallels were drawn between Guru Nanak and Luther and Calvin.[130] And both British scholar-administrators and Sikh reformers defined the Tat Khalsa, or 'pure Sikh', identity against those Sikhs they believed to be merging back into the amorphous mass of popular Hinduism. The notion of 'popular Hinduism' was a powerful tool for both Indian reformers attempting to redefine the boundaries of their own communities and for Europeans searching for a key to unlock the complexities of Indian history and society. The next chapter will trace the transplantation of this concept to Maori studies from the 1850s on, when Pakeha scholars suddenly 'discovered' Maori religion and came to believe that this religious tradition was a transplanted form of Hinduism.

4
'Hello Ganesha!': Indocentrism and the Interpretation of Maori Religion

Whereas the previous chapter established divergent trends in the representation of Indian and Polynesian religion until the 1850s, this chapter examines the subsequent emergence of Indocentric, or more specifically Hindu-centred, interpretations of Maori religion. From the 1850s there was a marked shift in Pakeha and British understandings of Maori culture as the 'discourse of negation' examined in Chapter 3 was undermined. Pakeha increasingly believed that Maori had gods, religious traditions and a form of socio-religious organization. Against the backdrop of the emergence of the Indocentric interpretations of Polynesian language and history traced in Chapter 2, several leading ethnographers and anthropologists saw Maori religion as a form of transplanted Hinduism; it was defined by its localized Indian gods, *tapu* (seen as a modified form of caste) and phallic worship.

This 'discovery' of Maori religion was not the product of metropolitan theorists making sense of the raw material provided by collectors in the colonial periphery, rather it was underpinned by political necessity and intellectual labour on the colonial frontier. Both Hiatt and Chidester have recently shown that missionaries, colonial administrators and ethnographers played a vital, and often overlooked, role in fashioning theoretical understandings of 'primitive religion'. While Hiatt's analysis of shifting interpretations of Aboriginal kinship and cosmology undercut the dominant image of colonial science as derivative and dependent on metropolitan initiative, Chidester's examination of comparative religion on the South African frontier has suggested that systems of colonial administration underpinned the 'discovery' of Xhosa, Zulu and Sotho-Tswana religious traditions.[1] This chapter adds further weight to these arguments, and locates the 'discovery' of Maori religion within two important and interrelated contexts: the textualization of Maori culture and the settler state's attempts to consolidate its often tenuous authority. The analysis of Maori religion and its insertion into an Indocentric tradition of comparative religion grew out of heightened Pakeha concern with Maori belief and practice in the wake of the northern wars of 1845–46. This conflict revealed the Maori ability to contest both the material and symbolic order of colonialism, marking the emergence of a series of anti-colonial traditions that exposed the limits of settler authority and the colony's dependence on military support from Australia, India and Britain. Thus, the growing interest of colonial officials in Maori beliefs reflected deep-seated anxieties about 'secret cults' and a desperation to master the idioms of indigenous political consciousness. Collections of traditions compiled by colonial administrators, essays discussing religious symbolism, and government discussions on the power of *tohunga* embody an important drive to 'know' the indigenous mind, to map its contours, to render it amenable to analysis and comparative discussion.

It is these complex engagements between scholarship and policy, Britain and its colonies, colonizer and colonized which form the core of this examination of Indocentric interpretations of Maori religion. The first part of this chapter identifies the major intellectual and political forces responsible for this major shift in British and Pakeha interpretations of Maori religion. The chapter then examines the deployment of India-derived models for the analysis of key aspects of Maori culture and religion, before concluding with an exploration of how this new understanding of Maori society as fundamentally religious penetrated the public sphere of colonial politics in the debates over rationality, religion and priestcraft that framed the Tohunga Suppression Act (1907).

Material transformations and textualizing traditions

This study has already traced the uneven development of ethnography on the New Zealand frontier until the 1840s, noting the linguistic difficulties and cultural impediments that limited early discussions of Maori 'religion'. While missionaries intent on policing emergent forms of vernacular Christianity hoped that they might accumulate a deeper understanding of traditional cosmology, it was the eruption of conflict in the Bay of Islands in the mid-1840s that stimulated a concerted effort on behalf of the colonial state to 'unveil' Maori religion.

In late 1845, when Nga Puhi chiefs Kawiti and Hone Heke were fighting government forces (which were largely dependent on the support of Heke's enemy, Tamati Waka Nene of Hokianga Nga Puhi), Sir George Grey replaced the humanitarian Robert Fitz-Roy as Governor. On the basis of his experience on the South Australian frontier, Grey stressed the value of ethnography as a foundation stone of colonial state-building.[2] In the preface to his ground-breaking *Polynesian Mythology* (1855), Grey explained the importance of Maori language and mythology to a governor who had taken over a war-torn colony: 'I soon perceived that I could neither successfully govern, nor hope to conciliate, a numerous and turbulent people, with whose languages, manners, customs, religion, and modes of thought I was quite unacquainted.' Grey noted that the 'rebel chiefs ... frequently quoted, in explanation of their views and intentions, fragments of ancient poems or proverbs, or made allusions which rested on an ancient system of mythology'. As Maori political discourse was grounded in 'these figurative forms', Grey believed that a close knowledge of Maori language and tradition was essential to the preservation of the Crown's authority.[3] In Grey's view the effective pacification and amalgamation of 'natives', whether Aborigines, Maori or Africans, was the primary duty of colonial governorship and this project was dependent on a sound knowledge of their social organization and worldview.

To achieve this end Grey provided several Maori with lodgings and wages in return for language instruction and recording various myths and historical narratives. The most important of these men was Wiremu Maihi Te Rangikaheke, a high-ranking member of Te Arawa. Te Rangikaheke quickly established a close working relationship with Grey. He lived with Grey in the Governor's residence, receiving £3 per month in return for his teaching and writing.[4] Until Grey's departure from New Zealand in 1853, Te Rangikaheke provided Grey with a series of manuscripts recounting various Maori traditions. These manuscripts, and the continuing dialogue between Te Rangikaheke and Grey which grew out of them, formed the basis for much of Grey's published work on Maori.

Grey's relationship with Te Rangikaheke was not unique. Edward Shortland, a leading surveyor and a Protector of the Aborigines, published two important works on Maori mythology, social organization and religious practice. His *The Southern Districts of New Zealand* (1851) and *Traditions and Superstitions of the New Zealanders* (1854) drew upon sources from a much wider geographical and tribal range, clarifying the extent of regional variation in Maori social life and cosmology.[5]

Meanwhile, the ethnographer John White was beginning to build a vast web of Maori correspondents. A range of important government positions in various parts of the North Island from the 1860s allowed White to extend this network, incorporating over 300 'informants', resulting in a huge collection of historical and mythological narratives.[6]

Thus, the increased willingness of Maori 'informants' to aid in the textualization of oral tradition underpinned this transformation of colonial knowledge. They provided Grey, Shortland and other collectors with versions of myths and narratives of the migrations from Hawaiki and recounted the deeds of their ancestors. Within pre-contact Maori society such knowledge possessed *mauri* (life force) and the communication of such knowledge was a highly *tapu* act. An elder would only slowly share ancestral knowledge with those members of the *whanau* or *hapu* who would respect and understand the *mauri* of the tradition. This careful guarding of knowledge frustrated many early nineteenth-century Pakeha searching for insight into the Maori world.

By the 1850s, deep-seated social and religious change modified this framework. The dissemination of Christian ideas from the 1830s began to undermine *tapu* and the mission station became a site where missionaries actively attempted to refashion Maori social organization by breaking *tapu*, attacking hereditary distinctions and stressing the primacy of the Christian family as the basic unit of society.[7] Concomitantly, involvement in the cosmopolitan world of Pacific whaling and participation in a trans-Tasman market economy exposed Maori to a range of new food plants (especially the potato), technology (especially the musket) and ideas. The enthusiastic and rapid appropriation of these innovations reshaped relationships both within and between kin groups. The influx of settlers from 1840 reoriented local patterns of production and the rhythms of tribal life, as many Maori communities living on the coasts and near Pakeha settlements became heavily involved in commercial agriculture and coastal shipping.[8]

Within the consolidation of this colonial market economy, knowledge production was also partly commercialized, as younger literate Maori enjoyed the remuneration offered by the ethnographers despite the reservations of older Maori about sharing knowledge with Pakeha.[9] John White's personal diary, for example, records his interactions with his informants at a daily level. It reveals a range of Maori responses to White's requests for information: some Maori demanded remuneration, others willingly entered into a dialogue about Maori traditions and also western culture, while others expressed a concern that in collecting these traditions White was violating *tapu*. For example, a *tohunga* named Te Takurua shared with White '2 ceremonies of priest-hood' and explained the magical uses of various plants to White in mid-1847. Te Takurua's grandfather scolded him for discussing these *tapu* matters with White. Both Te Takurua and his son soon died and the local Maori believed that their deaths were a direct result of violat-ing *tapu* by sharing traditions with White. However, the rise of a money-economy encouraged a new generation to rework this notion: Reilly has suggested that some 'informants' accepted that the pay-ments were made by Pakeha collectors as recognition of the *mauri* of the traditions.[10]

It is also possible that depopulation encouraged Maori to share their knowledge with Pakeha. The tumultuous inter-tribal wars fed by the competitive acquisition of firearms in the 1830s, and the introduction of new diseases (especially tuberculosis and venereal disease), had reduced the Maori population from between 80 000 and 120 000 in 1769 to approximately 60 000 at the end of the 1850s and 48 000 in 1874. The proverb that taught 'as the white man's rat has driven away the native rat, so the European fly drives away our own, and the clover kills our fern, so will the Maoris disappear before the white man himself' suggests that Maori feared a cultural crisis and eventual extinc-tion.[11] Thus, it seems that some Maori shared the Pakeha belief that print and literacy offered an important means of preserving Maori culture and these literate Maori were a moving force behind the textu-alization of their culture in the nineteenth century.[12] Maori's active acceptance of print culture coalesced with growing Pakeha interest in Maori cosmogony and mythology. Grey, and subsequent ethnogra-phers, set about editing and publishing the traditions they were collecting, believing that print might surpass medicine in preserving Maori culture. John White hoped that his writings would 'embalm' Maori knowledge and Grey noted that Maori knowledge was in jeop-ardy as the experts in tribal lore and myth were rapidly dying out.[13]

Fixing 'tradition'

These Pakeha scholars went beyond merely collecting traditions, to fix a coherent body of Maori myth and history. John White, for example, hoped to construct a complete picture of Maori tradition and typically instructed his informants to 'write as full as you can of all the History of the Maori, give everything you can no matter how trivial'.[14] By the late 1870s, with the assistance of key 'informants' such as Te

Whatahoro Jury, White had assembled a vast range of materials from different *iwi*, forming the basis for his *Ancient History of the Maori* (6 vols, 1887–90). These volumes were the culmination of a complex process of comparison, compression and translation, as White synthesized divergent and competing narratives into an encyclopaedic vision of traditional history.

White's *Ancient History*, like Grey's *Polynesian Mythology*, fashioned a standardized version of the indigenous past and created the scholarly framework for the analysis of Maori religion. Through textualization, Maori knowledge was 'disembodied', as print captured and disseminated knowledge to all literate Maori, removing knowledge transmission from the checks of the traditional elder/*tohunga*–junior relationship. Easily accessible, these codified collections of Maori history, legend and lore allowed Pakeha scholars to scrutinize traditions, searching for references to new gods, rituals or beliefs which could then be compared to other 'primitive' religious traditions. Freshly 'discovered' traditions, of occasionally dubious provenance, were added to this Maori mythological canon in the hope that a fuller picture of Maori beliefs could be constructed. Thus the allusive and elusive nature of Maori oral culture was finally captured in texts that could be carefully dissected with the aid of a growing number of Maori dictionaries, grammars and other Polynesian mythological collections.

This transformation in the colonial 'information order' was vitally important in the discovery of Maori 'religion'. The addition of a variety of new traditions and the continuing search for a 'religious' system facilitated the construction of new interpretations of Maori religion. Nowhere is this more visible than in the discovery of a supposedly monotheistic tradition. Jane Simpson has recently demonstrated that the processes of collection, evaluation and editing laid the foundation for later studies of Maori religion that argued that Maori were in fact monotheists, worshipping a god named Io.[15] Charles Davis, a respected linguist and chief translator to the government, argued that before colonization Maori did worship a Supreme Being, known as Ranginui or Io. This monotheism was an elite and secretive religion where God's name 'was held to be so sacred that none but the Priest might utter it at certain times and places'.[16] Following Davis's *The Life and Times of Patuone*, the supreme god Io regularly appeared in collections of mythology in the 1880s and 1890s.[17] However, until the close of the nineteenth century Io as the supreme god coexisted with, and was overshadowed by, the dominant ethnographic tradition that

emphasized a multitude of compartmental gods in the Maori cosmogony. Io's place as the God of Maori monotheism, as Simpson
shows, was only firmly secured in the twentieth century through a
heavily inter-textual body of scholarship created by Elsdon Best and
other Polynesian Society scholars.[18] Utilizing new material from Tuhoe
and Ngai Tahu informants and drawing on the work of Andrew Lang
on primitive monotheism, Best published an article in *Man* in 1913
that drew international attention to this hitherto neglected God, proclaiming that Io was the 'creative and eternal god' of Maori.[19]

The place of Io in 'traditional' Maori cosmogony remains hotly contested. While Io is the cornerstone for most recent reconstructions of
Maori cosmology, for some, Io is a product of the colonized imagination influenced by half a century's exposure to Christianity.[20] What is
certain is that the sudden appearance of Io in the public sphere of
scholarship was an important product of the textualization of Maori
mythology and history. Oral tradition, which narrators could shape
and adapt to serve their own interest or meet an audience's expecta-
tions, was now preserved in a multiplicity of published accounts. Yet
this process did not undermine Maori identity or mythology; rather it
provided a range of new sources for the articulation of identity and
understanding the past for an increasingly literate people. Published
accounts of mythology were open to contested readings and re-inter-
pretations, as the debates over the veracity of Io traditions themselves
illustrate. The Maori encounter with print culture unleashed complex
processes of cultural translation and negotiation, which profoundly
reshaped both Maori mentalities (as Chapter 5 illustrates) and Pakeha
understandings of Maori religion.

Maui, evolution and comparative religion

For many British and Pakeha commentators the immediate significance
of the mythological collections was that they allowed Maori religion
and mythology to be analysed for the first time. Although the emergence of Io as a supreme god in early twentieth-century scholarship
reflects a general European intellectual concern with 'high gods'
among 'primitive' peoples, no broad theoretical construct guided the
collection of mythology and folklore in the late 1840s and 1850s. The
tapu knowledge, which was previously beyond reach, was suddenly
accessible and Pakeha directed their energy to collecting and publishing this material rather than constructing a new model for the analysis
of Maori mythology.

But as Pakeha assembled and published more texts, important conclusions were drawn from Maori tradition. And as the textualization of Maori culture coincided with the rising intellectual authority of comparative mythology in Europe, this became an important analytical framework for the analysis of Maori religion. Although, as we saw in the previous chapter, scholars in the late eighteenth century and early nineteenth century were increasingly interested in comparative mythology and religion, Christianity remained the key reference point for any comparative enterprise. Attempts to identify parallels between Krishna and Christ and the Vedas and Christian doctrine upheld the centrality of Christian models for religious comparison. Those cultural traditions seen as 'natural religion' were also interpreted against the backdrop of Christianity. Pailin has shown that although the meaning of this term was disputed, all late eighteenth-century interpretations of 'natural religion' shared a vision of a universal religious sensibility that was underpinned by analytical frameworks grounded in Christian thought.[21]

In the late 1850s and early 1860s there was an important shift in this comparative tradition. From the 1860s on, European scholars suggested that Maori mythology provided an excellent example of 'primitive religion' and allowed the place of the Maori in the history of civilization to be assessed. This notion of 'primitive religion' drew on the older notion of 'natural religion', but within an intellectual milieu charged by biblical criticism, Darwinian evolution and geological discoveries that challenged literalistic readings of the Bible. These intellectual forces undercut the primacy of Christianity as a point of comparative reference, as scholars relied more heavily on anthropology and the natural sciences rather than Christian theology. By the end of the century, comparativists had produced works with titles such as *The Making of Religion, The Evolution of the Idea of God, The Supernatural: Its Origin, Nature and Evolution*, and Edward Caird, master of Balliol College, Oxford, had published a two-volume study simply entitled *The Evolution of Religion*.[22] Even Max Müller, a close associate of the liberal Anglicans at Cambridge, believed that the future of religion did not lie with 'historical Christianity' but rather with a new product of 'spiritual evolution', a syncretistic creed that drew on all branches of humanity's spiritual experience.[23]

For Max Müller, evolutionary processes dictated the past of religion as well as its future. He believed that while religious sensibilities generally evolved, becoming more sophisticated and refined, isolation and environmental difficulties could disrupt or even halt development. In his preface to William Wyatt Gill's important collection *Myths and Songs from the South Pacific* (1876), Max Müller argued that Polynesian mythology allowed unique access to the ancient Aryan past, because Polynesian society was actually frozen at the stage of Indian society at the time of *Rig Veda:*

> We know that mythopoeic phase among the Aryan and Semitic races, but we know it from a distance only, and where are we to look now for the living myths and legends, except among those who still think and speak mythologically, who are, in fact, at the present moment what the Hindus were before the days of Homer?[24]

He explained that mythology represented a 'complete period in thought'. Collections of mythology from the Pacific, which had only been opened to European influence recently, were invaluable for the exploration of the history of thought and society. It was as if 'the zoologist could spend a few days among the megatheria, or the botanist among the waving ferns of the forests, buried beneath our feet.' But among these fragments of the 'childhood of the world', Max Müller found scattered evidence of enlightenment that would 'comfort those who hold that God had not left Himself without a witness, even among the lowest outcasts of the human race.'[25]

Nine years later, in an 1885 article on solar mythology, Max Müller analysed the cycle of myths relating the feats of Maui. Maui, the *potiki* (last-born) son of primordial parents Rangi and Papa, overcame his junior status through his ingenuity and daring. His tricks and conquests shaped the world we live in: he fished up the land (the North Island is still called *Te Ika Maui* – the fish of Maui), stole fire for humanity from the fiery fingers of his ancestress Mahuika, and used the magical jaw-bone of Muriringa-whenua to beat the sun into submission and slow its movement across the sky. It was this last tale within the cycle that intrigued Max Müller. Maui, he argued, was an archetypal 'solar hero'. Like the Vedic god Yama (the son of the sun, the first man and later the god of the dead) Maui was born of a god but was a mortal who later became deified because of his daring exploits.[26]

Max Müller argued that the myths of Yama and Maui revealed the unity of humanity. He noted the dangers of philological comparison across linguistic families, but suggested that in mythology scholars could discern 'one common human nature' that lay beneath 'the diversity of human speech'. All religions, from the 'lowest' to the 'highest', venerated the Infinite and initially people saw the sun as the Infinite's symbol and embodiment. In the early stages of religious consciousness the sun assumed central importance, as riddles, myths, ritual and worship all focused on the sun's life-giving properties. This 'heliolatry' constituted the 'most widely spread form of early faith' and in this respect the special attention scholars had devoted to solar myths in the Greco-Roman world was misplaced.[27] Thus, Polynesian mythology revealed the ancient history of human thought and belief, as the Maui myths epitomized the earliest stages of religion when humanity's veneration fixed on the sun and its animating power.

Traditions relating to Maui were also prominent in E. B. Tylor's studies of primitive culture and religious evolution. Tylor asserted that 'all the world is one country' and synthesized a vast amount of material drawn from South Asia, the Pacific, Africa and North America. Tylor believed that a universalist worldview which treated 'mankind as homogeneous in nature, though placed in different grades of civilization' should be the foundation for the analysis of civilization.[28] His interpretation of religion was evolutionary, suggesting that the highest monotheistic and rational stages of religion had evolved out of the cruder religious beliefs that underpinned animism and primitive mythologies. He argued that mythology had its roots in the reverence for nature in primitive societies. Thus, nature worship was a consistent feature of all mythology and Maori mythology again proved a useful vehicle for establishing human kinship. Tylor identified Maui (whom he described as 'the New Zealand Sun-god') as the Maori parallel of Vishnu, as his fishing up of *Te Ika Maui* paralleled Vishnu's boar avatar who dredged up the earth on his great tusks.[29] Thus Tylor and Max Müller, the leading luminaries of comparative mythology, emphasized the importance of Polynesian sun myths and the strong parallels between Maori and Hindu mythology.

Colonial comparative mythology

Meanwhile from the 1850s, Pakeha scholars were exploring similar questions about the relationship between Hindu and Maori traditions. As we have seen in Chapter 2, the missionary-ethnographer Richard Taylor fashioned an Indocentric diffusionist framework for the analysis of Maori culture. This framework moulded Taylor's understandings of Maori religion, but where Tylor imagined the history of religion as mainly progressive, Taylor advocated a diffusionist interpretation, grounded in the older Evangelical theological traditions that emphasized degeneration. Taylor believed that as Maori emigrated from

Eurasia they became distanced from centres of civilization, losing the stimulus of cross-cultural interaction. Isolation from these 'leavening' influences froze Maori mythology and religion. He argued that the mythology of an 'isolated race like that of the New Zealander' embodied 'the most ancient remains of its history ... as well as peculiarities of its religion; and it is there amongst the fables and foolish tales, that some faint remains of ancient truth, are to be discerned.'[30] While Taylor believed that Maori were God's children, he suggested their isolation in the Pacific distanced them from Christian truth. Through this spiritual geography, which located the Pacific as the dark rim of human diffusion where reason decays and the spirit is sapped, Taylor clearly established the need for the introduction of Christianity. Pakeha had to introduce Maori to the Gospel and restore Maori to the folds of God.

Despite the widespread public debates over evolution in nineteenth-century New Zealand, the older degenerationist model adopted by Taylor for the study of Maori religion remained a powerful framework in the later nineteenth-century.[31] John White, whose work on Maori mythology enjoyed significant government support, confirmed the outlines of Taylor's analysis. White, like Taylor, reflected that Pakeha had to take Maori religion and mythology seriously:

> [t]he Maoris though far removed from the civilization of the rest of the world held opinions on those important questions too and if unable to answer them as satisfactorily as more highly favored members of the human family possibly such answers as they were able to give had no less influence on their lives and general character.[32]

Nevertheless, as White evaluated his collections, he too believed that the isolation of Maori in the Pacific meant that their beliefs were profoundly degraded. Geographic and cultural isolation had trapped 'so many generations' of Maori 'in a labyrinth of superstitions so servile in practice, and so degrading in their tendency' that they had become enslaved to the power of superstition, *tapa* and all-powerful priests.[33]

W. E. Gudgeon, the brother-in-law of Elsdon Best and New Zealand's Resident Commissioner in the Cook Islands between 1899 and 1909, synthesized many of these nineteenth-century interpretations in his research on Maori religion. He believed that Maori religion revealed their place in the universal history of religious sentiment, as in 'matters supernatural the mind of man follows much the same groove, be he

Caucasian, Mongol or Maori'. Gudgeon argued that they possessed an 'ancient religion' and that Maori were 'a most religious people'. The popular form of this religion was constructed around *tapu* (sacred or prohibited because of supernatural power), and was inherently legalistic as Maori fastidiously maintained the laws of *tapu*, as Indians observed caste, at risk of apostasy or death. Even this popular degraded and 'inferior' form of the religion revealed that Maori valued the 'most universal of all religious emotions' which is the 'recognition of all male and female principle[s] of life' as manifested in nature.[34] Gudgeon, however, was heavily influenced by the research of A. H. Howitt and Andrew Lang on primitive monotheism, and believed that, in addition to venerating nature, Maori worshipped a 'great god' and this constituted the highest form of Maori religion.[35] This God was only to be found in a 'purely abstract' system that was the domain of the priestly elite.

These arguments about *tapu* and the cleavage between elite and popular religious sensibilities echoed many of the interpretations of South Asian religion traced in Chapter 3. Gudgeon himself hinted at this 'Oriental' connection, and noted that this system echoed the 'the records of India or Egypt' and that presumably Maori carried their primitive monotheism from these homelands into the Pacific.[36] Thus, the Io cult was the original and superior form of Maori religion, while the later worship of a pantheon of 'anthropomorphic gods' and a society organized around the observance of *tapu* were the debased product of cultural degeneration.[37] Gudgeon's argument, therefore, drew on and harmonized three important models arising out of nineteenth-century studies of Maori religion: primitive monotheism, Indocentric diffusionism and Evangelical degenerationism. Gudgeon's weaving together of these arguments encapsulates the profound shifts arising out of the textualization of Maori oral traditions: where, less than fifty years before, missionaries, settlers and travellers denied the existence of Maori religion, spirituality was now seen as being at the core of Maori life.

Hindu-centrism: Indian gods in the Pacific

Thus far, this chapter has attempted to chart and explain general shifts in understandings of Maori religion in the second half of the nineteenth century as a result of the textualization of Maori tradition and the rise of comparative mythology. As we have already seen, both metropolitan and Pakeha scholars identified parallels between Maori religion and Hindu mythology. The impact of India on European mentalities meant that Hinduism was an important reference point for the analysis of African, Native American and Pacific cultures.[38] But in later nineteenth-century New Zealand, where linguistic affinities were commonly believed to establish Maori's Indian origins, some scholars went beyond noting affinities to suggest that Maori religion was essentially a Polynesian form of Hinduism. The dominance of the diffusionist models for the analysis of Maori religion meant that Maori mythic heroes and gods were often read as direct transplantations or localized forms of Indian gods.

In his *The Story of New Zealand* (1859), the former Indian army surgeon A.S. Thomson noted various connections between Maori and Indian religion. At this early stage, as the textualization of Maori culture was partial and Indocentric models were only crystallizing, Thomson did not try to reconstruct the relationship between Maori religion and Hinduism in any comprehensive way, rather he identified parallels which he believed established a significant cultural link. Maori called their gods *Atua*, which, Thomson argued, resembled 'the Sanscrit word Dewa and the Hindostanee term Ullah'.[39] He also argued that *tohunga* (ritual experts) possessed a secret ceremonial language which 'like the Sanscrit of the Brahmanical priesthood, was unknown among the people'. Moreover, Maori shared with Hindus a belief in the sacred colour red, a worldview grounded in 'the transmigration of souls' and the worship of 'wooden images'. Although Thomson was reluctant to trace Maori origins back beyond Malaya, he concluded that Maori religion revealed that they 'had intercourse with men holding the Hindu faith'. Maori religion was neither sophisticated nor highly elaborate, rather it was arrested at a rudimentary stage of development, belonging to 'the infancy of our race'.[40]

Thomson's use of the inclusive pronoun in this last quotation implied that Maori religion might be viewed within a broader pattern of Aryan religious development. Nevertheless, as Chapter 2 demonstrated, any identification of Maori as Aryan was contested in nineteenth-century New Zealand. Where A. S. Thomson was uncertain of the quality of the connection between Maori religion and Hinduism, the ethnologist W. H. Blyth asserted a direct link. In Blyth's view, the Maori form of Hinduism was not an Aryan creed: following J. T. Thomson's work Blyth suggested that Maori were of 'an An-Aryan, or Turanian origin'.[41] In contradistinction to Thomson's privileging of philology as a proof of the racial connection to South India, Blyth used mythological arguments, seeing a direct relationship between Hindu polytheism and Maori polytheism. He argued the Maori pantheon replicated the Turanian gods: '*Kali*, or *Uma*, appears as *Hema*, or *Houmea*; *Krishna* as *Karihi*; and *Dewaki*, the mother of Krishna, is transformed to *Tawaki*, a son of *Hema*'. Each pantheon, Turanian and Maori, was essentially a 'triad, consisting of father, mother, and germ'.[42] It was this Indian connection, Blyth argued, that explained why Maori cosmography and mythology was of 'an order far higher than might have been expected from a people of their position on the ethnological scale'. This surprising sophistication could be traced back to the cultural encounters that shaped the racial stock of Polynesians in their ancient Indian home. Where many Britons emphasized the cultural decay arising out of the mingling of Aryan and Turanian (or Dravidian) 'blood', Blyth argued hybridization improved Turanian and Dravidian cultures. This legacy was preserved in the 'more Caucasian cast of features' found in Maori 'chiefs and priests'.[43]

Alfred Kingcombe Newman extended Blyth's argument about the ethnic hybridity of Maori to form a comprehensive vision of Maori religion grounded in a racialized interpretation of South Asian history and religion. In Newman's view, the Polynesian form of the Hindu faith was not the pure Aryan faith of the Vedas; rather it was the hybridized religion born from the intermarriage between the invading Aryans and India's 'Gangetic' and 'Mongolic' peoples.[44] This intermarriage produced a range of new gods into the Hindu pantheons: Newman found evidence for 70 of these Hindu gods and 38 Hindu goddesses in Polynesia.[45] Newman noted that just as Hindu gods often had several names, Maori worshipped 'a few gods under many *aliases*'. Newman argued that a few names were perfectly preserved in the Pacific, such as Ira, Kali and Uma, but other parallels could be discerned in the similarity between the names of Indian and Maori gods, including 'Tangara' and 'Tangaroa', 'Devaki' and 'Tawhaki', 'Manu' and 'Oo-Manu', 'Rudra' and 'Ru and Rua', 'Sina' and 'Hina', and 'Dyo, Dyu, Io' and 'Io'.[46] Echoing Blyth's argument that a 'triad' underpinned Hindu and Maori pantheons, Newman identified a fundamental 'trinity of gods' in Hawai'i, if not in New Zealand.[47] Newman also discerned striking parallels between the 'first men' Manu and Maui: they were both closely associated with fire, survived a great flood alone and both failed to cheat death by re-entering the womb.[48]

Maori art furnished Newman with further 'proof' of the connections between Polynesian religion and the wider world of Hinduism. He identified traces of South Asian motifs and auspicious signs (especially the swastika) in Maori motifs, Pacific ornamentation and the Easter

Island pictographs. He believed that the essentially Hindu nature of Maori culture was substantiated by a *pare* (carved door lintel) that supposedly emulated Javanese representations of Vishnu and Garuda and the discovery of an 'idol' that was purportedly a local version of Ganesh. Newman recounted important confirmation of his belief in a Maori Ganesh cult: when an officer from the Indian army was examining Newman's collection of Maori sculpture, the officer 'suddenly exclaimed in the friendliest manner, "Hello, Ganesha!" just as though he were welcoming an old friend. I thought I was the only man who knew that Maoris carved the elephant god.' The officer reassured Newman that his Maori items were almost exact replications of 'little red image[s]' found 'at the end of houses in Multan'.[49]

Newman took the comparative method to its most extreme length, reading almost all available evidence as a proof of profound links between Maori and their north Indian home. He saw Maori as part of a larger racial and religious community, spanning India, South-East Asia and the Pacific, and this enabled him to draw on a huge range of ethnographic material produced within the region to bolster his argument. Comparative religion and philology always contained the implicit methodological danger that evidence which challenged a theory, or was simply neutral, could be disregarded at the expense of evidence which apparently established a particular theory. Newman, convinced of Maori's religious nature and their Indian origins, asserted a much stronger and direct connection between Maori religion and Hinduism than any other single scholar.

Religion and the crisis of imperial authority

Although the full elaboration of the connections that supposedly linked Maori religion and Hinduism was not achieved until the publication of Newman's work in the early twentieth century, India was a constant reference point in discussions of religion and colonial authority in New Zealand from the 1860s. The shock waves that rippled through the British empire in the wake of the Indian rebellions of 1857–58 provided a new stock of images and understandings of indigenous societies. Britons, both at home and in India, identified religion as one of the key causal factors in the rebellion and Evangelicals believed that the revolt revealed the corrupt nature of Hinduism and Islam. *The Church Missionary Intelligencer*, for example, argued in January 1858 that '[t]he social life of the Hindu abounds with iniquity.

Can humanity and compassion, have any place in the heart of that man who murders his daughters as quickly as they are born?'[50] The same journal forwarded a more novel interpretation five months later: Hinduism and Islam were imagined to be the New Zealand volcanoes Tongariro and 'Ruapaka' (Ruapehu). Muslims in India, like Tongariro, 'had continued to emit smoke' under British rule. Hinduism, on the other hand, had 'long been torpid and inactive' like Ruapehu. Suddenly the religious 'prejudices' of both communities had erupted into fanaticism and violence.[51]

In the wake of the Indian rebellion, many Britons regarded indigenous religions with considerable suspicion. Fears of 'native fanaticism' and sensationalized accounts of indigenous religion inscribed stronger boundaries between the rulers and ruled throughout the empire. Although the *Church Missionary Intelligencer* used the metaphor of Tongariro and Ruapehu to explain the situation in India, typically the flow of images and ideas went the other way. Ideas formulated in India about the dangers of indigenous religions proved particularly important in New Zealand during the wars of the 1860s, which according to some observers, were driven by the same religious fanaticism which underpinned the 1857–58 rebellion in India.

Many settlers identified religious passions as the root of the wars. This argument hinged on the textualization of Maori culture, the resultant 'discovery' of Maori religion and the profound imprint that the rebellion against British rule in India had throughout the empire. In December 1868, Governor G. F. Bowen wrote to the Duke of Buckingham to explain the wars that were racking New Zealand. Bowen believed that three factors caused the conflict: most importantly the 'outbreak of the Hauhau fanaticism', the removal of English forces that elevated 'Hauhau' and Kingitanga confidence, and the confiscation of portions of 'rebel' land. Bowen reflected that the intersection of these three causes exactly replicated the 'immediate causes of the Indian rebellion'.[52] Bowen continued:

> With regard to the first of these three causes, it may be observed that the religious and national fanaticism of the Hauhaus is analogous to the periodical outbreaks of a similar nature among the Malays (who are probably of kindred race with the Maoris), and among the Hindoos and Mussulmans of India. It may not be altogether impertinent to mention that the 'lily' fills the same place in the mysterious proclamations of the Maori King, as the 'lotus' filled in the missives of some of the native princes in Hindostan.[53]

Bowen, who obviously clung to a theory of Malay origins, was writing in the wake of attacks on settlers in Poverty Bay by the prophet Te Kooti and his followers, suggested that the Hauhau forces were carrying out atrocities 'as dreadful as any perpetrated during the great rebellion in India'. Bowen warned against the proposal to withdraw imperial troops from New Zealand, arguing that any withdrawal would be 'naturally similar to the impression which would have been made on the minds of Nana Sahib and the sepoy mutineers by an announcement of the immediate withdrawal of the English troops soon after the massacre at Cawnpore.'[54] Unless the Colonial Office maintained a strong force in New Zealand, the country would face 'a general rising of the disaffected natives' which would lead 'to tragedies as dreadful as Delhi and Cawnpore.'[55] The spectre of the rebellion was a powerful tool for a colonial administrator desperate to maintain resources in the face of 'native fanaticism'.

Maori phallic cults

Within two years of Bowen's letter an uneasy peace had been secured and Pakeha celebrated their 'victory' in the wars.[56] Britons in India also congratulated their fellow whites in New Zealand. An article entitled 'A Lesson from New Zealand' in *The Bombay Gazette* upheld the cooperation between the settler troops and 'friendly' Maori as a model for colonial warfare.[57] In the wake of the wars, Pakeha and the government closely monitored Maori religious movements. Fears of secret cults and new millennial movements constantly surfaced as the press reported a string of new prophets, healers, and cults.[58] Pakeha were suspicious of these Maori attempts to control the impact of colonization, fearful that Maori 'fanaticism' would lead to the resumption of war. The government used force in raids against the settlements of two prophets: Te Whiti-o-Rongomai's Parihaka in Taranaki (1881) and Rua Kenana's Maungapohatu in the Urewera (1917). Maori religious practice was a crucial issue for the government and scholars alike: government agents, missionaries and ethnographers attempted to uncover and analyse 'traditional' practices and their modern forms.

In light of these concerns, another aspect of Maori religion that drew particular scholarly interest in the late nineteenth and early twentieth century was phallus-worship. In part this interest was in keeping with the sensationalized accounts of Maori religion that became popular in the later nineteenth century, but an increased interest in the nature of 'primitive' religion was an equally important stimulus. Ethnographers and folklorists in the final decades of the nineteenth century attempted to discern patterns in mythology and social organization among 'primitive' peoples in the hope that fresh data would create a new image of the development of religion. This project involved a shift away from an approach that focused on theology or mythology alone, placing greater emphasis on magic, fertility and distinctive forms of socio-religious organization.[59] Pakeha interest in Maori phallic cults must be read against both the Pakeha concern to uncover Maori 'secret' religious practices and the broader history of European interest in phallic worship as a feature of 'natural' religion.

Indian phallus worship provided a particularly important reference point for Alfred Newman and Elsdon Best, as they set about unveiling the 'curious' and 'hidden' veneration of the phallus among Maori. Elsdon Best attempted to collect and analyse previously unrecorded traditions and practices during his research among the Tuhoe in the rugged and isolated Urewera. Correspondence with S. E. Peal, who believed that phallus worship was one of the 'racial customs' that linked the 'Mon-Anam' race in India, the Pacific and east Africa, encouraged Best's interest in fertility rites and phallic symbols. In a letter to Peal in 1895, Best reported that he was 'much pleased ... at having discovered the remnants of that most ancient cult – the worship of the phallic symbol, it never having been noted in N.Z. before.'[60] Best believed that Maori mythology and religion contained important 'survivals' from ancient forms of religious practice, especially phallus worship. He did not document these survivals until he published an article in *Man* in 1914, which recorded Maori beliefs 'concerning the inherent power of the organs of generation in the *genus homo.*'[61] In 1924, Best put these beliefs in a broader context, observing that 'barbaric man was much impressed by the mystery and powers of sex, that he extended it to things that we know to be sexless, and that he endowed certain natural phenomena with strange powers of fructification.' Although the Polynesians had abandoned any 'system of direct worship of the phallus' long ago, Best was able to discern elements in Maori mythology and ornamentation that echoed Indian phallus worship.[62] Best noted that childless women of the Tuhoe tribe venerated 'the phallic tree known as Te Iho o Kataka', believing that the tree's generative powers could aid conception and even determine the gender of the foetus.[63] He also suggested that the *tiki* ornaments worn by Maori women were 'fructifying' symbols that were personified forms of the 'linga'.[64]

Thus Best, no doubt encouraged by Peal's belief in the importance of phallic symbols, collected a range of traditions neglected by nineteenth-century ethnographers.[65] Unsatisfied with collection alone, Best pondered the broader significance of these traditions in a lengthy article on the gods Tane and Tiki. He argued that Tiki, who was the Creator according to certain traditions, was a personified form of the generative power of the phallus.[66] Tiki, Best noted, was closely associated in myths with *tuna*, the eel, which he believed echoed Aryan mythology: in ancient Persia Indra was worshipped in the form of a serpent and Ira or Indra were the names of 'the eel god of India'. Traces of this old Aryan form could be discerned in various Maori tales and incantations: one charm ended with the invocation '*ko Ira i, to ro wai*', or Ira of the water.[67] The phallic aspect of this Maori god was most obvious in a *waiata mate kaha*, a form of love song, which invoked 'the penis of Tiki, the redness of Tiki, the glow of virile Tiki'.[68] These traditions convinced Best that Tiki was 'the old sacerdotal Polynesian name for the linga or phallus' and these myths suggested that Maori mythology was in fact a form of Aryan mythology, modified as a result of their migration 'from a central source in pre-historic times'.[69]

Best further extended these arguments in *Tuhoe, Children of the Mist* (1925). Here Best argued that Maori socio-religious organization was structured around 'a masculine and feminine principle' as 'the expressions *tama tane* and *tama wahine*, implying male and female, are applied to almost everything under the sun'. This dichotomy was grounded in the spiritual and symbolic power of the genitals: the 'main ideas in connection with such are that the female organ represents destructive energy, and the male protective energy'. The operation of the 'feminine principle' in Maori society was opposed to the generative powers of the phallus and thus could be compared 'with Kali (also known as Uma), the Destructress, who is symbolized as the reproducer by the Yoni, or female generative principle'.[70] Best, convinced of Maori's Indian origins, clearly believed that the gendered representations of the gods in Hinduism were powerful tools for the analysis of the numerous Maori rites, chants and myths that concerned gender and sexuality.

Alfred Newman placed even heavier emphasis on these Indian connections and Maori 'phallic' worship was a cornerstone of his argument that attempted to establish that Maori religion was a form of Hinduism. In order to find proof for this argument Newman travelled to India in 1910, visiting Calcutta and Banaras. In these cities,

Newman found the evidence he was searching for: temples decorated with 'obscenities', sacred monkeys and other 'absurdities'. Newman, citing Monier-Williams, argued that Hinduism was 'a few traces of greatness swamped in a mass of barbaric worship', a characterization Newman believed to be applicable to Maori religion as well.[71]

Newman's understanding of Indian chronology and racial history shaped his representation of Maori religion. He subscribed to the racialized interpretation of Indian history examined in Chapter 1 – that Aryan invaders of the Punjab intermarried with 'Gangetic' and 'Mongolic' peoples as they pushed south and east into India. Out of this process, a 'three-quarter bred' Aryan race, the Aryan-Mongolic ancestors of Maori, was born. These Maori left India before the rise of Buddhism, migrating through Burma, the Malay peninsula, and Java, before peopling the Pacific (see Map on p. xi). Newman suggested that Maori left India around 1000 BCE, in his opinion approximately 2000 years after the composition of the Vedas.[72]

The timing of this migration was important for Newman's argument concerning Maori phallic worship. He suggested that Maori religion was conservative: each generation of Maori was 'a slave to the customs of its forefathers', fiercely defending oral tradition and custom.[73] The unchanging nature of Maori religion meant that Newman could argue that it was essentially the same as it was when Maori left India. Maori religion contained important non-Aryan accretions from the post-Vedic period, as it was the degraded product of the intermarriage between Aryan and Mongolic peoples in the wake of the Aryan invasion. The most important of these degenerated features was linga worship, a Mongolic custom that 'contaminated the purer Aryan religion'.[74] Traces of this linga worship could be discerned 'from Bengal and Orissa to Burma, Malay peninsula, Java, Hawaii and New Zealand' – indeed there was 'no break in the chain of linga worship' from India to the eastern Pacific. Newman suggested phallic worship took various forms in New Zealand. Childless women made offerings to 'an upright linga stone', buildings were adorned 'with lingas set on posts in profusion', and Maori, like their Indian and Indonesian cousins, venerated sacred red stones and constructed piles of stones as sites of worship.[75] Newman believed that the Maori term *oni*, used to denote 'the wrigglings of copulation', echoed the Hindi *yoni* – a link, he argued, that established a powerful conceptual continuity between Maori religion and Hinduism. These discoveries confirmed Fornander's earlier identification of remnants of phallus worship in Hawaii, and Maori phallus worship surely provided definite proof of the Indian origins of Polynesians.[76]

Tapu, rank and caste

These visions of Maori religion elaborated by Newman and Best attempted to explain the ways in which 'religious' beliefs shaped Maori ideas about gender, sex and the social order. Best's research on phallic worship among the Tuhoe attempted to find the principles within Maori mythology that provided the structural underpinnings of everyday life. Best believed that the fertility rites he uncovered and the oppositions between phallus and *yoni*, male and female, were important adjuncts to the system of *tapu* that structured Maori consciousness and society.

While, as Chapter 3 demonstrated, Evangelical missionaries defined Maori religion in negative terms, they nevertheless believed that there were important social conventions that defined and structured Maori life. The most important of these was *tapu*. The multiple meanings and practices of *tapu* remain contentious:[77] in the early nineteenth century Europeans normally conceived of *tapu* as things that were set apart, forbidden or beyond mundane contact.[78] This conception largely arose from European experiences of daily contact with Maori, where they were prohibited from having contact with certain areas (*kumara* plantations or burial grounds), people (pregnant women, the sick or chiefs) or certain 'pure' objects like cooked food.[79] Such experiences convinced Europeans that *tapu* underpinned Maori life. The artist Augustus Earle, who lived in the Bay of Islands in the late 1820s, suggested that 'taboo' constituted 'the principal part' of Maori social life.[80] A decade and a half later, the German naturalist Ernst Dieffenbach argued *tapu* 'comprises, indeed, everything that we would call law, custom, etiquette, prejudice, and superstition'.[81]

Closer acquaintance with Maori society led to a developing awareness amongst Pakeha of the complexities of *tapu* and from the 1840s a more sophisticated understanding of *tapu* began to emerge. These social rules, which governed the organization of space, personal contact and the preparation of food, were increasingly conceived of as a primitive religious institution. *Tapu* seemed to include some primitive notion of the sacred, but this religious component was distorted and degraded, and primarily served as a tool for the justification of social inequality. At the end of his long missionary career, the

Wesleyan James Buller reflected that Maori society was divided into three ranks: chiefs, commoners and slaves. These gradations were solely a result of the operation of *tapu*: '[i]t was the tapu that made the difference between chiefs and others.' *Tapu*, which expressed and protected distinctions of purity and sanctity, generated the hierarchical organization of Maori society.[82]

A member of the Legislative Council, William Brown, also forwarded this interpretation. Brown argued that *tapu* was of primary importance in considering Maori society because of 'the overwhelming influence which it exerts over them.' Brown felt that *tapu* primarily served the interests of the chiefly elite who were 'fully aware of the advantages of the *tapu*, finding that it confers on them, to a certain extent, the power of making laws and the superstition on which the tapu is founded will ensure the observance of them.'[83] *Tohunga* united the skills 'of priest, sorcerer, juggler, and physician' and wielded great influence due to the 'superstitious notions of the people' and this influence was further secured by the Maori's constant fear of evil.[84]

Such arguments about the relationship between *tapu* (or *tabu* in central and eastern Polynesia) and rank were common throughout colonial Polynesia, and by the mid-century *tapu* was frequently identified as the key socio-religious institution governing Polynesian life. Europeans frequently attacked *tapu* as an iniquitous and superstitious system, which clothed worldly ambition in the language of religion and magic. Hiram Bingham, a Protestant Missionary based in Hawaii and a member of the American Oriental Society, argued that *tapu* was created to justify immorality and licentiousness on the behalf of men. 'How must the observance of it, then, debase the public mind, cherish the vilest passions, banish domestic happiness, and shield priests and kings in their indulgences and oppression!'[85] Bingham's Polynesians were not the happy children of nature, rather they were the dupes of Satan ensnared in polytheism and a debased social system of 'immeasurable evil'.

These debates over Polynesian society and religion echoed British discourses on caste and Brahmanical tyranny in India. The role of *tapu* in Polynesian society was attacked on the same grounds as the British reformers in India attacked caste. James Mill's observation that 'the whole frame of Hindu society' rested on caste, was essentially the same argument that was being forwarded regarding *tapu*.[86] Just as Hindus were believed to be enslaved by the religious and social domination of the Brahmans, Maori *tohunga* (experts in communication with the spiritual world and masters of rituals and incantations) were seen to dominate Maori society with their 'superstitious observances'. Augustus Earle, for example, argued that *tohunga* 'easily work on the minds of the credulous and the ignorant. These impostors obtain great consideration, and their counsel and advice is most anxiously sought after'.[87]

However, there is no substantial evidence to suggest that the similarities in early nineteenth-century British representations of *tohunga* and Brahman were a product of a conscious application of British models created in India. In this case, it seems that hostile British attitudes to indigenous intermediaries between the supernatural and natural worlds arose out of Protestant hostility to 'priesthood'. As we have seen in the previous chapter, British Protestants consistently attacked Catholic priests as venial tyrants whose spiritual, social and political power retarded the development of Catholic countries. These arguments, which represented deep-seated Protestant understandings of religion and the place of religion in society, were a powerful thread in nineteenth-century British mentalities.[88] Thus, for the British observers, the *tohunga* and the Brahman effectively fulfilled the same functions and were guilty of the same sins as Catholic priests: they created spurious hierarchies and wove webs of superstition that ensnared the popular imagination.

If we shift our attention to Polynesia in the later nineteenth century, however, we can find examples of the explicit application of arguments about caste in discussions of *tapu*. Abraham Fornander, a judge and ethnographer based in Hawaii, provided a powerful overview of the interface between Polynesian religion and social organization. Fornander drew heavily on Max Müller's works and was an enthusiastic exponent of Polynesians' Aryan origins.[89] For Fornander, Polynesian social structure was underpinned by religious ideas and institutions transplanted by the Indo-Aryans, especially caste, that 'peculiar and exclusive division of society'. Fornander argued that these Polynesian forms of caste fossilized a social and religious system that predated the rise of 'Brahmanism'. Polynesian caste was an 'Arian heirloom from a pristine, pre-vedic age' which existed long before the degeneration of Indian Aryans through intermarriage.[90] Polynesian society, like the ancient Aryans of central Asia and north India, was essentially divided between 'the nobles' of 'the warrior class' and 'the cultivators, herdsmen, artisans, and general mass of the people'. Below these two primary groups, a class of slaves developed, creating the threefold division that characterized most of Polynesian society: caste, therefore, was conceived primarily as hierarchy based on social function.[91]

However, due to isolation in the Pacific, rather than through intermarriage with inferior peoples, Polynesian caste began to calcify in a degenerate form. Fornander argued that caste divisions had hardened allowing the 'priestly order' in Hawaii to maintain 'exclusive privileges' and they became a 'tabued caste', akin to the tyrannical Brahman. He suggested, however, that Maori culture developed along different lines, with the threefold division collapsing into only two groups: 'freemen' and 'slaves'.[92]

While Fornander believed that caste was primarily a hierarchy based on social function where *tapu* legitimized and supported these distinctions, late nineteenth-century observers in New Zealand tended to place greater emphasis on the centrality of *tapu* in actually engendering these divisions. Jesse Page, in his survey of the introduction of Christianity to New Zealand, suggested that *tapu* underlay 'all the religious ideas of the Maoris'.[93] *Tapu*, it seemed, had been transported into the Pacific via South-East Asia from India, as Page noted that '"tabooh" is a "Hindoo" word for a bier or coffin [Hindi – tabut]; and, in the ancient Sanskrit, "ta" means to mark, and "pu" to purify.'[94] This principle provided the structure that ordered Maori society into different ranks, shaping social relations and constituting the core of Maori religion. Page's description of *tapu* again echoes British indictments of Brahmanical tyranny: *tapu*, Page argued, 'is an unseen network of fear and misery to the native mind, and ensnares the heart of the people in the meshes of perpetual bondage and trouble.'[95] While Page identified *tapu* as the key religious institution in the Maori world, William Colenso believed that *tapu* was so powerful it had effectively replaced religion. Colenso argued, in his important 1868 essay 'On the Maori Races', that 'the observances of the *tapu* were in place of religion. Hence it was that the *tapu* was so rigidly upheld and enforced.' *Tapu* provided the social, spiritual and cultural glue that bound Maori society together.[96]

Not surprisingly, Alfred Newman addressed the relationship between *tapu* and caste in his attempt to delineate every connection between Indian and Maori culture. Newman believed that the migration of Maori from their Indian homeland had resulted in the greater modification of caste than the almost direct and unaltered transplantation of Indian religion and phallus worship. Against the backdrop of a Pakeha culture that (at least outwardly) emphasized mateship and opportunity, Newman attacked both caste and *tapu*. He argued that the Indian caste system, 'the most cruel and most revolting system imaginable', was only elaborated after Maori left India around 1000 BCE. But the *tapu* system, 'an allied system' to caste, 'was brought entire from India' to the Pacific by Maori. Newman, an adherent of a simple racialized interpretation of Indian history, believed that the essential difference between the two was that 'the caste system was a distinction of races, whereas the *tapu* system was a distinction between individuals.'[97] Because he believed that Maori were the first people in the Pacific, *tapu* could not function on a racial basis, rather it allowed the 'god-descended' chief to mark himself off from the rest of the population.[98] But in terms of social function, the two systems were similar in that they preserved the powers of the elite groups (or racial groups in India) in society, by establishing a code of 'no-touchism' that protected the sanctity and power of the elites from the defiling touch of the ordinary person. In both societies, these conventions, backed by the sanction of religious authority, provided the key socio-religious structure that governed everyday life.[99]

Religion and rationality: the Tohunga Suppression Act

Therefore, as Maori were drawn into the market economy, rebellious *iwi* were forcibly 'pacified' and ethnographers constructed an increasingly dense archive of material relating to cosmology, ritual and *tapu*, settlers imagined Maori mentalities as fundamentally religious. Within the colonial context of New Zealand, where politicians, freethinkers and migration agents celebrated the colony as a progressive social 'experiment', this assessment cast Maori as a threat to progress and enlightenment. The persistence of native 'superstition' and vernacular Christianities that railed against settler dominance (as examined in Chapter 5), suggested that the assimilation of Maori was a fragile project. Moreover, given the ongoing conflicts between the colonial state and 'rebel' Maori, this emphasis on Maori religiosity reflected fears about the limits of settler hegemony as well as concerns about the likelihood of assimilation. Where Europeans could divorce civil concerns and religion, public and private, Polynesians, like Hindus, were bound by the weight of their tradition: religion saturated every aspect of their existence.

These arguments, developed and refined over the nineteenth century, culminated in the debates over the Tohunga Suppression Act (1907). The chief proponent of this Act was James Carroll, the half-Maori representative for Waiapu (a European seat) and Native Minister in the Liberal Government. Drawing on broad support across party lines Carroll argued that this act was devised to control the actions of *tohunga* who claimed to be 'endowed with mystic powers and Divine authority, and who prey on credulity by claiming the power to predict and foretell events'.[100] Carroll hoped that the act could be used specifically against Rua Kenana, a Tuhoe prophet who had created Maungapohatu, a new settlement nestled under the sacred Tuhoe mountain of the same name. Carroll and his supporters hoped to check the influence of the 'notorious Rua', arguing that Rua had forced local Maori to stop working their lands and withdraw their children from school, and that Rua's influence was almost certain to breed 'stubborn and criminal resistance' against the Crown.[101] Rua's teachings were incompatible with Carroll's vision of an industrious, peaceable and prosperous Maori community.

Carroll's attacks on *tohunga* were based on a rationalistic and evolutionary interpretation of the history of religion and reflected fears of religiously inspired rebellion that were widespread among colonial administrations into the early twentieth century.[102] He noted that Rua had risen to prominence among the Tuhoe, an isolated tribe who tried to battle the evolutionary laws of nature as they 'resisted every stride, every advancement of civilization'. This evolutionary narrative was central to Carroll's championing of the modernization of Maori society. Carroll used his position as Native Minister to halt the alienation of Maori land and encourage cooperative farming as a means of rebuilding Maori society. Carroll was a prime mover behind the earlier Maori Councils Act (1900) that simultaneously devolved some power to *marae* councils, but also established a strict social code to improve Maori health. Carroll argued that the power of *tohunga*, including Rua, threatened to retard the 'evolution' born out of these 'progressive' reforms. Maori, Carroll suggested, were 'midway' in their cultural 'evolution', and prophets such as Rua jeopardized this progress. Maori's 'old doubts and fears' had not been totally extinguished, and they were 'scarcely ... beyond the tail end of barbarism'.[103] Carroll's argument drew widespread support from both Maori and Pakeha members. Dr John George Findlay, the Attorney-General, extended Carroll's arguments concerning the fragile state of Maori religious development. Findlay argued that the

Maori mind corresponds in a large measure with the mind of our own race not very many centuries ago ... we forget that it is not a great many years since we were just as credulous, and when men and women were put to death by us for offences of mysticism, witchcraft, and the like.

Such superstitions were difficult to extinguish as they were 'not only imbibed in the cradle, they come down to the individual throughout centuries of racial experience.' This experience was difficult to counteract, as such belief 'sometimes remains even after knowledge has dispelled the darkness'. Findlay suggested that the 'true remedy for the removal of superstition, for the removal of idolatry' was 'scepticism'. Primitive superstitions, such as faith in the power of *tohunga*, were out of step with the development of an increasingly secular society, with a social fabric moulded by 'progressive' social legislation that enfranchised women and provided a basic system of welfare relief.[104] Wi Pere, a Maori member of the Legislative Council, countered Findlay's advocacy of scientific rationalism, defending the cultural authority of Christianity. Pere proposed that Christianity and the teachings of 'Christ's Tohungas' were the most effective defence against the superstitious teachings of non-Christian *Tohunga*.[105] The goals of modernization were beyond dispute, even if the methods were open to debate.

Conclusion

These debates over the Tohunga Suppression Act demonstrate the powerful shift in Pakeha conceptions of the place of religion in Maori society in the later nineteenth century. The inherently religious nature of Maori was a matter of public concern, as it was not only seen to retard the evolution of a modern, rationalistic Maori society, but contained a powerful threat to the authority of the government. The positions adopted in this particular debate were not so much dictated by race, as by visions of the role of religion and science in a modern nation. Parliamentarians were united in a search for the best tools to promote the 'evolution' of Maori mind in the hope of eradicating Maori 'superstition' and challenges to the rule of law.

Although the language of colonial 'progressive reform' was scientific, as it invoked rationality and evolution while imagining New Zealand as a 'laboratory', Protestantism remained a crucial framework for discussions of religion.[106] Comparative religion historicized Protestantism, recognizing that it was part of the universal 'evolution' of religious sensibilities, but the structures and values of the Protestant tradition continued to mould discussions of non-Christian religion in profound ways. This chapter, and the previous one, have established the centrality of Protestantism as a cultural force that moulded British and Pakeha interpretations of both Maori and Indian religions. Not only did the Protestant tradition's heavy scriptural emphasis contribute to early nineteenth-century arguments that suggested Maori had no religion, but Protestant attacks on 'Popery' and priests shaped dominant British interpretations of the role of both Brahmans and *tohunga*.

However, British interpretations of non-European religions cannot be explained through reference to the power and longevity of Protestantism alone. This chapter has established that the northern wars of the 1840s and the growth of a market economy underpinned the textualization of tradition in the late 1840s and early 1850s. This important shift in colonial knowledge, together with the rising intellectual authority of comparative religion, prompted a reassessment of mythology and religion. The older discourse of negation was undermined as the Maori were increasingly conceived of as a religious people. This posed new questions: what were the sources, history and nature of this religion? From the 1850s, Pakeha answers to these questions were largely shaped by the concomitant debates over Polynesian origins. The diffusionist models, which suggested that Maori had migrated to the Pacific from an Indian homeland, encouraged Pakeha to analyse Maori religion against British understandings of Hinduism. Ideas concerning Polynesian religion did occasionally circulate back to discussions of Indian religion, but typically the flow of ideas was from British India to New Zealand.[107] India therefore functioned in the later nineteenth century as a subimperial centre, where new paradigms for the analysis of religion were created, tested and debated. Viewing Maori religion as a transplanted form of Hinduism reinforced the Indocentric diffusionist tradition of ethnology and inserted Maori into the broad sweep of both universal and imperial history. Many Maori, however, resisted this project. As we shall see in the next chapter, Maori prophetic leaders also embraced a diffusionist worldview: but in identifying as Israelites rather than Aryans they contested their incorporation into the symbolic and material webs of empire.

5
Print, Literacy and the Recasting of Maori Identities

Thus far, this study has charted the emergence of Indocentric frameworks for the analysis of Polynesian, but especially Maori, culture and history. As we have seen, complex webs of correspondence and emerging patterns of institutional exchange spanned disparate parts of the British empire (and reached out into other imperial and institutional knowledge systems), integrating scholars in the United Kingdom, Ireland, South Asia, the Malay peninsula, the Pacific islands and Australasia into new interpretative communities. I have particularly stressed the prominence of the Christian converts, scribal elites and other 'native experts' who shaped, contested and re-interpreted this thickening archive of ethnological material.

If we can understand this body of knowledge as a dialogic construct, the heavily intertextual product of competing voices speaking from a host of locations and subject positions, it is also important to recognize that some groups within the empire resisted these discourses or posited counter-discourses of group origins and identity. This chapter explores the various and competing rearticulations of community identity and history in New Zealand in the wake of contact with Euro-Americans. While Chapter 6 documents the active reappropriation of the 'Aryan' concept in the Hindi press and its centrality in the increasingly racialized discourses on Hindu identity and Indian nationhood, here I examine a set of indigenous discourses that countered, rather than reinterpreted, the Aryan theory. Maori elders, 'native teachers' and prophetic leaders embraced the Bible and the new skills of literacy as resources for an active recasting of indigenous identity within communities that were struggling to cope with depopulation, land alienation and renegotiation of chiefly sovereignty. Within these contexts, the notion that Maori were displaced Indo-Aryans had little appeal or cul-

146

tural power. Indigenous leaders instead fashioned arguments that empowered their communities in various ways; by identifying Maori as members of bi-racial church communities, as being 'loyal' to the Crown or, most intriguingly, as being God's chosen people destined to throw off Pakeha oppression and herald a millennial age of peace and prosperity.

Historiographical models

It is necessary to begin by locating this chapter within the existing historiography on colonialism, literacy and identity in the Pacific. Until the 1970s, the dominant model for the interpretation of colonialism in the Pacific was the 'fatal impact' model, an interpretation elaborated forcefully in Moorehead's popular history of the same name.[1] European intrusion into the Pacific was seen as calamitous, unleashing radical and rapid social change enacted by depopulation, the erosion of chiefly authority and the decay of traditional social systems and cultural values. Parsonson, in an influential 1967 article, identified literacy as a driving force behind this transformation of the Polynesian world, arguing that a 'literate revolution' was central in the dismantling of traditional belief systems in Polynesia.[2] This identification of colonialism as a fundamental rupture in indigenous history was challenged by the rise of a revisionist islander-centred interpretative tradition in the early 1970s, as historians strove to emphasize indigenous perspectives, important elements of cultural continuity that spanned pre-colonial, colonial and post-colonial periods, and the islanders' ability to shape the outcomes of cross-cultural contact.[3] But the centrality of cross-cultural violence and the extent of indigenous depopulation imposed real limits upon this revisionist thrust: Dening, for example, acknowledges that his influential vision of Pacific history still hinges upon the 'Fatal Impact of the Euro-Americans'.[4]

More specifically, within the New Zealand context, there have been two different interpretations of the place of literacy in Maori history. The first, the New Zealand version of 'the fatal impact' school, identifies literacy as a corrosive force that undermined the vitality of Maori oral tradition, and, as a result, played a central role in the construction of Pakeha hegemony. This model has exhibited considerable longevity, as some educationalists and historians continue to identify literacy and printing as key instruments for the construction of Pakeha hegemony, even equating literacy with becoming English.[5] The second position, which we might term the 'cultural continuity' argument, suggests that literacy and Christianity had limited impact on indigenous mentalities, emphasizing a fundamental cultural continuity with pre-European traditions. This interpretation was articulated most forcefully in McKenzie's seminal *Oral Culture, Literacy and Print in Early New Zealand: the Treaty of Waitangi*. This rich discussion of the career of William Colenso and the bibliographic history of the Treaty argued that the notion of a literacy revolution among Maori in the 1830s and 1840s was the product of a European 'literacy myth' promulgated by Evangelical missionaries. In McKenzie's view, print and Christianity had little effect on Maori mentalities in the nineteenth century: indeed, he suggested that this remains unchanged today, as 'the written and printed word is not the mode they [modern Maori] habitually use'.[6] Binney's landmark methodological article on 'Two forms of telling history' upheld this fundamental opposition between oral and written narratives and the historical sensibilities of Maori and Pakeha.[7]

This chapter counters both the 'fatal impact' and 'cultural continuity' interpretations, by stressing the ways in which Maori leaders quickly adapted to literacy and Christianity, charting their ability to fashion new cultural spaces and political idioms within the colonial order. Just as Ginzburg's miller in early modern Europe might read creatively, constructing an idiosyncratic and 'extravagant cosmology', literate Maori fashioned new worlds from the vernacular Bible, building histories and identities inconceivable a century before.[8] By the 1860s, indigenous leaders were articulating a diverse array of new identities and political agendas. Some identified primarily on sectarian lines as Anglican, Methodist or Roman Catholic, others aligned themselves with new pan-tribal political movements which attempted to restrict the flow of land and power to the settlers, while others still identified themselves as 'Tiu' or 'Hurai', literally Jews, as God's chosen people who were destined to cast off their Pakeha oppressors. These new identities were hybridized as they blended pre-colonial traditions and values with new ideas derived from the Old or New Testament. In this context, oral tradition and literacy were not mutually exclusive as Binney suggests, rather they were frequently interdependent. Within the political context of colonialism, leaders required both the *mana* (prestige, charisma) and oral skills of an old chief, but they also drew upon an encyclopaedic knowledge of the Bible in their letters, petitions and newspapers. As preachers, prophets, pamphleteers and warriors Maori leaders of the mid-nineteenth century moved between worlds, switching roles and shifting idioms as they negotiated the often treacherous waters of colonial politics.

Pre-colonial social structure and identity

The turbulence of the colonial period, with its host of prophetic movements, conflicts and controversies, often seems to counterpoint the apparent stability of 'tradition', the unchanging nature of 'pre-history'. This stark juxtaposition between history and tradition reflects not only the inability of historians to effectively recover indigenous agency, what Guha terms the 'rebel consciousness', but also reflects the weaknesses of analytical frameworks constructed by archaeologists and anthropologists for the interpretation of indigenous social structures.[9] Until recently, Maori social organization was understood through a structured, hierarchical and static model: the progression from *whanau* (family), to *hapu* (sub-tribe), to *iwi* (tribe) and finally to *waka* (tribal confederation).[10] As Sutton has pointed out, this model reflected the 'idealized' interpretative models developed in the study of other Polynesian contexts (especially Tikopia, Hawaii and Tahiti) that were transposed to the New Zealand context by Firth, and subsequently reinforced by the influence of Goldman's classic *Ancient Polynesian Society*.[11]

The *whanau–hapu–iwi–waka* progression is finally giving way under the weight of new research and the extensive body of evidence collected in the hearings of the Waitangi Tribunal. A new picture is beginning to emerge, one that places greater emphasis on the *hapu* as the central operational unit in the 'traditional' social system and, most importantly, emphasizes the historically contingent and dynamic nature of these units. We are increasingly aware that distinctions between *whanau* and *hapu*, and more particularly *hapu* and *iwi*, were finely shaded rather than rigidly inscribed. The complex interactions between resource exploitation, demographic change and political authority in shaping these units have been traced in Sutton's case study of the emergence of Nga Puhi and Ballara's history of Porangahau.[12] As the size and status of these descent groups shifted over time, visions of community and identity were revised and reconceptualized.[13]

The importance of these kin structures was expressed through *whakapapa* (genealogies). Customarily, *whakapapa* was the key repository and most important public expression of Maori identity. The narration of *whakapapa* not only recalled lines of descent, but also alluded to the actions and achievements of the shared ancestors that defined a *whanau* or *hapu*'s place in history and their relations with other kin-groups.[14] In this performative mode, the past and present were inter-woven; by recounting the heroism or cunning of a *tipuna* (ancestor) a narrator asserted the *mana* (prestige, status) of that *tipuna*'s descendants. Certain deeds or ancestors could be emphasized or glossed over according to the occasion or audience. Old victories could be selectively recalled or old wounds reopened, as the narrator asserted the *mana* of their ancestors and the *mana* of their modern kin-group.[15] Grievances, which had lain dormant for several generations, could suddenly erupt in conflict as *utu* (payment, retribution, revenge) was taken and *mana* was restored. Thus *whakapapa* (genealogy), as well as *korero* (talk, narratives) and *waiata* (songs), were (and are) combative forms of historical consciousness that encapsulate the competitive spirit at the heart of kin-group dynamics.[16]

The divisions fostered by competition and these combative historical modes were further compounded by regional variations. The geo- and biodiversity of New Zealand also meant that natural resources, modes of production and settlement patterns varied significantly. The people of Taitokerau (Northland) and Murihiku (the southern South Island) exploited different resources, constructed different settlements and organized their communities along slightly different lines. There was also significant variation within the shared Maori language and Maori in the southern South Island found it difficult to understand northern dialects.[17] Such linguistic, climatic and economic differences resulted in subtle variations of social organization and cosmology.[18] Social and cultural variation, together with the segmented structure and fluid development of pre-contact society, has led Cox to state: 'It is not possible ... to identify a single unified "traditional society" among the Maori.'[19]

Explorers and missionaries: a fatal impact?

The arrival of Cook's *Endeavour* in 1769 triggered a major shift in this sense of community and history. In the decades following Cook's visit as Maori increasingly dealt with Europeans, whom they deemed 'fairy folk', 'ghosts' or 'goblins', differences within the indigenous community became less important. Despite tribal rivalries and dialectal differences there was a new awareness of being 'tangata Maori': the ordinary people. 'Maori' as a collective noun had entered indigenous usage by 1801, and by the late 1820s and early 1830s it was in regular use.[20]

If encounters with Cook's crew created the first vague notions of 'Maori' as a meaningful category, it was the prolonged engagement with missionaries which initiated major change in the structure of indigenous communities and provided new ideas, skills and technologies which Maori appropriated as tools to articulate new visions of community, history and cosmology. Typically, New Zealand historians have seen the impact of the missionaries, and their religion, as corrosive. In his classic study of cultural contact, Wright argued that although the missionaries were initially subject to Maori control, in the long term Maori converted in the hope that Christianity would counteract the 'cultural confusion' unleashed by the introduction of European diseases, technology (especially muskets) and ideas.[21] For Sinclair, missionary 'ideas were as destructive as bullets': by the mid-1830s, Christianity had effectively undercut Maori agency, belief and culture and thereafter Pakeha were able to dictate the pattern of race relations.[22]

Although various historians have attacked this 'fatal impact' model by stressing Maori's active engagement with European ideas and technologies, insufficient attention has been paid to the ways in which Maori actively coopted missionary teaching and the Bible to fashion new visions of social structure, innovative readings of history and critiques of settler culture.[23] Certainly historians have shown a great deal of interest in religious anti-colonialism, particularly in the prophets Te Kooti, Te Whiti, Tohu and Rua Kenana who used elements of Christianity in their resistance against the colonial state. However, many of these surveys of Maori prophetic tradition have abstracted the more sensational elements of religious syncretism from the broader spectrum of Maori religious and political movements. This chapter suggests that Maori literacy, and the resulting engagement with the Bible, were not only central in the anti-colonial crusades of Maori prophets, but also provided a religious foundation, an ideological language and a stock of images which dominated Maori politics and reform from the 1830s through to the early twentieth century.

In a recent article on cross-cultural contact in the Pacific, Ian Campbell has suggested that the intellectual encounter between Polynesians and Europeans was largely constructive as it generated new identities, state formations and intellectual traditions.[24] The emergence of a new unified 'Maori' identity in the nineteenth century fits this pattern. While there is no doubt that Eurasian diseases and technologies (such as the musket) led to rapid depopulation and that missionaries pursued an interventionist programme, Maori were active, and often willing, agents in the reshaping of their own society and culture from the late 1820s on.

This agency is most obvious in the efforts of Maori leaders to reorganize indigenous society and resist the destructive effects of colonialism. The emergence of new pan-tribal, anti-colonial, prophetic and more conveniently Christian movements was the result of a complex dialogic process, where various Maori groups (differentiated by region, rank, *hapu*, *iwi* and, at a later stage, denomination) exchanged, contested and naturalized new ideas derived from the Bible. This dynamic engagement created new possibilities for the articulation of identity and generated new movements that stressed a pan-tribal identity. In a profound sense, much of New Zealand's history is a footnote to this dual engagement with print and Christianity.

The coming of print and Christianity

At first, missionary progress in printing for Maori was uneven. Although the first Maori book appeared within a year of the establishment of the CMS mission in the Bay of Islands, printing in Maori was hampered by a reliance on Sydney-based printers and the missionaries' limited linguistic ability.[25] It was not until Thomas Kendall's trip to England in 1819 that the first real steps towards creating a framework for linguistic analysis and translation were made. Kendall, who was accompanied by the chiefs Hongi and Waikato, collaborated with Professor Samuel Lee of Queens' College Cambridge to produce a basic Maori grammar that was published in 1820. From this point, the scholarly apparatus for translation and the analysis of Maori language made steady progress.[26] Despite initial uncertainties regarding the rendering of certain sounds, by the late 1820s the missionaries had fixed a sensible and easily comprehensible orthography.[27]

Thus, at the beginning of the 1830s the obstacles that had retarded early Maori-language printing were resolved, and the mission presses began to produce massive runs of Biblical texts.[28] The CMS press at Paihia produced three and a half million pages of Maori language texts between January 1835 and the beginning of 1840, and produced a further two million pages in 1840.[29] In 1841, 1843 and 1845 the Maori New Testament was reprinted in runs of 20 000. Even if each of these books lasted for only two years this meant that there were two New Testaments in circulation for every three Maori.[30]

In fact, Maori interest in the vernacular Bible predated this surge in printing. Although we must be cautious about missionary exaggeration of Maori interest in Scripture, frequent and consistent pleas by Maori for Bibles punctuate missionary sources, both published and private. Five years before the first adult Maori conversion, John King reported that Bay of Island Maori were visiting him regularly to discuss Scripture and asked the CMS to provide 'Psalters & Prayer Books'.[31] In December 1824 Richard Davis wrote to the CMS: 'A version of the Bible in the Maori language is greatly needed.'[32] By the mid-1830s this demand had become insatiable: in May 1836 Nathaniel Turner reported that Maori literacy was outstripping the supply of Bibles.[33] Demand for Scripture remained strong well into the 1840s. In the early 1840s, for example, William Williams reported that he had supplied Maori with 492 New Testaments in only eight days and that he could do with 3000 more.[34]

Although much has been made of Maori use of books for a range of magical, symbolic and even decorative purposes, books were primarily valued for the skills they symbolized and the knowledge they embodied.[35] Maori were primarily interested in the Bible because they were interested in Christianity, and literacy spread rapidly because it was seen as the key to God's teachings, Pakeha knowledge and church membership.[36] R. G. Jameson's detailed 1841 travelogue reported widespread literacy among those Maori between the ages of 10 and 30, and noted that this skill was highly valued.[37] By the mid-1850s, it was suggested that 'the majority' of the adult population could read and write.[38]

Thus, initially at least, literacy remained tightly tied to Christianity. The government newspaper *Ko Te Karere o Nui Tireni* upheld this connection, using print to inculcate a variety of 'lessons' that reinforced the authority of Christianity to a Maori audience that contained both a mix of denominations and a variety of attachments to missionary Christianity.[39] If print was an important tool for moral instruction, the spread of literacy also increased indigenous demand for more detailed exegesis: missionary sources record a significant body of Maori knowledge about Christianity.[40] The link between literacy and a genuine interest in Christianity is particularly clear in those regions first exposed to missionary teaching in the 1830s and 1840s. For example, Howe's research on the Thames-Waikato region clearly demonstrates a clear and consistent Maori interest in Christian theology in an area where literacy spread particularly rapidly.[41] Anderson's recent ethnohistory of the southern Maori clearly establishes the profound impact of print and Christianity in the south, which transformed an intensely hierarchical and competitive slave-holding society into an increasingly egalitarian Christian society where chiefly authority and kin-group conflict was greatly tempered.[42]

Literacy and social change: newspapers

While it would be misleading to entirely disentangle literacy and Christianity, it is important to recognize that missionaries were unable to restrict Maori to a purely 'scriptural literacy' (focusing narrowly on the Bible), as Maori deployed their skills in a variety of ways. Maori became enthusiastic letter-writers and this new form of communication reshaped both personal and political relationships. Letters, along with diaries and family notebooks, allowed Maori of all ranks and both genders to record a range of important forms of knowledge: land holdings, genealogies, songs and tales.[43] Literacy was particularly important for Maori women, keen to cement personal relationships with colonial administrators, to develop new political relationships and to substantiate their position as landowners.[44]

Beyond the interests of the individual and the kin-group, print also assumed greater cultural and political significance. We have already seen that, from the mid-1840s, an important group of younger literate Maori embraced the financial opportunities offered by the commercialization of knowledge, recording myths and historical narratives for colonial administrators and ethnographers. As well as becoming an important repository for traditional knowledge, print was an increasingly crucial social device within the terrain of a colonial market economy. Maori language newspapers were important spheres for the recruitment of labour, for notices regarding stolen items and wandering livestock, and for discussions of the latest developments in court and Parliament. Thus, the vernacular press was an important domain for the commercialization of Maori life. Maori-language newspapers detailed shipping movements and closely monitored fluctuations in the 'market' (*hoko*) and ran a variety of advertisements, providing valuable commercial knowledge for those Maori who attempted to locate economic and social niches within the developing order of colonial print capitalism.[45]

These advertisements are a rich source for tracing shifts in the social and intellectual terrain. While many advertisements were related to the colony's agricultural economy, others marked the emergence of new forms of economic activity. Most strikingly, some letters to the editor and advertisements reflected the desire of indigenous groups to inform both Maori and Pakeha of local attractions: Henare Te Pukuatua and Mohi Aterea of Whakarewarewa boasted of the miraculous cures of their local *wai puia* (hot springs), noting that 'many Pakeha have experienced the healing virtues of these waters, and they are all loud in praise of them'.[46] While entrepreneurs such as Te Pukuatua and Aterea used the new medium of print to compete within the colonial market and foster an emergent tourist trade, newspapers also fashioned new idioms for older forms of social competition. Hone Paraea of Rawene in the Hokianga responded to Te Pukuatua's and Aterea's advertisement. After questioning whether northern Maori would be able to afford to travel to Whakarewarewa unless Te Pukuatua and Aterea were prepared to pay for the journey themselves, Paraea appealed to 'Pakeha from beyond the seas' to visit the far north. The tribal lands of Nga Puhi, he assured readers, were renowned since ancient times (*'nga ra o namata'*) as a productive land and now boasted fruit from the tropics (*'nga whenua mahana'*) in addition to coal, kauri gum and an array of agricultural produce: in short, not a mere tourist destination, the home of Nga Puhi was 'verily a land flowing with milk and honey', ripe for agricultural and commercial development.[47]

Both the tone and content of Paraea's advertisement remind us of the important cultural values that underpinned the Maori transition to both print and the market economy. In responding so directly to the claims made on the behalf of Whakarewarewa and insisting on the superiority and multiplicity of the north's attractions, Paraea carried the tribal pursuit of *mana* into the new cultural space of print. While boasting of the value of the extractive industry of the north was indicative of the material shifts of the colonial order, Paraea's focus on food-stuffs reflected deep-seated cultural continuities. In boasting of Nga Puhi's possession of *'te panana, te painaaporo, me te arani'* (the banana, pineapple and orange) in addition to the traditional Polynesian crops and 'potato, maize, pumpkins, cucumbers, peaches, apples, pears, wheat, and sugar-cane', Paraea made the long-established equation between the accumulation of food-items and the *mana* of the *iwi*.[48] Paraea had effectively reworked the *hakari* (ritual feast), a key institution for the proclamation of economic and symbolic power to rival (or related) kin-groups, for the new age of print.[49]

Thus Maori-language newspapers emerged as an important political medium in the colony. The colonial government believed that the press was a valuable instrument for weaving Maori and Pakeha together. The first issue of *Ko Te Karere o Nui Tireni*, edited by the Protector of Aborigines George Clarke (a former CMS missionary) and

Edward Shortland, explained that it was published 'so that the Maori people would come to know the ways and customs of the Pakeha and the Pakeha would also come to know the customs of the Maori people.'[50] This newspaper was an important vehicle for the state to disseminate knowledge about the colonial legal system, and, most importantly, to reaffirm the centrality of the Treaty of Waitangi.[51] While *Te Karere* communicated the ideologies of the colonial state, it also provided an important political forum for Maori. Letters from individuals and from *iwi*, expounded new models for social relationships between the Maori and Pakeha, discussed the role of the colonial governor, and established (or contested) claims to lands and resources.[52] Some letters posed bold challenges to colonial policy and the editorial stance of Clarke and Shortland: 'Wakatupereru' (Agitator) dismissed the editor's claims that the Maori were beginning to accept Pakeha ways ('*te pakeha ritenga*'), emphasizing the persistence of Maori customs in the face of the inequalities of colonialism.[53] However, with the outbreak of conflict between Hone Heke and the Crown, 'loyal' northern Maori wrote letters that not only attacked the actions of Heke and proclaimed their allegiances to Tamati Waka Nene and the settler government, but also requested greater material support from the state, especially additional muskets and ammunition.[54] While there is no doubt that these requests reflected deep antipathies towards Hone Heke as much as support for the settler government, such letters are indicative of important shifts in the idiom of indigenous politics. By the 1840s, literacy was a political tool that could be used to articulate agendas beyond the *marae* (ceremonial meeting ground) and negotiate new social and military alignments.

Literacy: a social revolution?

However, these shifts did not amount to a sudden revolution in which the new skills of literacy completely replaced the older skills essential to collection, recitation and pedagogy in pre-colonial knowledge systems. The opposition between literate and oral cultures can be overdrawn[55] and this has certainly been the case in recent debates over the impact of literacy in colonial New Zealand. While the missionaries, desperate for funds and keen to substantiate claims of civilization and Christianization, may have overestimated the extent of literacy, McKenzie underestimates the impact of both printing and the Bible. By insisting that the 'literacy revolution' was a mere phantom created by missionary propaganda and asserting that late twentieth-century Maori culture remains largely oral, McKenzie effectively snap-freezes Maori culture in its 'traditional' pre-contact form. However, Polynesian cultures were not static and fragile: the historical and archaeological record attests to the ability of Polynesians to initiate and respond to rapid and momentous social change. The ability of Maori to engage in speculative trade to obtain muskets and their rapid incorporation of this new technology into their military strategy demonstrates Maori flexibility and adaptability.[56] These same qualities were evident in Maori responses to both Christianity and literacy: while the spread of these innovations may have been uneven and incomplete, they swiftly became an important part of Maori culture, social life and political discourse.

In fact, McKenzie's representation of Maori culture as emblematic of an 'oral' culture needs examination. There is substantial evidence that suggests Polynesian cultures did not conform to the classical model of 'oral culture' established in the early debates over the orality/literacy divide. For example, Finnegan's research on 'oral tradition' in Polynesia suggests that Maori society possessed several characteristics typical of 'literate' cultures rather than 'oral' cultures. She argued that pre-colonial Polynesian societies possessed several different modes of composition and knowledge retention. Some of these fit the standard image of oral composition, where an orator improvises to flesh out the memorized formulae that frame a performance, but others were based on a formalized process of prior composition and rehearsal.[57] She noted that in certain contexts, Maori stressed the importance of 'correct versions' and exact performances of particular compositions. Moreover, as Mitcalfe argued, Maori possessed clear notions of authorship for certain pre-colonial genres: famous 'poems', for example, were attributed to renowned authors.[58] This variety of Maori compositional modes sits uneasily with the typical opposition between oral and literate cultures. Finnegan's research intimates that some of these Maori traditions might have facilitated the adaptation to literacy and have allowed 'orality' and 'literacy' to 'interact and support each other'.[59] Thus, while literacy initiated widespread change in patterns of social communication it did not completely devalue older skills of memorization, improvisation and oratory.[60]

This insight opens up a new perspective on nineteenth-century Maori social and cultural history: Christianity and literacy were not 'more destructive than bullets', but rather provided new and important skills and ideas.[61] Most importantly, they underpinned new forms of discourse that redefined social relationships, analysed cultural change and discussed future prospects. Even within a context of depopulation and the alienation of tribal lands, Maori responded quickly and effectively to print capitalism, re-imagining their community in a range of ways that both drew upon tradition and incorporated new European ideas. If print disembodied Maori knowledge, removing knowledge transmission from the *marae* and from the relationships between the expert and their junior to the public space of newspapers, libraries and letter-writing, it allowed Maori to disembody European knowledge, disseminating new ideas, information and beliefs beyond the frontier of the missionary and the settlers.

The Bible and recasting Maori identity: Maori sectarianism

Maori adaptation and adoption of missionary Christianity was integral to this reformulation of identity. In the 1830s and 1840s, large numbers of Maori converted to Christianity and new Maori churches and Christian villages dotted the countryside. Although many missionaries and modern 'fatal impact' historians believed missionaries directed the rapid Christianization of Maori, in reality this conversion process was Maori-led.[62] 'Native teachers', many of whom were of humble origins or were ex-slaves, not missionaries, were the primary carriers of literacy and Christianity. For example, when William Williams arrived at Turanga (Gisborne), on the east coast of North Island, he discovered that a freed slave named Putoko had already converted 3000 Maori in the region.[63]

Conversion also reflected deep-seated social dynamics as the competitiveness of the pre-colonial culture drove the spread of Christianity. After their arrival, missionaries became a new currency in inter-*hapu* and inter-*iwi* competition. In 1819 John King noted that Maori chiefs 'are very disireous [sic] for missions one Chief says come & live with me – another says come & live with me … [they] are very impatient to wait until more [missionary] comes – they see – clearly see the temporal bennifit [sic] arising from the mission'.[64] With the arrival of the Wesleyan missionary Society in 1822, and then the establishment of a Roman Catholic mission in 1838, Maori were presented with new divisions to exploit. Religious affiliation was often determined by old agendas as denominational identity became a new vehicle for kin-group rivalries and, in turn, Christian identities became a means of re-inscribing boundaries between rival kin-groups. Thus Catholicism and

Methodism became, in Belich's phrase, 'denominations of dissent', allowing kin-groups to emphasize their autonomy from both the control of Pakeha and powerful Maori Anglican groups.[65]

The intensely sectarian programmes of the missionaries undoubtedly deepened these tensions. Both Wesleyan and Anglican missionaries drew on pre-existing Maori resentment of the French to launch anti-Catholic campaigns which were heavily reliant on print.[66] In response to the establishment of the Catholic mission the CMS produced *Te Anakaraiti* ('The Anti-Christ'), a pamphlet labelling the Pope the Anti-Christ. This was quickly followed by two more anti-Catholic pamphlets, in the form of dialogues between Rapu Pono (Searcher for Truth) and Aroha Pono (True Love), which detailed twelve 'errors' of the Catholic Church.[67] As a result of this anti-Catholic propaganda, Maori routinely called Jean-Baptiste Pompallier, the Catholic Bishop, the 'Anti-Christ'.[68] Pompallier reflected that the Catholic missionaries armed with 'only our voices and our pens' struggled as 'heresy [i.e. the Protestant missions] had two printing presses at its command', which allowed both the Anglicans and the Wesleyans to circulate 'pamphlets, tracts, and little books, which while teaching the first truths of salvation, were filled with all sorts of objections and calumnies against the minister and the faith of the Catholic Church.'[69] When W. B. Ullathorne, the English Catholic Vicar-General of Australia, visited New Zealand in 1840 to dispel the Maori belief that only the French were Catholics, he discovered that the Protestant missionaries had not only told Maori 'fantastic stories of the old anti-Catholic type', but that these anti-Catholic tales had been further sensationalized 'for the New Zealand palate'.[70] But Maori were not passive pawns in a European sectarian battle fought on New Zealand soil, as they exploited these sectarian tensions by playing on Protestant fears of 'Popery' to demand more frequent visits from missionaries and easier access to baptism.[71]

Maori also relished the frequent doctrinal debates between Protestant and Catholic missionaries.[72] Missionaries publicly disputed doctrines such as transubstantiation and the veneration of saints, sacraments such as the Eucharist, and church history, especially the function and history of the popes. While some missionaries clearly enjoyed these disputes, others doubted their efficacy as forums for instruction or feared their consequences.[73] James Stack (of the CMS) reflected that such debates were extremely dangerous in a society as competitive and combative as Maori. Stack noted, in a passage that unwittingly reveals the sectarian prejudices of even the most moderate of missionaries, that victories in these arguments filled Maori with excessive pride and fed sectarian tensions to such a degree that a 'heathen New Zealander in a few days is capable of conversion into a perfect counterpart of a dogmatical low Irish papist'.[74]

This deep-seated enthusiasm for doctrinal dispute, which no doubt appealed to the deeply competitive nature of Maori sensibilities, suggests the profound indigenization of Christianity. One of the most important consequences of printing was that Christianity and biblical interpretation were suddenly wrenched out of the hands of the missionaries. Initially, missionaries controlled access to, and provided the 'correct' interpretation of, Scripture. But ironically the circulation of the Maori Bible effectively undercut the missionary monopoly on Christian knowledge. Literate Maori, who might never have met a missionary, were able to read and interpret the Bible without any mediating influence. Consequently, Maori Christians interpreted the Bible in a variety of ways that unsettled the missionaries.[75] Even before the printing boom, Henry Williams noted that Maori Christians held 'ideas of an extravagant nature' and that missionaries had to be vigilant against the 'errors' which threatened to corrupt Maori Christianity.[76] With the extension of printing and the influence of 'native teachers', Maori adaptation of Christianity was greatly accelerated, producing a range of Maori Christianities from the relatively orthodox to the extremely heterodox. The people of Waokena, for example, developed a form of heterodox flagellant Christianity resulting from their literal interpretation of the Maori version of I Corinthians 9: 27.[77] Meanwhile, Maori in the Warea region of Taranaki followed 'Tikanga Hou', 'The New Custom', a pared down and indigenized form of Christianity. They insisted that three members of their congregation each embodied a different aspect of the Trinity, while the apostle Paul and the angel Gabriel were manifest in two other congregationalists. With God and his messengers living among them, the followers of Tikanga Hou dispensed with both prayer and scripture as conduits to the divine.[78]

It is important to emphasize, however, that the majority of Maori adhered to forms of Christianity that were doctrinally more orthodox and exhibited a strong connection to the denominational structures inherited from the missions. Even when many Maori began to socially and politically distance themselves from white missionaries during the New Zealand Wars, they continued to subscribe to mission doctrine, worship in mission churches and correspond with missionaries. Missionary teaching continued, in some communities at least, to enjoy intellectual and spiritual authority. From an early stage, some Maori were concerned with constructing 'correct' readings of Scripture, soliciting scriptural commentary and elucidation.[79] It is important to remember, however, that 'minihaere Maori' (missionary Maori) worshipped in churches, utilized a religious vocabulary and subscribed to a faith noticeably different from that found in the Anglican churches of England. The profound indigenization of missionary Christianity as a result of the three generations of teaching is embodied in the pewless interior, prominent *kowhaiwhai* patterning and the heavy use of ochre and carved work in Octavius Hadfield's church at Otaki.

Sandersons's study of Maori Christianity on the East Coast has shown the remarkable integration of missionary Christianity into Maori life. Even in the late 1850s and early 1860s, when missionaries feared that Maori were turning their back on 'true Christianity' and were becoming increasingly hostile to the Crown, 'most Maoris still considered themselves Christian in spite of their growing detachment from the missionaries and their morality.' In this particular regional context Christianity, Sanderson argues, was central in galvanizing a 'local patriotism' that stressed the autonomy of local *iwi* in the face of both rising Pakeha influence and the emergence of powerful pan-tribal movements.[80] William Williams, the CMS missionary based at Turanga (Gisborne), reported in 1863 that the local Rongowhakaata leader Anaru had rejected the overtures of the King Movement. Anaru asserted that Christianity, not the King Movement, was the basis of his own community's future: 'there was no unity except under the Gospel and no sure foundation but Christ.'[81] But Anaru's rejection of the King Movement came at a time when its leaders were formulating the most coherent, and politically explosive, vision of Maori Christian identity.

Christianity and unity: Kingitanga and its critics

Christianity played a crucial role in the elucidation of the ideology and aims of the King Movement, which was founded in 1857 by Waikato Maori in the hope that the alienation of Maori land could be controlled. New Zealand historians have primarily focused on the political aspects of the Movement: its ideological programme, its internal vicissitudes and its diplomatic weaknesses.[82] The King Movement has been seen as a key moment in the history of pan-tribalism or Maori 'nationalism' as the Maori began to reject European influences and assert their distinct identity and their 'nationhood'.[83] But, as Head warns us, the

King Movement was not a nativistic movement asserting Maori autonomy and rejecting Pakeha culture in its entirety.[84] While the movement's aim was to control the alienation of land and to limit Pakeha
influence in the 'King Country', its ideology and political language was
profoundly Christian. Iwikau Te Heuheu, who presided over the
investiture of Te Wherowhero Potatau as the first king, asserted the
primacy of Christianity in Kingitanga (the culture of the King
Movement):

> Potatau, this day I create you King of the Maori People. You and Queen
> Victoria shall be bound together to be one (*pai-here-tia kia kotahi*). The
> religion of Christ shall be the mantle of your protection; the law shall
> be the whariki mat for your feet, for ever and ever onward.[85]

This investiture ceremony reflected the remarkably swift integration of
Christianity into the construction and projection of political authority.
Not only did Iwikau Te Heuheu insist on the cohesive and protective
role of Christianity, but the Maori Bible was also the central ritual
object in the coronation.[86] Ultimately, the power of God sanctified and
legitimized the power of the new King.

The leadership of the King Movement consistently emphasized
Christianity, the love of Jesus, the primacy of the Gospel and potency of
the law. Matutaera Potatau or Potatau II (who in 1864 took the name
Tawhaio), the second Maori King, insisted that all Maori should live
'peaceably, so that you travel in the path of light and righteousness.'[87]
Under this programme the British Queen and law were to be respected, as
both derived their authority from God. In fact 'the law of God' was seen
to join the Maori King and the British Queen in a complementary relationship.[88] The Maori King was responsible for the maintenance of law
and order within Kingitanga's *aukati* (boundary), known by Pakeha as
'the King Country', while the Queen's sovereignty was recognized by all
New Zealanders, Maori and Pakeha, outside the *aukati*: 'The King on his
piece; the Queen on her piece, God over both; and Love binding them to
each other.'[89] Maori followers of the King believed this relationship was
grounded in the guarantee of *rangatiratanga* (chieftainship) provided in
the second article of the Treaty of Waitangi. One Kingite asserted this
goal through the metaphor of a *whare* (house): New Zealand was the
house, Maori formed the rafters on one side, Pakeha the rafters on the
other side, while God bound the structure together as the ridge-pole.[90]

Kingitanga ideology thus re-imagined the Maori as a national unit,
bound together by allegiance to the Christian God and the Bible.
Maori unity was symbolically asserted with the European term 'King'

for the new leader rather than Maori alternatives such as *Toihau* (Head), *Matua* (Parent) or *Ariki* (paramount Chief) that were grounded in the older language of tribal authority. The flag, another potent European symbol of nationality, was used to assert Maori nationhood: the Kingitanga flag was the flag accepted by 25 northern chiefs as a symbol of Maori unity in 1834.[91] These symbols asserted the *mana* (authority) of the King, representing his authority over the Maori, his power to control the buying and selling of land, and his maintenance of law and order within the *aukati*.

It is important to note that Christianity did not entirely supplant the older political traditions of *hapu* and *iwi* competition; rather Kingitanga was the product of the imbrication of the new European symbols and Christian ideologies with traditional political concerns. Even Wiremu Tamihana Te Tarapipi, for example, 'the Kingmaker', the chief advocate of Kingitanga and sponsor of Te Wherowhero, was motivated by a keen sensitivity to the interests of his tribe, Ngati Haua.[92] Key North Island chiefs supported the notion of a Maori King from 1856 in the hope that it would provide a vehicle for chiefly authority when the traditional tribal structures were under great strain from land alienation, migration and economic individualism. Thus the emergence and development of Kingitanga must also be viewed against the backdrop of inter- and intra-tribal relations in central North Island. Cleave reminds us that the structural basis of Kingitanga was the Tainui *waka*, and he suggests that the emergence of Kingitanga reflects the increasing emphasis placed on affinities within Tainui from the mid-eighteenth century. The culmination of this process, rooted in pre-colonial social change, was the emergence of strong alliances between the majority of the Tainui tribes. These ties were further strengthened in the early nineteenth century by the forcing out of Ngati Toa and their dissident leader Te Rauparahau from their homeland on the southern shores of the Kawhai harbour.[93] Although Te Rauparahau went on to establish a power base in the Kapiti region, from where he launched devastating raids on the tribes of the South Island, the more immediate result of Ngati Toa's expulsion was the construction of close, harmonious relations between the subunits of the Tainui *waka*. This new relationship was expressed through intermarriage and an increased stress on genealogical interrelationship between the *hapu* and *iwi* of Tainui; Cleave suggests that this 'syncretism of ... whakapapa' was a key precondition for the emergence of Kingitanga as a pan-tribal movement.[94]

Therefore the Christian symbols and language of Kingitanga can be read as an attempt to reinvent political authority as new social formations emerged and were consolidated. This was a crucial project, as deep-seated structural change within Maori society (which pre-dated colonization) continued to alter the balance of inter-*iwi* politics into the 1850s and the new colonial order increasingly threatened older political traditions. Christianity fundamentally challenged many of the foundations and expressions of chiefly authority. Traditionally, the ability to wage and win wars, the accumulation of slaves and the heightened *tapu* of the highborn were all markers of chiefly power. Missionaries attacked slave-holding, taught the children of the chiefly elite alongside the children of slaves and placed great emphasis on harmonious inter-tribal relations.[95] Kingitanga can be seen as a response of the old chiefly elite to these changes, as they fashioned an innovative vision of political power that would create a niche for themselves in the new colonial order.[96]

Nevertheless, while Christian ideology, ritual and language provided a powerful idiom for the pursuit of these goals, Christianity was also an important tool for those Maori unimpressed with the Kingitanga, or reluctant to join the movement because of the continuing importance of *iwi* rivalries. Donald McLean, the government's leading negotiator with Maori, reported from a *hui* (meeting) at Ngaruawahia in 1860 that a significant number of Maori felt that the King Movement would create racial conflict and feared that its aim was to 'elevate one section of the [Maori] people, to the exclusion of the whole from participation in any advantages to be derived from it.' McLean noted that Kingitanga's aim of the 'preservation of distinct nationality' was battling the 'mutual distrust' and 'jealousy' of the tribes.[97] At the congress of chiefs held at Kohimarama in 1860, many Maori leaders used Christianity to attack the King Movement and to assert their ongoing loyalty to the Queen and God. Ngati Kahungunu leaders from Gisborne, for example, reassured the Governor that they were loyal and that 'cultivation' and 'the buying of clothes, and vessels' were their interests, not war. 'The heart which has enmity towards God or man is an evil thing. Love to God and man is peace with God, the Queen, and her subjects.'[98] Christianity, then, was a flexible tool that could be used to assert loyalty to the Crown just as easily as it could be used to fashion new notions of Maori unity and nationhood.

Israelites not Aryans: the discourse of origins

Settler response to the King Movement was largely hostile, and those missionaries and humanitarians sympathetic to Kingitanga's appeal to

Christianity were unable to prevent the outbreak of war in 1860. However, the settler government was soon confronted with even more radical Maori challenges to its authority, in the form of prophetic leaders who drew on the Old Testament to identify the Maori as God's chosen people and to promise the end of Maori 'captivity'. As early as the 1830s and 1840s some Maori identified themselves as either the descendants of or as the modern Israelites. William Williams, for example, encountered several distinct Maori groups in the Wairoa region who had rejected Christianity and were calling themselves 'Jews' ('Tiu' or 'Hurai').[99] At this early stage Maori identification with the Jews was a form of religious dissent. As the missionaries translated the New Testament first, Maori encountered the Jews as unbelievers, heretics and the persecutors of Jesus. Just as some kin-groups dissented by identifying as Wesleyan or Catholic when their rivals were Anglican, Maori identification as 'Tiu' or 'Hurai' was a powerful means of rejecting missionary Christianity altogether.[100]

But the meaning of this Maori–Jewish affinity changed after the publication of Robert Maunsell's translation of the Old Testament from Hebrew to Maori in 1858. It appears that Maori found the Old Testament more accessible and powerful than the New Testament. The Old Testament's accounts of epic journeys and inter-tribal conflict were close to elements of Maori tradition: in 1864 John Gorst reported that Maori were 'exceedingly fond of reading the books of the Old Testament, in which they find described a state of civilization not unlike their own.'[101] The angry and vengeful god of the Hebrews was far closer to Maori *atua* (gods) than the God of the New Testament. The Christian God was, as one Maori observed, 'too quiet, too lazy, and so no good for the Maori'.[102]

The Old Testament's narratives of enslavement and hardship and its promise of salvation for God's chosen people held great appeal for Maori who had experienced the hardships of disease, depopulation, land-sales and war. Pai Marire (or Hau Hau),[103] the most important prophetic movement of the 1860s, consciously emphasized the Maori–Israelite link and its founder, Te Ua, signed himself as 'Te Ua Jew' or 'Te Ua a peaceable Jew'.[104] Te Ua's gospel 'Ua Rongopai' describes the Taranaki region, Te Ua's power-base, as '*waahi o Keenana*' (the land of Canaan) and '*Iharaaira*' (Israel). On the other hand, the oppressive and land-hungry Pakeha were '*nga Paarihi*' (the Pharisees) and '*nga Haaruki*' (the Sadduccees).[105] Kereopa, Te Ua's disciple, reaffirmed this opposition between Maori and Pakeha, Jew and

Pharisee, proclaiming: 'We are the Jews who were lost and have been persecuted.'[106]

Binney has shown that these Old Testament narratives of oppression and deliverance were integral to the teachings of the other great prophet of the 1860s, Te Kooti Arikirangi. Te Kooti, who was mission educated, initially served as an ammunition runner for government troops fighting against Pai Marire warriors. But, in 1865, Te Kooti was transported to the Chatham Islands for allegedly functioning as a Pai Marire spy. While imprisoned, Te Kooti fell ill and as he recovered he experienced a series of religious visions where the Archangel Gabriel told him of God's covenant with the Israelites. This revelation was the basis of Te Kooti's new religion, which subsequently developed into the Ringatu church. In 1868, Te Kooti led the escape of a group of prisoners from the islands, a group later known as the 'Exiles' or the 'Survivors'. Te Kooti thus became a Maori Moses, a leader who freed a persecuted group from bondage and functioned as a conduit for God's instructions to his Chosen People. In services, parables and prophecies Te Kooti consistently identified Maori as the Israelites and Pakeha as the Egyptian oppressors.[107] Over the next two decades, Te Kooti delivered a series of parables promising that he would drive the 'wicked' out of the Promised Land.[108] As Binney argues, these parables were the product of a powerful concordance between Old Testament notions of prophethood and *matakite*, the gift of foresight.[109] Te Kooti assured his followers that divine favour ensured success:

> Fear not because thy cry hath reached unto God, and God hath heard thy crying, hearken I will strengthen thee and will cause thee to know the things whereof I had spoken unto your forefathers, to Abraham to Isaac to Jacob and all their children down to David.[110]

As this quotation shows, by the 1860s the Maori identification with the Israelites had gone beyond a simple analogy between the Maori and Israelite experience of oppression. Te Kooti insisted that Abraham, Isaac, Jacob and David were the forefathers of the Maori. Te Ua also insisted that Maori actually were Jews. 'Ua Rongopai' ends with the injunction: *'kei hoki ki te Whare o Taapeta, engari e hoki ki te Whare o Heema'* – 'Do not return to the House of Japheth, but return to the House of Shem'.[111] Te Ua not only accepted the threefold division of humanity into the descendants of Japhet (Taapeta), Shem (Heema) and Ham (Hama) conveyed in missionary translations and texts, but identified Maori as the sons of Shem while Pakeha, in keeping with the dominant traditions of Mosaic ethnology, were the descendants of Japhet.[112]

It is important to note that just as there was a powerful similarity between the gifts of prophethood and *matakite*, the Old Testament's strong emphasis on genealogy was in keeping with Maori tradition where, as we have seen, *whakapapa* was fundamental to individual or group identity. In fact Christianity and pre-colonial tradition became increasingly imbricated and, as Christianity spread, Maori *whakapapa* began to assimilate the genealogies of the Old Testament. Noah and his sons were seen by some Maori as standing at the head of the *whakapapa* of the various human races. In one instance Noa (Noah) replaced Kaitangata as the father of Hema, a Maori personal name that coincided with the missionary transliteration of Shem, Noah's son and the father of the Semitic race![113]

This identification of Maori as both the descendants of the Old Testament's prophets and as a people suffering in the same way as the Israelites continued through the later nineteenth century and into the twentieth. The great prophet Te Whiti believed that Maori who flocked to his settlement at Parihaka in the 1870s were members of the twelve tribes of Israel.[114] In the early twentieth century, Rua Kenana, who was identified by many as the successor of Te Kooti, called his followers 'Iharaira' (the Israelites) and the region under their control 'Peura' (Beulah, the name of the restored Israel).[115]

Such beliefs were powerful responses, heavily shaped by new literacy skills and the translation and printing of Scripture, to the inequities of colonial society. Old Testament narratives of a chosen people breaking the bonds of oppression and enjoying God's favour obviously had an immediate appeal to a colonized people familiar with the Bible. Maori prophets, who derived their authority directly from Jehovah, possessed great *mana* and God sanctified their promises of Maori autonomy. By the 1860s literacy and the vernacular Bible had profoundly reshaped the indigenous identity and political discourse, providing powerful tools for the articulation of a range of visions of a Maori future free from the inequities of colonialism.

Conclusion

Not surprisingly, Maori exhibited little or no interest in the Pakeha debates over their origins. Although the scribe Whatahoro encouraged Best and Smith's belief that Maori were the descendants of Indian

Aryans and one minor prophet claimed that God communicated to him through a magical rupee, Maori themselves had limited interest in any Indian connection.[116] The notion of an Aryan people was foreign and too irrelevant to be of any significance in nineteenth-century Maori thought. But the idea of the Israelites was also foreign and irrelevant in the period of earliest contact as well. However, with the spread of Christianity and literacy and the increasing marginalization of Maori in the colonial economy, the belief that Maori were a chosen people destined to overthrow their oppressors held an obvious appeal. Contrary to McKenzie's assertion that the Bible was 'alien' and 'irrelevant', it became the most important source for the recasting of Maori identity from the mid-1830s on. Thus in the New Zealand context, there were two parallel but largely independent discourses on racial origins. Maori identification with the Israelites coexisted with, and implicitly challenged, the common Pakeha belief that colonizer and colonized both belonged to the Aryan family. The Maori case clearly shows that there were profound limits to the 'colonization of consciousness'.[117] Maori were able to quickly adapt new ideas and skills to formulate new visions of community, the past and the future. While muskets and disease took their toll on the Maori population, any 'fatal impact' was limited to a material level. The strength of nineteenth-century Maori Christian, Kingitanga and prophetic traditions reveals the ways in which literate Maori used print to disembody Pakeha knowledge and to fashion new powerful religious identities and political idioms that challenged Pakeha claims to hegemony.

6
The Politics of Language, Nation and Race: Hindu Identities in the Late Nineteenth Century

Although nineteenth-century India and New Zealand both gave rise to anti-colonial movements, the social sources and political ideologies of Indian and Maori anti-colonialism were markedly different. Where the previous chapter established that Maori countered British and Pakeha anthropological theories about their origins with historical and spiritual narratives fashioned out of an active appropriation of scriptural literacy, British Orientalist knowledge itself was central in the new nationalist and Hindu identities fashioned by South Asian elites. This chapter examines the role of this intellectual and cultural encounter in the construction of anti-colonial and nationalist ideologies in India, extending Chapter 4's discussion of the interrelationship between Orientalism and indigenous reform in the construction of Sikhism.

In the colonial period, South Asians reassessed the Aryan idea, to offer new interpretations of Indo-Aryan history and fashion an ethnic and religious basis for Hindu nationalism. The Aryas, deeply embedded in Sanskritic tradition and its vision of the past, were seen as forming the foundation of both Hindu tradition and the lineage of the modern Indian nation. Various Hindu groups forwarded divergent interpretations of the Arya community: for some it was a vehicle for stressing kinship with the British rulers and praising the gifts of the Raj, for others it was an inclusive term which was to underpin their vision of Indian nationalism, and for others still it was a tool to inscribe rigid lines between communities, to offer a narrow and particularizing definition of their racial and religious identity. This chapter will explore these debates, endeavouring to reveal the distinct voices and competing interpretations that moulded indigenous identities and political discourse. Most importantly, I hope to extend recent work by Raychaudhuri on the Bengali intelligentsia and Dalmia's study of Bharatendu Harishchandra and the nationalization of Hinduism, by emphasizing the Indians' use of language as an analytical and political tool in the later nineteenth century.[1] In order to produce a contextualized reading of these debates over Aryanism, however, we need to first examine the origin and shifting meaning of 'Arya' within South Asian cultural traditions.

Sources: 'Arya' and the Vedas

As we have already seen, the Vedic texts (*Samaveda, Rigveda, Artharveda* and *Yajurveda*), composed in the second millennium BCE, record the migrations of pastoralist people who called themselves 'Arya'. These texts have been a vital source for the scholarly reconstruction of Indo-European religion and have served as the basis for the development of much subsequent Hindu tradition. Not only do these texts contain hymns dedicated to the gods of the Aryas, Indra, Agni and Varuna, but they also depict the social world of the Aryan peoples who entered the Indus valley from the Central Asian steppes. The *Rig Veda*, the earliest of the Vedic collections, emphasized the cultural distinctions between the Aryan invaders and the non-Aryan inhabitants of the Indus Valley. Although inter-tribal conflict within the Aryas is prominent in the hymns, a stronger cultural opposition is drawn between the Aryas and the indigenous people of north India.[2]

The *Rig Veda* depicts indigenous tribes such as the Pani and Dasa as godless, savage and untrustworthy. The Pani are cattle-thieves who seek to deprive the pastoralist Aryas of their main source of wealth. The Dasa are savages, whose darker complexion, godless society and different language diverged significantly from the culture of the invaders.[3] The other adjectives used to describe the Dasa also posit a rigid cultural opposition between Arya and Dasa: the Dasa are barbarians (*rakshas*), those without fire (*anagnitra*) and flesh-eaters (*kravyad*).[4] The usage of Pani and Dasa were extended beyond tribal names, to become terms for savage or barbarian peoples in general and they also came to describe the workings of demonic force. The Aryas, on the other hand, were a noble people protected by their gods Agni and Indira. This linguistic opposition was continued into later Sanskritic tradition where *dasa* came to mean slave and *arya* came to mean noble or honourable. Hence one might be said to be *aryaguna* (exhibiting noble qualities), be *aryabuddhi* (noble-minded), be *aryavesha* (respectably dressed) or live in an *aryadesha* (an Aryan region).[5]

Most importantly the Arya/non-Arya opposition underpinned forms of social organization, especially caste. The exclusion of the non-Aryan peoples, such as the dark-skinned Dasa or Pani, from the social world of Aryan north India was a central moment in the emergence of the caste system. An opposition between light and dark, Arya and non-Arya recurs throughout the *Rig Veda*.[6] Although the terms used to signify descent groups and ties of kinship in the Vedas, such as *jati*, *gotra* and *kula*, should be not be understood as purely racial terms in the western sense, they do convey a strong sense of descent and cultural community.[7] Colour became a central issue in the elaboration of the Aryan social vision: *varna* was the Sanskrit term for both colour and the theoretical fourfold model of Indian society.[8]

Thapar has warned against a simple racialized reading of the importance of colour in this social schema, suggesting that the fourfold division of the *varna* system was largely symbolic rather than racial.[9] She argues that in ancient Indian society caste was a system of organizing marriage relations to control descent and thus determined both ritual and social status.[10] The opposition between Arya and Dasa was, therefore, one of descent and social function rather than phenotypical characteristics. While other ancient texts contrast Aryas against non-Indian *mleccha*s (barbarians), Halbfass argues that these *mleccha*s were 'nothing but a faint and distant phenomenon at the horizon of the [ancient] indigenous tradition.'[11] *Mleccha*, moreover, was predominantly a cultural term denoting foreigners who did not speak Sanskrit and did not perform Vedic rituals. Foreign invaders (Greeks, Huns and Shakas) who adopted local beliefs and practices, and accepted the ritual authority of the Brahmans, could be incorporated into the *varna* structure as *kshatriya*s.[12]

Brockington has suggested that this flexibility was eroded over time. In the *Mahabharata* and post-Vedic legal texts, those foreign *kshatriya*s who accepted the responsibility of defending Brahmanical authority were termed *vratyakshatriya* ('degenerate *kshatriya*'), while those who disregarded the Brahmans became outcastes. Thus, the epics reveal that the incorporation of foreigners became provisional and their status slowly declined. As the *varna* model became more rigid the 'rough equality' extended to the *mleccha*s in the Vedic hymns and early epics and was replaced by increasing contempt.[13] Taking this evidence – the existence of cultural taxonomies, an awareness of colour as a marker of community and a greater reluctance to incorporate foreigners within the *varna* model – we can discern in the Vedas and epics a strengthening understanding of cultural difference as the basis of community. Thapar is correct that the Vedic view of community lacks the heavy emphasis on biology and rigid categorization found in nineteenth-century European definitions of race, but these ancient interpretations of community provided crucial material for the elaboration of a racialized understanding of Hindu identity in the nineteenth century.[14]

Arya, religion and race

There is no substantial evidence to suggest that there was any significant shift in meaning of the term 'Arya' in medieval or early modern India. It was still used mainly as a descriptive term for the descendants of the Aryas who invaded India and dominated the plains of Hindustan. Indeed the Gangetic plains of north India, Rajasthan and Punjab were termed Aryavarta, the land of the Arya. European traders soldiers and missionaries who visited India from the late fifteenth century were not seen as Arya. Europeans were dismissed as *faringi*, derived from the Persian term for 'Franks', the sworn enemies of Muhammad and the *Qur'an*, or any number of Sanskrit derivatives: *mleccha* (barbarian or outcaste), *yavana* (Greek or Westerner) or, as in the case of the French General Dupleix, *hunapati* (Hun Lord).[15]

Where medieval sources such as Rajashekhara's *Kavyamimamsa* (*c.* 900 CE) constructed rudimentary regional typologies of complexion (describing north Indians as *gaura* (fair), while those from the east were *shyama* (dusky), nineteenth-century Indian sources reveal a social vision where race assumed increasing importance.[16] The extension of British political control, direct or indirect, over the bulk of South Asia undoubtedly promoted this process. Unequal social relationships across racial lines created a heightened awareness of race among Indians, as the racialized structures of the army, judiciary and civil administration emphasized the importance of race as a marker of difference.

But new ideas, as well as the racial inequalities of colonialism, promoted views of history and society that emphasized the centrality of race. As we have seen from the 1760s members of the Indian service gentry, *pandits* and *munshis* had participated in the dialogic construction of Indological knowledge. However, Indians were not simply producers of knowledge, they were active consumers of Indology as well. Indeed many Indians, fluent in Sanskrit and various vernacular languages, embraced philological methods developed in Europe to construct visions of Indian society that variously confirmed, modified or challenged the findings of their British counterparts. The idea of an Aryan racial group proved remarkably flexible as it was used to create a wide variety of interpretations of India's past and a multiplicity of racial and religious visions of community.

Some Indians, particularly those in close contact with Europeans or in British employ, embraced Orientalism to express loyalty to *amgrezi raj* (British rule). Krishna Bihari Sen, Principal of Maharaja's College, Jaipur, for example, celebrated the claims of Max Müller and other European philologists that Indians and Europeans were 'Arian Brethren'. Sen, a keen scholar of philology, proclaimed in 1876: 'What a sublime spectacle is afforded by the present concourse of nations. The Hindu and Englishman are brothers! ... Philosophy has evolved a strange unity out of the hopeless variety of races. Let that unity be the groundwork of future peace and brotherhood.'[17] One year later Keshab Chandra Sen, a close friend of Max Müller, argued that the Raj was 'a reunion of parted cousins, the descendants of two different families of the ancient Aryan race.' Chandra Sen suggested that British rule was 'destined to promote the true interests and lasting glory of both nations.'[18]

Other South Asians, however, while loyal to the British, were more interested in the religious and cultural applications of the Aryan theory. Krishna Mohan Banerjea, an Honorary Member of the Royal Asiatic Society of London and chaplain to the Bishop of Calcutta, used philology to pursue two different agendas. Firstly, he enlisted philology as a powerful weapon against racial prejudice, examining a range of ancient languages to disprove the contention found in various official publications that Hindustan meant 'black-place' or 'negro-land'.[19] The comparative method could be used to expose scurrilous etymologies and establish cross-cultural kinship. Secondly, Banerjea hoped that comparative philology would guide the reform of Hinduism through a critical evaluation of the Vedas and Hindu history more generally. He argued, for instance, that the Vedic evidence clearly established that the Aryas migrated to north India from Central Asia. The dominance of the Brahmans only dated from this period and Banerjea hoped that a careful analysis of the Vedas would explode the 'myths' which invested Brahmans with ancient origins and unquestioned religious authority.[20]

As a Christian, Banerjea sought not only to undermine Brahmanical 'tyranny', but also to establish the compatibility of the Vedas with Christian doctrine. He noted that Indian mythology recorded tales of a huge flood and suggested that Manu was the 'Indo-Arian ideal of

Noah'.[21] He suggested, therefore, that a close comparative examination of Sanskrit revealed the true place of Indians in universal history. Banerjea argued that 'arya' was a derivative of the Hebrew *ari* (loin), and if the initial sound of this Hebrew word was aspirated the result was *hari*, the Sanskrit word for loin. On the basis of such linguistic evidence, Banerjea asserted that the Indo-Aryans were 'Japhetic' but also had close contact 'with the children of Shem'. Thus, Banerjea reconciled the Biblical narrative with ancient Indian sources, declaring that 'Sacred history' was 'abundantly confirmed by Arian records'.[22]

Ramachandra Ghosha, Banerjea's close friend and fellow member of the Royal Asiatic Society, also embraced comparative philology as the basis for his scholarship. Ghosha's *The Indo-Aryans, their History, Creed and Practice* (1881) began by praising the works of 'occidental *savans*' whose work 'elucidated many knotty problems' pertaining to the literature and history of ancient India. Ghosha, echoing Banerjea's attack on Brahmanical authority, argued that the greatest contribution of European Indologists was the editing and publication of ancient texts that 'undermined the dishonorable attempts of the Brahmans, who debarred all but themselves from reading the Veda'. The printing press and the creation of an informed Indian public were powerful weapons in the battle against Brahmanical tyranny and for the modernization of the Hindu mind. In keeping with this aim, Ghosha's text was an admirably clear reconstruction of Indo-Aryan history: his preface noted that the 'labyrinth[s] of heterogeneous materials' so loved by European authorities often created confused and unreadable texts.[23]

Ghosha accepted the linguistic unity of the Aryan family and posited that the various branches of this family had 'hitherto guided the van of civilization'.[24] However, while few nineteenth-century observers in India or Europe would have challenged Ghosha's contention that Aryans were at the forefront of the emergence of civilization, his interpretation of subsequent Indo-Aryan history diverged from the models forwarded by both British authorities and Brahmans. Following the research of William Jones and H. T. Colebrooke, the dominant British view of Indian history was degenerationist. Although the Vedas marked a 'Golden Age' in human history, the civilized and highly sophisticated Indo-Aryan society had declined slowly over the long march of the centuries. The increasing hybridity of the Indo-Aryans tarnished the purity of their language and religion, as Sanskrit and Vedic monotheism were debased by later non-Aryan accretions. Hinduism fell under the tyrannical control of the Brahmans and the pure hymns of the Vedas were lost under layers of meaningless idolatry, ritual and phallic worship.[25] Brahmanical interpretations also forwarded a degenerationist model, as modern human history was taking place in *Kali yuga,* the fourth and final stage of the cosmological cycle. As the world edged towards destruction in Shiva's dance (*tandava*), wars, famine and human weakness dominated society. Only the inauguration of a new world by Shiva would restore moral and political equilibrium.[26]

Ghosha challenged these degenerationist interpretations, positing an alternative developmental model for Indian intellectual history. The Vedas, which combined sublime truths with 'many puerilities and repulsive legends', shed light on the 'primitive' history of the Indo-Aryans when they had only just begun to construct a civilized society.[27] Indeed, Ghosha noted that before departing their central Asian homeland, the Indo-Aryans were 'savages' who 'lived upon the flesh of wild animals'. Slowly they developed a sedentary lifestyle becoming pastoralists living in clans.[28] At this stage, they migrated to north India, where their society continued to develop with the elaboration of political structures and composition of the Vedas. Although these hymns were undeniably beautiful, they conveyed 'conceptions of the Godhead ... of a fluctuating and undecided character'. It was only when the *Upanishads* were composed that a 'proper philosophical age' dawned. Gradually the Indian mind developed a purer monotheistic religious conception and moved closer to the theological basis of Christianity, but this progress was slow, uneven and incomplete, as 'tradition and habit' inclined Indo-Aryans to revert to polytheism.[29] Britain's mission in South Asia was to halt this backsliding and to aid the Hindu mind to 'evolve' towards the monotheism of Christianity.

While Ghosha's developmental account of Indian religious thought challenged degenerationist interpretations of Hinduism, he readily accepted the racialized reading of the Vedas forwarded by European Indologists. Ghosha suggested that the Indo-Aryans embarked on a war of destruction against the indigenous people of India, which arose out of both cultural difference and racial antipathy. The Indo-Aryans, Ghosha argued:

> always justified their conduct towards the latter [the aborigines] because they [the aborigines] were irreligious, and because they worshipped no Vaidik gods. The Indo-Aryans, as they were naturally fair of complexion, of majestic appearance, civilized, and much more advanced in thought, looked down upon the aborigines who were of beastly and unsightly appearance.[30]

Ghosha accepted the terminology of colonial ethnography and racial science as he described the linga-worshipping Dasa (or Dasyu) as 'Turanian', a designation used by Max Müller and others to describe the indigenous population of India. These Turanian peoples were excluded from the caste system. Indeed, Ghosha argued that caste was underpinned by racial antipathy and was 'purely an ethnological institution', confirming the interpretations commonly forwarded by colonial ethnographers such as Ghosha's contemporary W. W. Hunter.[31]

Dayananda Sarasvati and the Arya Samaj

The works of Banerjea and Ghosha reflected the views of a small class of western-educated Bengalis who embraced Christianity and British colonial knowledge, as they strove to 'modernize' India through the extension of literacy, Christianity, science and democracy.[32] The Aryan theory was easily assimilated into their programmes for cultural revivification through cross-cultural exchange and the dissemination of Christianity. But Indian Christians were not alone in seeing embracing the Aryan theory as part of a drive for spiritual renewal and social reform: both Hindu nationalists and reformist Hindu leaders were alert to the potency of the theory.

One of the most influential reinterpretations of the Aryan theory and the Indo-Aryan past was fashioned by Dayananda Sarasvati, the founder of the Arya Samaj. Dayananda, born into a Gujarati Brahman family in 1824, ran away from home to become a *sannyasi* at the age of 22. As an ascetic in search of *moskha* (liberation), Dayananda travelled through much of north and central India, visiting holy sites and learning yoga and grammatical theory from renowned masters. He wandered for many years, spending a year in the mountains north of Haridwar and journeying south into the jungle-clad Vindhya range, before arriving in Mathura, the great centre of Krishna devotion, in late 1860.[33] For nearly three years in Mathura Dayananda studied with Virjananda, a renowned grammar guru, immersing himself in the Sanskrit grammatical tradition and gaining first-hand experience of popular Hinduism at one of India's great pilgrimage centres. This experience was pivotal in Dayananda's career, as he accepted Vrijananda's emphasis on the superiority of the books of the ancient *rishis* and developed a dim view of popular Hinduism.[34] After leaving Mathura in 1863, Dayananda recast himself as a Hindu reformer, set on expunging the 'degenerate' features of modern religion and urging a return to the

Vedas as a source of spiritual enlightenment and social wisdom. Dayananda, who initially preached against the excesses of popular Hinduism in Sanskrit, embraced vernacular preaching, the foundation of schools, and the use of the printing press as weapons for his crusade.[35] Although, as we shall see, he was a fierce opponent of Christianity, Dayananda drew on the very methods central to evangelical programmes in India and his reforming career combined the roles of *sannyasi*, preacher and pamphleteer.

In 1875, he established the Arya Samaj, a voluntary organization (echoing the Protestant missionary societies) dedicated to reforming modern Hindu belief and practice along Vedic lines. This group quickly established a strong following in Punjab and emerged as one of the most influential reformist movements of the late nineteenth century.[36] In that same year, Dayananda wrote *Satyarth Prakash*, a Hindi treatise on the reform of Indian belief and practice. The basis of this text was his identification of the Vedas as the foundation stone of Hinduism, a source of great wisdom and of vital historical value. Drawing on both Indological research and the Hindu model of historical degeneration, Dayananda depicted the Vedic period as a Golden Age when civilization first emerged and Indian culture was at its apogee.[37] Originally, he argued, all humanity lived in Tribishtapa (Tibet), while the rest of the world remained uninhabitated. These first humans divided themselves into two groups: the noble, moral and learned Aryas and the lowly, immoral and backward Dasyus. The Aryas, tired of bitter conflict with the Dasyus, left Tribishtapa journeying to Aryavarta, an uninhabited land renowned for its wealth. Here the Aryas settled after defeating various savage peoples living to the north and west.

Society in Aryavarta was sophisticated. Vehicles propelled by a combination of fire, wind and water established that the Aryas were technologically advanced as well as spiritually enlightened. Aryavarta, the Aryan homeland, became the base of Arya power, and their influence spread all over the world, disseminating Vedic religion to East Asia, Egypt, Europe and even America. This religion was pure, as the Vedas were the product of divine revelation and as a result provided the perfect model for social organization. In the post-Vedic period society began to decline. Power-hungry Brahman and sectarian tendencies began distorting the religion around the time of the *Mahabharata*. Once introduced, these influences grew increasingly powerful, until Hinduism was riddled with conflict and idol-worship, meaningless pilgrimages, fraudulent miracles and a lust for worldly power. Dayananda's evocation of a lost Golden Age and cry for reform was more strikingly degenerationist than even the most hostile Evangelical attacks on popular Hinduism.[38]

The further decay of Hinduism could only be halted by a return to the teachings of the Vedas, and in *Satyarth Prakash* Dayananda thoroughly rejected the claims of Christianity. Missionary influence was greatly feared by many Punjabis and Dayananda actively contested missionary claims that 'the fertilizing stream of the gospel' was about to rejuvenate and reform Punjabi religion.[39] He presented a critique of Christianity based on a very literal reading of both the Old Testament and the New Testament and an unwavering belief in the Vedas as the only source of revelation.[40] Using dialogues where an imaginary Christian explained doctrine to a sceptical commentator, Dayananda suggested that the Christian God was not really a god at all. In fact his carefully selected Biblical evidence and his dialogues showed that the Christian God had a body (*sakar*) and this corporeality meant that he was not all-knowing (*sarvagya*) or all-pervading (*viyapak*). The Christian God failed the Vedic model of God as 'eternal, pure, conscious, free, beginningless and endless' (*nitya, shuddh, buddh, sukta svabhav, anadi, ananadi*). God's preference for Abel's meat sacrifice over Cain's fruit offering was the action of a man (*manushyon ki banai*), in fact a flesh-eating man (*manashari*), rather than a god. Moreover, the Christian God's insistence that animals were created for humanity and God's willingness to receive animal sacrifices were characteristics of a barbarian (*jangli wala* – literally a man of the jungle) and a cruel man (*hinsak manushya*). Dayananda dismissed Jesus as a lowly *barhai* (carpenter) and *karigar* (craftsman) devoid of supernatural prowess (*kuch karamati nahim*).[41] These critiques reflected a strong tradition in Brahmanical thought and apologetics established from the 1830s, which stressed the antiquity and absolute authority of the Vedas against the 'historical' nature of Christianity.[42]

But not only did Dayananda reject the powers of the Christian God and Jesus's claims to prophethood, but he suggested that Christianity was an exclusively European religion, full of barbaric customs and designed to serve white colonialism. Dayananda saw the Christian emphasis on God as a judge as echoing the reality of colonialism, where non-European people were being judged against an essentially European moral code. Indeed for Dayananda, Christianity and European culture were basically indistinguishable, as he used *saf guna* (white race) as a synonym for Christian.[43]

Thus in *Satyarth Prakash* we can observe the increasing late nineteenth-century emphasis on cultural difference and race.

Admittedly Dayananda believed that Indian society should be restructured along the clean simple lines of the fourfold *varna* model, on the basis of morality and social function, rather than ethnicity.[44] But Dayananda's outright rejection of Christianity, his dismissal of Christians as brutish *jangli log* (wild people), and his insistence on the unrivalled glories of the Vedic Golden Age reveal an important ethnic subtext which emphasized cultural and, as his use of *saf guna* suggests, racial difference. Although Harishchandra Chintamani, a leading Bombay Arya Samaji, initiated close ties between the Theosophical Society and the Samaj between 1878 and 1880, Arya Samajis placed little emphasis on the unity of the Aryan race.[45] One Arya Samaj ideologue noted late in the nineteenth century: 'I do not use the word Arya in the sense in which it is taken by the modern Europeans ... I mean by it the inhabitants of Aryavarta and of Aryavarta only.'[46] Har Bilas Sarda, a leading Arya Samaj writer based in Ajmer, not only downplayed racial affinities, but made 'Hindu superiority' the cornerstone of his vision of Arya history. In his *The Hindu Superiority* (1906), he challenged the location of the Aryan homeland in central Asia, suggesting that all human society developed initially in Aryavarta. From this central point, north Africa, the Middle East, Europe, Britain, east Asia and America were colonized. But Aryavarta alone remained the centre of true civilization, populated by an inherently cultured and sophisticated race that headed the 'scale of nations'.[47]

Tilak and the rewriting of the history of civilization

Where Dayananda was primarily concerned with the spiritual renewal of Hindu Aryas, nationalist leaders coopted the Aryan theory in their search for a cohesive ideological tool to reify Hindu/Indian nationhood. Of the early nationalists, Balwantrao Gangadhar Tilak, the leading ideologue of the 'Extremist' faction of the Indian National Congress and co-founder of the Indian Home Rule Leagues during the First World War, offered the most striking reinterpretation of Indo-Aryan history. Tilak published two works, *Orion, or Researches into the Antiquity of the Vedas* (1892) and *The Arctic Home of Vedas* (1903), which set out his argument. Tilak, drawing on a Hindu cosmogony with a vast temporal scope, had no trouble accepting the 'latest and most approved geological facts and opinions', which greatly extended the timescale of history. He suggested that the ancient home of the Aryas was not central Asia but rather in the Arctic during the 'Tertiary period'. Originally, the Arctic was temperate, but the advent of an ice age between 10 000 BCE and 8000 BCE transformed it into an 'ice-bound land unfit for the habitation of man'. From 8000 BCE the Aryas left their Arctic home moving south into Europe and central Asia and by 6000 BCE had settled in the southern tracts of the central Asian steppes, displacing pre-existing communities and carrying with them an advanced culture: this was the Vedic culture carried south into India in the final southern push of the great migration.[48]

These Indo-Aryans retained their cultural sophistication and military superiority, but those Aryas who settled in northern Europe began to slide into barbarism. The sophistication of the Indo-Aryans was enshrined in the Vedas that were transmitted 'accent for accent' for maybe as long as six millennia. Therefore the Indo-Aryans, Tilak argued, were precociously civilized, attaining a level of civilization that was commensurate with the glories of Egypt at the height of its power, but predating the peak of Nile civilization by several thousand years.[49]

Thus Tilak extended and reinterpreted the work of European Indologists, rebutting arguments that European culture developed earlier and more quickly than Indian culture, and asserting the sophistication of Vedic culture. *The Arctic Home of the Vedas* opened with a discussion of his debts to Max Müller. Max Müller's work on the *Rig Veda* and the history of Sanskrit literature was not only a key reference point for Tilak, but Max Müller also provided him with material and personal assistance. Tilak wrote much of *The Arctic Home of the Vedas* while imprisoned for sedition. Max Müller sent Tilak a copy of his edition of the *Rig Veda* to read in prison and led the press campaign for Tilak's release.[50] Tilak made good use of the latest Orientalist research, supplementing Max Müller with Rhys and Taylor's works on Aryan origins and Warren's research on ancient languages.[51] Most importantly, Tilak extended the image of a Vedic Golden Age created by Jones, Colebrooke and Max Müller, using it to assert the primacy, vigour and superiority of Indo-Aryan culture.

Elsewhere, Tilak suggested that this superiority was manifest in the Devanagari script used for Sanskrit and later Hindi. He argued that all Indian languages should be written in a standardized script and Devanagari was best suited for this purpose. He noted that European Sanskritists had 'declared the Devanagari alphabet is more perfect than any which obtains in Europe'. He firmly rejected suggestions that the Roman script might be the best tool for standardization as it was 'entirely unsuited to express the sounds used by us ... sometimes a single [Roman] letter has three or four sounds, sometimes a single sound is represented by three or four letters.' Devanagari, he argued, could be used to build a pan-Indian community by uniting 'the Aryan ... and the Dravidian or Tamil character' and promoting linguistic comprehension across regional boundaries.[52]

Thus Tilak's contributions to debates over language and history were central to his programme that proclaimed Arya superiority, reclaimed national self-esteem and posited potential Indian unity. Here it is important to note that Tilak drew upon an older Indian astrological and geographical tradition as well as the latest Indological research. His periodization of Arya history in *The Arctic Home* was based on an astrological calendar. The period between 8000 and 5000 BCE was termed the Aditi period as in this period the 'vernal equinox was then in the constellation of Purvasu, and ... Aditi is the presiding deity of Punarvasu'. The two subsequent periods were named after the Orion and Krittika vernal equinoxes.[53] Astrological knowledge thus became a key tool for Tilak as he pushed back the date for the composition of the Vedas from Müller's 1200 BCE to before 4000 BCE.[54] This debate over the dating of the Vedas can be read as a skirmish in the ongoing contest between Indian astral sciences and western historians over Indian chronology.[55] Tilak believed that rationalist European science was not necessarily inimical to Hinduism, arguing that science could be easily accommodated into pre-existing Indian traditions.[56] Bayly has therefore suggested that Tilak was able to command social and political respect because he spanned both long-existing indigenous and newly founded colonial knowledge communities.[57] This observation illuminates Tilak's researches into the Vedas, which clearly show his attempts to synthesize Indian and western traditions to create a history that established the sophistication and superiority of Vedic India.

'Arya', anti-colonialism and Hindu nationalism

While some Indians used comparative philology's proofs of linguistic affinity to celebrate the Raj, the dominant trend in the later nineteenth century was for Indian reformers and scholars to downplay racial affinity or to assert Indo-Aryan superiority. The active appropriation of European Orientalist learning was a powerful strand in the articulation of nationalist agendas and, contrary to Inden's assertion, British research on India's history and languages was never hegemonic as it could be selectively adapted and harnessed to serve Indian ends.[58]

This has been well established by Raychaudhuri's research on the Bengali intelligentsia, which identified a strand in nineteenth-century

Bengali thought that reinterpreted Indological scholarship to form a powerful anti-colonial ideology:

> The central message ... was clear and simple: Hindu superiority and the unacceptability of western civilization. Indian Hindus were the most superior Aryans, no, even the only true Aryans. Everything in popular Hindu practice was based on higher reasoning and could be explained in a scientific way. All the discoveries of western science and technology had been anticipated by the ancient Aryans.

Sasadhar Tarkachudamani, an advocate of what Raychaudhuri terms an 'aggressive chauvinistic' Hinduism, went so far as to argue that 'only India could produce human beings complete in every sense'.[59] Other Bengalis rejected the notion of kinship with Europeans on quotidian grounds: they were not edified by the prospect of being cousins with 'beef-eating, whiskey-drinking Englishmen'.[60]

The stark inequalities of colonial political economy also moulded Hindu mentalities. The reconstruction of British authority, the continued denial of political representation to Indians and increasing British racial arrogance created widespread disenchantment within Indian elites. Vishnu Krishna Chiplunkar, the distinguished man of letters, suggested that while many Bengalis benefited under British rule, this did not offset the fact of colonization that was 'extremely baneful to us'. The later works of Bharatendu Harishchandra (poet, editor and 'the father of modern Hindi') dwelt on the destructive impact of *amgrezi raj* (English rule) and used the Aryan theory to downplay divisions within Hinduism, stressing the congruence between the nation and a unified Hindu tradition.[61] Balkrishna Bhatt, editor of the anti-colonialist *Hindi Pradip*, depicted the Queen of England (*Englandeshwari*) as a duplicitous tyrant intent on the financial and political subjection of *Bharat Janani* (Mother India). Bhatt vividly communicated this perceived hunger for power in an exchange where *Bharat Janani* imagines *Englandeshwari* consuming her flesh.[62]

Thus Indian ideologues harnessed the Arya concept in their attempts to construct a sense of nationhood in opposition to British rule and racial arrogance. The Bengali historian Rajanikanta Gupta's *Arya Kirti* 'The Glorious Deeds of the Aryas', which drew heavily on Tod's *Annals and Antiquities of Rajasthan*, celebrated Indo-Aryan masculinity, military prowess and courage.[63] Chowdhury has recently demonstrated that *Arya Kirti* was part of a broader project in which Bengali historians embraced the Aryan theory to fashion an alternative vision of Indian history, which celebrated Indo-Aryan superiority, asserted Hindu nationhood and, most importantly, reinvested the Bengali with the masculinity denied by the 'effeminate Bengali' of the British imagination.[64]

Others stressed the political and social sophistication of the Aryas. Ramachandra Ghosha, for example, argued that the Indo-Aryans evolved rapidly, becoming feudal agriculturists before they reached north India.[65] Bankimchandra Chatterjee affirmed this interpretation, but regretted that Aryan nationhood dissipated as the population differentiated itself into numerous small communities.[66] Other scholars rewrote the Aryan theory to include groups that the dominant interpretations depicted as being outside the bounds of Arya community. Aurobindo Ghose suggested that despite cultural differences, Dravidians and Aryas were descended from the same racial stock and the gulf between the two communities was narrowing. Aurobindo, like Lala Lajpat Rai, suggested that most Indian Muslims were indigenous converts, therefore they were also the heirs to the glories of the Vedas and Aryavarta.[67]

However, these attempts to utilize the Aryan theory in the fashioning of a more inclusive vision of nationhood were largely unsuccessful. As we have seen, the Vedas and the epics constructed a clear opposition between Aryas and non-Aryas, an opposition that was accepted and developed by colonial ethnography. In the south, the notion of the independence of the Dravidian languages, especially Tamil, was elaborated into a potent Tamil identity. Tamil revivalists and political leaders articulated a distinctive Dravidian identity that was defined against a Sanskritic, Aryan, Brahmanical 'other'.[68] The strength of Dravidianism posed a stern question to north Indian advocates of the Aryan theory: what place was there for Dravidians in the Indian nation?

Some leaders simply accepted the superiority of the Indo-Aryans of the north. Mahadeva Govind Ranade, a founding member of the Indian National Congress, believed the Aryas were the chosen race in India, but they constantly fought a battle against the degenerating effects of the non-Aryan Jats, Muslims, and Dravidians: India's struggle for freedom was dependent on re-Aryanization.[69] Rajnarayan Basu, a Bengali writer and nationalist, believed that high-caste Dravidians were in fact Aryans, as they were afforded high ritual status under the *varna* caste system. True Aryas, he continued, accepted the epics and the *Puranas* as the key sources of their history and identity. So while he included high-caste southern Hindus as Aryas, he believed Muslims had no claim on the glories of Arya history and believed that 'any deep-rooted association' between Hindus and Muslims was impossible.[70] Partha Chatterjee has shown that Bengali literature and textbooks constructed an image of Indian nationhood that followed Orientalists in blaming India's 'medieval decline' on the increasing influence of Muslim rule, which, in the reformers' eyes, undermined the sophistication of Hindu culture. These Bengali nationalists imagined Indian history and nationhood in explicitly Hindu terms.[71]

Therefore the inherent limitations of the Aryan concept, and the strength of regional identities, presented stern challenges to any attempt to use it as the basis for Indian nationalism at an all-India and pan-community level. Aryan theories, however, proved a potent tool for the refashioning of Hindu history and identity within north India. The Arya Samaj's insistence that Hinduism was the religion of the Aryas and should be based on the Vedas encouraged a rediscovery of the Hindu/Arya past. Hindu reformers and politicians, including Dayananda Sarasvati, forwarded a vision of Indian history that evoked a Vedic golden age followed by prolonged decline. This narrative was confirmed by four generations of Indological research and was embedded in colonial textbooks. Tarinichandra Chattopadhyay's *The History of India*, perhaps the most influential textbook in nineteenth-century Bengal, argued:

> What distinguishes the giant from the dwarf ... is nothing compared to the difference between the ancient and the modern Hindu ... In those [ancient] days Hindus would set out on conquest and hoist their flags in Tartar, China and other countries; now a few soldiers from a tiny island long away are lording it over the land of India ... Then the Hindus would sail their ships to Sumatra and other islands ... Now the thought of a sea voyage strikes terror in to the heart of a Hindu ...[72]

Chatterjee has demonstrated that such narratives were central to the constitution of a Hindu 'nationalist' consciousness in Bengal. This degenerationist vision of India's past asserted the superiority of ancient Indian civilization, the corrupting influence of Islam and the necessity for cultural regeneration. At the same time, however, it promised the possibility of advance in the future, if the descendants of the Aryas united together to battle the corrosive influence of Islam that subjected the Hindu nation, and worked to reform the abuses that had distorted the pure creed developed in the Vedas. Chatterjee notes that although this history was variously imagined as sometimes 'Bengali, sometimes Hindu, sometimes Arya, sometimes Indian', the essential structure of the degenerationist narrative and the exclusion of Muslims were constant.[73]

Conclusion: Arya and the definition of Hindu identity

Thus the allied forces of the civilizing mission, Indology and indigenous reform authorized an interpretation of India's past that was central in transforming Indian mentalities in the second half of the nineteenth century. As Indians sought a cohesive ideology that could be used to fight for greater representation and ultimately freedom from *amgrezi raj*, they looked to the past for possible sources for a shared identity and political inspiration. Although the rise and fall of great dynasties and little kingdoms marked India's history, Hindus found in the Vedas and the epics a history of their Arya ancestors. By extolling the virtue and superiority of the ancient Aryas, Hindu ideologues were able to contest British claims of inherent racial superiority. By the turn of the century 'Arya', together with Pratapnarayan's formula 'Hindi, Hindu, Hindustan', became a stock phrase in the vocabulary of Hindu nationalism. The notion of a Golden Vedic Age, created by the military might, technological sophistication and moral purity of the Aryas provided cohesion for a Hindu population divided by variations in belief, practice, caste and language. This pride in the Aryan past penetrated all levels of society and became embedded in even the most populist definitions of *Hindutva* (Hinduness). Raychaudhuri observes that in colonial Bengal even 'street corner shops' used Arya in their names.[74] Throughout north India today 'Arya' is common in the names of guest houses, book shops and dispensaries.

While this term was actively used in the anti-colonial struggle, it also promoted the hardening of boundaries between India's Muslim and Hindu communities. As we have seen, these ideas penetrated popular textbooks and accordingly it became commonplace for Hindus to blame Muslims for the supposed decline of Hindu culture under the Mughals, and for most Hindus Muslims could not be included in any Arya-based community. These rigid oppositions, between Muslim and Hindu, Indo-Aryan and all others, increasingly dominated the ideological elaboration of Hindu nationalism in the twentieth century. Extreme groups, such as the ultra-communalist Hindu Mahasabha and the Rashtriya Swayamsevak Singh, praised the racial visions of Hitler and Mussolini and emphasized the racial basis of Hindu nationalism. Although, as Jaffrelot has shown, Hindu nationalists never fully assimilated European racial and eugenic thought, the visions of *Hindutva* in the twentieth century have become more rigid and exclusive.[75]

But communal consciousness and nationalist ideologies were never simply 'derivative discourses' borrowed from European models.[76] The negotiation of Hindu identity, as this chapter has demonstrated, was the product of a complex interaction between ancient tradition, nineteenth-century reform movements, and dominant interpretations of Indian history. The importance of history as a legitimating tool means that we must view the construction of Indian religious identities against the *longue durée* of the South Asian cultural tradition, the rise of Islam and European colonialism. Although this chapter has supported the view that the late nineteenth century witnessed heightened communal consciousness, the increased pace of the development of religious identities was fed by the lived past and the interpretation of ancient texts.

The resulting visions have, of course, outlasted colonial rule. The Aryas remain a key touchstone in South Asian culture and politics. Over the last two decades, the Hindu right, eager to proclaim both the Aryas and Hinduism as the product of the national soil, has launched numerous attacks on British Orientalism and the 'Aryan Invasion Theory'. Such attempts to construct 'nativist' visions of the South Asian past not only deny the complex networks and exchanges that have shaped the region's past, but also repudiate history altogether. The editorial of the December 1994 issue of *Hinduism Today*, a leading monthly journal aimed both at a domestic Indian market and the communities of the Indian diaspora, proclaimed that 'History' was a 'Hoax' and suggested:

The bad news ... is that history is always inaccurate and often injurious. The good news is that India and Hinduism live beyond history ... Other faiths, excluding some tribal and pagan paths, are rooted in events. They began on such and such a day, were born with the birth of a prophet or the pronouncements of a founder. Thus they are defined, circumscribed by history. Not Hinduism. She has no founder, no birthday to celebrate. Like Truth, she is eternal and unhistorical.[77]

Professional historians hesitate to give credence to such views, but *Hinduism Today* has a circulation of around 135 000 readers, and a host of recent texts proclaiming the Aryas as the 'autochthon of India' have been greeted with enthusiasm.[78]

Most importantly, such arguments are currently promulgated as the basis of Hindu identity and the Indian nation-state. The Bharatiya

Janata Party (BJP), which dominates if not controls Indian politics, casts itself as the defender of Hinduism and equates Hinduism and India, effacing the reality of religious difference.[79] In upholding the Vedas as the basis for its social programme and its advocacy of Sanskritizing projects, the BJP forwards a narrow vision of the nation, disempowering 'secularized' Hindus, Dalits, tribals, Christians and Muslims. This vision of Hindu nationalism is only possible by denying the power struggles and imperial exchanges that both moulded the emergence of Indian nationalism and repeatedly reinscribed the meaning of the 'Arya' category. Within the South Asian context at least, the story of Aryanism continues, as it remains a central discursive formation in post-colonial politics.

Conclusion: Knowledge, Empire, Globalization

This study has demonstrated the centrality of Aryanism in British imperial culture, not only in British India, but also in South-East Asia, the Pacific and Britain itself. Within the British empire in the long nineteenth century Aryanism became a crucial heuristic device in colonial politics, popular journalism and imperial ethnology. Sir William Jones's ethnological essays, which insisted on a common cultural genealogy shared by Indians and Europeans, did not locate European origins in a 'harmless and distant' Orient as Said suggests: rather it fundamentally unsettled divisions between Europe and Asia, Britain and India, colonizer and colonized. The Aryan idea was both powerful and troubling. It seemed to unlock the broad sweep of universal history (and the place of the British empire within that grand narrative), but also caused much anxiety. What cultural bonds did Britons and Indians (or Polynesians) really share? If these ties of kinship were substantial, on what basis could imperial authority be constructed? The divergent visions of the Aryan theory examined in this study and the intensity of the debates that surrounded this notion reflected the moral and political weight of these questions.

Sir William Jones's discovery of linguistic affinities between Sanskrit, Latin and Greek was the basis for a fundamental reconceptualization of Indian history and culture. In 'unlocking' the mysteries of Sanskrit, in tracing the affinities between Greco-Roman mythology and Hindu tradition and in locating ancient Indian history within a Judeo-Christian chronological framework, Jones disciplined India, making it amenable to the emergent disciplines of history and ethnology. But Jones's legacy was ambivalent: his work did not simply inscribe colonial authority by proclaiming British ascendancy over Indian knowledge. Rather, Jones's research established a new comparative framework for the writing of universal history, a model that located

Asia, and India specifically, at the very heart of the history of civilization, shattering the images of a wild and exotic India that haunted the European imagination from the Renaissance through to the mid-eighteenth century.

Within a colonial context, where racial boundaries were strictly policed and imperial authority carefully protected, Jones's discovery of Indo-European commonalities was particularly challenging. Chapter 1 traced the intense battles over the implications of Aryan kinship, as administrators, historians, journalists and ethnographers attempted to impose order onto the Indian past and to reduce the complexity of South Asian culture into meaningful interpretations. Where late eighteenth-century Orientalists like Jones celebrated the sophistication of the Vedic period and its contributions to 'Civilization' (while frequently decrying the 'decayed' nature of contemporary Indian society), from the 1820s these ancient glories and the authority of the Jonesian tradition itself were increasingly undercut as evangelical and utilitarian reformers pushed for the East India Company to assume a more aggressive position towards indigenous customs. Within this context, the cultural affinities between Indians and Britons were frequently downplayed or the Aryan theory was used to naturalize, justify and celebrate British colonialism of South Asia: Britain, younger and more energetic, was reinvigorating the increasingly decrepit culture of its ailing relative.

As British interpretations of India increasingly privileged race, British scholars and administrators dwelt not only on racial differences between Indians and Europeans, but also placed greater emphasis on the clash between Aryan and Dravidian elements in Indian history. Within the fraught terrain of colonial life 'Aryan' and 'Dravidian' increasingly functioned as racial, rather than linguistic, signifiers. Although race never completely supplanted language as an analytical tool, as George Grierson's monumental *Linguistic Survey of India* illustrates, race did increasingly dominate popular, administrational and academic discourses on India. This centrality of race was enshrined in the *Imperial Gazetteer of India*: in the 1909 edition British understandings of India were so racialized that even the geology of India was divided into Dravidian and Aryan periods![1]

I have suggested that these debates over Aryan origins had an important impact in Britain itself in a period where the history and boundaries of 'Britishness' were openly debated. Although most Britons, like Europeans more generally, might have invested local traditions and regional identities with the greatest importance, elite groups were increasingly concerned with the national and racial past.[2] The very nature of the Aryan idea, which suggested that cultural bonds linked diverse European and non-European peoples, engaged the interest of a wide variety of scholars, politicians and religious thinkers in Europe. This idea was adopted and deployed unevenly: compared to their Scottish and German counterparts, English scholars were generally slow to show an interest in the idea or its methodological basis – comparative philology. While Scottish scholars quickly deployed the comparative method to refine their developmental models for the history of civilization, both Orientalism and philology were slow to make an impact south of the border. The Aryan idea finally gained some influence in England through the work of James Cowles Prichard, whose training in Scotland and a profound interest in German thought underpinned his engagement with Orientalism. In the face of the Anglo-Saxon revival and the rise of polygenist anthropology, Prichard used the Aryan concept to not only posit shared origins for 'Celtic' and 'Anglo-Saxon' Britons, but also to insist on an ancient cultural link between Britain and India. Prichard's vision of a shared Aryan history underpinning the empire jostled with older notions of the British as Teutons, Israelites or 'a Mongrel half-bred Race ... In whose hot Veins now Mixtures quickly ran'.[3]

Although Victorian Britons could not arrive at a consensus regarding the ultimate origins of their ethnic stock, it is clear that the cultural entanglements of empire, where migration, military service and missionary projects brought Britons to the colonies and colonials to Britain, made questions of ethnic origins and the boundaries between peoples urgent. Thus history and ethnology were invested with particular cultural significance as they were central in the definition of both national and imperial identities. In suggesting that the encounter with India had important consequences for identities in the metropole, this study reaffirms recent works that suggest that metropolitan society was not insulated from the effects of empire, rather the imperial venture played a pivotal role in the constitution of material culture, cultural patterns and identities in Britain itself.[4]

We have also seen the divergent ways in which the Aryan idea was inserted into various forms of colonial nationalism, indigenous social reform and anti-colonial prophetic movements. For some Indian reformers, such as Dayananda Sarasvati, Orientalism's stress on the glories of the ancient Aryans was an important source for arguments that urged a return to the 'pure' Hinduism of the Vedas. But it was a short journey from Dayananda's celebration of Indo-Aryan purity to the more militant proclamations of Hindu superiority made by later Arya Samajis and nationalists such as Har Bilas Sarda.[5] Chapter 6 noted that Bengali Hindu reformers and intellectuals embraced Aryan theory particularly enthusiastically, using it to attack British stereotypes of the effeminate *babu*, reclaiming a 'virile history' which drew heavy inspiration from the work of the Orientalist James Tod.[6] While this study has added further depth to our knowledge of Bengali and Arya Samaji views of history and race, it has also shown that the Aryan theory was harnessed by a largely overlooked group of Indian Christians and administrators. For these groups who had vested material and social interest in British power, the Aryan idea allowed them to construct a vision of a harmonious and egalitarian colonial society characterized by Indian loyalty to the Crown and racial fraternity. Even these 'loyalists', therefore, offered a critique of British racial thought, proclaiming Indian equality as the bedrock of their distinctive social and religious agenda. Thus, the notion of an Aryan racial community was both profoundly contested and highly flexible, and any attempt to see it simply as a metropolitan ideology that could be transplanted to colonial contexts to justify British superiority is misleading.[7]

Chapter 5 underlined this point forcibly. Maori leaders exhibited limited interest in the ongoing Pakeha debates over the location of Hawaiki and the ultimate source of Maori culture. For the Maori, theories that cast them as migrants from India, whether from the Aryan north, from the Dravidian south or from the strongholds of tribal culture, had little appeal. Instead, a succession of leaders, from Te Ua, the founder of Pai Marire, to Te Kooti, the great prophet-warrior, through to the later prophet-reformers Te Whiti and Rua Kenana, insisted that the Maori were 'Tiu' or 'Hurai' (Jews) or 'Iharaira' (the Israelites). Their arguments were both an appeal to the power of Old Testament narratives of deliverance and the result of the interweaving of Biblical knowledge and Maori political idioms. The most telling evidence of this imbrication was the assimilation of Noah and Shem into Maori *whakapapa* (genealogies), the basis for both individual and community identity. While we can see this identification with the Israelites as testament to the transformative power of colonialism and missionary activity, it was also a discourse of resistance and empowerment that countered the authority claims of Pakeha history and ethnology.

I have insisted throughout this study that these various interpretations and counter-interpretations of the Aryan idea must be located within the specific cultural contexts from which they were fashioned. In particular, this study has insisted that we must place these ethnological and historical texts within the changing patterns of knowledge production. Chapter 1 detailed the complex conjuncture of economic and political change in Bengal from the 1760s, which allowed the East India Company to draw upon religious experts and scribal communities. Through the studious maintenance of Indo-Islamic courtly tradition, the Company cast itself as a patron of learning and an upholder of cultural continuity, while simultaneously exerting growing pressure on regional kingdoms and local economies. The colonial state thus set about opening up new reservoirs of knowledge in addition to new sources of revenue as it keenly appreciated the value of military intelligence, commercial information and a 'mastery' of local customs. In a similar vein, the shift to Indocentric interpretations of Maori culture initiated by Richard Taylor was dependent upon economic, technological and social forces that underpinned the textualization of Maori culture. Once collected, edited, translated and printed, Maori traditions were effectively disembodied and, as such, they were amenable to comparative analysis, allowing Taylor to identify a shared Aryan heritage as an antidote to racial conflict.

Thus, it is clear that we must pay close attention to the diverse forces that shaped the production of historical and ethnological texts. We must not reduce colonial knowledge to being an instrument deployed at will to protect and maintain imperial authority. Neither the painless transplantation of metropolitan ideology nor the uncontested imposition of administrational exigency, colonial knowledge must be seen as the product of complex local engagements (whether in Bengal, Punjab, the Bay of Islands or even in Britain itself), struggles over meaning and power enacted within the unequal power relations of colonialism. As Eugene Irschick has insisted, the colonial social order was 'a negotiated, heteroglot construction shaped by both weak and strong, the colonized and colonizer, from the present to the past.'[8] Irschick's study of land tenure in the Madras hinterland traces the interplay between the demands of colonial administrators and the authority of indigenous knowledge traditions, stressing the 'dialogic' nature of British colonial knowledge. He warns that 'we can no longer presume' that British understandings of India were the 'product of an "imposition" by the hegemonic colonial power onto a mindless and subordinate society.'[9] Local aspirations and colonial agendas were in a constant dialogue, a dynamic process of exchange where claim and counter-claim led each interest group to modify its position almost constantly.

Such local engagements, however, occurred within a wider imperial world. The localized bodies of knowledge examined here must also be read as part of an Enlightenment and post-Enlightenment project that attempted to produce a detailed picture of the 'great map of mankind'.

Chronologically, this study began in the 1760s with the penetration of British commercial and scientific agents into parts of Asia and the Pacific that Europeans knew little about. The cluster of scholars at the forefront of this project (Cook, Banks, the Forsters, Jones) were central in constructing a global picture of both natural and human history. Detailed ethnographic observation in India and the Pacific, the translation of new languages, and the collection and analysis of indigenous traditions, allowed Europeans to study human variation and trace cultural affinities in greater detail. By 1800, European scholars had firmly established linguistic ties between north India and Europe and the fundamental affinity of the languages of the central and eastern Pacific, and had begun to explore the historical relationships between Eurasia and the Pacific.

Most importantly, we have seen that this global project was facilitated by a series of intellectual exchanges created by publication, correspondence and the foundation of new scholarly societies dedicated to the production of ethnographic and historical knowledge. Many of these individuals, institutions and networks were closely related to the agents of British expansion (the East India Company, the Royal Society, missionary organizations and colonial learned societies), and these imperial networks facilitated the rapid transmission of ideas and information. These networks thickened and multiplied in the nineteenth century, quickening the pace of the intellectual transactions within the empire. Extensive collections of ethnographic material had been gathered by European explorers, traders and missionaries in Asia and the Pacific by 1850, creating variegated bodies of knowledge which could be used to create increasingly sophisticated comparative studies of 'primitive cultures' and human history.

This knowledge underpinned the work of metropolitan synthesizers like E. B. Tylor or Max Müller and, equally importantly, it also allowed ethnographers in the colonies to locate their studies within a broader comparative context. But, even as this process of accessing indigenous knowledge was in its infancy, important new models emerged in the 'peripheries'. While Sir William Jones's innovative comparative vision drew on his classical education and his extensive knowledge of Persian, it was fundamentally dependent on his engagement with Sanskritic and Indo-Islamic traditions. Innovative work was also carried out on the New Zealand frontier: Richard Taylor's identification of Maori as fellow Aryans in the midst of the racial hatred unleashed by the New Zealand Wars was not only an attempt to counteract the centrifugal forces that threatened the colony, but also reoriented the analysis of

Maori culture toward India. Colonial officials, surveyors and anthropologists devoted greater effort to tracing affinities between Maori religion and Hinduism. By the 1890s and early 1900s, *tapu* had been identified as a transplanted form of caste, Elsdon Best had uncovered phallus worship among the Tuhoe, Alfred Newman had identified some 70 Hindu gods and 38 Hindu goddesses in Polynesia, and (from Assam) Samuel Peal had argued that Maori were descendants of the Nagas of the Gangetic basin and upper Burma.

These examples remind us that, by its very nature, colonial knowledge was itself profoundly hybridized at two levels. Firstly, British understandings of both South Asian and Maori society were dependent on indigenous expertise, as these forms of 'local' knowledge were not only believed to be more effective guides to policy-making, but were also more likely to be accepted by indigenous communities. Through their use of indigenous language, institutions and customs, colonial authorities hoped that their policies would be invested with authority and would gain greater cultural and political purchase. Secondly, the flows of personnel, policies and ideas that gave the empire its fundamental structure shaped the development of colonial cultures in ways that we are only beginning to understand. Because of their very nature as colonial societies, the development of India or New Zealand was never solely driven by internal forces; rather the reality of their integration into the webs of empire continued to mould their economic fortunes, social structures and cultural patterns.

Finally, it is important to conclude by underlining the central methodological emphases of this study. The importance of the cultural traffic and imperial networks uncovered in this work means that we must move beyond the nation-state as the organizing unit for the writing of the history of imperialism. In its place I have advocated a multi-sited imperial history that uses webs as its organizing analytical metaphor, an approach that views empires as integrative structures that knit, often forcibly, previously disparate and unconnected points together into a shared space.

The metaphor of the web also embodies the multiple positions that any given location might occupy within the structure of empire: one culture, city or institution could simultaneously be subordinate to the metropole, but in turn function as a important hub of its own set of important networks. This argument was stimulated by recent work on Ireland's place within the empire. It is increasingly clear that Ireland was both, in some senses at least, a colony but also an imperial centre in its own right. While the west of Ireland, for example, felt the full brunt of British power and was particularly impoverished during the famine years, it also became an important node within the imperial system. The East India Company army had recruited soldiers from the region since the late eighteenth century and with the foundation of the Queen's College in Galway in 1845 the British drew upon the small middle-class of the region. A steady flow of men from the west, both Catholic and Protestant, used their college education as preparation for imperial service, becoming colonial officials, administrators of prisons, asylums and hospitals, and, in the case of M. A. Macauliffe, a leading Orientalist.[10]

This study has made similar points with regard to New Zealand, which dominated Pacific studies and increasingly assumed the mantle of an imperial power in the Pacific islands, while remaining a British colony and a vital larder for Britain. Even more markedly, British India was the site of imperial innovation and intellectual endeavour, standing at the centre of numerous imperial circuits of exchange, including the expansive and dense personal, publishing, governmental and cultural networks that transmitted Aryanism from British India into South-East Asia, the Pacific and beyond.[11]

Such networks were powerful agents of globalization. Throughout this study I have suggested that globalization offers a useful analytical lens for imperial history: an argument grounded in a belief that globalization itself has multiple histories, pasts that were embedded in the processes of empire building.[12] The imperial globalization generated by British commerce, conquest and colonization had two important effects. Firstly, and most obviously, imperial networks brought previously unconnected regions together into a system, albeit a highly uneven one, of exchange and movement. Secondly, it transformed worldviews: globalization was (and is) as much a state of mind as a series of capital flows or migratory movements. The British empire transformed the ways in which people, both in Britain and in the colonies, thought about the world. From the 1760s, largely because of the drive of British interests into the Pacific and Asia which was so pivotal in constructing a truly global picture of geography, Britons were not only able to comprehend the world as (more fully) global, but also increasingly saw their empire in global terms. This sense of global interconnectedness reached beyond the political and commercial elite. An author of a popular volume of 'improving literature' observed in 1786: '[b]y the amazing progress of navigation and commerce, within the last two or three centuries, all parts of the world are now connected: the most distant people are become well acquainted, who for thousands of years, never heard of one another's existence.'[13]

The discourses of Aryanism were an important product of these new 'connections'. Born out of the colonial encounter in South Asia, the Aryan idea became a crucial element of the culture of empire, whether in British India, South-East Asia, the Pacific or in Britain itself, as it seemed to offer a powerful framework for explaining both the past and present of the empire. In charting the transmission of the theory and the ways in which it was quickly reworked and indigenized in various colonial contexts, this study has begun to construct a fuller picture of the long history of the idea, a global history that is fundamentally entwined with the British empire's reach into the Asia-Pacific region.

Notes

Abbreviations

AR	*Asiatic[k] Researches*
ATL	Alexander Turnbull Library, Wellington
BL	British Library, London
CMS	Church Missionary Society
CO	Colonial Office Records, PRO, London
GBPP	*Great Britain Parliamentary Papers*
HL	Hocken Library and Archives, Dunedin
JPS	*Journal of the Polynesian Society*
ML	Mitchell Library, Sydney
MR	*Missionary Register*
NA	National Archives, Wellington, New Zealand
NZPD	*New Zealand Parliamentary Debates*
OIOC	Oriental and India Office Collections, BL
PRO	Public Record Office, Kew
PSC	Polynesian Society Collection, ATL
WMS	Wesleyan Missionary Society

Introduction: Aryanism and the Webs of Empire

1. Eric R. Wolf, *Europe and the People without History* (Berkeley, CA, 1982), 3.
2. Marshall G. S. Hodgson, *Rethinking World History: Essays on European, Islam and World History*, Edmund Burke III ed. (Cambridge, 1993); Sanjay Subrahmanyam, 'Connected histories: notes towards a reconfiguration of early modern Eurasia', *Modern Asian Studies*, 31 (1997), 735–62; Andre Gunder Frank, *ReOrient: Global Economy in the Asian Age* (Berkeley, CA, 1998).
3. David Hancock, *Citizens of the World: London Merchants and the Integration of the British Atlantic Community, 1735–1785* (Cambridge, 1995); P. J. Cain and A. G. Hopkins, *British Imperialism: Innovation and Expansion, 1688–1914* (London, 1993). Hopkins has articulated a rather different vision in his recent 'Back to the future: from national history to imperial history', *Past and Present*, 164 (1999), 198–243.
4. Most notably Antoinette Burton, *At the Heart of the Empire: Indians and the Colonial Encounter in Late Victorian Britain* (Berkeley, CA, 1998); Shompa Lahiri, *Indians in Britain: Anglo-Indian Encounters, Race and Identity, 1880–1930* (London, 2000); John M. Mackenzie (ed.), *Imperialism and Popular Culture* (Manchester, 1986).
5. Sudipta Kaviraj, 'The imaginary institution of India', *Subaltern Studies VII: Writings on South Asian History and Society* (Delhi, 1993), 1–39. Also see Antoinette Burton, 'Who needs the nation? Interrogating British history', *Journal of Historical Sociology*, 10 (1997), 227–48.

6. J. G. A. Pocock, 'British history: a plea for a new subject', *New Zealand Journal of History*, 8 (1974), 3–21 and 'The limits and divisions of British history: in search of the unknown subject', *American Historical Review*, 87 (1982), 311–36.

7. C. W. Dilke, *Greater Britain: A Record of Travel in English-Speaking Countries during 1866 and 1867*, 3 vols (London, 1868).

8. W. W. Hunter, *Annals of Rural Bengal* (Calcutta, 1868); James Fergusson, *History of Indian and Eastern Architecture* (London, 1876).

9. Mary Louise Pratt, *Imperial Eyes: Travel Writing and Transculturation* (London, 1992); I. C. Campbell, 'Culture contact and Polynesian identity in the European age', *Journal of World History*, 8 (1997), 29–55.

10. Reginald Horsman, 'Origins of racial Anglo-Saxonism in Great Britain before 1850', *Journal of the History of Ideas*, 37 (1976), 387–410; Edward A. Hagan, 'The Aryan myth: a nineteenth-century Anglo-Irish will to power', in *Ideology and Ireland in the Nineteenth Century*, Tadhg Foley and Sean Ryder eds (Dublin, 1998), 197–206.

11. Raymond Schwab, *Oriental Renaissance: Europe's Rediscovery of India and the Orient, 1680–1880*, trans. Gene Patterson-Black and Victor Reinking (New York, 1984).

12. Jane Rendall, 'Scottish Orientalism: from Robertson to James Mill', *Historical Journal*, 25 (1982), 43–69.

13. J. D. Lang, *A View of the Origin and Migrations of the Polynesian Nation; demonstrating their ancient discovery and progressive settlement of the Continent of America* (London, 1834).

14. Joan Leopold, 'The Aryan theory of race', *Indian Social and Economic History Review*, 7 (1970) and 'British applications of the Aryan theory of race to India, 1850–1870', *English Historical Review*, CCCLLII (1974), 578–603; Romila Thapar, 'The theory of Aryan race and India: history and politics', *Social Scientist* 24 (1996), 3–29.

15. Thomas R. Trautmann, *Aryans and British India* (Berkeley, CA, 1997), 217–21; Tapan Raychaudhuri, *Europe Reconsidered. Perceptions of the West in Nineteenth Century Bengal* (Delhi, 1988).

16. Paul Rabinow, 'Representations are social facts: modernism and post-modernism in anthropology', in James Clifford and G. Marcus (eds), *Writing Culture: The Poetics and Politics of Ethnography* (Berkeley, CA, 1986).

17. Andrew E. Barnes, 'Aryanizing projects: African collaborators and colonial transcripts', *Comparative Studies of South Asia, Africa, and the Middle East* 17 (1997), 46–68; Hagan, 'The Aryan myth: a nineteenth-century Anglo-Irish will to power', 197–206; Mónica Quijada Mauriño, 'Los "Incas Arios": Historia, lengua y raza en la construcción nacional Hispanoamericana del siglo XIX', *Histórica*, 20 (1996), 243–69.

18. J. S. Mill, 'The East India Company's Charter', *Writings on India by John Stuart Mill. Collected Works of John Stuart Mill, volume 30*, J. M. Robson, M. Moir and Z. Moir eds (Toronto, 1990), 33.

19. Radhika Mongia, 'Race, nationality, mobility: a history of the passport', *Public Culture* 11 (1999), 527–56; Antoinette Burton (ed.), *Gender, Sexuality, and Colonial Modernities* (London, 1999).

20. Richard Drayton, *Nature's Government: Science, Imperial Britain, and the 'Improvement' of the World* (New Haven, CT, 2000), xviii, 221–68.

21. Jorge Luis Borges, 'Museum: On rigor in science', *Dreamtigers*, trans. Mildred Boyer and Harold Morland (Austin, TX, 1964), 90.

22. Most notably W. H. Sleeman, *Ramaseeana, or a Vocabularly of the Peculiar Language used by the Thugs* (Calcutta, 1836).

23. C. A. Bayly, *Empire and Information. Intelligence Gathering and Social Communication in India, 1780–1870* (Cambridge, 1996), 171–4, 331–2.

24. Ranajit Guha, *Elementary Aspects of Peasant Insurgency in Colonial India* (Oxford, 1983).

25. Katherine Prior, 'Making history: the state's intervention in urban religious disputes in the North-West Provinces in the early-nineteenth century', *Modern Asian Studies*, 27 (1993), 179–203. On archives as 'state memory' see Matt K. Matsuda, *The Memory of the Modern* (New York, 1996).

26. See M. P. J. Reilly, 'John White. Part II: Seeking the exclusive Mohio: White and his Maori informants', *New Zealand Journal of History*, 24 (1990), 45–55; Bayly, *Empire and Information*, 56–141.

27. Warren Hastings, 'Letter to Nathaniel Smith', from *The Bhagvat-Geeta, The British Discovery of Hinduism in the Eighteenth Century*, P. J. Marshall ed. (Cambridge, 1970), 189–91; Sir George Grey, *Polynesian Mythology, and ancient traditional history of the New Zealand race, as furnished by their priests and chiefs* (London, 1855), iii–vii.

28. Th. Hahn, *An Index of the Grey Collection in the South African Public Library* (Cape Town, 1884); Anon, *General Catalogue of Grey Collection, Free Public Library* (Auckland, 1888).

29. Benita Parry, 'Problems in current theories of colonial discourse', *Oxford Literary Review*, 9 (1987), 39.

30. For example, Hone Mohi Tawhai in Parliamentary Debates in 1880. See John Caselberg (ed.), *Maori is My Name: Historical Maori Writings in Translation* (Dunedin, 1975), 121–2.

31. C. A. Bayly, 'Informing empire and nation: publicity, propaganda and the press, 1880–1920', *Information, Media and Power through the Ages*, Hiram Morgan ed. (Dublin, 2001); Lachy Paterson, '*Te Hokioi* and Haiti'. Conference paper in author's possession.

32. Harold Innis, *Staples, Markets and Cultural Change: Selected Essays*, Daniel Drache ed. (Montreal, 1995); Benedict Anderson, *Imagined Communities. Reflections on the Origin and Spread of Nationalism*, rev. edn (London, 1991).

33. Susan O'Brien, 'A transatlantic community of Saints: the Great Awakening and the first Evangelical network, 1735–1755', *American Historical Review*, 91 (1986), 811–32.

34. For example, *Te Karere Maori*, 1:5 (1 June 1855) and 5:13 (30 June 1858); *Te Korimako*, 36 (15 January 1885).

35. Schwab, *Oriental Renaissance*, 52–4.

36. John Stenhouse, '"A disappearing race before we came here": Doctor Alfred Kingcombe Newman, the dying Maori and Victorian scientific racism', *New Zealand Journal of History*, 30 (1996), 124–40; Shaun Broadley, 'Science, race and politics: an intellectual biography of A. K. Newman' (University of Otago, Honours thesis, 1994).

37. These uncatalogued works are in the Polynesian Society's closed stack collection at the Alexander Turnbull Library.

38. Percy S. Smith to Newman, 2 March 1907, and Newman to Smith, 5 March 1907, PSC, MS-Papers-1187–268.

39. Richard H. Grove, *Green Imperialism: Colonial Expansion, Tropical Island Edens, and the Origins of Environmentalism, 1600–1860* (Cambridge, 1995)

and *Ecology, Climate and Empire: Colonialism and Global Environmental History, 1400–1940* (Cambridge, 1997); S. B. Cook, *Imperial Affinities. Nineteenth Century Analogies and Exchanges between India and Ireland* (New Delhi, 1993); Andrew Porter, 'North American experience and British missionary encounters in Africa and the Pacific, c. 1800–50', *Empire and Others. British Encounters with Indigenous Peoples 1600–1850*, Martin Daunton and Rick Halpern eds (London, 1999).

40. Gauri Viswanathan, *Masks of Conquest: Literary Study and British Rule in India* (London, 1989).

41. *Panjab Notes and Queries*, 1: 1 (October 1883), 6; S. E. Peal, 'The ancestors of the Maori', *JPS*, 6:24 (December 1897), 174–6; Elsdon Best, 'Maori beliefs concerning the human organs of generation', *Man*, 14 (1914), 132–4.

Chapter 1 The Emergence of Aryanism: Company Orientalism, Colonial Governance and Imperial Ethnology

1. For example, C. A. Bayly, *The Imperial Meridian. The British Empire and the World 1780–1830* (London, 1989); H. V. Bowen, 'British conceptions of global empire, 1756–83', *Journal of Imperial and Commonwealth History*, 26 (1998), 1–27.

2. C. A. Bayly, 'The first age of global imperialism, c.1760 to 1830', *Journal of Imperial and Commonwealth History*, 26 (1998), 28–47.

3. Vincent Harlow, *The Founding of the Second British Empire, 1763–93*, 2 vols (London, 1952–64). For recent reworkings of this vision see P. J. Marshall, 'Britain without America – a second empire?', *The Oxford History of the British Empire. The Eighteenth Century*, P. J. Marshall ed. (Oxford, 1998), 576–95; and more provocatively Bayly, *Imperial Meridian, passim*.

4. For example, Kate Teltscher, *India Inscribed: European and British Writing on India* (Delhi, 1995).

5. Clive to the Court of Directors, 30 September 1765, *Fort William–India House Correspondence. Vol. IV: 1764–1766*, C S. Srinivasachari ed. (Delhi, 1962), 337–8.

6. C. A. Bayly, *Empire and Information. Intelligence Gathering and Social Communication in India, 1780–1870* (Cambridge, 1996), 16, 90; Bernard S. Cohn, *Colonialism and Its Forms of Knowledge: the British in India* (Princeton, NJ: 1996), 117–19.

7. Bayly, *Empire and Information*, 44–8.

8. Court of Directors to Select Committee in Bengal, 17 May 1766, *Fort William-India House Correspondence IV*, 183–4

9. Public Letter from Court of Directors to Council in Bengal, 10 April 1771, *Fort William-India House Correspondence. Vol VI: 1770–1772*, K. D. Bhargava ed. (Delhi, 1960), 107–8; Public Letter from Court of Directors to Council in Bengal, 28 August 1771, ibid., 119–20; Public Letter from Council in Bengal to Court of Directors, 3 November 1772, ibid., 418–19; Secret Letter from Council in Bengal to Court of Directors, 15 November 1771, ibid., 328; *Gentleman's Magazine*, 41 (1771), 402.

10. Public Letter from Court of Directors to Council in Bengal, 28 August 1771, *Fort William-India House Correspondence VI*, 122–4.

11. O. P. Kejariwal, *The Asiatic Society of Bengal and the Discovery of India's past 1784–1838* (Delhi, 1988), 25.
12. H. T. Colebrooke, *Remarks on the Husbandry and Internal Commerce of Bengal. Extracted from: Remarks on the present state of the husbandry and commerce of Bengal by H. T. Colebrooke and Lambert* (Calcutta, 1804).
13. Balt. Solvyns, *A Collection of Two Hundred and Fifty Coloured Etchings: descriptive of the manners, customs, and dresses of the Hindoos* (Calcutta, 1796) and *Les Hindous, ou description de leurs moeurs, coutumes et cérémonies*, 4 vols (Paris, 1808–12).
14. Francis Buchanan, *A Journey from Madras through the countries of Mysore, Canara and Malabar*, 3 vol (London, 1807).
15. H. H. Wilson, *The Mackenzie Collection: a descriptive catalogue of the Oriental manuscripts, and other articles illustrative of the literature, history, statistics and antiquities of the south of India collected by Colin Mackenzie* (Calcutta, 1828); Nicholas Dirks, 'Colonial Histories and Native Informants: Biography of an Archive', *Orientalism and the Postcolonial Predicament. Perspectives on South Asia,* Carol A. Breckenridge and Peter van der Veer eds (Philadelphia, 1993), 279–313.
16. Public Letter from Council in Bengal to Court of Directors, 3 November 1772, *Fort William-India House Correspondence VI*, 428.
17. David Kopf, *British Orientalism and the Bengal Renaissance. The Dynamics of Indian Modernization 1773–1835* (Berkeley, CA, 1969), 17, 19 n. 32, 27.
18. On 'symbolic capital' see Pierre Bourdieu, *Language and Symbolic Power: the Economy of Linguistic Exchanges,* John B. Thompson ed. (Cambridge, 1991).
19. Javed Majeed, '"The Jargon of Indostan": an exploration of jargon in Urdu and East India Company English', *Languages and Jargons. Contributions to a Social History of Language,* Peter Burke and Roy Porter eds (Cambridge, 1995), 187
20. H. H. Wilson, *A Glossary of Judicial and Revenue Terms, and of useful words occurring in official documents relating to the administration of the government of British India* (London, 1855).
21. Warren Hastings, 'Letter to Nathaniel Smith', from *The Bhagvat-Geeta, The British Discovery of Hinduism in the Eighteenth Century,* P. J. Marshall ed. (Cambridge, 1970), 191.
22. Brian A. Hatcher, 'Indigent Brahmans, industrious pandits: bourgeois ideology and Sanskrit pandits in colonial Calcutta', *Comparative Studies of South Asia, Africa and the Middle East,* 16 (1996), 20.
23. Garland Cannon, *Oriental Jones* (Bombay, 1964), 131. By August 1787 he reported: 'I have more Brahmanical teachers than I can find time to hear.' Jones to John Shore, 16 August 1787, *The Letters of Sir William Jones,* Garland Cannon ed. (Oxford, 1970), II, 762.
24. Nathaniel Brassey Halhed, *A Code of Gentoo Laws* (1776) in *British Discovery of Hinduism,* 157; P. J. Marshall, 'Introduction', *British Discovery of Hinduism,* 10–12.
25. Jones to Lee, 28 September 1788, *Letters of Sir William Jones,* II, 821.
26. Rosane Rocher, 'The Career of Radhakanta Tarkavagisa: an eighteenth-century pandit in British employ', *Journal of the American Oriental Society,* 109 (1989), 628.
27. N. K. Sinha, *The Economic History of Bengal,* 2 vols (Calcutta, 1962), II, 147–57.

28. David Kopf, *British Orientalism and the Bengal Renaissance. The dynamics of Indian Modernization 1773–1835* (Berkeley, CA, 1969), 57.

29. S. N. Mukherjee, *Calcutta: Myths and History* (Calcutta, 1977), 87–8; Brian A. Hatcher, *Idioms of Improvement: Vidyasagar and Cultural Encounter in Bengal* (Delhi, 1996), 36–7.

30. H. T. Colebrooke to his father, 3 February 1797, *Sir Thomas Edward Colebrooke, The Life of H.T. Colebrooke* (London, 1873), 89.

31. Bayly, *Empire and Information*, 80.

32. Ibid., 83–8.

33. J. H. Little, *The House of Jagat Seth*, N.K. Sinha ed. (Calcutta, 1967).

34. Peter Marshall, 'Masters and banians in eighteenth-century Calcutta', *The Age of Partnership: Europeans in Asia before Dominion*, Blair Kling and M.N. Pearson eds (Honolulu, HI, 1979), 191–213.

35. Rosane Rocher, 'British orientalism in the eighteenth century: the dialectics of knowledge and government', *Orientalism and the Postcolonial Predicament. Perspectives on South Asia*, Carol Breckenridge and Peter van der Veer eds (Philadelphia, PA, 1993), 217.

36. M. Martin (ed.) *The Despatches, Minutes and Correspondence of the Marquess of Wellesley*, 2 vols (London, 1837), II, 346.

37. Kopf, *British Orientalism*, 110–18.

38. Sisir Kumar Das, *Sahibs and Munshis: an Account of the College of Fort William* (Calcutta, 1978), 7–21, 107.

39. *AR*, I, vii-viii.

40. Kejariwal, *Asiatic Society*, 32. Garland Cannon has also suggested that Jones blazed a path 'toward world humanism and universal tolerance'. Garland Cannon, *The Life and Mind of Oriental Jones: Sir William Jones, the Father of Modern Linguistics* (Cambridge, 1990), 361.

41. Lord Teignmouth, *Memoirs of the Life, Writings, and Correspondence of Sir William Jones* (London, 1804), 228.

42. For his distrust of the pandits see his letter to Charles Chapman, *Letters*, II, 683. On forgery see J. D. M. Derret, *Religion, Law and State in India* (London, 1968), 245.

43. Teignmouth, *Jones Memoirs*, 352.

44. William Jones, 'On the Origin and Families of Nations', *AR*, 3 (1792), 479–92.

45. Jones did not identify the genetic relationship between Sanskrit and Hindi. He noted that the purest form of Hindi or Hindustani (he used both terms) was spoken around Agra and that '[f]ive words in six, perhaps, of this language were derived from the *Sanscrit*'. He accounted for Hindustani's lexical debt to Sanskrit in the general trend of linguistic borrowing by conquered peoples. Jones argued at a grammatical level, 'particularly the inflexions and regimen of verbs', Hindi varied greatly from Sanskrit and therefore they were genealogically unrelated. William Jones, 'On the Hindu's [sic]', *AR*, 1 (1788), 348.

46. Ibid., 348–9.

47. While others, including Nathaniel Brassey Halhed (see his *Grammar of the Bengal Language* (Hooghli, 1778), iii), had hinted at this connection, Jones's argument was assertive, convincing and widely disseminated.

48. Hans Aarsleff, *The Study of Language in England, 1780–1860* (Princeton, NJ, 1967), 14–7.

49. Jones, 'On the Hindu's', 343. This criticism was directed against Jacob Bryant's *A New System, or an analysis of Ancient Mythology*, 3 vols (London, 1774–6). Bryant argued that Egyptians, Indians, Greeks and Italians had shared origins and carried their religions to Japan and China. Jones restated this criticism more broadly in his ninth Discourse as he attacked 'the licentiousness of etymologists in transposing and inserting letters, in substituting at pleasure any consonant for another of the same order, and in totally disregarding the vowels', 'On the origin and families of nations', *AR*, 3, 199–200.

50. Jones, 'Discourse on the Arabs', ibid., 53.

51. Roy Harris and Talbot J. Taylor, *Landmarks in Linguistic Thought. The Western Tradition from Socrates to Saussure* (London, 1989), 44.

52. William Jones, 'On the origins and families of nations', *AR*, 3, 487.

53. Ibid., 479–80, 490–1.

54. Trautmann, *Aryans and British India*, 42–7.

55. Ibid., 53–4.

56. *The Works of Sir William Jones, with a Life of the Author by Lord Teignmouth*, 13 vols (London, 1807), III, 325; Alun David, 'Sir William Jones, Biblical Orientalism and Indian scholarship', *Modern Asian Studies*, 30, 1 (1996), 177.

57. Lord Kames, *Sketches of the History of Man*, 2 vols (Edinburgh, 1774), I, 39–40; Samuel Shuckford, *Sacred and Profane History of the World Connected*, 5th edn (London, 1819 [1728]); David, 'Biblical Orientalism', 175.

58. Schwab, *Oriental Renaissance*, 71.

59. Javed Majeed, *Ungoverned Imaginings: James Mill's The History of British India and Orientalism* (Oxford, 1992), 15.

60. William Jones. 'On the mystical poetry of the Persians and Hindus', *AR*, 3 (1792), 171.

61. His initial aim was to revise the date of the beginning of the *Kaliyuga* from 3102 BC to enable him to reconstruct the dates of the great Hindu kings. He drew on the knowledge of his Pandit Ramlochan and utilized Radhakanta Sharman's (Hasting pandit) *Puranarthaprakasa*, which outlined Puranic chronology. For a critical account of Jones's studies of Indian chronology see Mukherjee, *Sir William Jones*, 100–8.

62. *The Sanscrit Dictionary* (Serampore, 1808) was based on the *Amarakosha*, a popular Sanskrit lexicographical work. For Colebrooke's insights into Hindu legal tradition see H.T. Colebrooke, *Miscellaneous Essays*, 2 vols (London, 1837), I, 477–480.

63. Colebrooke made this observation in his paper on 'The Sanscrit and Prakrit languages' which he presented to the Asiatic Society on 7 January 1801: ibid., I, 24.

64. Ibid., I, 1–3.

65. Colebrooke insisted that modern Hindus 'seem to misunderstand their numerous texts'. Colebrooke, 'On the religious ceremonies of the Hindus', *Miscellaneous Essays*, I, 196.

66. Jones, 'On the Hindu's [sic]', *AR*, I, 347.

67. Mukherjee, *Sir William Jones*, 24–5; Kejariwal, *Asiatic Society*, 76. For the shifting importance of Greece and Rome in eighteenth- and nineteenth-century British thought see Frank M. Turner, *Contesting Cultural Authority. Essays in Victorian Intellectual Life* (Cambridge, 1993), chs 9–11.

68. See Cannon (ed.), *Letters*, II, 718 n. 1.

69. Mukherjee, *Sir William Jones*, 99; Roseanne Rocher, 'Sanskrit: discovery by Europeans', 36–54. On Panini see Hartmut Scharfe, *A History of Indian Literature. Volume 5, Part 2, Grammatical Literature* (Wiesbaden, 1977), 88–117.

70. E.g. Sir William Jones, *A Discourse on the Institution of a Society for Enquiring into the History of Asia, delivered at Calcutta, January 15th, 1784* (London, 1784) and William Jones to James Burnett, Lord Monboddo, 24 September 1788, *Letters of Sir William Jones*, II, 818. Schwab has suggested that *Asiatick Researches* 'spread with remarkable speed and pervasiveness among scholars and writers in England, Germany, and France'. Schwab, *Oriental Renaissance*, 52.

71. Johann Freidrich Kleuker translated William Jones's articles from *AR*, into German from 1795: Schwab, *Oriental Renaissance*, 53, 94–8.

72. A similar argument is made in Richard Drayton, 'A l'école des Français: les sciences et le deuxième empire britannique (1783–1830)', *Revue Française d'Histoire D'Outre-Mer* 86 (1999), 91–118.

73. See George W. Stocking, Jr, *Victorian Anthropology* (New York, 1987), 23; P. J. Marshall and Glyndwr Williams, *The Great Map of Mankind: British Perceptions of the World in the Age of Enlightenment* (London, 1992), 258.

74. Schwab, *Oriental Renaissance*, 58; Mukherjee, *Sir William Jones*, 114–6.

75. Schwab, *Oriental Renaissance*, 58–9.

76. Ibid., 71–2. Schlegel described Sanskrit as 'the actual source of all languages, of all thoughts and poetry of the human spirit', quoted in Rocher, 'Sanskrit: discovery by Europeans', 36–53.

77. Sheldon, Pollock, 'Deep Orientalism? Notes on Sanskrit and power beyond the Raj', *Orientalism and the Postcolonial Predicament. Perspectives on South Asia*, Carol A. Breckenridge and Peter van der Veer, eds (Philadelphia, 1993), 83.

78. Notable exceptions include Jane Rendall, 'Scottish Orientalism: from Robertson to James Mill', *Historical Journal*, 25 (1982), 43–69; Bruce Lenman, 'The Scottish enlightenment, stagnation and empire in India, 1792–1813', *Indo-British Review: a Journal of History*, 21 (n.d.), 53–62; Martha McLaren, 'Philosophical history and the ideology of the Company state: the historical works of John Malcolm and Mountstuart Elphinstone', ibid., 130–43.

79. William Robertson, *An Historical Disquisition Concerning the Knowledge which the Ancients had of India* (London, 1791), 335–6; Rendall, 'Scottish Orientalism', *passim*.

80. Hamilton, 'Wilkins's *Sanscrit Grammar*', *Edinburgh Review*, XIII (January 1809), 372.

81. For example, *Asiatic Annual Register*, 1 (1800), 209–24 and 2 (1801), 1–22. Also see Rosane Rocher, *Alexander Hamilton (1762–1824): A Chapter in the Early History of Sanskrit Philology* (New Haven, CT, 1968).

82. Francis Buchanan, 'Notices on the Birman Empire', *AR*, 5 (1801), 219.

83. See James A. Boon, *Affinities and Extremes: Crisscrossing the Bittersweet Ethnology of East Indies History, Hindu-Balinese Culture, and Indo-European Allure* (Chicago, 1990), 28–49.

84. John Leyden, 'On the languages and literature of the Indo-Chinese nations', *AR*, 10 (1808), 162.

85. John Crawfurd, *History of the Indian Archipelago. Containing an Account of the Manners, Arts, Languages, Religions, Institutions, and Commerce of its Inhabitants*, 3 vols (Edinburgh, 1820), II, 8–9; also see II, 46–7.

86. Crawfurd suggested that Maori, with their brown skins and 'lank' hair were part of the superior 'Brown' race of the archipelago, unlike the

Australian Aborigines who had 'frizzled' hair and were thus linked to the Papuans (the Archipelago's 'Negroes'). Crawfurd, *History*, I, 25 n.

87. Colin Kidd, *British Identities before Nationalism: Ethnicity and Nationhood in the Atlantic World, 1600–1800* (Cambridge, 1999).

88. Charles Vallancey, *An Essay on the Antiquity of the Irish language: Being a collation of the Irish with the Punic language* (Dublin, 1772), 3.

89. Francis Wilford, 'On Egypt and other countries adjacent to the Cali River, or Nile of Ethiopia, from the ancient books of the Hindus', *AR*, 3 (1792), 295–462.

90. J. C. Walker, *Historical Memoirs of Irish Bards* (London, 1786). For Jones's doubts about Vallancey's work see Jones to the second Earl Spencer and to Joseph Cooper Walker, 11 September 1787, *Letters*, II, 768–71.

91. Many of these are detailed in Keith Jeffrey (ed.), *An Irish Empire? Aspects of Ireland and the British Empire* (Manchester, 1996).

92. Sylvester O'Halloran, *An Introduction to the Study of the History and Antiquities of Ireland* (London, 1772), i.

93. Lawrence Parsons, *Observations on the bequest of Henry Flood* (Dublin, 1795).

94. Kidd, *British identities before nationalism*, 176.

95. L. C. Beaufort, 'An Essay upon the state of Architecture and Antiquities, previous to the landing of the Anglo-Normans in Ireland', *Transactions of the Royal Irish Academy*, XV (1828), 115.

96. Ibid., 110–13, 115–16, 195, 199–206

97. Ulick J. Bourke, *The Aryan origin of the Gaelic race and Language, showing the present and past literary position of Irish Gaelic* (London, 1875); Joep Leerssen, *Mere Irish and Fior-Ghael: Studies in the Idea of Irish Nationality, Its Development and Literary Expression prior to the Nineteenth Century* (Cork, 1996), 140.

98. Aarsleff, *Study of Language*, 162–5.

99. Richard Symonds, *Oxford and Empire. The Last Lost Cause?* (London, 1986), 101–5.

100. George Stocking, Jr, 'Introduction', James Cowles Prichard, *Researches into the Physical History of Man* (Chicago, 1973 [1813]), xii. For biographical information see J. C. Trevor, 'Prichard's life and works', *Man*, 49 (1949), 124–7.

101. Stocking, 'Introduction', xvi-xvii.

102. It is likely that he was influenced by this spate of research both directly and indirectly, as we have seen that teaching at Edinburgh University was profoundly shaped by comparative philology in the Jonesian mould, and Prichard himself attended Stewart's lectures on moral philosophy. Ibid., xv–xvi, xxxix.

103. Prichard, *Researches*, 460, 524. Indeed Jones's influence was even visible in Prichard's medical dissertation of 1808: George W. Stocking Jr, *Victorian Anthropology*, 50.

104. Prichard, *Researches*, 244–7; Dr Thomas Hodgkin, 'Obituary of Dr. Prichard', *Journal of the Ethnological Society of London*, 2 (1850), 190.

105. James Cowles Prichard, *An Analysis of Egyptian Mythology: To Which is Subjoined a Critical Examination of the Remains of Christian Chronology* (London, 1819), ii, vi–vii.

106. Prichard, *Researches*, 471; Trautmann, *Aryans and British India*, 169–71.

107. James Cowles Prichard, *The Eastern Origin of the Celtic Nations Proved by a Comparison of their Dialects with the Sanskrit, Greek, Latin and Teutonic*

Languages. Forming a Supplement to the Researches into the Physical History of Mankind (London, 1831), 42–3, 345.

108. Adolphe Pictet, *De l'affinité des langues celtiques avec le Sanscrit* (Paris, 1838).

109. See his stress on environmental and climactic forces in James Cowles Prichard, *The Natural History of Man; comprising inquiries into the modifying influence of physical and moral agencies on the different tribes of the human family* (London, 1843).

110. Poliakov, *Aryan Myth*, 49–50.

111. Aarsleff, *Study of Language*, 182–209;

112. Thomas Arnold, *Introductory Lectures on Modern History, with the Inaugural Lecture Delivered in Dec., 1841* (Oxford, 1842), 33–5

113. Robert Young, *Colonial Desire. Hybridity in Theory, Culture and Race*, (London, 1995), 66–89.

114. Gwyneth Tyson Roberts, "Under the Hatches": English Parliamentary Commissioners' views of the people and language of mid-nineteenth-century Wales', *The Expansion of England: Race, Ethnicity and Cultural History*, Bill Schwarz ed. (London, 1996), 171–97.

115. Young, *Colonial Desire*, 72–9.

116. J. R. Green, *A Short History of the English people* (London, 1874); William Stubbs, *The Constitutional History of England*, 3 vols (Oxford, 1874–8). The popularity of these works undercuts Young's assertion that Teutonism 'collapsed with the unification of Germany in 1871'. Young, *Colonial Desire*, 73.

117. O. Michael Friedman, *Origins of the British Israelites: the Lost Tribes* (San Francisco, 1993).

118. Brothers also suggested that both Africans and Indians were members of the Semitic family as well, as they were descendants of Ophir. Richard Brothers, *A letter to his Royal Highness the Prince Regent, the lords, commons, and people of the United Kingdom* (London, 1821).

119. Daniel Defoe, 'The True Born Englishman', from frontispiece, Benedict Anderson, *Imagined Communities. Reflections on the origin and spread of nationalism*, rev. edn (London, 1991). This notion of hybridity continued strongly in the mid nineteenth century. In 1861 John Crawfurd stated: 'We are but hybrids, yet, probably not worse for that.' 'On the Classification of the races of man', *Transactions of the Ethnological Society of London*, 1 n. s. (1861), 354–78, the quotation is at 357. Others were more enthusiastic about the 'mongrel' nature of the English; the *London Review*, for example, argued 'We Englishmen may be proud of the results to which a mongrel breed and a hybrid race have led us.' *London Review*, 16 February 1861.

120. R. G. Latham, *The Ethnology of the British Islands* (London, 1852), 259.

121. Ibid., 260.

122. Martin Maw, *Visions of India. Fulfilment Theology, the Aryan Race Theory, and the Work of British Protestant Missionaries in Victorian India* (Frankfurt, 1990), 23–4.

123. See Ronald W. Neufeldt, *F. Max Muller and the Rig-Veda: a Study of Its Rôle in His Work and Thought* (Calcutta, 1980).

124. F. Max Müller, *Physical Religion. The Gifford Lectures delivered before the University of Glasgow in 1890* (London, 1898), 17–18.

125. Friedrich Max Müller, 'On the relation of the Bengali to the Arian and aboriginal languages of India', *Report of the British Association for the Advancement of Science* (1847), 319–50; Kidd, *British Identities before Nationalism, passim.*

126. F. Max Müller, 'The last results of the Sanskrit researches in comparative philology', *Christianity and Mankind: Volume I, Outlines of the Philosophy of Universal History*, C. C. J. Bunsen ed. (London, 1854), 129–30.

127. Max Müller, *Physical Religion*, 19.

128. On these terms see Joan Leopold, 'British applications of the Aryan theory of race to India, 1850–1870', *English Historical Review*, 352 (1972), 578–9.

129. Cited in Nirad K. Chaudhuri, *Scholar Extraordinary. The Life of Professor the Rt. Hon. Friedrich Max Müller P.C.* (London, 1974), 317–18.

130. Joan Leopold, 'The Aryan theory of race', *The Indian Social and Economic History Review*, 7 (1970), 271.

131. John Crawfurd, 'On the Aryan or Indo-Germanic theory', *Transactions of the Ethnological Society of London*, 1 n. s. (1861), 268–86; 'On the classification of the races of man', *Transactions of the Ethnological Society of London*, 1 n.s. (1861), 355–87; 'Language as a test of the races of man', *Transactions of the Ethnological Society of London*, 3 n. s. (1865), 2.

132. G. Cowell, *Life and Letters of E. B. Cowell* (London, 1904), 139.

133. W. H. Russell, *My Indian Mutiny Diary*, M. Edwardes ed. (London, 1957), 86. For other views over the use of 'nigger' in the Indian context see 'Mr Laing and the Niggers', *The Indian Empire*, 4 (June 1862), 627–8; Anon., 'Morals in the Punjab', *The Bombay Miscellany*, 4 (August 1862), 449.

134. J. W. Kaye, *History of the Sepoy War in India*, 3 vols (London, 1864–76), III, 365.

135. Even Sir William Jones resented his economic dependence on Indian moneylenders and merchants. C.A. Bayly, *Imperial Meridian. The British Empire and the World 1780–1830* (London, 1989), 148.

136. Brian Stanley, 'Christian Responses to the Indian Mutiny of 1857', *Studies in Church History. Volume 20: The Church and War*, W. T. Sheil ed. (London, 1980), 277–89.

137. Thomas Metcalf, *Ideologies of the Raj* (Cambridge, 1995), 45.

138. Ibid., 47–8.

139. Nancy Paxton, 'Mobilizing chivalry: rape in British novels about the Indian Uprising of 1857', *Victorian Studies*, 36 (1992), 5–30; Jenny Sharpe, 'The unspeakable limits of rape: colonial violence and counter-insurgency', *Genders*, 10 (1991), 32.

140. Ashis Nandy, *The Intimate Enemy: Loss and Recovery of Self Under Colonialism* (Delhi, 1988), 37–8, 69–70.

141. John Muir, *Original Sanskrit Texts on the origin and progress of the religions and institutions of India*, 1st edn, 3 vols (London, 1858–61 [vol. II – 1860]), II, 265–6. The tables run from 233–62.

142. Ibid., II, 212.

143. Ibid., II, 282.

144. 'The scorching rays of the Indian sun, the high temperature of an Indian climate, and the peculiar diet afforded by an Indian soil, acting on the Indo-Arians during the long period of 3,000 years or more since they first settled in Hindusthan, appear amply sufficient to account for the various

peculiarities of complexion, of feature, and of corporeal structure which now distinguish that section of the Indo-European family from the kindred branches to the west.' Ibid., II, 283.

145. Trautmann, *Aryans and British India*, 190–1.

146. John Crawfurd, 'On the Aryan or Indo-Germanic theory', *Journal of the Ethnological Society of London*, I n.s. (1861), 285.

147. John Muir, *Original Sanskrit Texts on the origin and history of the people of India, their religion and institutions*, 3rd edn, 3 vols (London, 1874), II, 279–86, quotation is at 286.

148. Muir, *Original Sanskrit Texts*, 1st edn, I, 1.

149. On Ballantyne and Banaras see C. A. Bayly, 'Orientalists, informants and critics in Banaras, 1790–1860', typescript in author's possession.

150. *The Times of India*, 24 May 1862.

151. Samuel Laing, *Lecture on the Indo-European Languages and Races* (Calcutta, 1862), 17. Laing was himself a follower of Zarathustra – see his *A Modern Zoroastrian* (London, 1887).

152. Laing, *Lecture*, 13–14, 22–3. For a defence of African intellectual capabilities provoked by Laing's comments see *The Englishman*, 19 May 1862.

153. Henry Sumner Maine, *The Effects of Observation of India on Modern European Thought* (London, 1875), 253.

154. Mathew H. Edney, *Mapping an Empire: the Geographical Construction of British India, 1765–1843* (Chicago, 1997).

155. Zénaïde A. Ragozin, *Vedic India as Embodied Principally in the Rig-Veda* (London, 1895), 103. Emphasis added.

156. Stephen P. Cohen, *The Indian Army: Its Contribution to the Development of a Nation* (Berkeley, CA, 1971), 45–9; David Omissi, *The Sepoy and the Raj: the Indian Army, 1860–1940* (London, 1994).

157. Lionel Caplan, *Warrior Gentlemen: 'Gurkhas' in the Western Imagination* (London, 1995).

158. Robert Caldwell, *A Comparative Grammar of the Dravidian or South-Indian Family of Languages* (London, 1874 [1856]), 67. For his reservations about the use of these linguistic groups as racial categories see 107–11.

159. B. H. Hodgson, *Preeminence of the Vernaculars* (Serampore, 1839), 26.

160. B. H. Hodgson, 'Ethnography and geography of the Sub-Himalayas', *Journal of the Asiatic Society of Bengal*, 16 (1847), 544–9; 'The aborigines of Central India', ibid., 550–8; 'Aborigines of Southern India', ibid., 18 (1849), 350–9.

161. Hodgson's theory, however, was degenerationist, as he argued that Turanian aborigines were in fact civilized initially, but their culture declined because of the Aryan invasion.

162. For example, H. S. Maine, *Dissertations on Early Law and Customs* (London, 1883), 233; Maine, *Village-communities in the East and West: Six lectures delivered at Oxford* (London, 1871), 233; J. W. Jackson, *Ethnology and phrenology, as an aid to the historian* (London, 1863), 105–6, 118.

163. For example, George Campbell, *Memoirs of My Indian Career*, C. E. Bernard ed. 2 vols (London, 1883), I, 194–5.

164. Anthony King, *Colonial Urban Development* (London, 1976), chs 5 and 8.

165. James Fergusson, *History of Indian and Eastern Architecture*, 1st edn (London, 1876), 34, 91. Also see H. H. Cole, *Catalogue of the Objects of Indian Art Exhibited in the Kensington Museum* (London, 1874), 10.

166. Fergusson, *History*, 406–8.

167. James Fergusson, *On the Study of Indian Architecture* (London, 1867), 10.
168. Fergusson, *History*, 37–41.
169. Ibid., 345–55, 362, 365.
170. Joan Leopold, 'British applications of the Aryan theory of race to India, 1850–1870', *English Historical Review*, CCCLII (July 1974), 585.
171. On Maine's debt to comparative philology see J. W. Burrow, *Evolution and Society. A Study in Victorian Social Theory* (Cambridge, 1966), 148–53.
172. Maine, *Observation of India*, 30.
173. Ibid., 2.
174. Clive Dewey, 'The Influence of Sir Henry Maine on agrarian policy in India', *The Victorian Achievement of Sir Henry Maine*, Alan Diamond ed. (Cambridge, 1991), 359–362 and Gordon Johnson, 'India and Henry Maine', ibid., 384–5.
175. While Trautmann explores north/south, Aryan/Dravidian oppositions and has revealed a deep-seated rivalry between southern Indologists based in Madras and those based in Calcutta, his study overlooks important regional variations within discourses on Aryanism in north India.
176. F. Max Müller, *Physical Religion*, 86.
177. Vincent A. Smith, 'Greco-Roman Influence on the Civilization of Ancient India', *Journal of the Asiatic Society of Bengal*, 58 (1889), 122–37.
178. H. P. Blavatsky, *The Secret Doctrine: Volume II – Anthropogenesis*, 3 vols (Adyar, 1979 [1888]), 411n.
179. Mrinalini Sinha, *Colonial Masculinity: the 'Manly Englishman' and the 'Effeminate Bengali' in the late Nineteenth Century* (Manchester, 1995).
180. J. D. Cunningham, *History of the Sikhs* (London, 1849), ch. 1.
181. Ibid., 17, 19, 23.
182. Archaeology Survey of India, *Reports*, 23 vols (Shimla, 1871–88), I, 70.
183. R. C. Temple, 'A survey of the incidents in modern Indian folk-tales', *Tales of the Punjab Told by the People*, Flora Annie Steel comp. and trans. (Lahore, 1894), 358–9.
184. Denzil Ibbetson, *Panjab Castes. Being a Reprint of the chapter on 'The Races, Castes and Tribes of the People' in the Report on the Census of the Panjab published in 1883* (Lahore, 1916), 3.
185. W. W. Hunter saw the racial ethnography of Bengal as the product of a huge race war between the Aryan invaders and the 'rude' Aboriginal tribes of the region. See W. W. Hunter, *The annals of rural Bengal; the ethnical frontier of Lower Bengal with the ancient principalities of Beerbhoom and Bishenpore* (London, 1871).
186. Denzil Ibbetson, *Panjab Castes*, 7–8.
187. Ibid., 5. The best assessment of Ibbetson's place in Indian anthropology is Susan Bayly, 'Caste and "race" in the colonial ethnography of India', *The Concept of Race in South Asia*, Peter Robb ed. (Delhi, 1997), 165–218, especially 204–14.

Chapter 2   Indocentrism on the New Zealand Frontier: Geographies of Race, Empire and Nation

1. Helen Wallis, 'Terra Australis, Australia and New Zealand. Voyages, discoveries and concepts', *Australian and New Zealand Studies*, Patricia McLaren-Turner ed. (London, 1985), 184–93.

2. Robert Clancy, *The Mapping of Terra Australis* (Macquarie Park, NSW, 1995) Maps 6.13 and 6.38–6.40, 83, 100–1.

3. *Oxford English Dictionary*, I, 569; John Callander, *Terra Australis Cognita*, 3 vols (Edinburgh, 1766–8), I, 49.

4. Douglas Sutton suggests that a 'consensus view' accepts that: 'first, the geographical settlement of New Zealand was the same as for Easter Island and Hawaii; second, this central Eastern Polynesian homeland includes the Marquesas, Societies, Southern Cooks, with Mangareva, the Australs and Pitcairn.' Douglas G. Sutton, 'Conclusion: Origins', *The Origins of the First New Zealanders*, Douglas G. Sutton ed. (Auckland, 1994), 251. The Maori, as Polynesians, are part of the Austronesian family, a broad linguistic and ethnic grouping who can be traced back to the speakers of Proto-Austronesian in southern China and Taiwan approximately 3500 BCE.

5. J. C. Beaglehole (ed.), *The Endeavour Journal of John Banks, 1768–1771*, 2 vols (Sydney, 1962), I, 35–6.

6. J. C. Beaglehole (ed.), *The Journals of Captain James Cook on His Voyages of Discovery. The Voyage of the Endeavour, 1768–1771* (Cambridge, 1955), 286–7. Cf. Beaglehole, *Journal of John Banks*, II, 35–6.

7. Cook stated that he could not 'preswaid [*sic*] my self that ever they came from America and as to a Southern Continent I do not believe any such thing exists unless in a high Latitude'. Beaglehole, *Journals of Captain Cook 1768–1771*, 286–8.

8. On Hawaiki and Maori tradition see Margaret Orbell, *Hawaiki: a New Approach to Maori Tradition* (Christchurch, 1991).

9. John Hawkesworth, *An Account of the Voyages undertaken by the Order of His Present Majesty for Making Discoveries in the Southern Hemisphere ...*, 3 vols (London, 1783), III, 474. Hawkesworth did add one phrase from Cook's vocabulary: 'What do you call this or that?' Presumably he preferred Banks's vocabulary because it distinguished between 'northern' and 'southern' Maori. Ibid., 474–5.

10. Alun David, 'Sir William Jones, Biblical Orientalism and Indian Scholarship', *Modern Asian Studies*, 30,1 (1996), 173–84.

11. Samuel Marsden, Journal, 9 November 1819, in *The Letters and Journals of Samuel Marsden 1765–1838*, J. R. Elder ed. (Dunedin, 1932), 219.

12. Ibid. See Elsmore, *Maori and Old Testament*, 63–4; Sorrenson, *Maori Origins*, 13–5.

13. Marsden , Journal, 9 November 1819, *Journals*, 219.

14. Kendall to CMS, 3 July 1820, *Marsden's Lieutenants*, J. R. Elder ed. (Dunedin, 1934), 162.

15. Elsmore, *Maori and Old Testament*, 64.

16. Cf. Elsmore's suggestion that Lee subscribed to the theory. Ibid., 63.

17. Samuel Lee, *A grammar and vocabulary of the language of New Zealand* (London, 1820), 3.

18. George Lillie Craik, *The New Zealanders* (London, 1830), 235.

19. Ibid., 202.

20. Ibid., 159.

21. R. Maunsell, *Grammar of the New Zealand Language* (Auckland, 1842), xii-xiii. Maunsell acknowledged his debt to Lee's 'theory of Hebrew tenses' which allowed him to find a 'satisfactory solution' to tense structures in Maori, ibid., xiii.

22. William Barret Marshall, *A Personal Narrative of Two Visits to New Zealand in His Majesty's Ship Alligator, A. D. 1834* (London, 1836), 68.
23. Joel Samuel Polack, *New Zealand: being a narrative of travels and adventures during a residence in that country between 1831 and 1837* (London, 1838), I, 358.
24. Ibid., I, 385
25. Alexander Marjoribanks, *Travels in New Zealand, with a map of the country* (London, 1845), 23.
26. J. D. Lang, *View of the Origin and Migrations of the Polynesian Nation* (London, 1834).
27. Cited in Howe, *Singer*, 49.
28. Franz Bopp, *Über die Verwandtschaft der malayisch-polynesischen Sprachen: mit den indisch-europäischen* (Berlin, 1841); William Marsden, 'Remarks on the Sumatran languages', *Archaelogia: or, miscellaneous tracts relating to antiquity 7* (1782), 154–8.
29. J. R. Logan, 'Ethnology of the Indo-Pacific Islands', *Journal of the Indian Archipelago and Eastern Asia*, 5 (1851), 211–43 and n.s. 3 (1859) 211–43.
30. Tony Ballantyne, 'Print, politics and Protestantism: New Zealand, 1769–1860', *Information, Communications, Power*, Hiram Morgan ed. (Dublin, 2001), 152–76.
31· Sorrenson, *Maori Origins*, 16. Michael Belgrave concurs with this assessment as he suggested that the Semitic model 'reached its most sophisticated form in the work of the Rev. Richard Taylor.' Belgrave, 'Archipelago of exiles. A study in the imperialism of ideas: Edward Tregear and John MacMillan Brown' (University of Auckland, MA thesis, 1979), 36.
32. Richard Taylor, *A Leaf from the Natural History of New Zealand* (Wellington, 1848), xviii-xix. My emphasis.
33. Richard Taylor, *Te Ika a Maui, or New Zealand and its inhabitants* (London, 1855), 184, 189–90.
34. Ibid., 184.
35. Taylor, *Te Ika a Maui*, 184. It is interesting to note in light of Sorrenson's argument that at least one contemporary reviewer felt that the central thrust of *Te Ika a Maui* was to establish this Indian link: Anon., 'Review of *Te Ika a Maui*', *Supplement to the Record*, 11 April 1856. A copy of this review is held in Taylor Papers, ATL, MS-Papers-0254:0254a-019.
36. Taylor, *Te Ika a Maui*, 185.
37. Ibid., 190, 191–2, 196.
38. Richard Taylor, *Our Race and its origin* (Auckland, 1867), 4, 7–9.
39. Ibid., 14, 24. Also see his sketch 'Taken from paintings in the Ajunta Caves 200 miles NE of Bombay.' ATL, Taylor Papers, MS-Papers-025–026.
40. Taylor, *Our Race*, 28. He cites Max Müller's *History of Ancient Sanskrit Literature*, 13.
41. Taylor clearly suggests that the Europeans reacted positively to the strength of Maori resistance. At the onset of war the Europeans tended to look with contempt upon the 'niggers', but now, because of the 'calm' and 'skill' the Maori exhibited in the war the Maori were seen as equals, as 'brave and skilful'. *Our Race*, 38–9.
42. Richard Taylor, *Te ika a Maui: or, New Zealand and its inhabitants*, 2nd edn (London, 1870), 33.
43. Ibid., 48–53, 57.

44. The standard work on Maori demographic history is Ian Pool, *Te Iwi Maori: a New Zealand Population, Past, Present &and Projected* (Auckland, 1991).

45. Edward Shortland, *A Short Sketch of the Maori Races* (Dunedin, 1865), 9–10.

46. Ibid., 8.

47. Edward Shortland, *How to Learn Maori* (Auckland, 1883), 2.

48. Edward Shortland, *Maori Religion and Mythology* (London, 1882), 2.

49. Ibid., 3.

50. Sorrenson, *Maori Origins*, 19; James Belich, 'Myth, race and identity in New Zealand', *New Zealand Journal of History*, 31 (1997). Belgrave does note the work of J.T. Thomson, but only in so far as it provided a stimulus for Tregear's work: Belgrave, 'Archipelago of Exiles', 38.

51. *New Zealand Gazette*, 9 March 1868.

52. Sir George F. Bowen 'Anniversary Address of the President, His Excellency Sir George F. Bowen', *Transactions and Proceedings of the New Zealand Institute*, 3 (1870), 6; Richard Drayton, 'A l'école des Français: les sciences et le deuxième empire britannique (1783–1830)', *Revue Française d'Histoire D'Outre-Mer*, 86 (1999), 91–118.

53. Bowen, 'Anniversary Address', 6.

54. C. J. Abraham, 'On the Celtic origin of the English vowel sounds', *TPNZI*, 1 (1868), 125.

55. Ibid., 127

56. George W. Stocking Jr, *Victorian Anthropology* (New York, 1987), xii–xiii.

57. About 75 per cent of these were Irish Catholic, composing 13.9 per cent of the total population. Donald Harman Akenson, *The Irish Diaspora: A Primer* (Toronto, 1996), 67–9.

58. Rory Sweetman, '"The importance of being Irish": Hibernianism in New Zealand, 1869–1969', *A Distant Shore: Irish Migration and New Zealand Settlement*, Lyndon Fraser ed. (Dunedin, 2000), 135–9.

59. Charles Fraser, 'On university education, as adapted to the circumstances and prospects of the Colony of New Zealand', *TPNZI*, 1, (1868), 194.

60. On 'Munshi Abdullah' and the cosmopolitan world of the Straits see Anthony Milner, *The Invention of Politics in Colonial Malaya: Contesting Nationalism and the Expansion of the Public Sphere* (Cambridge, 1995), 10–30; J. T. Thomson, *Translations from the Hakayit Abdullah* (London, 1874); J. T. Thomson papers, HL, AG-726.

61. John Turnbull Thomson, 'On Barata Numerals', *TPNZI*, 5 (1872), 131.

62. Ibid., 135–8.

63. Thomson, 'Barat or Barata fossil words', *TPNZI*, 11 (1878), 158.

64. Ibid., 160.

65. On the language and politics of race in colonial science see John Stenhouse, '"A disappearing race before we came here": Doctor Alfred Kingcombe Newman, the dying Maori and Victorian scientific racism', *NZJH* (1996), 124–140. For Thomson's concerns with the conduct of colonial science see J. T. Thomson, *An Outline of the Principles and Details connected with the Colonial Survey of the Province of Otago* (Dunedin, 1861) and *An Exposition of Processes and Results of the Survey System of Otago* (Dunedin, 1875).

66. J. T. Thomson, 'Original Exploration in the Scottish Settlement of Otago, and Recent Travel in Other Parts of N. Z.', *Royal Scottish Society of Arts*, 10 (1878), 96.

67. Ibid., 96, 114.

68. For a recent reassessment of the Scottish Enlightenment's impact in New Zealand see Erik Olssen, 'Mr Wakefield and New Zealand as an experiment in post-Enlightenment experimental practice', *New Zealand Journal of History*, 31 (1997), 197–218.

69. Thomson, 'Original Exploration', 101.

70. He also suggested that the English too would exhibit the Malay's 'self-indulgent patriarchal tendencies' if placed in a tropical environment. John Turnbull Thomson, *Some Glimpses into Life in the Far East* (London, 1864), 60, 253–4.

71. John Turnbull Thomson, *Rambles with a Philosopher or, Views at the Antipodes by an Otagoian* (Dunedin, 1867), 86–7.

72. He pursued this project by overlaying Maori place names with a new layer of names drawn from the borderlands. See W. H. Roberts, *Place Names and the Early History of Otago and Southland* (Invercargill, 1913).

73. R. C. Barstow, 'Stray thoughts on Mahori or Maori migrations', *TPNZI*, 9 (1876), 242; J. D. Lang, *A View of the Origin and Migrations of the Polynesian Nation; demonstrating their ancient discovery and progressive settlement of the Continent of America* (London, 1834).

74. W. H. Blyth, 'On "the Whence of the Maori"', *TPNZI*, 9 (1886), 544.

75. Ibid., 516. Cf. Thomson, 'Barat or Barata fossil words', 165.

76. Edward Tregear, *The Aryan Maori* (Wellington, 1885), 1–2, 5–6.

77. Howe, *Singer in a Songless Land*, 58–9, 209–10 n. 22; Sorrenson, *Origins*, 22; Belgrave, 'Archipelago of Exiles', 46–7.

78. Howe, *Singer in a Songless Land*, 58–9, 209–10 n. 22.

79. Tregear, *Aryan Maori*, 1.

80. A. S. Atkinson, 'The Aryo-Semitic Maori', *TPNZI*, 9 (1886), 552–76.

81. See, for example, his discussion of sound shifts and philological methodology in 'The Track of a Word', *TPNZI*, 9 (1886), 482–3, 486.

82. *New Zealand Herald*, 19 September 1885.

83. This review, which is undated and has no publication details, is pasted inside the front cover of Hocken Library's copy of the 1885 edition of *The Aryan Maori*.

84. For a summary of the reviews see *New Zealand Mail*, 19 March 1886.

85. Abraham Fornander, *An Account of the Polynesian Race, Its Origin and Migrations, and the Ancient History of the Hawaiian People to the Times of Kamehameha I*, 3 vols (London, 1878–85). See K. R. Howe, 'Some origins and migrations of ideas leading to the Aryan Polynesian theories of Abraham Fornander and Edward Tregear', *Pacific Studies*, 11 (1988), 67–81.

86. Howe, *Singer*, 56. Tregear to John White, 8 October 1885, ATL, John White collection, MS-Papers-0075–076.

87. Among these works are: 'A Flitting Ghost', *The Westminster Review* (1887), 404–413; 'The Thunder Axe', *Nature*, 38 (1888), 565; 'The Maori and the Moa', *Journal of the Anthropological Institute*, 17 (1888), 292–304; 'The Maoris of New Zealand', *Journal of the Anthropological Institute*, 19 (1890), 97–123; 'Compulsory Immigration', *Westminster Review* (1888), 382.

88. Howe, *Singer*, 64–5.

89. James Belich, 'Myth, race and identity in New Zealand', *NZJH*, 31 (1997), 18. Sinclair argued that 'it was widely believed that Maori were a "branch of the Caucasian race"'. Keith Sinclair, *A Destiny Apart: New Zealand's Search for*

National Identity (Wellington, 1986), 198. Sorrenson seems confused in his use of terminology: he identifies the dominant 'idea of an Indian or Caucasian origin': Sorrenson, *Maori Origins*, 33. Not only does this conflate two distinct geographic/cultural regions (and Sorrenson does not discuss any theorist who argued that Maori were Caucasian), but it also neglects the debates over whether Maori descended from Indian Aryans, Dravidians or tribal peoples.

90. Tregear, *Aryan Maori*, 103.

91. Raymond Schwab, *Oriental Renaissance: Europe's Rediscovery of India and the East, 1680–1880*, Gene Patterson-Black and Victor Reinking trans (New York, 1984). Cf. Tony Ballantyne, 'The "Oriental Renaissance" in the Pacific: Orientalism, language and ethnogenesis in the British Pacific', *Migracijske Teme: A Journal for Migration and Ethnic Studies*, 15 (1999), 423–50.

92. Tregear was a regular contributor to the leading free-thought journal *The Monthly Review* and its earlier and more openly theosophical incarnation *Hestia*. These journals are discussed in Robert S. Ellwood, *Islands of the Dawn. The Story of Alternative Spirituality in New Zealand* (Honolulu, 1993), 99–101.

93. F. D. Fenton, *Suggestions for a History of the Origin and Migration of the Maori People* (Auckland, 1885). 60, 87–8.

94. Gerald Massey, *The Natural Genesis*, 2 vols (London, 1883), I, 9.

95. Gerald Massey, *A Book of the Beginnings*, 2 vols (London, 1881), I, 26. Anne McLintock has recently analysed some of the relationships between gender, sexuality and colonial geography articulated in passages such as this: *Imperial Leather. Race, Gender and Sexuality in the Colonial Contest* (New York, 1995), 1–3, 21–30.

96. Massey, *A Book of Beginnings*, II, 597.

97. Ibid., II, 537, 596–7.

98. For biographical information see Peal's obituary in *The Calcutta Englishman*, 12 August 1897; for Smith's views on Peal's contribution to New Zealand ethnography see his draft obituary PSC, MS-Papers-1187–226.

99. Peal to Smith, 1892 [marked received 16 April], PSC, MS-Papers-1187–270.

100. S. E. Peal, 'The Ancestors of the Maori', *JPS*, 6: 24 (December 1897), 174–6.

101. Peal to Smith, recd. 16 April 1892, PSC, MS-Papers-1187–270.

102. Peal to Smith, 15 October 1894, ibid.

103. Peal to Smith, 17 January 1892 and 25 January 1893, ibid.

104. See J. Smith to MacDonald, undated, PSC, Polynesian Society Outward Letters 1894–1907, 80–115–02/18.

105. Percy S. Smith, *Hawaiki, the Original Home of the Maori* (Wellington, 1898), with subsequent editions in 1904, 1910 and 1921; 'Aryan and Polynesian points of contact: the story of Te Niniko', *JPS*, 19 (1910); 'The fatherland of the Polynesians: Aryan and Polynesian points of contact', *JPS*, 28 (1919).

106. Peter Buck [Te Rangi Hiroa], *Vikings of the Sunrise* (New York, 1938), 35.

107. Raymond Firth, *Primitive Economics of the New Zealand Maori* (Wellington, 1929). Also see his 'Economic psychology of the Maori', *Journal of the Royal Anthropological Institute of Great Britain and Ireland*, 55, (1925), 340–62.

108. The 'Tartar' or 'Mongol' origins of the Chinese were emphasized as an important marker of difference, for example *Dunedin Punch*, 23 December 1865.

109. *NZPD*, 95 (1896), 247–8.

110. Ibid., 94 (1896), 426.
111. Ibid., 94 (1896), 254.
112. Radhika Viyas Mongia, 'Race, nationality, mobility: a history of the passport', *Public Culture*, 11 (1999), 527–55.
113. William Pember Reeves, *State experiments in Australia and New Zealand*, 2 vols (London, 1902), II, 329.
114. *Franklin Times*, 18 December 1925.

Chapter 3   Systematizing Religion: from Tahiti to the Tat Khalsa

1. S. N. Balagangadhara, *'The Heathen in his Blindness': Asia, the West, and the Dynamic of Religion* (Leiden, 1994).
2. Jonathon Z. Smith, *Imagining Religion: from Babylon to Jonestown* (Chicago, 1982), xi; Michel de Certeau, *The Practice of Everyday Life*, S. Rendall trans. (Berkeley, CA, 1984), 50.
3. Talal Asad, *Genealogies of Religion: Discipline and Reasons of Power in Christianity and Islam* (Baltimore, MD, 1993), 28–9.
4. Balagangadhara, *'The Heathen in his Blindness'*, 241–2.
5. Peter Harrison, *'Religion' and the Religions in the English Enlightenment* (Cambridge, 1990), 20–5.
6. Smith, *Imagining Religion*, 49; Richard King, *Orientalism and Religion: Postcolonial Theory, India and the 'Mystic East'* (London, 1999), 10–11.
7. For example, R. Po-Chia Hsia, *Social Discipline in the Reformation: Central Europe, 1550–1750* (London, 1989).
8. Keith Thomas, *Religion and the Decline of Magic* (New York, 1971), 25–77,
9. This phrase is borrowed from Mary Louise Pratt, *Imperial Eyes: Travel Writing and Transculturation* (London, 1992).
10. David Chidester, *Savage Systems: Colonialism and Comparative Religion in Southern Africa* (Charlottesville, VA, 1996), 12.
11. Bernard Smith, *European Vision and the South Pacific, 1768–1850: a Study in the History of Art and Ideas* (Oxford, 1960) and *Imagining the Pacific: in the Wake of the Cook Voyages* (London, 1992).
12. Cited in Michael Ross, *Bougainville* (London, 1978), 118.
13. Joseph Banks, *The Endeavour Journal of Joseph Banks 1768–1771*, J. C. Beaglehole ed., 2 vols (Sydney, 1962), II, 29.
14. O. H. K. Spate, *Paradise Found and Lost* (Rushcutters Bay, NSW, 1988), 246; G. Chinard, 'Introduction', to Denis Diderot, *Supplément au Voyage de Bougainville* (Paris, 1955), 72–8.
15. J. R. Forster, *Observations Made During a Voyage Round the World* (London, 1778), 318–32.
16. See, for example, Cook's account of an *ahu*: Beaglehole, *Journals of Captain Cook 1768–1771*, I, 113.
17. For a full discussion of Uawa and Te Aitanga-a-Hauiti at the time of Cook's visit see Salmond, *Two Worlds*, 156–9, 169–84.
18. Banks, Journal, 25 October 1769, *Endeavour Journal of Joseph Banks*, I, 420.
19. Cook, *Captain James Cook: Vol. I, The Voyage of the Endeavour 1768–1771*, 538–9.

20. Salmond, *Two Worlds*, 265.
21. For example, Banks, Journal, 5 December 1769 and 5 February 1770, *Endeavour Journal of Joseph Banks*, I, 446–7, 462–3. Tupaia also told Banks that he should not trust Maori as they were 'given to lying', Banks, Journal, 5 February 1770, ibid., 462.
22. John Hawkesworth (ed.) *An account of the voyages undertaken by the order of His Present Majesty for making discoveries in the Southern Hemisphere*, 3 vols (London, 1773), III, 472.
23. Ibid., III, 472–3.
24. *GBPP*, 1837–8 (680) XXI, 46.
25. Kendall to Thomas Hassall, 9 April 1823, MS 71/49, HL; Kendall to Josiah Pratt, 11 April 1823, MS 71/51, HL.
26. *MR* (1819), 466.
27. *MR* (1820), 308.
28. Jane Samson, *Imperial Benevolence: Making British Authority in the Pacific Islands* (Honululu, HI, 1998), 24–43.
29. For a contemporary criticism of this policy see J. S. Polack, *Manners and Customs of New Zealand*, 2 vols (London, 1838), I, 147.
30. William Colenso, 'On the Maori Races of New Zealand', *TPNZI*, 1 (1868), appendix, 43.
31. William Williams, *Christianity Among the New Zealanders* (London, 1867), 18.
32. James W. Stack to W. M. S., 29 March 1826, ATL, micro coll. 3/reel 18.
33. Rt Revd Jean Baptiste François Pompallier, *Early History of the Catholic Church in Oceania* (Auckland, 1888), 36.
34. Augustus Earle, *Narrative of a Residence in New Zealand. Journal of a Residence in Tristan da Cunha*, E. H. McCormick ed. (Oxford, 1966), 126.
35. Elsdon Best, *Some Aspects of Maori Myth and Religion* (Wellington, 1922), 9.
36. Owen Chadwick, *The Victorian Church. Part One* (London, 1966), 441.
37. Richard Davis to CMS, HL, 29 April 1829, MS 66 item 23; Davis to CMS, 14 October 1827, HL, MS 66 item 14.
38. Samuel Marsden, Journal, 11 March 1830, *The Letters and Journals of Samuel Marsden 1765–1838*, J. R. Elder ed. (Dunedin, 1932), 462.
39. Williams, *Christianity Among the New Zealanders*, 20, 36.
40. P. J. Marshall and Glyndwr Williams, *The Great Map of Mankind. British Perceptions of the World in the Age of Enlightenment* (London, 1982), 98.
41. Cited in P. J. Marshall (ed.) *The British Discovery of Hinduism in the Eighteenth Century* (Cambridge, 1970), 24.
42. Joseph Priestly, *A Comparison of the Institutes of Moses with those of the Hindoos and other Ancient Nations* (Northumberland, 1799), 33.
43. Marshall, *British Discovery*, 109, 185.
44. Rosane Rocher, 'British Orientalism in the eighteenth century: the dialectics of knowledge and government', *Orientalism and the Postcolonial Predicament. Perspectives on South Asia*, Carol Breckenridge and Peter van der Veer, eds (Philadelphia, 1993), 230; C. J. Fuller, *The Camphor Flame: Popular Hinduism and Society in India* (Princeton, NJ, 1992).
45. Luke Scrafton, *Reflections on the government, & c., of Indostan: and a short sketch of the History of Bengal, from the year 1739 to 1756* (Edinburgh, 1761), 5.
46. Wilkins carried on to call Brahma 'the Almighty' and described Brahmans as 'Unitarians'! Charles Wilkins, 'The Translator's Preface', from the Bhagavat-Geeta', *European Discovery of Hinduism*, Marshall ed., 193–4.

47. Monier Monier-Williams, *Indian Wisdom or Examples of the Religious, Philosophical, and Ethical Doctrines of the Hindus* (London, 1875), xxvi.
48. Monier-Williams, *Hinduism* (London, 1877), 11–13, 134, 151.
49. Charles Grant, 'Observations on the State of Society among the *Asiatic* Subjects of *Great Britain'*, Appendix to *Report from the Select Committee on the Affairs of the East India Company with Minutes of Evidence Volume I*, *GBPP*, 1831– (734) VIII.
50. Walter L. Arnstein, *Protestant versus Catholic in Mid-Victorian England* (Columbia, MO, 1982), 214.
51. For example, Ingram Cobbin, 'Essay on Popery', *Foxe's Book of Martyrs*, William Bramley-Moore ed. (revd edn, London, 1875), xi.
52. Allan K. Davidson, *Evangelicals and Attitudes to India 1786–1813. Missionary Publicity and Claudius Buchanan* (n.p., 1990), 47.
53. J. Long, *Handbook of Bengal Missions in Connection with the Church of England* (London, 1848), 93–4.
54. Grant, 'Observations on the State of Society among the *Asiatic* Subjects of *Great Britain'*, 59–60.
55. James Mill, *The History of British India. Fifth edition with notes and continuation by Horace Hayman Wilson*, 10 vols (London, 1858), I, 229, 267, 277.
56. H. H. Wilson, *Two Lectures on the Religious Practices and Opinions of the Hindus; delivered before the University of Oxford on the 27th and 28th February, 1840* (Oxford, 1840), 4, 26, 37. Also see H. H. Wilson, *Sketch of the Religious Sects of the Hindus* (Calcutta, 1846), 5.
57. Wilson, *Two Lectures*, 35.
58. Wilson, *Sketch*, 5.
59. Sir Alfred C. Lyall, *Asiatic Studies Religious and Social* (London, 1882), 288.
60. Ibid., 1–2, 288–9.
61. Sir Alfred Lyall, *Natural Religion in India. The Rede Lecture Delivered in the Senate House on June 17, 1891* (Cambridge, 1891), 12, 10.
62. Lyall, *Asiatic Studies*, 287–8.
63. Lyall, *Natural Religion*, 10, 12, 39.
64. Thomas Metcalf, *Ideologies of the Raj* (Cambridge, 1995), 137.
65. See, for example, the introduction and notes to Ganda Singh, *Early European Accounts of the Sikhs* (Calcutta, 1962).
66. Buddh Singh Arora collaborated with Lala Ajaib Singh Suraj of Malerkotla to produce his Persian history *Rizalah dar Ahwal-i-Nanak Shah Darvesh* – see British Library Add. MSS 26273.
67. Singh, *Early European Accounts of the Sikhs*, 13–14.
68. Charles Wilkins, 'Observations and Inquiries concerning the Seeks and their College, at Patna', *AR*, 1 (1788), 292.
69. Monier-Williams, *Hinduism*, 142n; Monier Monier-Williams, *Brahmanism and Hinduism or Religious Thought and life in India based on the Veda and other sacred books of the Hindus*, 3rd edn (London, 1887), 161.
70. Ibid., 177–8.
71. J. D. Cunningham, *A History of the Sikhs* (London, 1849).
72. R. N. Cust, *Essay on the Common Features, which appear in all forms of religious belief* (London, 1895), 13.
73. Ibid., 20. CMS missionaries in New Zealand also insisted that salvation was open to all humanity. See, for example, John King, Journal, 26 March

1823 and 13 April 1823, HL, MS 73 item 12; and James Kemp, Journal, 18 May 1823 and 31 December 1824, HL, MS 70 item 16.

74. Cust, *Essay*, 312.

75. R. N. Cust, *Pictures of Indian Life Sketched with the Pen from 1852 to 1881* (London, 1881), 313.

76. R. N. Cust, *The Life of Baba Nanuk, the founder of the Sikh sect of the Hindu Religion in the Punjab. For the use of schools* (Lahore, 1859), 7.

77. Ibid. Cf. his later interpretation in R. N. Cust, *Orientation of Early Christian Missionaries in Asia and Africa* (London, 1891), 262–3.

78. On the *janam-sakhi*s see W. H. McLeod, *Guru Nanak and the Sikh Religion* (Oxford, 1968) and *Early Sikh Tradition* (Oxford, 1980).

79. Cust, *Baba Nanak*, 20.

80. Ibid., 21. Cust was a prime mover behind the decision that the government of India should sponsor the translation of the *Adi Granth*. R. N. Cust, *Orientation of Early Christian Missionaries*, 262, 265.

81. Ibid., 264–5, 327.

82. Lepel Henry Griffin, *Ranjit Singh* (Delhi, 1957 [1892]), 28.

83. Lepel Henry Griffin, *The Rajas of the Punjab. Being the history of the principal states of the Punjab and their political relations with the British Government* (Lahore, 1870), 2.

84. *C.M.S. Intelligencer*, 2: 7 (July 1851), 148, 156.

85. N. G. Barrier, 'Trumpp and Macauliffe: western students of Sikh history and religion', *Historians and Historiography of the Sikhs*, Ganda Singh ed. (New Delhi, 1978), 166–85.

86. Ernest Trumpp, *The Adi Granth, or the Holy Scriptures of the Sikhs, translated from the original Gurmukhi, with introductory essays* (London, 1887), v–vi.

87. Ibid., vii–vii.

88. Barrier, 'Trumpp and Macauliffe', 169.

89. Trumpp, *Adi Granth*, vii.

90. For Trumpp's demands for extra fees and the growing hostility towards Trumpp among the Punjab government see: Lepel H. Griffin to Secretary to Government of India, *Punjab Home Proceedings*, October 1871, A/4, and C. U. Aitchison, Secretary to Government of India to Punjab Government, *Punjab Home Proceedings*, April 1872, A/15.

91. Trumpp, *Adi Granth*, vii, cxii.

92. Trumpp provides examples of these 'prayers'. Ibid., cxii n. 4–n. 5.

93. Ibid., cxvi.

94. Lepel H. Griffin, Officiating Secretary, Punjab Government to Secretary to the Government of India, *Punjab Home Proceedings*, April 1872, A/15.

95. Trumpp, *Adi Granth*, vii–viii.

96. Barrier, 'Trumpp and Macauliffe', 171.

97. M. A. Macauliffe, 'The Fair at Sakhi Sarvar', *Calcutta Review*, LX (1875), 78–101.

98. Max Arthur Macauliffe, *The Sikh Religion. Its Gurus, sacred writings and authors*, 6 vols (Oxford, 1909), I, xxxix.

99. M. A. Macauliffe, *How the Sikhs became a Militant People* (Paris: 1905), selection reprinted in *Panjab Past and Present*, 26 (October 1982), 504.

100. Macauliffe, *The Sikh Religion*, I, v.

101. Ibid., I, vi–vii.

102. Ibid., I, vii.
103. Ibid., I, ix.
104. Eugene F. Irschick, *Dialogue and History: Constructing South India, 1795–1895* (Berkeley, CA, 1994).
105. See the letter they addressed to Macauliffe printed in Macauliffe, *The Sikh Religion*, I, xii.
106. Ibid., I, xxix.
107. Undated excerpt from *The Khalsa*, Macauliffe, *The Sikh Religion*, xi.
108. Richard Fox, *Lions of the Punjab: Culture in the Making* (Berkeley, CA, 1985), 140–1.
109. Harjot Oberoi, *The Construction of Religious Boundaries: Culture, Identity and Diversity in the Sikh Tradition* (Delhi, 1994), 372–3.
110. G. T. Vigne, *Travels in Kashmir, Ladak, Iskardo, the countries adjoining the mountain-course of the Indus, and the Himalaya, north of the Panjab* (London, 1842), 54.
111. W. T. Osborne, *The Camp and Court of Ranjit Sing* (London, 1840), 69, 64, 62.
112. See, for example, the summation of the military characteristics of the Sikhs in J. Craufurd, 'India, as connected with a Native Army', *The Journal of the United Service Institution*, 2 (1859), 185.
113. George St P. Lawrence, 'The Sikh and European Soldiers of Our Native Forces', *Journal of the United Service Institution*, 11 (1868), 89.
114. Report of the Eden Commission, 15 November 1879, OIOL, Military Department Papers: Military Collections, L/MIL/7/5445.
115. MacMunn, *The Armies of India*, 139–40. On the 'Sikh look' see Simeran Man Singh Gell, 'The origins of the Sikh "look": from Guru Gobind to Dalip Singh', *History and Anthropology*, 10 (1996), 37–83.
116. On the British as arbiters of tradition see Nicholas Dirks, 'The policing of tradition: colonialism and anthropology in Southern India', *Comparative Studies in Society and History*, 39 (1997), 182–212.
117. R. W. Falcon, *Handbook on Sikhs for the use of Regimental Officers* (Allahabad, 1896), 61–2.
118. Ibid., 15, 71–3, 98–102.
119. Vincent Eyre, *The Sikh and European Soldiers of Our Indian Forces. A Lecture* (London, 1867), 7–8.
120. For example, A. A. Roberts to R. Montgomery, 20 March 1858, *Mutiny Records. Reports in Two Parts*, 2 vols (Lahore, 1911) I, 234; Colonel H. St G. M. McRae, *Regimental History of the 45th Rattray's Sikhs. Volume I, 1856–1914* (London, 1933), 19.
121. On Jats and the composition of the *Panth* see W. H. McLeod, *Who is a Sikh? The Problem of Sikh Identity* (Oxford, 1989), 40–1.
122. Oberoi, *Construction*, 362–3.
123. Rajiv A. Kapur, *Sikh Separatism. The Politics of Faith* (London, 1986), 64.
124. Falcon, *Handbook*, 21.
125. H. M. Clark, 'The Decay of Sikhism', *Panjab Notes and Queries*, 3 (1885), 20.
126. Macauliffe, *Sikh Religion*, I, lvii. In a similar vein David Petrie praised the colonial state for 'buttressing the crumbling edifice of the Sikh religion' but warned that the maintenance of a separate Sikh identity was an ongoing project. David Petrie, *Recent Developments in Sikh Politics, 1900–1911, a Report* (Amritsar, 1911), 52.

127. Oberoi, *Construction, passim.*
128. K. S. Talwar, 'The Anand Marriage Act', *The Panjab Past and Present*, 2 (1968), 400–10.
129. Undated excerpt from *The Khalsa*, Macauliffe, *The Sikh Religion*, xi.
130. It seems these parallels have been accepted by some Sikhs. When I visited the Golden Temple in October 1996 the Assistant Information Officer observed that Nanak lived at the same time as Luther and he too tried to create a 'pure' religion.

Chapter 4   'Hello Ganesha!': Indocentrism and the Interpretation of Maori Religion

1. David Chidester, *Savage Systems: Colonialism and Comparative Religion in Southern Africa* (Charlottesville, VA, 1996); L. R. Hiatt, *Arguments about Aborigines* (Cambridge, 1996).
2. George Grey, *Journals of Two Expeditions of Discovery in North-west and Western Australia, during the years 1837, 38, and 39, under the authority of Her Majesty's Government* (London, 1841); *A Vocabulary of the Dialects of south-western Australia* (London, 1840). For Grey's impact see Hiatt, *Arguments about Aborigines*, 18–20, 84–6, 96, 115.
3. Sir George Grey, *Polynesian Mythology, and Ancient Traditional History of the New Zealand Race, as Furnished by their Priests and Chiefs* (London, 1855), iii–iv, vii.
4. Jenifer Curnow, 'Wiremu Maihi Te Rangikaheke: his life and work', *JPS*, 94 (1985), 97–147.
5. See Giselle M. Byrnes, '"The Imperfect Authority of the Eye": Shortland's southern journey and the calligraphy of colonization', *History and Anthropology*, 8 (1994), 207–235.
6. John White, *The ancient history of the Maori, his mythology and traditions*, 6 vols (Wellington, 1887–90); M. P. J. Reilly, 'John White: an examination of his use of Maori oral tradition and the role of authenticity' (MA thesis, Victoria University of Wellington, 1985), 375–80.
7. Tony Ballantyne, 'The mission station as "The Enchanter's Wand": Protestant missionaries, Maori and the notion of the household', *Archaeological Review from Cambridge*, 13 (1994), 100–1.
8. For example, Bill Dacker, *Te Mamae me te Aroha: The Pain and the Love. A History of Kai Tahu Whanui in Otago, 1844–1994* (Dunedin, 1994), 31–3.
9. John White, 'Journal written at Mata', 14, 19 June, 1 July, 17 September 1847, qMS 2201, ATL.
10. Michael Reilly, 'John White. Part II: Seeking the exclusive Mohio: White and his Maori informants', *NZJH*, 24 (1990), 55.
11. Cited in Samuel Butler, *A First Year in the Canterbury Settlement*, A. C. Brassington and P. B. Maling eds (Auckland, 1964), 50. Also see R. Bourke to Lord Glenelg, 9 September 1837, enclosure C, J. Busby to Colonial Secretary, New South Wales, 16 June 1837, *GBPP*, 1838 (585) XXXIX, 7–8.
12. At the Treaty of Waitangi negotiations Tamati Waka Nene instructed Lieutenant Governor William Hobson to 'remain for us a father, a judge, a peacemaker ... You must preserve our customs'. T. Lindsay Buick, *The Treaty of Waitangi* (Wellington, 1914), 120.

13. John White, *Te Rou; or, the Maori at home* (London, 1874), v; Grey, *Polynesian Mythology*, x.

14. Ledger Book, John White Papers, MS-Papers-0075 ATL; Reilly, 'John White: Part II', 48.

15. Jane Simpson, 'Io as Supreme Being', *History of Religions*, 37 (August 1997), 50–85.

16. C. O. Davis, *The Life and Times of Patuone, the Celebrated Ngapuhi Chief* (Auckland, 1876), 13–14.

17. See, for example, John White, *Ancient History*, I, 32; Edward Tregear, *The Maori-Polynesian Comparative Dictionary* (Christchurch, 1891), 106; T. G. Hammond, 'Atua Maori', *JPS*, 30 (1899), 89–92.

18. Simpson, 'Io as Supreme Being', 60–81.

19. Elsdon Best, 'The cult of Io, the concept of a supreme deity as evolved by the Ancestors of the Polynesians', *Man*, 57 (1913), 98–103. The quotation is at 99.

20. Compare Simpson's article with James Irwin, *An Introduction to Maori Religion* (South Australia, 1984), 33–5; Jonathon Z. Smith, *Imagining Religion: From Babylon to Jonestown* (Chicago, 1982), 66–89; Margaret Orbell, 'Io: a high god', *The Illustrated Encyclopedia of Maori Myth and Legend* (Christchurch, 1995), 72–5.

21. Pailin, *Attitudes to Other Religions*, 23–7, 45.

22. Andrew Lang, *The Making of Religion* (London, 1898); Grant Allen, *The Evolution of the Idea of God* (New York, 1897); J. H. King, *The Supernatural: its Origin, Nature and Evolution* (London, 1892); Edward Caird, *The Evolution of Religion*, 2 vols (Glasgow, 1893).

23. F. Max Müller, *The Life and Letters of the Right Honourable Friedrich Max Müller. Edited by his wife*, 2 vols (London, 1902), II, 135.

24. F. Max Müller, 'Preface', in William Wyatt Gill, *Myths and Songs from the South Pacific* (London, 1876), vi.

25. Ibid., vi–vii, xviii.

26. F. Max Müller, 'Solar myths', *Nineteenth Century*, 18 (December 1885), 918.

27. Ibid., 901, 906–7; R. M. Dorson, *The British Folklorists: A History* (London, 1968), 163.

28. E. B. Tylor, *Primitive Culture*, I, 5–7.

29. Tylor, *Primitive Culture*, I, 248.

30. Richard Taylor, *Te Ika Maui*, 1st edn (London, 1855), 12.

31. On these debates see John Stenhouse, 'The "battle" between science and religion over evolution in nineteenth century New Zealand' (Massey University, PhD thesis, 1985).

32. John White, 'A chapter from the Maori Mythology on the Soul of Man ... ', undated manuscript, ATL, John White papers, MS-Papers-0075–087.

33. John White, 'Notes on Maori Religion and Superstitions', undated manuscript, ibid., MS-Papers-0075–086.

34. W. E. Gudgeon, 'Maori Religion', *JPS*, 55 (1907), 107, 110.

35. Simpson, 'Io as supreme being', 68.

36. Gudgeon, 'Maori religion', 109–110.

37. Ibid., 108.

38. For example, Thomas Trautmann, *Lewis Henry Morgan and the Invention of Kinship* (Berkeley, CA, 1987), 71–3, 88–9, 104–13.

39. A. S. Thomson, *The Story of New Zealand: past and present – savage and civilized*, 2 vols (London, 1859), I, 108–9.

40. Ibid., I, 112, 114–16, 120.
41. Blyth, '"Whence"', 516. Cf. J. T. Thomson, 'Barat or Barata fossil words', 165.
42. Blyth, '"Whence"', 529, 541.
43. Ibid., 516.
44. Alfred Newman, *Who are the Maoris?* (Christchurch, n. d. [*c.* 1912]), 19–33.
45. Ibid., 198–200, 207–8.
46. Ibid. For a discussion of the parallel functions and worship of Rudra and Ru and Rua see ibid., 185–9.
47. Ibid., 198. Newman rejected the term 'Polynesian' preferring 'Maori' for the peoples of the central and eastern islands of the mid-Pacific. '"Polynesian" is a useless term. Maori was their common name. It links them with their cradle-land and connects them with their ancient history. In Asia in the dim twilight of a far past they were Maoris, and they are Maoris to-day in the Pacific.' Ibid., 76.
48. Ibid., 172–84.
49. Ibid., 274.
50. *C.M.S. Intelligencer*, 9 (1858), 27.
51. Ibid., 125.
52. In Bowen's opinion the causes of the Indian rebellion were: '(A.) Religious and national fanaticism. (B.) The recent reduction in the number of English troops employed in India. (C.) The annexation of the entire territories of the King of Oude.' Governor G. F. Bowne to His Grace the Duke of Buckingham and Chandos, 7 December 1868. *GBPP*, 1868–9 [307] XLIV, 313.
53. Ibid., 314
54. Ibid., 315.
55. Ibid.
56. James Belich has deconstructed this interpretation: James Belich, *The New Zealand Wars and the Victorian Interpretation of Racial Conflict* (Auckland, 1986).
57. *The Bombay Gazette*, 6 March 1869.
58. One of the most intriguing of these prophets was Himiona (Simeon), based near Maketu, who claimed to have religious powers derived from mystical visions of a rupee ('*na te rupi*'). *The Bay of Plenty Times*, 16 January 1882.
59. Bryan S. Turner, 'Introduction: the study of religion', *The Early Sociology of Religion. Volume I. Readings in Nineteenth Century Theory*, Bryan S. Turner ed. (Routledge, 1997), 1–14.
60. Best to Peal undated, but in response to Peal's letter dated 31 August 1895, PSC, MS 80–115–02/02. Peal's letter to Best has not survived, but the phrasing of Best's letter suggests that he was replying to specific questions raised by Peal. Best also sent Peal a newspaper clipping describing a Maori 'phallic cult', Best to Peal May–June 1893, PSC, MS-Copy-Micro-146.
61. Elsdon Best, 'Maori beliefs concerning the human organs of generation', *Man*, 14 (1914), 132–4.
62. Elsdon Best, *The Maori*, 2 vols (Wellington, 1924), I, 294.
63. Te Iho o Kataka literally means 'the Umbilical Cord of Kataka'. This tree was favoured by the god Tane, who placed the severed umbilical cords of his children on the tree (including the umbilical cord of his child Kataka), and invested the tree with the power to enhance women's fertility. Best suggested that this practice echoed the veneration of trees in South Asia,

such as the sacred cedar of Gilgit, discussed in Isaline Philpot's *The sacred tree: or, the tree in religion and myth* (London, 1894). Best, *The Maori*, I, 297.

64. Ibid., I, 294.

65. See the chants, rituals and myths related to the power of phallus printed in Eldson Best, *Tuhoe: Children of the Mist*, 2 vols (New Plymouth, 1925), especially 828–9, 1135.

66. Best notes that Tiki was often understood as the first man created by the Gods. Best argues that this tradition is a 'popular' notion, a folk version of the myth that is freely shared by one and all. However, he stressed that in the 'sacerdotal' version of the myth of creation, a purer tradition that was shared only by the priestly elite, Tiki was understood as the Creator. Elsdon Best, 'Maori personifications. Anthropogeny, solar myths and phallic symbolism: as exemplified in the demiurgic concepts of Tane and Tiki', *JPS*, 32 (1923), 53–6.

67. Ibid., 57.

68. Ibid., 61.

69. Ibid., 58.

70. Best, *Tuhoe*, 1129. Previously Best recorded that Te Arawa described female genitalia as '*whare o aitua*' – the abode of misfortune – and that generally served as an 'emblem of trouble, if not death itself'. Best, 'Human organs of generation', 132.

71. Newman, *Who are the Maoris?*, 158–9.

72. Ibid., 19–33, 140–2, 145–9. Newman first outlined his theory of migration from the Punjab, down the Ganges and through South-East Asia into the Pacific in a letter to Smith in 1906. Newman to Smith, 29 September 1906, PSC, MS-1187–268.

73. Newman, *Who are the Maoris?*, 151. 'Religion is the most *conservative*, the embodiment of the life history of the race.' Newman to Smith, 28 June 1906, PSC, MS-1187–268.

74. Newman, *Who are the Maoris?*, 215, 217–19.

75. Ibid., 217–19.

76. Newman to Smith, 14 December 1906, 12 March 1907, PSC, MS-1187–268.

77. Jean Smith, *Tapu Removal in Maori Religion* (Wellington, 1974); Te Uira Manihera, Ngoi Pewhairangi and John Rangihau, 'Learning and Tapu', *Te Ao Hurihuri*, 9–14; Maori Marsden, 'God, man and universe: a Maori view', Ibid., 118–38.

78. For example, Joel Samuel Polack, *Manners and Customs of the New Zealanders*, 2 vols (London, 1840), I, 274.

79. There are numerous instances of this, the most notable being George French Angas, *Savage Life and Scenes in Australia and New Zealand*, 2 vols (London, 1847), I, 320; Richard Cruise, *Journal of a Ten Months Residence in New Zealand* (London, 1823), 32; F. E. Maning, *Old New Zealand*, (Auckland, 1973 [1887]), 39; William Yate, *An Account of New Zealand* (London, 1835), 137 .

80. Earle, *Narrative*, 128.

81. Ernst Dieffenbach, *Travels in New Zealand*, 2 vols (London, 1843), II, 105.

82. James Buller, *Forty Years in New Zealand* (London, 1878), 222.

83. William Brown, *New Zealand and its Aborigines* (London, 1845), 11–12.

84. Ibid., 80.

85. Hiram Bingham, *A Residence of Twenty-One Years in the Sandwich Islands; or the Civil, Religious, and Political History of Those Islands* (Hartford, 1849), 21.

86. James Mill, *The History of British India*, Horace Hayman Wilson ed, 5th edn, 10 vols (London, 1858), I, 127.
87. Earle, *Narrative*, 127.
88. Walter L. Arnstein, *Protestant versus Catholic in Mid-Victorian England* (Columbia, MO, 1982), 214; Owen Chadwick, *The Victorian Church. Part One* (London, 1966), 441.
89. K. R. Howe, 'Some origins and migrations of ideas leading to the Aryan Polynesian theories of Abraham Fornander and Edward Tregear', *Pacific Studies*, 11 (1988), 67–81.
90. Abraham Fornander, *An Account of the Polynesian Race its Origin and Migrations and the ancient history of the Hawaiian people to the times of Kamehameha I*, 3 vols (London, 1878–85), I, 109, 112.
91. Ibid., I, 111
92. Ibid., I, 110–1.
93. Jesse Page, *Among the Maoris or Daybreak in New Zealand. A record of the Labours of Samuel Marsden, Bishop Selwyn, and Others* (London, n. d. [1864?]), 77.
94. Ibid., 77. This is an almost direct quotation from A. S. Thomson, see A. S. Thomson, *The Story of New Zealand*, 2 vols (London, 1859), I, 100–1.
95. Page, *Among the Maoris*, 79.
96. Colenso, 'On the Maori races', *TPNZI*, 1 (1868), appendix, 43.
97. Newman, *Who are the Maoris?*, 160–1. Newman wrote to Smith arguing that *tapu* was the key Polynesian social custom and that it was 'surely like caste'. Alfred Newman to Percy Smith, 10 July 1906, PSC, MS-1187–268.
98. Newman, *Who are the Maoris?*, 76–9, 161.
99. Ibid., 159–61.
100. *NZPD*, 139 (1907), 510.
101. Ibid., 511.
102. Cf. William R. Pinch, *Peasants and Monks in British India* (Berkeley, CA, 1996).
103. *NZPD*, 139 (1907), 511.
104. Ibid., 140 (1907), 373.
105. Ibid., 375, 382.
106. Cf. Sharpe, *Comparative Religion*, 47–71.
107. See, for example, Risley's use of *tapu* in his discussions of race and caste: H. H. Risley, 'The study of ethnology in India', *Journal of the Anthropological Institute*, 20 (1891), 259.

Chapter 5   Print, Literacy and the Recasting of Maori Identities

1. Alan Moorehead, *The Fatal Impact: an Account of the Invasion of the South Pacific 1767–1840* (London, 1966). A similar argument of cultural crisis was elaborated in Harrison M. Wright, *New Zealand 1769–1840: Early Years of Western Contact* (Cambridge, MA, 1967).
2. Gordon Parsonson, 'The literate revolution in Polynesian', *Journal of Pacific History*, 2 (1967), 39–58.
3. Most notably I. C. Campbell, 'Culture contact and Polynesian identity in the European age', *Journal of World History*, 8 (1997), 29–55.

4. Greg Dening, 'Writing, rewriting the beach: an essay', *Rethinking History*, 2 (1998), 143–72, here 160.

5. For example, Kuni E. H. Jenkins, 'Te ihi, te mana, te wehi o te ao tuhi : Maori print literacy from 1814–1855: literacy, power and colonization', (University of Auckland MA, 1991) and *Becoming Literate, Becoming English* (Auckland, 1993).

6. D. F. McKenzie, *Oral Culture, Literacy and Print in Early New Zealand: the Treaty of Waitangi* (Wellington, 1985), 15 n. 19.

7. Judith Binney, 'Maori oral narratives, Pakeha written texts: two forms of telling history', *New Zealand Journal of History*, 21 (1987), 16–28.

8. Carlo Ginzburg, *The Cheese and the Worms: the Cosmos of a Sixteenth-Century Miller*, John and Ann Tedeschi eds (Baltimore, MD, 1992), 27–54, here 32.

9. Compare the analytical strategies of Ranajit Guha, *Elementary Aspects of Peasant Insurgency in Colonial India* (Delhi, 1983), 15, with James Belich, *The New Zealand Wars and the Victorian Interpretation of Racial Conflict* (Auckland, 1986).

10. For example, Elsdon Best, *The Maori as He Was* (Wellington, 1952 [1924]), 96.

11. Douglas G. Sutton, 'Organization and ontology: the origins of the northern Maori chiefdom, New Zealand', *Man*, n. s. 25 (1990) 667; Raymond Firth, *We, the Tikopia* (London, 1936) and Irving Goldman, *Ancient Polynesian Society* (Chicago, 1970).

12. Angela Ballara, 'Porangahau: the formation of an eighteenth-century community in Southern Hawke's Bay', *New Zealand Journal of History*, 29 (1995), 3–18; Douglas Sutton (ed.), *The Archaeology of the Kainga: a Study of Precontact Maori Undefended settlements at Pouerua, Northland, New Zealand* (Auckland, 1994).

13. For example, Angela Ballara, 'The Origins of Ngati Kahungunu' (Victoria University of Wellington, PhD thesis, 1991).

14. 'Genealogy is the backbone of all Maori history': Binney, 'Two forms of telling history', 21.

15. Ibid., 23–4.

16. Ibid., 21, 24.

17. Watkin, Journal, 5–7 June 1840 and 8 September 1840, ML.

18. See Margaret Orbell, *Maori Folktales in Maori and English* (London, 1968), xiv; Katharine Luomala, *Maui-of-a-thousand-tricks: His Oceanic and European Biographers* (Honolulu, HI, 1949).

19. Lindsay Cox, *Kotahitanga: the Search for Maori Political Unity* (Auckland, 1993), 17.

20. H. W. Orsman, *The Dictionary of New Zealand English: a Dictionary of New Zealandisms on Historical Principles* (Auckland, 1997), 809–10.

21. 'For the Maoris to turn to Christianity there had to be things happening which they could not explain in terms of their own culture': Harrison M. Wright, *New Zealand 1769–1840: Early Years of Western Contact* (Cambridge, MA, 1967), 143–4.

22. Keith Sinclair, *A History of New Zealand*, 3rd edn (London, 1980), 42.

23. Belich, *Making Peoples*, 156–178; J. M. R. Owens, *The Unexpected Impact; Wesleyan Missionaries and Maoris in the Early 19th Century* (Auckland, 1973); K. R. Howe, 'The Maori Response to Christianity in the Thames-Waikato Area, 1833–1840', *NZJH*, 7 (1973), 28–46.

24. I. C. Campbell, 'Culture contact and Polynesian identity in the European age', *Journal of World History* (1997), 29–55.

25. Thomas Kendall, *A Korao no New Zealand; or, the New Zealander's First Book; being An Attempt to compose some Lessons for the Instruction of the Natives* (Sydney, 1815).

26. Samuel Lee, *A Grammar and Vocabulary of the Language of New Zealand* (London, 1820).

27. Compare the 19 consonants (including 'ng') of Kendall and Lee's grammar with the nine consonants of the later grammars. Eventually ten consonants were settled upon, with the aspirated form 'wh' differentiated from 'w'. See Colenso's comments on this process: William Colenso, *Fifty Years Ago in New Zealand* (Napier, 1888), 24–7, 47–9.

28. The first portion of Maori scripture was printed in 1827: 400 copies of a 31-page pamphlet containing seven hymns and various portions of Scripture were produced in Sydney.

29. *MR* (1840), 512 and (1841), 510; Harrison Wright, *New Zealand, 1769–1840*, (Cambridge, MA, 1959), 53. For a review of these processes see Tony Ballantyne, 'Print, politics and Protestantism: New Zealand, 1769–1860', *Information, Communications, Power*, Hiram Morgan ed. (Dublin, 2001), 152–76.

30. D. F. McKenzie, *Oral Culture, Literacy and Print in Early New Zealand: the Treaty of Waitangi* (Wellington, 1985), 28.

31. John King to Josiah Pratt, 1 July 1820, HL, MS 72 item 4.

32. J. N. Coleman, *A Memoir of the Rev. Richard Davis* (London, 1865), 61. Davis had only arrived in New Zealand in August of that year.

33. Nathaniel Turner to WMS, 27 May 1836, reprinted in *Missionary Notices*, 256 (April 1857), 453–4.

34. *MR* (1842), 475.

35. For example, Michael Jackson, 'Literacy, Communications and Social Change: the Maori case, 1830–1870' (University of Auckland, MA thesis, 1967), 135; McKenzie, *Oral Culture, Literacy and Print in Early New Zealand*, 30.

36. K. R. Howe, 'The Maori response to Christianity in the Thames-Waikato area, 1833–1840', *NZJH*, 7 (April 1973), 39.

37. R. G. Jameson, *New Zealand, South Australia and New South Wales* (London, 1841), 260–2.

38. John Morgan, 16 September 1858, cited in Parr, 'Maori literacy 1843–1867', 217. Also see Charles Hursthouse, *An Account of the Settlement of New Plymouth* (London, 1849) 30; *MR* (1849), 485.

39. *Ko Te Karere o Nui Tireni*, 1 January 1845, 2–3.

40. For example, William Yate, *An Account of New Zealand and of the Church Missionary Society's Mission in the Northern Island* (London, 1835), 239–40; Richard Taylor, *The Past and Present of New Zealand: with its prospects for the future* (London, 1868), 20.

41. Howe, 'The Maori response to Christianity in the Thames-Waikato area', 28–46. Missionary records suggested that 800 to 1000 Maori could read in the Thames region by 1839. *MR* (1840), 379.

42. Atholl Anderson, *The Welcome of Strangers. An Ethnohistory of Southern Maori A. D. 1650–1850* (Dunedin, 1998), 220–4.

43. For example, 'Whakapapa and waiata recorded by Te Whatahoro [1862]', qMS-0204, ATL; H. T. Whatahoro Jury, 'Notebook with information about Maori land tenure', MS-Papers-0189-B052, ATL.

44. For example, Katrinia Taoatoe to Isaac Featherson, 8 August 1862, MS-Papers-0075-9D, ATL; Mere Te Rere to Governor Grey, 22 September 1862, MS-0075-96, ATL.

45. Discussions of the market are ubiquitous, for example *Te Karere Maori*, 1 July 1855, 14–15 and 30 June 1856, 15–16.

46. *Te Waka Maori o Niu Tirani*, 2 May 1876, 107.

47. Ibid., 25 July 1876, 10. '*Tena koia, kia panuitia atu ki nga Pakeha haere mai i rawahi nga tikanga o o matou kainga, o Hokianga, Kaipara, Whangarei, Peiwhairangi, Mangonui, me te takiwa katoa o Ngapuhi raua ko te Rarawa – he pono ra ia he whenua tenei e rerengia ana e te waiu, e te honi.*' For criticisms of this commercialization see ibid., 27 June 1876.

48. Ibid., 25 July 1876, 10

49. On this dynamic see Ann Parsonson, 'The expansion of a competitive society', *NZJH*, 14 (1980), 45–60 and F. Allan Hanson and Louise Hanson, *Counterpoint in Maori Culture* (London, 1983).

50. '*He pukapuka ra tenei, kia mohio ai te tangata maori ki nga tikanga me nga ritenga o te Pakeha kia mohio ai ano hoki te Pakeha ki nga ritenga o te tangata maori.*' Ko *Te Karere o Nui Tireni*, 1 January 1842.

51. Ibid., 1 February 1842, 5–8 and 1 March 1842, 11.

52. For example, ibid., 1 March 1843, 11–12 and 1 February 1844, 10–11.

53. Ibid., 1 March 1844, 15–7.

54. Ibid., 1 February 1845, 6.

55. See Ruth Finnegan, *Literacy and Orality: Studies in the Technology of Communication* (Oxford, 1988).

56. See Belich, *Making Peoples*, 140–155; James Belich, *The New Zealand Wars and the Victorian Interpretation of Racial Conflict* (Auckland, 1988).

57. Finnegan, *Literacy and Orality*, 91–101.

58. Barry Mitcalfe, *Maori Poetry. The Singing Word* (Wellington, 1974), 7.

59. Finnegan, *Literacy and Orality*, 110.

60. For example, Lawrence M. Rogers ed., *The Early Journals of Henry Williams 1826–40* (Christchurch, 1961), 456.

61. Cf. Sinclair, *A History of New Zealand*, 42.

62. Belich, *Making Peoples*, 168–9; Philip Turner, 'The Politics of Neutrality: The Catholic Mission and the Maori 1838–1878' (University of Auckland, MA thesis, 1986).

63. Bronwyn Elsmore, *Mana from Heaven: a Century of Maori Prophets in New Zealand* (Tauranga, 1989), 44.

64. King to Josiah Pratt, 4 November 1819, HL, MS 73 item 1.

65. Belich, *Making Peoples*, 219.

66. Maori in the north of North Island were consistently wary of the 'Wiwis', the French, in the wake of reprisals following the death of the explorer Marion du Fresne. Hugh Carleton, *The Life of Henry Williams* (Wellington, 1948), 254–5. British missionaries also feared that the French might pre-empt the annexation of New Zealand, and in the wake of annexation French influence was suspected to lie behind Maori resistance to the Treaty of Waitangi and the northern war of 1845-6. William Colenso, *The*

Authentic and Genuine History of the Signing of the Treaty of Waitangi (Wellington, 1890), 34; James Stack to CMS, 4 April 1840, HL, CN/O78.

67. William Colenso, *He Pukapuka Waki; he wakakite atu i nga henga o te Hahi o Roma* [A Book of Errors, revealing the errors of the Church of Rome] (Paihia, 1840); *Ko te tuarua o nga Pukapuka Waki* [The Second Book of Errors] (Paihia, 1840).

68. Jean-Baptiste François Pompallier, *Early History of the Catholic Church in Oceania* (Auckland, 1888), 44.

69. Ibid., 44.

70. W. B. Ullathorne, *The Autobiography of Archbishop Ullathorne with selections from his letters* (London, 1891), 177–8.

71. For example, 'Report of the Revd. G. A. Kissling, Hick's Bay, for the year 1844', HL, C/NO 56.

72. Jane Thomson, 'The Roman Catholic mission in New Zealand, 1838–1870' (Victoria University of Wellington, MA thesis, 1966), 230–2.

73. For example, James Buller, *Forty Years in New Zealand*, 297 cf. Thomson, 'Roman Catholic mission', 77–85.

74. James Stack to CMS, 13 August 1844, HL, CN/O 78.

75. For a similar observation see Howe, 'The Maori response to Christianity in the Thames-Waikato area', 36.

76. Henry Williams, Journal, 5 September 1834. Rogers, *Early Journals*, 389.

77. 'But I keep under my body, and bring it into subjection: lest that by any means, when I have preached to others, I myself should be a castaway. 'In an early missionary translation this was rendered as 'E kuru ana ahau I taku tinana', 'I beat my body with my fists.' Elsmore, *Like Them That Dream*, 51; 42. Elsmore incorrectly identifies the passage as I Corinthians 9: 2.

78. Taylor, *Past and Present*, 41–2.

79. Ibid., 20.

80. See Kay Sanderson, 'Maori Christianity on the East Coast', *NZJH*, 17 (1983), 175.

81. Frances Porter (ed.), *The Turanga Journals* (Wellington, 1974), 592.

82. Ann Parsonson, for example, suggests that the King Movement was a 'notable failure'. She attributes the ineffectiveness of the movement to an absence of a precise and cohesive ideology, deep-seated internal conflicts and the 'capricious' loyalty of many of the King's followers. Ann Parsonson, 'The pursuit of mana', 154–5.

83. Sorrenson emphasizes this: 'It was an attempt to forge the tribes into a Maori nation – a nation within a nation.' Sorrenson, 'Maori and Pakeha', *The Oxford History of New Zealand*, W. H. Oliver ed. (Wellington, 1981), 180.

84. Lyndsay Head, 'Te Ua and the Hauhau Faith in the light of the Ua Gospel Notebook' (University of Canterbury, MA thesis, 1983).

85. James Cowan, *The New Zealand Wars. A History of the Maori Campaigns and the Pioneering Period*, 2 vols (Wellington, 1922), I, 446.

86. Lindsay Cox notes that a Maori Bible was prominent in the ritual of coronation and this same Bible has been used in the coronation of the five subsequent monarchs. Lindsay Cox, *Kotahitanga*, 52.

87. Head, 'Te Ua and the Hauhau Faith', 76–7.

88. This relationship was communicated in the Kingitanga symbol of two upright sticks, one symbolizing the Maori King and one the British

Queen, joined by a third representing the law. Alan Ward, *A Show of Justice: Racial 'Amalgamation' in Nineteenth Century New Zealand* (Auckland, 1973), 101.

89. *The New Zealander*, 3 July 1858.

90. Claudia Orange, *The Treaty of Waitangi* (Wellington, 1987), 143.

91. Cox, *Kotahitanga*, 50; Thomas Buddle, *The Maori King Movement* (Auckland, 1860), 8. This flag, a red St George's cross on a white background with a blue field containing a red cross and four white stars in the upper left corner, became a powerful symbol for Maori. Not only did it allow the chiefs' ships duty-free entry into Australian ports, but the chiefs believed that the flag recognized New Zealand as a separate country but affirmed a special tie to England.

92. Cox, *Kotahitanga*, 49.

93. On Te Rauparaha see W. T. L. Travers, *The Stirring Times of Te Rauparaha (Chief of the Ngatitoa)* (Christchurch, 1906 [1872]); T. Lindsay Buick, *An Old New Zealander, or, Te Rauparaha, the Napoleon of the south* (London, 1911).

94. Cleave, 'Tribal and state-like political formations', *JPS*, 92 (1983), 58–62, the quote is at 58.

95. James Kemp to CMS, 24 July 1824, HL, MS 70 item 15; A. J. Ballantyne, 'Reforming the Heathen Body: C.M.S. Missionaries, Sexuality, and Maori 1814–1850', (University of Otago, BA Hons thesis).

96. Head and Mikaere note that Christianity and literacy were essential in this new political order: 'After about 1850, no Maori leader with more than local aspirations was unable to read and write'. Lyndsay Head and Buddy Mikaere, 'Was 19th century Maori society literate?' *Archifacts*, 2 (1988), 19.

97. Donald McLean, 'Report of Meeting at Ngaruawahia 21–9 May 1860', enclosure 1, in Governor Gore Browne to Duke of Newcastle, 27 June 1860, *GBPP*, 1861 (2789), 71–3.

98. Tamati Hapimana, Te Rangituawaru, Tamihana Ratapu and Te Waka Perohuka, 'Reply from Ngati Kahungunu, No. 1', 14 July 1860, ibid., 101.

99. See Williams's journal entries in late October and November 1840, William Williams, Journal, ATL.

100. Richard Taylor reflected that Te Atua Wera, a prophet in the Bay of Islands in the late 1830s who emphasized the Maori–Jew connection, was supported by those Maori who 'opposed the Gospel' believing that as Judaism preceded Christianity, Judaism 'must be the mother Church'. Taylor, *Past and Present*, 41.

101. John Gorst, *The Maori King* (Auckland, 1959 [1864]), 103.

102. Cited in Elsmore, *Like Them That Dream*, 72–3.

103. Pai Marire means 'good and peaceful'. The followers of Te Ua would repeatedly chant 'hau' as a charm as they went into battle, hence the name 'Hauhau'.

104. Paul Clark, *'Hauhau': the Pai Marire Search for Maori identity* (Auckland, 1975), 17.

105. Lyndsay Head, 'The Gospel of Te Ua Haumene', *JPS*, 101 (1992), 14–15, 16–17, 28–9.

106. William Greenwood, *The Upraised Hand, or The Spiritual Significance of the Rise of the Ringatu Faith* (Wellington, 1942), 15.

107. Greenwood, *The Upraised Hand*, 25; W. Hugh Ross, *Te Kooti Rikirangi: General and Prophet* (Auckland, 1966), 52.

108. Binney, 'Myth and explanation in the Ringatu tradition', *JPS*, 93 (1984), 368–70.
109. Ibid., 348.
110. Ross, *Te Kooti*, 31
111. Head, 'The Gospel of Te Ua Haumene', 28–9.
112. For example, one 1847 CMS text described Europeans (including Pakeha presumably) as '*ngaa taangata o Ooropi*', the descendants of 'Hapeta' (Japheth); cf. Te Ua's transliteration 'Taapeta'. CMS, *He Whakapapa, ara Nga Mahi menga aha noa a te Atua raua ko tana Hahi* (Auckland, 1847). Cited in Head, 'The Gospel of Te Ua Haumene', 36 n. 78
113. L. G. Kelly, 'Some problems in the study of Maori genealogies', *JPS*, 49 (1940), 241.
114. Elsmore, *Like Them That Dream*, 119.
115. Isaiah 62:4.
116. *The Bay of Plenty Times* reported on 16 January 1882 that a prophet named Himiona (Simeon) founded a new religious tradition among Arawa Maori in the Maketu region. Himiona claimed that his teachings came from a rupee ('*na te rupi*') which would float in front of his eyes. Various letters appeared on the rupee and these letters alluded to certain chapters and verses in the Bible.
117. See Jean Comaroff, 'The colonization of consciousness', *Economy and Society*, 18 (1989), 267–96.

Chapter 6   The Politics of Language, Nation and Race: Hindu Identities in the Late Nineteenth Century

1. Tapan Raychaudhuri, *Europe Reconsidered. Perceptions of the West in Nineteenth Century Bengal* (Delhi, 1988), especially 79, 178–82, 262–3, 296–7; Vasudha Dalmia, *The Nationalization of Hindu Traditions: Bharatendu Harishchandra and Nineteenth-century Banaras* (Delhi, 1997).
2. For example, *Rig Veda*, 7. 33 and 7. 82.
3. Ibid., 1. 33.
4. Thomas R. Trautmann, *Aryans and British India* (Berkeley, CA, 1997), 197.
5. Arthur A. Macdonell, *A Sanskrit–English Dictionary* (London, 1893), 42.
6. See, for example, Wendy Doniger O'Flaherty (trans. and ed.), *The Rig Veda: An Anthology* (Harmondsworth, 1981), 122 n. 9.
7. Romila Thapar, *Interpreting Early India* (Delhi, 1992), 27.
8. This model is elaborated in the later hymns in the *Rig Veda*. *Rig-Veda*, 10. 90; Romila Thapar, *A History of India. Volume 1* (Harmondsworth, 1966), 39–40.
9. In the *Mahabharata*, each *varna* was associated with a particular colour: *Brahman* – white, *Kshatriya* – red, *Vaishya* – yellow; *Shudra* – black. Thapar, *Interpreting Early India*, 29.
10. Romila Thapar, 'Ideology and the interpretation of early Indian history', *Interpreting Early India*, 12.
11. Wilhelm Halbfass, *India and Europe – an Essay in Understanding* (New York, 1988), 187.
12. Romila Thapar, *Ancient Indian Social History* (Delhi, 1978), 155, 173.

13. John Brockington, 'Concepts of race in the Mahabharata and Ramayana', *The Concept of Race in South Asia*, Peter Robb ed. (Delhi, 1995), 101, 106, 108.
14. Sheldon Pollock suggests that this world-view constituted a 'pre-form of racism'. Sheldon Pollock, 'Deep orientalism? Notes on Sanskrit and power beyond the Raj', *Orientalism and the Postcolonial Predicament*, C. A. Breckenridge and P. van der Veer eds (Philadelphia, PA, 1993), 107.
15. Henry Yule and Arthur Coke Burnell (eds), *Hobson-Jobson* (London, 1886), 352–4; Trautmann, *Aryans and British India*, 13–14. On *faringi* see: Chandra Richard de Silva, 'Beyond the Cape: the Portuguese encounter with the peoples of South Asia', *Implicit Understandings*, Stuart B. Schwartz ed. (Cambridge, 1994), 300–3.
16. Madhav Deshpande, *Sanskrit and Prakrit: Sociolinguistic Issues* (Delhi, 1993), ch. 6. On Rajashekhara see A. K. Warder, 'Classical literature', *A Cultural History of India*, A. L. Basham ed. (Oxford, 1975), 189–90.
17. Krishna Bihari Sen, 'The romance of language', *Essays on Swami Dayanand Saraswati and the Arya Samaj*, Lala Jivan Das ed. (Lahore, 1902), no. 7, 12.
18. Keshab Chandra Sen, 'Philosophy and madness in religion', *Sources of Indian Tradition*, William Theodore de Bary ed., 2 vols (New York, 1964), II, 67.
19. C. A. Bayly, *Empire and Information. Intelligence Gathering and Social Communication in India, 1780–1870* (Cambridge, 1996), 311.
20. K. M. Banerjea, *The Arian Witness: or the Testimony of the Arian Scriptures in Corroboration of Biblical History and the Rudiments of Christian Doctrine* (Calcutta, 1875), 15, 79.
21. Ibid., 154–67. The quotation comes from 158.
22. Ibid., 93–4, 193.
23. Ramachandra Ghosha, *The Indo-Aryans, their History, Creed and Practice* (Calcutta: 1881), vi.
24. Ibid., 1–2. Quotation is at 1.
25. For example Monier Monier-Williams, *Hinduism* (London, 1877), 12–13, 134.
26. Editorial note to S. Radhakrishnan, 'Hinduism', *The Cultural History of India*, A. L. Basham ed. (Oxford, 1975), 81.
27. Ghosha, *The Indo-Aryans*, 2: *History of Hindu civilization, as illustrated in the Vedas and their appendages* (Calcutta, 1889), 2.
28. On South Asian dietic theories of character and culture. See C. A. Bayly, *Empire and Information*, 25, 301–3; Francis Zimmermann, *The Jungle and the Aroma of Meats. An Ecological Theme in Hindu Medicine* (Berkeley, CA, 1987).
29. Ghosha, *Indo-Aryans*, 3, 51, 56.
30. Ghosha, *History of Hindu Civilization*, 134–5.
31. W. W. Hunter suggested that the ancient history of India revealed two races of 'widely different origin, struggling for mastery' and as Indian society degenerated caste became increasingly elaborated, rigid and 'cruel'. W. W. Hunter, *Annals of Rural Bengal* (Calcutta, 1868), 89–101.
32. See Gyan Prakash, *Another Reason: Science and the Imagination in Modern India* (Princeton, NJ, 1998), 71–82.
33. The sources for this biographical sketch are the three installments of an English translation of his Hindi biography reprinted in *The Theosophist*, 1 (October 1879), 9–13; (December 1879), 66–8; 2 (November 1880), 24–6. This biography ends in 1857, as no further installments were published in *The Theosophist* following Dayananda's break with the Theosophical Society

in 1880. The other source is the excellent biography J. T. F. Jordens, *Dayananda Sarasvati: His Life and Ideas* (Delhi, 1978).

34. Virjananda's distinction between between *arsha* and *anarsha* works, the works of *rishi*s (the 'real sages' of ancient India) and less insightful mundane works is discussed in Jordens, *Dayananda Sarasvati*, 36–7, 102–3.

35. Ibid., ch. 3.

36. For the rules of the Samaj see Lekhram, *Maharshi Dayananda Sarasvati ka Jivan Charitra*, Pandit Harishchandra Vidyalankar ed. (Delhi, 1972), 270–2.

37. For Dayananda's relationships with Indologists and knowledge of their works see Leopold, 'The Aryan theory of race', 288–9; Jordens, *Dayananda Sarasvati*, 40, 56, 95, 157.

38. This summary is based on Shri Paramahansa Vrajat Acharya and Shri Maddayananda's Hindi edition of *Satyarth Prakash* (Ajmir, 1937 vikrami samvat [c. 1880 AD]).

39. *C.M.S. Intelligencer*, 2: 7 (July 1851), 156.

40. The best example of Dayananda's rigid literalism is his reaction to Revelation 9: 16 which describes the 200 000 horses in heaven. Dayananda found this notion revolting, as surely this would have resulted in heaven being littered with dung (*lid*) and filled with a terrible stench (*durganh*). Acharya and Maddayananda (eds), *Satyarth Prakash*, 504.

41. Ibid., 461–2, 466, 475–6, 493–5.

42. Cf. Richard Fox Young, *Resistant Hinduism: Sanskrit Sources on Anti-Christian Apologetics in Early Nineteenth-century India* (Vienna, 1981), 135.

43. Acharya and Maddayananda (eds), *Satyarth Prakash*, 492.

44. For Dayananda's views on caste see Revd. Rodolf Hoernle's report in Lala Lajpat Rai, *A History of the Arya Samaj*, Shri Ram Sharma ed., (Bombay, 1967), 35–6

45. Dayananda, for example, firmly rejected the claims of a Christian missionary who identified as a fellow Aryan, as the missionary believed in 'false teachings' and did not accept the Vedas as the only true source of religious knowledge. Har Bilas Sarda, *Life of Dayanand Saraswati* (Ajmer, 1946), 526.

46. Anon., 'What we were and what we are', *Essays on Swami Dayanand*, no. 3, 15 n. 7.

47. Har Bilas Sarda, *Hindu Superiority – an Attempt to Determine the Position of the Hindu Race in the Scale of Nations* (New Delhi, 1975 [1906]).

48. Bal Gangadhar Tilak, *The Arctic Home in the Vedas, Being Also a New Key to the Interpretation of Many Vedic Texts and Legends* (Poona, 1903), 418–19, 429, 464.

49. Ibid., 434, 443, 456, 464.

50. Ibid., iii.

51. For example, ibid., 4, 428–9.

52. Bal Gangadhar Tilak, 'On the Devanagri character: address to the Nagari Pracharini Conference, Benares, 1905', *Speeches of Bal Gangadhar Tilak (Delivered During 1889–1918)* (Madras, n. d.), 59–64. Tilak echoed Dayananda's advocacy of Hindi as a national language and his belief in the superiority of the Devanagari script. See Jordens, *Dayananda Sarasvati*, 223–5.

53. Tilak, *The Arctic Home*, 453–4.

54. As this was the period when the vernal equinox was in Orion he named his first exploration of Vedic history *Orion, or Researches into the Antiquity of the*

Vedas by B. G. Tilak, BA, LLB (London, 1892). Also see Leopold, 'The Aryan theory of race', 275.

55. Bayly, *Empire and Information*, 264; S. N. Mukherjee, *Sir William Jones. A Study in Eighteenth Century British Attitudes to India* (Cambridge, 1968), 100–8.

56. He observed, for example: '*Vedanta* and *Yoga* have been fully vindicated by modern science.' Tilak, 'On the greatness of Hinduism to Bharata Dharma Mahamandala Benares, 3 January 1906', *Speeches*, 70. He also praised the creation of Hindi terms for western science apparatus and techniques. Tilak, 'Devanagari', 64.

57. Bayly, *Empire and Information*, 363.

58. C. f. Ronald Inden, *Imagining India* (Oxford, 1989).

59. Tapan Raychaudhuri, *Europe Reconsidered*, 9, 34. There was considerable debate amongst pandits over the exact status of non-Indians, particularly their caste and ritual status. See, for example, Young, *Resistant Hinduism*, 90–1.

60. Trautmann, *British Aryans and India*, 219n.

61. Sudhir Chandra, *The Oppressive Present. Literature and Social Consciousness in Colonial India* (Delhi, 1994), 20, 29; Dalmia, *The Nationalization of Hindu Traditions*, especially ch. 6.

62. *Hindi Pradip*, March 1878.

63. Indira Chowdhury-Sengupta, 'The effeminate and the masculine: nationalism and the concept of race in colonial Bengal', *The Concept of Race*, 290–1.

64. Indira Chowdhury, *The Frail Hero and Virile History: Gender and the Politics of Culture in Colonial Bengal* (Delhi, 1998).

65. Ghosha, *The Indo-Aryans*, 2–3.

66. Cited in T. W. Clark, 'The role of Bankimchandra in the development of nationalism', *Historians of India, Pakistan and Ceylon*, C. H. Philips ed. (London, 1961), 2.

67. Leopold, 'The Aryan theory of race', 283.

68. Charles Ryerson, *Regionalism and Identity: the Tamil Renaissance and Popular Hinduism* (Madras, 1988) and Sumathi Ramaswamy, 'En/gendering language: the poetics of Tamil identity', *Comparative Studies in Society and History*, 35 (1993), 687–8, 694.

69. Mahadeva Govind Ranade, *Religious and Social Reform*, M. B. Kolasker ed. (Bombay, 1902), 98–100.

70. Chowdhury-Sengupta, 'The effeminate and the masculine', 287.

71. Partha Chatterjee, 'History and the nationalization of Hinduism', *Representing Hinduism: the Construction of Religious Traditions and National Identity*, Vasudha Dalmia and Heinrich von Stietencron, eds (Delhi, 1995), 103–28. For an insightful survey of representations of Muslims in the medieval south, especially Andhra Pradesh, see Cynthia Talbot, 'Inscribing the other, inscribing the self: Hindu–Muslim identities in pre-colonial India', *Comparative Studies in Society and History*, 37 (1995), 679–722.

72. Cited in Chatterjee, 'History and nationalization of Hinduism', 117.

73. Ibid., 114.

74. Raychaudhuri, *Europe Reconsidered*, 33.

75. Christophe Jaffrelot, 'The Idea of a Hindu Race', 327–54.

76. Partha Chatterjee, *Nationalist Thought and the Colonial World: a Derivative Discourse?* (London, 1986).

77. *Hinduism Today*, 16 (December, 1994).

78. For example, S. K. Biswas, *Autochthon of India and the Aryan Invasion* (New Delhi, 1995); Paramesh Choudhury, *The Aryan Hoax, that Dupes the Indians* (Calcutta, 1995); David Frawley, *The Myth of the Aryan Invasion of India* (New Delhi, 1994); Navaratna Srinivasa Rajaram, *Aryan Invasion of India: the Myth and the Truth* (New Delhi, 1993) and *The Politics of History: Aryan Invasion Theory and the Subversion of Scholarship* (New Delhi, 1995); Shrikant G. Talageri, *The Aryan Invasion Theory: a Reappraisal* (New Delhi, 1993).
79. See Thomas Blom Hansen and Christophe Jaffrelot (eds), *The BJP and the Compulsions of Politics in India* (Oxford, 1998).

Conclusion: Knowledge, Empire, Globalization

1. *The Imperial Gazetteer of India. The Indian Empire: vol. I Descriptive*, 26 vols (Oxford, 1907–9), 64–102.
2. Cf. Linda Colley, *Britons: Forging the Nation, 1707–1837* (London, 1992), 373.
3. Daniel Defoe, 'The True Born Englishman', from frontispiece, Benedict Anderson, *Imagined Communities. Reflections on the Origin and Spread of Nationalism*, rev. edn (London, 1991).
4. For example, Antoinette Burton, *At the Heart of the Empire: Indians and the Colonial Encounter in Late-Victorian Britain* (Berkeley, CA, 1998); Michael Fisher (eds), *The Travels of Dean Mahomet* (Berkeley, CA, 1997); Rozina Visram, *Ayahs, Lascars and Princes* (London, 1986).
5. Har Bilas Sarda, *Hindu Superiority – an attempt to determine the position of the Hindu race in the scale of nations* (New Delhi, 1975 [1906]).
6. Indira Chowdhury Sengupta, *The Frail Hero and Virile History: Gender and the Politics of Culture in Colonial Bengal* (Delhi, 1998).
7. For example, James Belich, 'Myth, race and identity in New Zealand', *NZJH*, 31 (1997) 9–22.
8. Eugene F. Irschick, *Dialogue and History: Constructing South India, 1795–1895* (Berkeley, CA, 1994), 10.
9. Ibid., 8.
10. Tadhg Foley, *From Queen's College to National University: Essays towards an Academic History of NUI, Galway* (Galway, 1999).
11. But Indians themselves, we must note, had limited success in accessing these networks, in part because of the racialized reinterpretation of the Aryan idea (forwarded by Hunter, Risley and others) which denied the intellectual and political equality of South Asians.
12. A. G. Hopkins, 'Back to the future: from national history to imperial history', *Past and Present*, 164 (1999), 198–243.
13. Hester Chapone, *Letters on the Improvement of the Mind and Miscellanies in Prose and Verse*, 2 vols (Dublin, 1786), I, 145.

Bibliography

Manuscripts

Alexander Turnbull Library, Wellington:
  Atkinson Papers
  Best Papers
  Lee Papers
  Peal Papers
  Polynesian Society Collection
  Taylor Papers
  White Papers

Cambridge University Library, Cambridge:
  Lee Papers

  Hocken Library and Archives, Dunedin:
  Davis Letters and Journals
  Kemp Letters and Journals
  King Letters and Journals
  Kissling Correspondence, CN/O 56
  Stack Correspondence, CN/O78
  Thomson Papers

Mitchell Library, Sydney:
  Watkin Papers

National Archives, Wellington:
  Governor – Miscellaneous Inwards Correspondence

Oriental and India Office Library, London:
  Cust Papers
  Orme MS XIX

Public Record Office, Kew:
  Colonial Office records – New Zealand CO, 209 series.
  Pickersgill Journal

Primary sources

Official publications and proceedings

Appendices to the Journal of the House of Representatives, 1863–91.
Archaeology Survey of India, *Reports* (23 vols, Shimla 1871–88).
Great Britain Parliamentary Papers: Colonies. Irish University Press Series.

The Imperial Gazetteer of India, 26 vols (Oxford 1907–9).
Military Department Papers: Military Collections.
Mutiny Records. Reports in Two Parts (Lahore, 1911).
New Zealand Gazette (1868).
New Zealand Parliamentary Debates (1896, 1907).
Punjab Home Proceedings (1871–75).

Periodicals

Archaelogia: or, miscellaneous tracts relating to antiquity (1782).
Asiatic Annual Register (1800–1).
Asiatic[k] Researches (1788–1810).
The Bay of Plenty Times (January 1882).
The Bombay Gazette (March 1869).
The Bombay Miscellany (August 1862).
The Calcutta Englishman (August 1897).
Calcutta Review (1875–81).
Church Missionary Intelligencer (1849–89).
Dunedin Punch (1865).
Edinburgh Review (1809).
The Englishman (1862).
Franklin Times (1925).
Gentleman's Magazine (1771).
Hindi Pradip (1878).
The Indian Christian Intelligencer (1878).
The Indian Empire (1862).
Journal of the Anthropological Institute (1874–91).
Journal of the Asiatic Society of Bengal (1847–89).
Journal of the Ethnological Society of London (1850).
Journal of the Indian Archipelago and Eastern Asia (1851).
Journal of the Polynesian Society (1892–1923).
Journal of the Royal Anthropological Institute (1884–91).
The Journal of the United Service Institution (1859–68).
Ko Te Karere o Nui Tireni (1842–45).
Man (1913–14).
Missionary Notices (1857).
Missionary Register (1813–54).
Nature (1888).
The New Zealander (1858).
New Zealand Herald (1885).
The New Zealand Mail (March 1886).
Nineteenth Century (1885).
Panjab Notes and Queries (1883–86).
Proceedings of the Asiatic Society of Bengal (1873).
Report of the Australasian Association for the Advancement of Science (1891–93).
Royal Scottish Society of Arts (1878).
Société de Géographie Bulletin (1832).
Taranaki Herald (1864).
Tasmanian Journal of Natural Science (1842).

Te Karere Maori (1855–58)
Te Korimako (1885).
Te Waka Maori o Niu Tirani (1876).
The Theosophist (1879–80).
The Times of India [overland summary edition] (1862).
Transactions and Proceedings of the New Zealand Institute (1868–91).
Transactions of the Ethnological Society of London, n.s. (1861–69).
Transactions of the Royal Irish Academy (1828).
Wellington Independent (1864).
Westminster Review (1887–88).

Books

Acharya, Shri Paramahansa Vrajat and Shri Maddayananda (eds), *Satyarth Prakash* (Ajmir, 1937 vikrami samvat [c. 1880 AD]).
Allen, Grant, *The Evolution of the Idea of God* (New York, 1897).
Angas, George French, *Savage Life and Scenes in Australia and New Zealand*, 2 vols (London, 1847).
Anon., *General catalogue of Grey collection, Free Public Library* (Auckland, 1888).
Arnold, Thomas, *Introductory Lectures on Modern History, with the Inaugural Lecture Delivered in Dec., 1841* (Oxford, 1842).
Banerjea, K. M., *The Arian Witness: or the testimony of the Arian Scriptures in corroboration of biblical history and the rudiments of Christian Doctrine* (Calcutta, 1875).
Beaglehole, J. C. (ed.), *The Endeavour Journal of Joseph Banks, 1768–1771*, 2 vols, (Sydney, 1962).
Beaglehole, J. C. (ed.), *The Journals of Captain James Cook on His Voyages of Discovery. The Voyage of the Endeavour, 1768–1771* (Cambridge, 1955).
Bhargava K. D. (ed.), *Fort William–India House Correspondence. Vol VI: 1770–1772* (Delhi, 1960).
Bingham, Hiram, *A Residence of Twenty-One Years in the Sandwich Islands; or the Civil, Religious, and Political History of Those Islands* (Hartford, 1849).
Blavatsky, H. P., *The Secret Doctrine: Volume II – Anthropogenesis*, 3 vols (Adyar, 1979 [1888]).
Bopp, Franz, *Über die verwandfschaft der Malayisch-Polynesischen sprache mit den Indo-Europäischen* (Berlin, 1841).
Bourke, U. J., *The Aryan origin of the Gaelic Race and Language, showing the present and past literary position of Irish Gaelic* (London, 1875).
Bramley-Moore, William (ed.), *Foxe's Book of Martyrs*, revd edn (London, 1875).
Brothers, Richard, *A Letter to His Royal Highness the Prince Regent, the Lords, commons, and people of the United Kingdom* (London, 1821).
Brown, William, *New Zealand and its Aborigines* (London, 1845).
Bryant, Jacob, *A New System, or an Analysis of Antient Mythology*, 3 vols (London, 1774–76).
Buchanan, Francis, *A Journey from Madras through the countries of Mysore, Canara and Malabar*, 3 vols (London, 1807).
Buck, Peter [Te Rangi Hiroa], *Vikings of the Sunrise* (New York, 1938).
Buddle, Thomas, *The Maori King Movement* (Auckland, 1860).
Buick, T. Lindsay, *An Old New Zealander, or, Te Rauparaha, the Napoleon of the south* (London, 1911).

Buick, T. Lindsay, *The Treaty of Waitangi* (Wellington, 1914).

Buller, James, *Forty Years in New Zealand: including a Personal Narrative, an Account of Maoridom, and of the Christianization and Colonization of the Country* (London, 1878).

Bunsen, C. C. J., *Christianity and Mankind: Volume I Outlines of the Philosophy of Universal History* (London, 1854).

Bunsen, C. C. J., *God in History, or the Progress of Man's faith in the Moral order of the world*, trans. S. Winkworth, 2 vols (London, 1868).

Butler, Samuel, *A First Year in the Canterbury Settlement*, A. C. Brassington and P. B. Maling eds (Auckland, 1964).

Caird, Edward, *The Evolution of Religion*, 2 vols (Glasgow, 1893).

Caldwell, Robert, *A Comparative Grammar of the Dravidian or South-Indian Family of Languages* (London, 1874 [1856]).

Callander, V., *Terra Australis cognita*, 3 vols (Edinburgh 1766–68).

Campbell, George, *Memoirs of my Indian Career*, C. E. Bernard ed. 2 vols (London, 1883).

Cannon, Garland (ed.), *The Letters of Sir William Jones*, 2 vols (Oxford, 1970).

Chapone, Hester, *Letters on the Improvement of the Mind and Miscellanies in Prose and Verse*, 2 vols (Dublin, 1786).

Cole, H. H., *Catalogue of the Objects of Indian Art Exhibited in the Kensington Museum* (London, 1874).

Colebrooke, H. T., *Miscellaneous Essays*, 2 vols (London, 1837).

Colebrooke, H. T., *Remarks on the Husbandry and Internal Commerce of Bengal. Extracted from: Remarks on the present state of the husbandry and commerce of Bengal by H. T. Colebrooke and Lambert* (Calcutta, 1804).

Coleman, J. N., *A Memoir of the Rev. Richard Davis* (London, 1865).

Colenso, William, *The Authentic and Genuine History of the Signing of the Treaty of Waitangi* (Wellington, 1890).

Colenso, William, *Fifty Years Ago in New Zealand* (Napier, 1888).

Colenso, William, *He Pukapuka Waki; he wakakite atu i nga henga o te Hahi o Roma* (Paihia, 1840).

Colenso, William, *Ko te tuarua o nga Pukapuka Waki* (Paihia, 1840).

Cowell, G., *Life and Letters of E. B. Cowell* (London, 1904).

Craik, George Lillie, *The New Zealanders* (London, 1830).

Creagh, General Sir O'Moore, *Indian Studies* (London, n. d.).

Cruise, Richard, *Journal of a Ten Months Residence in New Zealand* (London, 1823).

Cunningham, J. D., *History of the Sikhs* (London, 1849).

Cust, R. N., *Essay on the Common Features, which Appear in all Forms of Religious Belief* (London, 1895).

Cust, R. N., *The Life of Baba Nanuk, the founder of the Sikh sect of the Hindu Religion in the Punjab. For the use of schools* (Lahore, 1859).

Cust, R. N., *Orientation of Early Christian Missionaries in Asia and Africa* (London, 1891).

Cust, R. N., *Pictures of Indian Life Sketched with the Pen from 1852 to 1881* (London, 1881).

Das, Lala Jivan (ed.), *Essays on Swami Dayanand Saraswati and the Arya Samaj* (Lahore, 1902).

Daunton, Martin and Rick Halpern (eds), *Empire and Others. British Encounters with Indigenous Peoples 1600–1850* (London, 1999).

Davis, C. O., *The Life and Times of Patuone, the Celebrated Ngapuhi Chief* (Auckland, 1876).

de Bary, William Theodore (ed.), *Sources of Indian Tradition*, 2 vols (New York, 1964).

Diderot, Denis, *Supplément au Voyage de Bougainville* (Paris, 1935).

Dieffenbach, Ernst, *New Zealand, and its Native Population* (London, 1841).

Dieffenbach, Ernst, *Travels in New Zealand*, 2 vols (London, 1843).

Dilke, C.W., *Greater Britain: a record of travel in English-speaking countries during 1866 and 1867*, 3 vols (London, 1868).

Dow, Alexander (trans. and ed.), *The History of Hindostan*, 2 vols (London, 1768).

Earle, Augustus, *Narrative of a Residence in New Zealand. Journal of a Residence in Tristan da Cunha*, E. H. McCormick ed. (Oxford, 1966).

Elder, J. R. (ed.), *The Letters and Journals of Samuel Marsden 1765–1838* (Dunedin, 1932).

Elder, J. R. (ed.), *Marsden's Lieutenants* (Dunedin, 1934).

Eyre, Vincent, *The Sikh and European Soldiers of Our Indian Forces. A Lecture* (London, 1867).

Falcon, R. W., *Handbook on Sikhs for the use of Regimental Officers* (Allahabad, 1896).

Fenton, Francis Dart, *Suggestions for a History of the Origin and Migration of the Maori People* (Auckland, 1885).

Fergusson, James, *On the Study of Indian Architecture* (London, 1867).

Fornander, Abraham, *An Account of the Polynesian Race, its origin and migrations; and the ancient history of the Hawaiian people to the times of Kamehameha I*, 3 vols (London, 1878–85).

Forster, Georg, *A Voyage Round the World, in His Britannic Majesty's Sloop, Resolution, commanded by Capt. James Cook*, 2 vols (London, 1777).

Forster, Johann Reinhold, *Observations Made During a Voyage Round the World: on physical geography, natural history, and ethic philosophy* (London, 1778).

Ghosha, Ramachandra, *History of Hindu civilisation, as illustrated in the Vedas and their appendages* (Calcutta, 1889).

Ghosha, Ramachandra, *The Indo-Aryans, their History, Creed and Practice* (Calcutta, 1881).

Gill, William Wyatt, *Myths and Songs from the South Pacific* (London, 1876).

Gorst, John, *The Maori King* (Auckland, 1959 [1864]).

Green, J. R., *A Short History of the English people* (London, 1874).

Grey, George, *Journals of Two Expeditions of Discovery in North-west and Western Australia, during the years 1837, 38, and 39, under the authority of Her Majesty's Government* (London, 1841).

Grey, George, *Polynesian Mythology, and Ancient Traditional History of the New Zealand race, as Furnished by their Priests and Chiefs* (London, 1855).

Grey, George, *A Vocabulary of the Dialects of South-western Australia* (London, 1840).

Griffin, Lepel Henry, *The Rajas of the Punjab. Being the history of the principal states of the Punjab and their political relations with the British Government* (Lahore, 1870).

Griffin, Lepel Henry, *Ranjit Singh* (Delhi, 1957 [1892]).

Griffith, Ralph T. H., *The Hymns of the Rigveda. Translated with a Popular Commentary*, J. L. Shastri ed. (revd edn (Delhi, 1973).

Hahn, Th., *An Index of the Grey Collection in the South African Public Library* (Cape Town, 1884).

Halhed, Nathaniel Brassey, *Grammar of the Bengal Language* (Hooghli, 1778).

Harlow, Ray (ed.), *A Word-List of South Island Maori* (Dunedin, 1987).

Hawkesworth, John (ed.), *An Account of the Voyages Undertaken by the Order of His Present Majesty for Making Discoveries in the Southern Hemisphere*, 3 vols (London, 1773).

Hodgson, B. H., *Preeminence of the Vernaculars* (Serampore, 1839).

Hunter, W. W., *Annals of Rural Bengal* (Calcutta, 1868).

Hursthouse, Charles, *An Account of the Settlement of New Plymouth* (London, 1849).

Ibbetson, Denzil, *Panjab Castes. Being a Reprint of the chapter on 'The Races, Castes and Tribes of the People' in the Report on the Census of the Panjab published in 1883* (Lahore, 1916).

Jackson, J. W., *Ethnology and Phrenology, as an Aid to the Historian* (London, 1863).

Jameson, R. G., *New Zealand, South Australia and New South Wales* (London, 1841).

Jones, William, *A Discourse on the Institution of a Society for Enquiring into the History of Asia, delivered at Calcutta, January 15th, 1784* (London, 1784).

Jones, William, *The Works of Sir William Jones, with a Life of the Author by Lord Teignmouth*, 13 vols (London, 1807).

Kames, Lord, *Sketches of the History of Man*, 2 vols (Edinburgh, 1774).

Kaye, J. W., *History of the Sepoy War in India*, 3 vols (London, 1864–76).

Kendall, Thomas, *A Korao no New Zealand; or, the New Zealander's first book; being an attempt to compose some lessons for the instruction of the natives* (Sydney, 1815).

King, J. H., *The Supernatural: its Origin, Nature and Evolution* (London, 1892).

Laing, Samuel, *Lecture on the Indo-European Languages and Races* (Calcutta, 1862).

Laing, Samuel, *A Modern Zoroastrian* (London, 1887).

Lang, Andrew, *The Making of Religion* (London, 1898).

Lang, J. D., *A View of the Origin and Migrations of the Polynesian Nation; demonstrating their ancient discovery and progressive settlement of the Continent of America* (London, 1834).

Latham, R. G., *The Ethnology of the British Islands* (London, 1852).

Lee, Samuel, *A grammar and vocabulary of the language of New Zealand* (London, 1820).

Long, J., *Handbook of Bengal Missions in Connection with the Church of England* (London, 1848).

Lyall, A. C., *Asiatic Studies Religious and Social* (London, 1882).

Lyall, A. C., *Natural Religion in India. The Rede Lecture Delivered in the Senate House on June 17, 1891* (Cambridge, 1891).

Macauliffe, M. A., *How the Sikhs became a Militant People* (Paris, 1905).

Macauliffe, Max Arthur, *The Sikh Religion. Its Gurus, sacred writings and authors*, 6 vols (Oxford, 1909).

MacMunn, G. F., *The Armies of India* (London, 1911).

McRae, Colonel H. St G. M., *Regimental History of the 45th Rattray's Sikhs. Volume I, 1856–1914* (London, 1933).

Maine, H. S., *Dissertations on Early Law and Customs* (London, 1883).

Maine, Henry Sumner, *The Effects of Observation of India on Modern European Thought* (London, 1875).

Maine, H. S., *Village-communities in the East and West* (London, 1871).

Maning, F. E., *Old New Zealand* (Auckland, 1973 [1887]).

Marjoribanks, Alexander, *Travels in New Zealand, with a map of the country* (London, 1845).

Marshall, William Barret, *A Personal Narrative of Two Visits to New Zealand in His Majesty's Ship Alligator, A. D. 1834* (London, 1836).

Martin, M. (ed.), *The Despatches, Minutes and Correspondence of the Marquess of Wellesley*, 2 vols (London, 1837).

Massey, Gerald, *A Book of the Beginnings*, 2 vols (London, 1881).

Massey, Gerald, *The Natural Genesis*, 2 vols (London, 1883).

Maunsell, R., *Grammar of the New Zealand Language* (Auckland, 1842).

Max Müller, F., *Biographies of Words* (London, 1888).

Max Müller, F., *Contributions to the Science of Mythology* (New York, 1897).

Max Müller, F., *A History of Sanskrit Literature* (London 1859).

Max Müller, F., *Lectures on the Origin and Growth of Religion as Illustrated by the Religions of India. The Hibbert Lectures for 1878* (London, 1878).

Max Müller, F., *The Life and Letters of the Right Honourable Friedrich Max Müller. Edited by his wife*, 2 vols (London, 1902).

Max Müller, F., *Natural Religion* (London, 1889).

Max Müller, F., *Physical Religion. The Gifford Lectures delivered before the University of Glasgow in 1890* (London, 1898).

Max Müller, F., *Science of Mythology*, 2 vols (London, 1897).

Max Müller, F., *Selected Essays on Language, Mythology and Religion*, 2 vols (London, 1881).

Mill, James, *The History of British India*, Horace Hayman Wilson ed. 5th edn, 10 vols (London, 1858).

Monier-Williams, Monier, *Brahminism and Hinduism or Religious Thought and life in India based on the Veda and other sacred books of the Hindus*, 3rd edn (London, 1887).

Monier-Williams, Monier, *Hinduism* (London, 1877).

Monier-Williams, Monier, *Indian Wisdom or Examples of the Religious, Philosophical, and Ethical Doctrines of the Hindus* (London, 1875).

Muir, John, *Original Sanskrit Texts on the origin and progress of the religions and institutions of India*, 1st edn, 3 vols (London, 1858–61).

Muir, John, *Original Sanskrit Texts on the origin and progress of the religions and institutions of India*, (3rd edn, 3 vols (London, 1874).

Newman, Alfred, *Who are the Maoris?* (Christchurch, n.d. [1912]).

O'Flaherty, Wendy Doniger (trans. and ed.), *The Rig Veda: An Anthology* (Harmondsworth, 1981).

O'Halloran, Sylvester, *An Introduction to the Study of the History and Antiquities of Ireland* (London, 1772).

Osborne, W. T., *The Camp and Court of Ranjit Sing* (London, 1840).

Page, Jesse, *Among the Maoris or Daybreak in New Zealand. A record of the Labours of Samuel Marsden, Bishop Selwyn, and Others* (London, n.d. [1864?]).

Parsons, Lawrence, *Observations on the Bequest of Henry Flood* (Dublin, 1795).

Petrie, David, *Recent Developments in Sikh Politics, 1900–1911, a Report* (Amritsar, 1911).

Philpot, Isaline, *The Sacred Tree: or, the tree in religion and myth* (London, 1894).

Pictet, Adolphe, *De l'affinité des langues celtiques avec le Sanscrit* (Paris, 1838).

Polack, Joel Samuel, *Manners and Customs of the New Zealanders*, 2 vols (London, 1840).

Polack, Joel Samuel, *New Zealand: being a narrative of travels and adventures during a residence in that country between 1831 and 1837*, 2 vols (London, 1838).

Pompallier, Jean-Baptiste François, *Early History of the Catholic Church in Oceania* (Auckland, 1888).

Porter, Frances (ed.), *The Turanga Journals* (Wellington, 1974).

Prichard, James Cowles, *An Analysis of Egyptian Mythology: To Which is Subjoined a Critical Examination of the Remains of Christian Chronology* (London, 1819).

Prichard, James Cowles, *The Eastern Origin of the Celtic Nations Proved by a Comparison of their Dialects with the Sanskrit, Greek, Latin and Teutonic Languages. Forming a Supplement to the Researches into the Physical History of Mankind* (London, 1831).

Prichard, James Cowles, *The Natural History of Man; comprising inquiries into the modifying influence of physical and moral agencies on the different tribes of the human family* (London, 1843).

Prichard, James Cowles, *Researches into the Physical History of Man*, George Stocking Jr., ed. (Chicago, 1973 [1813]).

Priestly, Joseph, *A Comparison of the Institutes of Moses with those of the Hindoos and other Ancient Nations* (Northumberland, 1799).

Ragozin, Zénaïde A., *Vedic India as Embodied Principally in the Rig-Veda* (London, 1895).

Ranade, Mahadeva Govind, *Religious and Social Reform*, M. B. Kolasker ed. (Bombay, 1902).

Rendall, George H., *The Cradle of the Aryans* (London, 1889).

Roberts, W. H., *Place Names and the Early History of Otago and Southland* (Invercargill, 1913).

Robertson, William, *An Historical Disquisition Concerning the Knowledge which the ancients had of India* (London, 1791).

Robson, J. M., M. Moir and Z. Moir (eds), *Writings on India by John Stuart Mill. Collected works of John Stuart Mill, volume 30* (Toronto, 1990).

Rogers, Lawrence M. (ed.), *The Early Journals of Henry Williams 1826–40* (Christchurch, 1961).

Russell, W. H., *My Indian Mutiny Diary*, M. Edwardes ed. (London, 1957).

Sarda, Har Bilas, *Hindu Superiority – an attempt to determine the position of the Hindu race in the scale of nations* (New Delhi, 1975 [1906]).

Scrafton, Luke, *Reflections on the Government, &c., of Indostan: and a short sketch of the History of Bengal, from the year 1739 to 1756* (Edinburgh, 1761).

Shortland, Edward, *How to Learn Maori* (Auckland, 1883).

Shortland, Edward, *Maori Religion and Mythology* (London, 1882).

Shortland, Edward, *A Short Sketch of the Maori Races* (Dunedin, 1865).

Shuckford, Samuel, *Sacred and Profane History of the World Connnected*, (5th edn (London, 1819 [1728]).

Singh, Ganda (ed.), *Early European Accounts of the Sikhs* (Calcutta, 1962).

Sleeman, W. H., *Ramaseeana, or a vocabularly of the peculiar language used by the Thugs* (Calcutta, 1836).

Smith, Percy S., *Hawaiki, the Original home of the Maori* (Wellington, 1898).

Solvyns, F. Baltazard, *Les Hindous, ou description de leurs moeurs, coutumes et céré-monies*, 4 vols (Paris, 1808–12).

Srinivasachari, C. S. (ed.), *Fort William-India House Correspondence. Vol. IV: 1764–1766* (Delhi, 1962).

Steel, Flora Annie (comp. and trans.), *Tales of the Punjab Told by the People* (Lahore, 1894).

Stubbs, William, *The Constitutional History of England*, 3 vols (Oxford, 1874–78).

Taylor, Richard, *A Leaf from the Natural History of New Zealand* (Wellington, 1848).

Taylor, Richard, *Our Race and its Origin* (Auckland, 1867).

Taylor, Richard, *The Past and Present of New Zealand: with its prospects for the future* (London, 1868).

Taylor, Richard, *Te Ika a Maui, or New Zealand and its inhabitants*, 1st edn (London, 1855).

Taylor, Richard, *Te Ika a Maui, or New Zealand and its inhabitants*, 2nd edn (London, 1870).

Teignmouth, Lord, *Memoirs of the Life, Writings, and Correspondence of Sir William Jones* (London, 1804).

Tenant, William, *Indian Recreations: consisting chiefly of strictures on the domestic and rural economy of the Mohommedans and Hindoos*, 2 vols (London, 1804).

Thomson, A. S., *The Story of New Zealand* (London, 1859).

Thomson, John Turnbull, *An Exposition of Processes and Results of the Survey System of Otago* (Dunedin, 1875).

Thomson, John Turnbull, *An Outline of the Principles and Details connected with the Colonial Survey of the Province of Otago* (Dunedin, 1861).

Thomson, John Turnbull, *Rambles with a Philosopher or, Views at the Antipodes by an Otagoian* (Dunedin, 1867).

Thomson, John Turnbull, *Social Problems: an inquiry into the law of influences* (London, 1878).

Thomson, John Turnbull, *Some Glimpses into Life in the Far East* (London, 1864).

Tilak, Bal Gangadhar, *The Arctic Home in the Vedas, Being Also a New Key to the Interpretation of Many Vedic Texts and Legends* (Poona, 1903).

Tilak, Bal Gangadhar, *Orion, or Researches into the Antiquity of the Vedas by B. G. Tilak, BA, LLB* (London, 1892).

Tilak, Bal Gangadhar, *Speeches of Bal Gangadhar Tilak (Delivered During 1889–1918)* (Madras, n.d.).

Travers, W. T. L., *The Stirring Times of Te Rauparaha (Chief of the Ngatitoa)* (Christchurch, 1906 [1872]).

Trumpp, Ernest, *The Adi Granth, or the Holy Scriptures of the Sikhs, translated from the original Gurmukhi, with introductory essays* (London, 1887).

Tregear, Edward, *The Aryan Maori* (Wellington, 1885).

Tregear, Edward, *The Maori–Polynesian Comparative Dictionary* (Christchurch, 1891).

Tylor, E. B., *Primitive Culture: Researches into the Development of Mythology, Philosophy, Religion, Art and Custom*, 2 vols (London, 1871).

Ullathorne, W. B., *The Autobiography of Archbishop Ullathorne with selections from his letters* (London, 1891).

Vallancey, Charles, *An Essay on the Antiquity of the Irish language: Being a collation of the Irish with the Punic language* (Dublin, 1772).

Vallancey, Charles, *A Grammar of the Iberno-Celtic, or Irish language* (Dublin, 1773).

Vigne, G. T., *Travels in Kashmir, Ladak, Iskardo, the countries adjoining the mountain-course of the Indus, and the Himalaya, north of the Panjab* (London, 1842).

Wade, William, *A Journey in the Northern Island of New Zealand* (Hobart, 1842).

Walker, J. C., *Historical Memoirs of Irish Bards* (London, 1786).

White, John, *The ancient history of the Maori, his mythology and traditions*, 6 vols (Wellington, 1887–90).

White, John, *Te Rou; or, the Maori at home* (London, 1874).

Wilkins, Charles, *The Bhagvat-geeta, or Dialogues of Kreeshna and Arjoon; in eighteen lectures* (London, 1785).

Wilkins, Charles, *The Heetopades of Veeshnoo-Sarma, in a series of connected fables, interspersed with moral, prudential, and political maxims; translated from an ancient manuscript in the Sanskreet language* (Bath, 1787).

Williams, William, *Christianity Among the New Zealanders* (London, 1867).

Wilson, H. H., *A Glossary of judicial and revenue terms, and of useful words occurring in official documents relating to the administration of the government of British India* (London, 1855).

Wilson, H. H., *The Mackenzie Collection: a descriptive catalogue of the oriental manuscripts, and other articles illustrative of the literature, history, statistics and antiquities of the south of India collected by Colin Mackenzie* (Calcutta, 1828).

Wilson, H. H., *Sketch of the Religious Sects of the Hindus* (Calcutta, 1846).

Wilson, H. H., *Two Lectures on the Religious Practices and Opinions of the Hindus; delivered before the University of Oxford on the 27th and 28th February, 1840* (Oxford, 1840).

Yate, William, *An Account of New Zealand* (London, 1835).

Secondary sources

Books

Aarsleff, Hans, *The Study of Language in England, 1780–1860* (Princeton, NJ, 1967).

Akensen, Donald Harman, *Half the World from Home. Perspectives on the Irish in New Zealand* (Wellington, 1990).

Akenson, Donald Harman, *The Irish Diaspora: A Primer* (Toronto, 1996).

Anderson, Atholl, *The Welcome of Strangers. An Ethnohistory of Southern Maori A. D. 1650–1850* (Dunedin, 1998).

Anderson, Atholl, *When All the Moa Ovens Grew Cold: Nine Centuries of Changing Fortune for the Southern Maori* (Dunedin, 1983).

Anderson, Benedict, *Imagined Communities. Reflections on the Origin and Spread of Nationalism*, revd edn (London, 1991).

Arnstein, Walter L., *Protestant versus Catholic in Mid-Victorian England* (Columbia, MO, 1982).

Asad, Talal, *Genealogies of Religion: Discipline and Reasons of Power in Christianity and Islam* (Baltimore, MD, 1993).

Asher, R. E. (ed.), *The Encyclopedia of Language and Linguistics*, 10 vols (Oxford, 1994).

Balagangadhara, S. N., *'The Heathen in his Blindness': Asia, the West, and the Dynamic of Religion* (Leiden, 1994).

Basham, A. L. (ed.), *A Cultural History of India* (Oxford, 1975).

Bayly, C. A., *Empire and Information. Intelligence Gathering and Social Communication in India, 1780–1870* (Cambridge, 1996).

Bayly, C. A., *Imperial Meridian. The British Empire and the World 1780–1830* (London, 1989).

Bayly, C. A., *Indian Society and the Making of the British Empire* (Cambridge, 1988).

Bebbington, David, *Evangelicalism in Modern Britain: a History from the 1730s to 1980s* (London, 1989).

Beekes, R. S. P., *Comparative Indo-European Linguistics: an Introduction* (Amsterdam, 1995).

Belich, James, *Making Peoples: a History of the New Zealanders from Polynesian Settlement to the End of the Nineteenth Century* (Auckland, 1996).

Belich, James, *The New Zealand Wars and the Victorian Interpretation of Racial Conflict* (Auckland, 1986).

Best, Elsdon, *The Maori*, 2 vols (Wellington, 1924).

Best, Elsdon, *Some Aspects of Maori Myth and Religion* (Wellington, 1922).

Biswas, S. K., *Autochthon of India and the Aryan Invasion* (New Delhi, 1995).

Boon, James A., *Affinities and Extremes: Crisscrossing the Bittersweet Ethnology of East Indies History, Hindu–Balinese Culture, and Indo-European Allure* (Chicago, 1990).

Bourdieu, Pierre, *Language and Symbolic Power: the Economy of Linguistic Exchanges*, John B. Thompson ed. (Cambridge, 1991).

Breckenridge, Carol A. and Peter van der Veer (eds), *Orientalism and the Postcolonial Predicament. Perspectives on South Asia* (Philadelphia, PA, 1993).

Buckland, C. E. (ed.), *Dictionary of Indian Biography* (Delhi, 1971).

Burke, Peter and Roy Porter (eds), *Languages and Jargons. Contributions to a Social History of Language* (Cambridge, 1995).

Burrow, J. W., *Evolution and Society. A Study in Victorian Social Theory* (Cambridge, 1966).

Burton, Antoinette, *At the Heart of the Empire: Indians and the Colonial Encounter in Late Victorian Britain* (Berkeley, CA, 1998).

Burton, Antoinette (ed.), *Gender, Sexuality, and Colonial Modernities* (London, 1999).

Cain, P. J. and A. G. Hopkins, *British Imperialism: Innovation and Expansion, 1688–1914* (London, 1993).

Cannon, Garland, *The Life and Mind of Oriental Jones: Sir William Jones, the Father of Modern Linguistics* (Cambridge, 1990).

Caplan, Lionel, *Warrior Gentlemen: 'Gurkhas' in the Western Imagination* (London, 1995).

Carleton, Hugh, *The Life of Henry Williams* (Wellington, 1948).

Chandra, Sudhir, *The Oppressive Present. Literature and Social Consciousness in Colonial India* (Delhi, 1994).

Chatterjee, Partha, *Nationalist Thought and the Colonial World: a Derivative Discourse?* (London, 1986).

Chaudhuri, K. N., *The Trading World of Asia and the East India Company, 1600–1760* (Cambridge, 1978).

Chaudhuri, Nirad K., *Scholar Extraordinary. The Life of Professor the Rt. Hon. Friedrich Max Müller P. C.* (London, 1974).

Chidester, David, *Savage Systems: Colonialism and Comparative Religion in Southern Africa* (Charlottesville, VA, 1996).

Choudhury, Paramesh, *The Aryan Hoax, that Dupes the Indians* (Calcutta, 1995).

Chowdhury, Indira, *The Frail Hero and Virile History: Gender and the Politics of Culture in Colonial Bengal* (Delhi, 1998).

Clancy, Robert, *The Mapping of Terra Australis* (Macquarie Park, NSW, 1995).

Clark, Paul, *'Hauhau'. The Pai Marire Search for Maori Identity* (Auckland, 1975).

Clifford, James, and G. Marcus (eds), *Writing Culture: the Poetics and Politics of Ethnography* (Berkeley, CA, 1986).

Cohen, Stephen P., *The Indian Army: Its Contribution to the Development of a Nation* (Berkeley, CA, 1971).

Cohn, Bernard S., *Colonialism and Its Forms of Knowledge: the British in India* (Princeton, NJ, 1996).

Collison, R. L., *A History of Foreign Language Dictionaries* (Southampton, 1982).

Cook, S. B., *Imperial Affinities. Nineteenth Century Analogies and Exchanges Between India and Ireland* (New Delhi, 1993).

Cowan, James, *The New Zealand Wars. A History of the Maori Campaigns and the Pioneering Period*, 2 vols (Wellington, 1922).

Cox, Lindsay, *Kotahitanga: the Search for Maori Political Unity* (Auckland, 1993).

Crook, Nigel (ed.), *The Transmission of Knowledge in South Asia. Essays on Education, Religion, History and Politics* (Delhi, 1996).

Crosby, Alfred W., *Ecological Imperialism. The Biological Expansion of Europe, 900–1900* (Cambridge, 1986).

Dacker, Bill, *Te Mamae me te Aroha: The Pain and the Love. A History of Kai Tahu Whanui in Otago, 1844–1994* (Dunedin, 1994).

Dalmia, Vasudha, *The Nationalization of Hindu Traditions: Bharatendu Harishchandra and Nineteenth-century Banaras* (Delhi, 1997).

Dalmia, Vasudha and Heinrich von Stietencron (eds), *Representing Hinduism: the construction of religious traditions and national identity* (Delhi, 1995).

Das, Sisir Kumar, *Sahibs and Munshis: an Account of the College of Fort William* (Calcutta, 1978).

Davidson, Allan K., *Evangelicals and Attitudes to India 1786–1813. Missionary Publicity and Claudius Buchanan* (n.p., 1990).

de Certeau, Michel, *The Practice of Everyday Life*, S. Rendall trans. (Berkeley, CA, 1984).

Department of Internal Affairs (NZ), *The Dictionary of New Zealand Biography. Volume One, 1769–1869* (Wellington, 1990).

Derret, J. D. M., *Religion, Law and State in India* (London, 1968).

Deshpande, Madhav, *Sanskrit and Prakrit: Sociolinguistic Issues* (Delhi, 1993).

Deshpande, Madhav M. and Peter Edwin Hook (eds), *Aryan and Non-Aryan in India* (Ann Arbor, MI, 1979).

Diamond, Alan (ed.), *The Victorian Achievement of Sir Henry Maine* (Cambridge, 1991).

Dorson, R. M., *The British Folklorists: A History* (London, 1968).

Drayton, Richard, *Nature's Government: Science, Imperial Britain, and the 'Improvement' of the World* (New Haven, CT, 2000).

Edney, Matthew H., *Mapping an Empire: the Geographical Construction of British India, 1765–1843* (Chicago, 1997).

Ellwood, Robert S., *Islands of the Dawn. The story of Alternative Spirituality in New Zealand* (Honolulu, 1993).

Elsmore, Bronwyn, *Like Them That Dream. The Maori and the Old Testament* (Tauranga, 1985).

Elsmore, Bronwyn, *Mana from Heaven: a Century of Maori Prophets in New Zealand* (Tauranga, 1989).

Finnegan, Ruth, *Literacy and Orality: Studies in the Technology of Communication* (Oxford, 1988).

Firth, Raymond, *Economics of the New Zealand Maori*, 2nd edn (Wellington, 1959).

Firth, Raymond, *The Primitive Economics of the Maori* (London, 1929).

Firth, Raymond, *We, the Tikopia* (London, 1936).

Fisher, Michael (ed.), *The Travels of Dean Mahomet* (Berkeley, CA, 1997).

Foley, Tadhg, *From Queen's College to National University: Essays towards an Academic History of NUI, Galway* (Galway, 1999).

Foley, Tadhg and Sean Ryder (eds), *Ideology and Ireland in the Nineteenth Century* (Dublin, 1998).

Fox, Richard, *Lions of the Punjab: Culture in the Making* (Berkeley, CA, 1985).

Frank, Andre Gunder, *ReOrient: Global Economy in the Asian Age* (Berkeley, CA, 1998).

Fraser, Lyndon (ed.), *A Distant Shore: Irish Migration and New Zealand Settlement* (Dunedin, 2000).

Frawley, David, *The Myth of the Aryan Invasion of India* (New Delhi, 1994).

Friedman, O. Michael, *Origins of the British Israelites: the Lost Tribes* (San Francisco, 1993).

Fuller, C. J., *The Camphor Flame: Popular Hinduism and Society in India* (Princeton, NJ, 1992).

Gidwani, Bhagwan S., *Return of the Aryans* (New Delhi, 1994).

Ginzburg, Carlo, *The Cheese and the Worms: the Cosmos of a Sixteenth-century Miller*, John and Ann Tedeschi eds (Baltimore, MD, 1992).

Goldman, Irving, *Ancient Polynesian Society* (Chicago, 1970).

Goody, Jack, *The Interface between the Written and the Oral* (Cambridge, 1987).

Green, R. C. and M. Kelly (eds), *Studies in Oceanic Culture History*, 2 vols (Honolulu, HI, 1971).

Greenwood, William, *The Upraised Hand, or The Spiritual Significance of the Rise of the Ringatu Faith* (Wellington, 1942).

Grewal, J. S., *Guru Nanak in Western Scholarship* (Shimla, 1992).

Grove, Richard H., *Ecology, Climate and Empire: Colonialism and Global Environmental History, 1400–1940* (Cambridge, 1997).

Grove, Richard, *Green Imperialism: Colonial Expansion, Tropical Island Edens and the Origins of Environmentalism, 1600–1860* (Cambridge, 1995).

Grove, Richard H., Vinita Damodaran and Satpal Sangwan (eds), *Nature and the Orient: the Environmental History of South and Southeast Asia* (Delhi, 1998).

Guha, Ranajit, *Elementary Aspects of Peasant Insurgency in Colonial India* (Oxford, 1983).

Guha, Ranajit (ed.), *Subaltern Studies IV. Writings on South Asian History and Society* (Delhi, 1985).

Halbfass, Wilhelm, *India and Europe – an Essay in Understanding* (New York, 1988).

Hancock, David, *Citizens of the World: London Merchants and the Integration of the British Atlantic Community, 1735–1785* (Cambridge, 1995).

Hanson, F. Allan and Louise Hanson, *Counterpoint in Maori Culture* (London, 1983).

Harlow, Ray. *Otago's First Book: The Distinctive Dialect of Southern Maori* (Dunedin, 1994).

Harlow, Vincent, *The Founding of the Second British Empire, 1763–93*, 2 vols (London, 1952–64).

Harris, Roy and Talbot J. Taylor, *Landmarks in Linguistic Thought. The Western Tradition from Socrates to Saussure* (London, 1989).

Harrison, Peter, *'Religion' and the Religions in the English Enlightenment* (Cambridge, 1990).

Hatcher, Brian A., *Idioms of Improvement: Vidyasagar and Cultural Encounter in Bengal* (Delhi, 1996).

Hiatt, L. R., *Arguments about Aborigines* (Cambridge, 1996).

Hodgson, Marshall S., *Rethinking World History: Essays on Europe, Islam, and World History*, Edmund Burke III ed. (Cambridge, 1993).

Hogg, Richard M. (ed.), *The Cambridge History of the English Language. Volume I The Beginnings to 1066* (Cambridge, 1992).

Howe, Kerry, *Singer in a Songless Land: a Life of Edward Tregear, 1846–1931* (Auckland, 1991).

Innis, Harold, *Staples, Markets and Cultural Change: Selected Essays*, Daniel Drache ed. (Montreal, 1995).

Irschick, Eugene, *Dialogue and History. Constructing South India, 1795–1895* (Berkeley, CA, 1994).

Irwin, James, *An Introduction to Maori Religion* (Bedford Park, South Australia, 1984).

Jeffrey, Keith (ed.), *An Irish Empire? Aspects of Ireland and the British Empire* (Manchester, 1996).

Jenkins, Kuni E. H., *Becoming Literate, Becoming English* (Auckland, 1993).

Jones, Pei Te Hurunui, *King Potatau* (Wellington, 1959).

Jordens, J. T. F., *Dayananda Sarasvati: His Life and Ideas* (Delhi, 1978).

Kapur, Rajiv A., *Sikh Separatism. The Politics of Faith* (London, 1986).

Kejariwal, O. P., *The Asiatic Society of Bengal and the Discovery of India's Past 1784–1838* (Delhi, 1988).

Kidd, Colin, *British Identities before Nationalism: Ethnicity and Nationhood in the Atlantic World, 1600–1800* (Cambridge, 1999).

King, Anthony, *Colonial Urban Development* (London, 1976).

King, Michael (ed.), *Te Ao Hurihuri: Aspects of Maoritanga* (Auckland, 1992).

King, Richard, *Orientalism and Religion: Postcolonial Theory, India and the 'Mystic East'* (London, 1999).

Kling, Blair and M. N. Pearson (eds), *The Age of Partnership: Europeans in Asia before Dominion* (Honolulu, HI, 1979).

Kopf, David, *British Orientalism and the Bengal Renaissance. The Dynamics of Indian Modernization 1773–1835* (Berkeley, CA, 1969).

Lach, Donald, *Asia and the Making of Europe, Volume III: Book 2* (Chicago, 1993).

Lahiri, Shompa, *Indians in Britain: Anglo-Indian encounters, race and identity, 1880–1930* (London, 2000).

Leerssen, Joep, *Mere Irish and Fíor-Ghael: Studies in the Idea of Irish Nationality, Its Development and Literary Expression Prior to the Nineteenth Century* (Cork, 1996).

Little, J. H., *The House of Jagat Seth*, N. K. Sinha ed. (Calcutta, 1967).

Luomala, Katharine, *Maui-of-a-thousand-tricks: His Oceanic and European biographers* (Honolulu, HI, 1949).

Macdonell, Arthur A., *A Sanskrit–English Dictionary* (London, 1893).

Mackenzie, John M. (ed.), *Imperialism and Popular Culture* (Manchester, 1986).

Mackenzie, John, *Orientalism: History, Theory, and the Arts* (Manchester, 1995).

McLeod, W. H., *Early Sikh Tradition: a Study of the Janam-sakhis* (Oxford, 1980).

MacLeod, Roy and Philip H. Rehbock (eds), *Darwin's Laboratory: Evolutionary Theory and Natural History in the Pacific* (Honolulu, 1994).

McLeod, W. H., *Guru Nanak and the Sikh Religion* (Oxford, 1968).

McLeod, W. H., *Who is a Sikh? The Problem of Sikh Identity* (Oxford, 1989).

McLintock, Anne, *Imperial Leather. Race, Gender and Sexuality in the Colonial Contest* (New York, 1995).

Majeed, Javed, *Ungoverned Imaginings. James Mill's The History of British India and Orientalism* (Oxford, 1992).

Manuel, Frank E., *The Eighteenth Century Confronts the Gods* (Cambridge, MA, 1959).
Marshall, P. J., *Bengal: the British Bridgehead. Eastern India, 1740–1828* (Cambridge, 1987).
Marshall, P. J., *East India Fortunes: the British in Bengal in the Eighteenth Century* (Oxford, 1976).
Marshall, P. J. (ed.), *The Oxford History of the British Empire. The Eighteenth Century* (Oxford, 1998).
Marshall, P. J. and Glyndwr Williams, *The Great Map of Mankind. British Perceptions of the World in the Age of Enlightenment* (London, 1982).
Masuzawa, Tomoko, *In Search of Dreamtime. The Quest for the Origin of Religion* (Chicago, 1993).
Matsuda, Matt K., *The Memory of the Modern* (New York, 1996).
Maw, Martin, *Visions of India. Fulfilment Theology, the Aryan Race Theory, and the Work of British Protestant Missionaries in Victorian India* (Frankfurt, 1990).
McKenzie, D. F., *Oral Culture, Literacy and Print in Early New Zealand: the Treaty of Waitangi* (Wellington, 1985).
McLaren-Turner, Patricia (ed.), *Australian and New Zealand Studies* (London, 1985).
Metcalf, Thomas, *Ideologies of the Raj* (Cambridge, 1995).
Metcalf, Thomas R., *An Imperial Vision. Indian Architecture and Britain's Raj* (London, 1989).
Milner, Anthony, *The Invention of Politics in Colonial Malaya: Contesting Nationalism and the Expansion of the Public Sphere* (Cambridge, 1995).
Mitcalfe, Barry, *Maori Poetry. The Singing Word* (Wellington, 1974).
Moorehead, Alan, *The Fatal Impact: an Account of the Invasion of the South Pacific 1767–1840* (London, 1966).
Morgan, Hiram (ed.), *Information, Media and Power through the Ages* (Dublin, 2001).
Mukherjee, S. N., *Calcutta: Myths and History* (Calcutta, 1977).
Mukherjee, S. N., *Sir William Jones. A Study in Eighteenth Century British Attitudes to India* (Cambridge, 1968).
Neufeldt, Ronald W., *F. Max Müller and the Rig-Veda: a Study of Its Role in His Work and Thought* (Calcutta, 1980).
Oberoi, Harjot, *The Construction of Religious Boundaries: Culture, Identity and Diversity in the Sikh Tradition* (Delhi, 1994).
Oliver, W. H. (ed.), *The Oxford History of New Zealand*, 1st edn (Wellington, 1981).
Omissi, David, *The Sepoy and the Raj: the Indian Army, 1860–1940* (London, 1994).
Orange, Claudia, *The Treaty of Waitangi* (Wellington, 1987).
Orbell, Margaret, *Hawaiki: a New Approach to Maori Tradition* (Christchurch, 1991).
Orbell, Margaret, *The Illustrated Encyclopedia of Maori Myth and Legend* (Christchurch, 1995).
Orbell, Margaret, *Maori Folktales in Maori and English* (London, 1968).
Orsman, H. W., *The Dictionary of New Zealand English: a Dictionary of New Zealandisms on Historical Principles* (Auckland, 1997).
Pandey, Gyanendra, *The Construction of Communalism in Colonial North India* (Delhi, 1992).
Pinch, William R., *Peasants and Monks in British India* (Berkeley, CA, 1996).
Po-Chia Hsia, R., *Social Discipline in the Reformation: Central Europe, 1550–1750* (London, 1989).
Poliakov, Leon, *The Aryan Myth: a History of Racist and Nationalist Ideas in Europe*, Edmund Howard trans. (London, 1973).

Pool, Ian, *Te iwi Maori: a New Zealand Population, Past, Present and Projected* (Auckland, 1991).

Prakash, Gyan, *Another Reason: Science and the Imagination in Modern India* (Princeton, NJ, 1998).

Pratt, Mary Louise, *Imperial Eyes: Travel Writing and Transculturation* (London, 1992).

Preus, J. Samuel, *Explaining Religion: Criticism and Theory from Bodin to Freud* (New Haven, CT, 1987).

Prichard, Muriel Lloyd, *An Economic History of New Zealand to 1939* (Auckland, 1970).

Pyenson, Louis, *Empire of Reason; Exact Sciences in Indonesia, 1840–1940* (Leiden, 1989).

Rai, Lala Lajpat, *A History of the Arya Samaj*, Shri Ram Sharma ed. (Bombay, 1967).

Rajaram, Navaratna Srinivasa, *Aryan Invasion of India: the Myth and the Truth* (New Delhi, 1993).

Rajaram, Navaratna, *The Politics of History: Aryan Invasion Theory and the Subversion of Scholarship* (New Delhi, 1995).

Raychaudhuri, Tapan, *Europe Reconsidered. Perceptions of the West in Nineteenth Century Bengal* (Delhi, 1988).

Richards, Thomas, *The Imperial Archive: Knowledge and the Fantasy of Empire* (London, 1993).

Robb, Peter (ed.) *The Concept of Race in South Asia* (Delhi, 1997).

Robins, R. H., *A Short History of Linguistics*, 4th edn (London, 1997).

Rocher, Rosane, *Alexander Hamilton (1762–1824): A Chapter in the Early History of Sanskrit Philology* (New Haven, CT, 1968).

Ross, Michael, *Bougainville* (London, 1978).

Ross, W. Hugh, *Te Kooti Rikirangi: General and Prophet* (Auckland, 1966).

Ryerson, Charles, *Regionalism and Identity: the Tamil Renaissance and Popular Hinduism* (Madras, 1988).

Said, Edward, *Culture and Imperialism* (New York, 1993).

Salmond, Ann, *Two Worlds: First Meetings between Maori and Europeans 1642–1772* (Auckland, 1991).

Samson, Jane, *Imperial Benevolence: Making British Authority in the Pacific Islands* (Honululu, HI, 1998).

Sarda, Har Bilas, *Life of Dayanand Saraswati* (Ajmer, 1946).

Scharfe, Hartmut, *A History of Indian Literature. Volume 5, Part 2, Grammatical Literature* (Wiesbaden, 1977).

Scholefield, G. H. (ed.), *Dictionary of New Zealand Biography*, 2 vols (Wellington, 1940).

Schwab, Raymond, *Oriental Renaissance: Europe's Rediscovery of India and the East, 1680–1880*, Gene Patterson-Black and Victor Reinking trans. (New York, 1984).

Schwarz, Bill (ed.), *The Expansion of England: Race, Ethnicity and Cultural History* (London, 1996).

Schwartz, Stuart B. (ed.), *Implicit Understandings: Observing, Reporting, and Reflecting on Encounters Between Europeans and Other Peoples in the Early Modern Era* (Cambridge, 1994).

Sharpe, Eric J., *Comparative Religion: a History* (London, 1975).

Sheil, W. T. (ed.), *Studies in Church History. Volume 20: The Church and War* (London, 1980).

Sinclair, Keith, *A History of New Zealand*, 3rd edn (London, 1980).

Singh, Fauja (ed.), *Historians and Historiography of the Sikhs* (New Delhi, 1978).

Singh, Ganda (ed.), *Sources of the Life and Teachings of Guru Nanak* (Patiala, 1969).

Singh, Harbans, *Guru Nanak and Origins of the Sikh Faith* (Bombay, 1969).

Sinha, Mrinalini, *Colonial Masculinity: the 'Manly Englishman' and the 'Effeminate Bengali' in the Late Nineteenth Century* (Manchester, 1995).

Sinha, N. K., *The Economic History of Bengal*, 2 vols (Calcutta, 1962).

Smith, Bernard, *European Vision and the South Pacific, 1768–1850: a Study in the History of Art and Ideas* (Oxford, 1960).

Smith, Bernard, *Imagining the Pacific: in the Wake of the Cook Voyages* (London, 1992).

Smith, Jean, *Tapu Removal in Maori Religion* (Wellington, 1974).

Smith, Jonathon Z., *Imagining Religion: From Babylon to Jonestown* (Chicago, 1982).

Sorrenson, M. P. K., *Maori Origins and Migrations. The Genesis of Some Pakeha Myths and Legends* (Auckland, 1979).

Spate, O. H. K., *Paradise Found and Lost* (Rushcutters Bay, NSW, 1988).

Stocking, George W. Jr, *Victorian Anthropology* (New York, 1987).

Sutton, Douglas (ed.), *The Archaeology of the Kainga: a Study of Precontact Maori Undefended Settlements at Pouerua, Northland, New Zealand* (Auckland, 1994).

Sutton, Douglas G. (ed.), *The Origins of the First New Zealanders* (Auckland, 1994).

Sutton, Douglas (ed.), *Saying So Doesn't Make It So: Papers in Honour of B. Foss Leach* (Dunedin, 1989).

Symonds, Richard, *Oxford and Empire. The Last Lost Cause?* (London, 1986).

Talageri, Shrikant G., *The Aryan Invasion Theory: a Reappraisal* (New Delhi, 1993).

Teltscher, Kate, *India Inscribed: European and British Writing on India* (Delhi, 1995).

Thapar, Romila, *Ancient Indian Social History* (Delhi, 1978).

Thapar, Romila, *A History of India. Volume 1* (Harmondsworth, 1966).

Thapar, Romila, *Interpreting Early India* (Delhi, 1992).

Thomas, Keith, *Religion and the Decline of Magic* (New York, 1971).

Thomas, Nicholas, *Colonialism's Culture: Anthropology, Travel and Government* (Cambridge, 1994).

Thomas, Nicholas, *Out of Time: History and Evolution in Anthropological Discourse* (Cambridge, 1989).

Trautmann, Thomas R., *Aryans and British India* (Berkeley, CA, 1997).

Trautmann, Thomas, *Lewis Henry Morgan and the Invention of Kinship* (Berkeley, CA, 1987).

Turner, Bryan S. (ed.), *The Early Sociology of Religion. Volume I. Readings in Nineteenth Century Theory* (Routledge, 1997).

Turner, Frank M., *Contesting Cultural Authority. Essays in Victorian Intellectual Life* (Cambridge, 1993).

Vidyalankar, Pandit Harishchandra (ed.), *Maharshi Dayananda Sarasvati ka Jivan Charitra* (Delhi, 1972).

Visram, Rozina, *Ayahs, Lascars and Princes* (London, 1986).

Viswanathan, Gauri, *Masks of Conquest: Literary Study and British Rule in India* (London, 1989).

Ward, Alan, *A Show of Justice: Racial 'Amalgamation' in Nineteenth Century New Zealand* (Auckland, 1973).

Wolf, Eric R., *Europe and the People without History* (Berkeley, CA, 1982).

Wright, Harrison M., *New Zealand 1769–1840: Early Years of Western Contact* (Cambridge, MA, 1967).

Young, Robert, *Colonial Desire. Hybridity in Theory, Culture and Race* (London, 1995).

Young, Richard Fox, *Resistant Hinduism: Sanskrit Sources on Anti-Christian Apologetics in Early Nineteenth-century India* (Vienna, 1981).

Young, R. F. and S. Jebanesan, *The Bible Trembled: the Hindu–Christian Controversies of Nineteenth-century Ceylon* (Vienna, 1995).

Zimmermann, Francis, *The Jungle and the Aroma of Meats. An Ecological Theme in Hindu Medicine* (Berkeley, CA, 1987).

Articles

Ballantyne, Tony, 'The mission station as "the enchanter's wand": Protestant missionaries, Maori and the notion of the household', *Archaeological Review from Cambridge*, 13 (1994), 98–112.

Ballantyne, Tony, 'The "Oriental Renaissance" in the Pacific: Orientalism, language and ethnogenesis in the British Pacific', *Migracijske Teme: a Journal for Migration and Ethnic Studies*, 15 (1999), 423–50.

Ballara, Angela, 'Porangahau: the formation of an eighteenth-century community in Southern Hawke's Bay', *New Zealand Journal of History*, 29 (1995), 3–18.

Barnes, Andrew E., 'Aryanizing projects: African collaborators and colonial transcripts', *Comparative Studies of South Asia, Africa, and the Middle East*, 17 (1997), 46–68.

Bayly, C. A., 'The first age of global imperialism, c. 1760 to 1830', *Journal of Imperial and Commonwealth History*, 26 (1998), 28–47.

Belich, James, 'Myth, race and identity in New Zealand', *New Zealand Journal of History: Koha: Essays in Honour of M. P. K. Sorrenson*, 31, 9–22.

Binney, Judith, 'Maori oral narratives, Pakeha written texts: two forms of telling history', *New Zealand Journal of History*, 21 (1987), 16–28.

Binney, Judith, 'Myth and explanation in the Ringatu tradition', *Journal of the Polynesian Society*, 93 (1984), 345–98.

Bowen, H. V., 'British conceptions of global empire, 1756–83', *Journal of Imperial and Commonwealth History*, 26 (1998), 1–27.

Burton, Antoinette, 'Who needs the nation? Interrogating British history', *Journal of Historical Sociology*, 10 (1997), 227–48.

Byrnes, Giselle, '"The imperfect authority of the eye": Shortland's southern journey and the calligraphy of colonisation', *History and Anthropology*, 8 (1994), 207–35.

Campbell, I. C., 'Culture contact and Polynesian identity in the European age', *Journal of World History*, 8 (1997), 29–55.

Comaroff, Jean, 'The colonization of consciousness', *Economy and Society*, 18 (1989), 267–96.

Curnow, Jenifer, 'Wiremu Maihi Te Rangikaheke: his life and work', *Journal of the Polynesian Society*, 94 (1985), 97–147.

David, Alun, 'Sir William Jones, Biblical Orientalism and Indian scholarship', *Modern Asian Studies*, 30 (1996), 173–84.

Dening, Greg, 'Writing, rewriting the beach', *Rethinking History*, 2: 2 (1998), 143–72.

Dirks, Nicholas, 'The policing of tradition: colonialism and anthropology in Southern India', *Comparative Studies in Society and History*, 39 (1997), 182–212.

Drayton, Richard, 'A l'école des Français: les sciences et le deuxième empire britannique (1783–1830)', *Revue Française d'Histoire D'Outre-Mer*, 86 (1999), 91–118.

Gell, Simeran Man Singh, 'The origins of the Sikh "look": from Guru Gobind to Dalip Singh', *History and Anthropology*, 10: 1 (1996), 37–83.

Hanson, Alan, 'The making of the Maori: culture invention and its logic', *American Anthropologist*, 91 (1989), 890–902.

Hatcher, Brian A., 'Indigent Brahmans, industrious pandits: bourgeois ideology and Sanskrit pandits in colonial Calcutta', *Comparative Studies of South Asia, Africa and the Middle East*, 16 (1996), 20.

Head, Lyndsay and Buddy Mikaere, 'Was 19th century Maori society literate?', *Archifacts*, 2 (1988), 17–20.

Hopkins, A. G., 'Back to the future: from national history to imperial history', *Past and Present*, 164 (1999), 198–243.

Horsman, Reginald, 'Origins of racial Anglo-Saxonism in Great Britain before 1850', *Journal of the History of Ideas*, 37 (1976), 387–410

Howe, K. R., 'The Maori response to Christianity in the Thames-Waikato area, 1833–1840', *New Zealand Journal of History*, 7, 28–46.

Howe, K. R., 'Some origins and migrations of ideas leading to the Aryan Polynesian theories of Abraham Fornander and Edward Tregear', *Pacific Studies*, 11, 67–81.

Kelly, L. G., 'Some problems in the study of Maori genealogies', *JPS*, 49 (1940), 235–42.

Lenman, Bruce, 'The Scottish enlightenment, stagnation and empire in India, 1792–1813', *Indo-British review: a journal of history*, 21 (n.d.), 53–62.

Leopold, Joan, 'The Aryan theory of race', *Indian Social and Economic History Review*, 7 (1970).

Leopold, Joan, 'British applications of the Aryan theory of race to India, 1850–1870', *English Historical Review*, CCCLLII (1974), 578–603.

McLaren, Martha, 'Philosophical history and the ideology of the Company state: the historical works of John Malcolm and Mountstuart Elphinstone', *Indo-British Review: a Journal of History*, 21 (n.d.), 130–43.

Mauriño, Mónica Quijada, 'Los "Incas Arios": Historia, lengua y raza en la construccion nacional Hispanoamericana del siglo XIX', *Histórica* 20 (1996), 243–69.

Mongia, Radhika, 'Race, nationality, mobility: a history of the passport', *Public Culture*, 11 (1999), 527–56

O'Brien, Susan, 'A transatlantic community of Saints: the Great Awakening and the first Evangelical network, 1735–1755', *American Historical Review*, 91 (1986), 811–32.

Olssen, Erik, 'Mr Wakefield and New Zealand as an experiment in post-Enlightenment Practice', *New Zealand Journal of History*, 31 (1997), 197–218.

Parr, C. J., 'Maori Literacy, 1843–1867', *Journal of The Polynesian Society*, 71 (1963), 211–34.

Parsonson, Ann, 'The expansion of a competitive society', *New Zealand Journal of History*, 14 (1980), 45–60.

Parsonson, Gordon, 'The literate revolution in Polynesian', *Journal of Pacific History*, 2 (1967), 39–58.

Paxton, Nancy, 'Mobilizing chivalry: rape in British novels about the Indian uprising of 1857', *Victorian Studies*, 36 (1992), 5–30.

Pocock, J. G. A., 'British history: a plea for a new subject', *New Zealand Journal of History*, 8 (1974), 3–21.

Pocock, J. G. A., 'History and sovereignty: the historiographical response to Europeanization in two British cultures', *Journal of British Studies*, 31 (1992), 358–89.

Pocock, J. G. A., 'The limits and divisions of British history: in search of the unknown subject', *American Historical Review*, 87 (1982), 311–36.

Reilly, M. P. J., 'John White: the making of a nineteenth-century writer and collector of Maori tradition', *New Zealand Journal of History*, 23 (1989), 157–72.

Reilly, M. P. J., 'John White. Part II: seeking the exclusive Mohio: White and his Maori informants', *New Zealand Journal of History*, 24 (1990), 45–55.

Rendall, Jane, 'Scottish Orientalism: from Robertson to James Mill', *Historical Journal*, 25 (1982), 43–69.

Rocher, Rosane, 'The career of Radhakanta Tarkavagisa: an eighteenth-century pandit in British employ', *Journal of the American Oriental Society*, 109 (1989), 628.

Sanderson, Kay, 'Maori Christianity on the East Coast', *New Zealand Journal of History*, 17 (1983), 166–84.

Sharpe, Jenny, 'The unspeakable limits of rape: colonial violence and counter-insurgency', *Genders*, 10 (1991), 25–46.

Simpson, Jane, 'Io as supreme being', *History of Religions*, 37 (1997), 50–85.

Singh, Ganda, 'Colonel Polier's account of the Sikhs', *Panjab Past and Present*, 4: 2 (1972), 232–53.

Sorrenson, M. P. K., 'The whence of the Maori: some nineteenth century exercises in scientific method', *Journal of the Polynesian Society*, 86 (1977), 449–78.

Stenhouse, John, '"A disappearing race before we came here": Doctor Alfred Kingcombe Newman, the dying Maori and Victorian scientific racism', *New Zealand Journal of History*, 30 (1996), 124–40.

Stocking, George W. Jr, 'What's in a name? The origins of the Royal Anthropological Institute: 1837–1871', *Man*, n.s. 6 (1971), 369–90.

Subrahmanyam, Sanjay, 'Connected histories: notes towards a reconfiguration of early modern Eurasia', *Modern Asian Studies*, 31 (1997), 735–62.

Talbot, Cynthia, 'Inscribing the other, inscribing the self: Hindu–Muslim identities in pre-colonial India', *Comparative Studies in Society and History*, 37: 4, 679–722.

Talwar, K. S., 'The Anand Marriage Act', *Panjab Past and Present*, 2 (1968), 400–10.

Thapar, Romila, 'The theory of Aryan race and India: history and politics', *Social Scientist*, 24 (1996), 3–29.

Trevor, J. C., 'Prichard's life and works', *Man*, 49 (1949), 124–7.

Ward, Alan, 'Historical claims under the Treaty of Waitangi', *Journal of Pacific History*, 28 (1993), 181–203.

Webster, Stephen, 'Maori *hapuu* and their history', *Australian Journal of Anthropology*, 8 (1997), 307–35.

Unpublished dissertations and papers

Ballantyne, A. J., 'Reforming the Heathen Body: C. M. S. Missionaries, Sexuality, and Maori 1814–1850' (University of Otago, BA Hons thesis, 1993).

Ballara, Angela, 'The Origins of Ngati Kahungunu' (Victoria University of Wellington, PhD thesis, 1991).

Bayly, C. A., 'Orientalists, Informants and Critics in Banaras, 1790–1860' (typescript in author's possession).

Belgrave, Michael, 'Archipelago of Exiles. A study in the imperialism of ideas: Edward Tregear and John MacMillan Brown' (University of Auckland, MA thesis, 1979).

Broadley, Shaun, 'Science, race and politics: an intellectual biography of A. K. Newman' (University of Otago, BA Hons thesis, 1994).

Byrnes, Giselle, 'Inventing New Zealand: surveying, science, and the construction of cultural space, 1840s–1890s' (University of Auckland, PhD thesis, 1995).

Head, Lyndsay, 'Te Ua and the Hauhau Faith in the light of the Ua Gospel Notebook' (University of Canterbury, MA thesis, 1983).

Jackson, Michael, 'Literacy, Communications and Social Change: the Maori case, 1830–1870' (University of Auckland, MA thesis, 1967).

Jenkins, Kuni E. H., 'Te ihi, te mana, te wehi o te ao tuhi : Maori print literacy from 1814–1855: literacy, power and colonization' (University of Auckland, MA thesis, 1991).

Keenan, Danny, 'Haere whakamua, hoki whakamuri, going forward, looking back: tribal and hapu perspectives of the past in 19th century Taranaki' (Massey University, PhD thesis, 1994).

Paterson, Lachy, 'Te Hokioi and Haiti'. Conference paper in author's possession.

Prior, Katherine, 'The British Regulation of Hinduism in North India, 1780–1900' (University of Cambridge, PhD thesis, 1990).

Reilly, M. P. J., 'John White: an examination of his use of Maori oral tradition and the role of authenticity' (Victoria University of Wellington, MA thesis, 1985).

Sethi, Anil, 'The creation of religious identities in the Punjab, c. 1850–1920', (University of Cambridge, PhD thesis, 1998).

Stenhouse, John, 'The "battle" between science and religion over evolution in nineteenth century New Zealand' (Massey University, PhD thesis, 1985).

Thomson, Jane, 'The Roman Catholic mission in New Zealand, 1838–1870' (Victoria University of Wellington, MA thesis, 1966).

Turner, Philip, 'The Politics of Neutrality: The Catholic Mission and the Maori 1838–1878' (University of Auckland, MA thesis, 1986).

Index

Aborigines 118, 120
Abraham 95
Abraham, C. J. 69–70
Adi Granth 103, 105–8, 110
Africa 130, 135
Agni 170
ahu 88
Ajmer 179
Akbar Nama 29
Allahabad 24
Allard, Hugo 56
American Oriental Society 139
amgrezi raj 173, 182, 185
Amritsar 107
Anand Marriage Act 116
anti-Catholicism 98
anti-colonialism 11, 169, 181–5
Anderson, Atholl 153
Anderson, Benedict 12
Anglicanism 148, 159, 161, 165
Anglo-French rivalry 25
Anglo-Irish settlers 36–7
Anglo-Saxon revival 39–40
Anglo-Sikh Wars 113
anthropology 79–82, 125
architecture 51–2
archives 8–13, 59, 91, 94
ardas 107
Argentina 8
ariki 60, 163
art
    South Asian 51, 131
    Maori 13, 131–2
    Pacific 131–2
Aryan 'invasion' 49, 186
Aryanism
    and the Bible 27–8
    in British nationalism 6
    in India 26–55, 146, 169–87,
        188–91, 195–6
    and Indian nationhood 49
    and military recruitment
        49–50

and mythology 136
in New Zealand 56–82, 130,
    145–6, 167–8, 195–6
in the Pacific 7, 126, 140, 188,
    195–6
in Punjab 52–5
Aryas 5, 42, 137, 169–87
Arya Samaj 176–9, 184, 190–1
Aryavarta 172, 177, 179, 183
Arnold, Matthew 41
Arnold, Thomas 40, 69
Asad, Talal 85
Asiatic[k] Researches 32
Asiatic Restriction Bill 80
Asiatic Society of Bengal 5, 26
astrology 180
Assam 78
Atkinson, A. S. 74–5
atua 130, 165
aukati 162–3
Australasia 56, 146
Australia 2, 6, 18, 56, 80, 90, 119,
    120
Awadh 102

babu 46
Ballantyne, J. R. 47
Ballara, Angela 149
Banerjea, Krishna Mohan 173, 176
banians 25
Banaras 136
Banaras Sanskrit College 46–7
Banks, Joseph 32, 57–8, 88–90, 94,
    193
Barrier, N. G. 108
Barstow, R. C. 73
Bastian, Adolf 75
Basu, Rajnarayan 183
Bay of Islands 11, 138, 152, 192
Bayly, C. A. 10, 24, 181
Beaufort, L. C. 37–8
Belgrave, Michael 76
Belich, James 76, 159

Bengal 7, 20–5, 49, 137, 170–189, 176, 181–4, 185, 190, 191–2
Berar 100
Best, Elsdon 15, 16, 78, 79, 80, 124, 128, 135–6, 138, 167, 194
Bhagavad-Gita 96
BJP 187
Bible 11, 28
  Maori engagement with 151–3, 165–8
  New Testament 148, 165
  Old Testament 148, 165–68
  as an 'Oriental text' 28–9, 58, 60–1
Biblical criticism 125
Bihar 20
Bingham, Hiram 139
Binney, Judith 148, 166
Blavatsky, Madame 53
Blyth, W. H. 73, 130–1
Bombay Gazette 134
Bopp, Franz 62, 67, 70
Bouchet, Jean 95
Bourke, Ulick 38
Bowen, C. C. 80
Bowen, Sir G. F 69, 133–4
Brahma 95
Brahmans 85, 95–6, 99, 100–1, 104, 139–41, 145, 171, 173–4, 177–8
British empire
  analytical models 1–3, 14–17, 188–97
Britishness 2–3, 40–1, 69–70, 98, 189
Brockington, John 171
Brothers, Richard 41
Brown, William 138
Browne, James 102, 111
Bryant, Jacob 29
Buchanan, Claudius 98
Buchanan, Francis 22, 34
Buck, Peter (Te Rangi Hiroa) 79
Buddhism 105, 137
Buller, James 93, 139
Bunsen, Baron 42
Burke, Edmund 32
Burma 137, 194

Caird, Edward 125
Calcutta 15, 16, 23, 48, 136
Caldwell, Rev. Robert 50

Calvin 117
Cambridge 60
Campbell, Ian 151
Caroline Islands 87
Carroll, James 142–3
caste 54, 139
  and history 97, 104
  and Maori 129, 138–42
  and military service 49
  in Pacific 60, 140–1
  in the Vedas 171–2
Catholicism 86, 93, 98, 140, 148, 158–9, 165
Celticism 6, 12, 35–8, 41, 69
Chatterjee, Bankimchandra 183
Chatterjee, Partha 184
Chattopadhyay, Tarinichandra 184
Chatham Islands 166
Chidester, David 86, 118
Chinese 28, 81–2
Chiplunkar, Vishnu Krishna 182
Christianity 82–7
  and comparative mythology 125
  and Maori 144, 148–68
  racialization of 45–6
  and the Vedas 173–6
  vernacularization of 84, 86, 91, 119, 142, 148, 159–60
Church Missionary Intelligencer 132, 133
Church Missionary Society 58–61, 90–4, 106, 152–3, 159
citizenship 80–1
Clark, Henry Martyn 115
Clarke, George 155
Cleave, Peter 163
Colebrooke, H. T. 21, 24, 30–2, 174, 180
Colenso, William 93, 141, 148
College of Fort William 25–6, 30
'company Orientalism' 18–23, 25
colonial science 23–6, 48–52, 62–79
communalism 102, 111–6, 181–6
comparative mythology 125, 127–9
comparative philology
  Aryan/Dravidian opposition 50
  and Celticism 39–40, 69
  in India 26–30, 46–7, 173–4, 181
  methodology 27–9, 72, 75–6, 190

comparative philology (*continued*)
  in New Zealand   60–1, 69–71,
    132
  and Polynesian languages   57–8
  and Sir William Jones   26–30, 71
  in Southeast Asia   33–5
Cook, Captain James   18, 57–8,
    89–90, 150–1, 193
Cook Islands   128
Cook, S. B.   14
Cowell, E. B.   44–5
Cox, Lindsay   150
Craik, George Lillie   60
Crawfurd, John   34–5, 47, 62, 65
Cunningham, Alexander   53–4
Cunningham, J. D.   53, 103
Cust, Robert Needham   103–5, 108

Dalits   187
Dalmia, Vasudha   170
Darwin, Charles   65
Darwinism   47, 65, 125
Das, Nobin Chandra   13
Dasa   170–1, 176
Dasam Granth   105–8
Davis, Charles   123
Davis, Richard   93–4, 153
de Brosses, Charles   56
de Commerson, Philibert   87
Defoe, Daniel   41
Degeneration
  in New Zealand   72, 77–8, 127–9
  in South Asia   30–2, 43, 48,
    50–2, 55, 97, 103–4, 174–8,
    184–5
Delhi   24, 102, 134
Dening, Greg   147
devanagari script   180
Dewaki   131
dharma   86
dialogics   109–11, 146, 192
Diderot, Denis   88
Dieffenbach, Ernst   138
Dilke, C. W.   3, 75
Disraeli, Benjamin   45
Dow, Alexander   95
Dravidian   50
Drayton, Richard   9
Duke of Buckingham   133

Earle, Augustus   93, 94, 138, 140
East India Company   18–26, 189,
    193, 195
  as *diwan*   20–1, 94
  Evangelical critiques of   98–9
  and F. Max Muller   42
Easter Island   64, 131
Eden Commission   113
Edinburgh   34
education   70
Edwards, W. F.   41
Egypt   77–8
Elephanta   64, 66
Elsmore, Bronwyn   59
Enlightenment   87–8, 90, 94–5
'ethnic theology'   29, 58–9, 64, 77
eugenics   185
Eurasia   128
Euro-Americans   146,147
Evangelicalism   91, 94, 97–9, 103–5,
    106–9, 138
evolution   65, 78, 128

Falcon, R. W.   114, 115
'fatal impact'   146, 151, 158, 169
Fenianism   70
Fenton, Francis Dart   77, 79
Fergusson, James   51–2
Findlay, John George   143–4
Finnegan, Ruth   157
Firishtah, Muhammad Qasim   29
Firth, Raymond   80, 82, 149
Fitz-Roy, Robert   120
Fornander, Abraham   75, 137, 140–1
Forster, Georg   32–3, 35–6, 193
Forster, Johann Reinhold   88, 193
Fox, Richard   111–3, 116
Fraser, Charles   70
frontiers   4, 86
Froude, J. Anthony   75
'further India'   33–5, 56

Galway   195
Ganesh   132
Garuda   132
gender
  in colonial South Asia   46, 49–50,
    53, 113, 182–3, 191
  in Maori society   136, 138

Genesis, as ethnological model 28, 39, 42, 58
German Romanticism 33–4, 190
Ghose, Aurobindo 183
Ghosha, Ramachandra 174–6, 183
Gill, William Wyatt 75, 78, 126
Ginzburg, Carlo 148
Gisborne (Turanga) 158, 161, 164
globalization 195–6
Goethe 32
Goldman, Irving 149
Gorakhnath 103
Gorst, John 165
Grant, Charles 97–9
granthis 106–7, 114
Green, J. R. 41
Grey, Sir George 10–11, 120–4
Grierson, George 189
Griffin, Lepel Henry 105, 108
Grove, Richard 14
Gudgeon, W. E. 128–9
Guha, Ranajit 10, 149
Gupta, Rajanikanti 182
Guru Gobind Singh 105, 107, 114
Guru Nanak 103–7, 114, 116

Hadfield, Octavius 64, 161
Halbfass, Wilhelm 171
Hale, Horatio 78
Haileybury 34
Halhed, Nathaniel Brassey, 23
Ham 29, 42, 77
Hamilton, Alexander 34
hapu 149–50, 151, 163
Haridwar 176
Harishchandra, Bharatendu 170, 182
Harlow, Vincent 18–9
Harrison, Peter 86
Hastings, Warren 10, 22–5, 95
Hauhauism (Pai Marire) 133–4, 165–6, 191
Hawaii 75, 88, 131, 137, 139, 140–1, 149
Hawaiki 57–9, 67, 121
Hawkesworth, John 57–8, 90
Head, Lindsay 161
Heke, Hone 120, 156
Herder 33

Hiatt, L. R. 118
Hika, Hongi 60, 120
Hindi Pradip 182
Hinduism
 Brahmanical models of 95–6
 and Buddhism 105
 and Christianity 95–6, 101, 117, 173, 176–9
 'classical' 95
 'high' (*vaidik* or *shastrik*) 94–7
 as 'jungle' 97, 99–102
 law 23, 96
 and Maori religion 130–2, 194
 and nationalism 169–87
 'popular' (*laukik*) 85, 94–7, 115–16, 117
 Shaivism 97, 104
 and Sikhism 112
 Tantrism 97, 104
 Vaishnavism 97
Hinduism Today 186
Hindu Mahasabha 185
hindutva 185
Hitler, Adolf 185
Hodgson, Brian 50
Hokianga 155
Howe, K. R. 74, 153
Howell, J. Z. 36
Howitt, A. H. 129
hui 164
Hume, David 40
Hunter, W. W. 54, 176

Ibbetson, Denzil 54
Imperial Gazetteer of India 189
Imperial Legislative Council 116
Inden, Ronald 181
'Indocentrism' 66–8, 74–81, 127, 129, 146
Indo-European 43
Indian Home Rule Leagues 179
Indian rebellion 133–4
Indian National Congress 179, 183
Indonesia 137
Indra 136, 170
Innis, Harold 12
'information panics' 10
Io 123–4, 129
Iran 28

Ireland   8, 12, 18, 19, 35–8, 146,
    194–5
Irish Enlightenment   19, 36–7
Irschick, Eugene   11, 192
Islam   45, 106, 132, 133, 184
Israelites   145
iwi   142, 149, 151, 156, 161, 163–4

Jaffrelot, Cristophe   185
Jagat Seth   25
Jaipur   173
Jameson, R. G.   153
*janam-sakhi*s   104
Japhet   29, 42
Jats   108, 114
Java   78, 132, 137
Jones, Sir William   5–6, 23, 26–30,
    42, 44, 99, 174, 180, 188–9, 193
    influence   32–6, 39, 56–7, 60, 66,
        67, 71, 77
Jury, Te Whatahoro   123, 167

Kabir   103
Kadir, Abdullah Abdul   71
Kali   131, 136
Kali yuga   176
Kapiti   163
Kames, Lord   29
Kanpur   45–6, 134
Kapur, Rajiv A.   115
Kaviraj, Sudipta   2
Kaye, J. W.   45
Kejariwal, O. P.   21
Kemble, John   6, 40
Kendall, Thomas   59–60, 92, 152
Khalsa   105, 107–8
khande ki pahul   114–15
Khalsa, The   111
Khan, Muhammad Reza   21
Kidd, Colin   37, 58
King Country   162
King, John   152, 158
Kingitanga   133, 161–9
Knox, Robert   41
Kohimarama   164
korero 150
Kororareka (Russell)   61
Ko Te Karere o Nui Tireni   153

Krishna   95, 125, 131, 176
Krishnanagar   27

Lang, Andrew   129
Lahore   53, 106
Laing, Samuel   48, 55, 66
Lambert, A.   21
Lang, Andrew   124
Lang, J. D.   6–7, 62, 73
language
    as test for race   40, 46–8, 71–2, 78
    history of   26–31
    'fossils'   71–2
languages
    Anglo-Saxon   6, 40, 70
    Arabic   35
    Bahasa Malay   35, 60, 64, 73
    Bengali   50
    Celtic   40
    Dravidian   50, 183
    Egyptian   77
    'Greater Polynesian'   35
    Greek   27, 46, 64, 70, 188
    Hebrew   59, 61
    Hindi   30–1
    Javanese   35
    Latin   27, 46, 70, 188
    Malayo-Polynesian   62, 67
    Maori   58–66, 75, 91, 150, 152
    Persian   22–3
    Punjabi   50, 107, 108
    Rajasthani   50
    Sanskrit   5, 23, 26–33, 39, 40,
        42–3, 46–7, 64–6, 70, 99, 141,
        171–2, 174, 176–7, 180, 188
    Tahitian   58, 89
    Tamil   183
    Tongan   60
    Turanian   50–1, 53–4,
    Welsh   40
Latham, R. G.   41
Lee, Samuel   60, 64, 152
Leyden, John   35, 62
literacy   84, 86, 146–68
Logan, J. R.   62
London   15
Long, James   98
Lucknow   24

Luther, Martin 117
Lyall, A. C. 100–101

Macauliffe, Max Arthur 108–11,
   115–16, 195
Mackenzie, Colin 22
McKenzie, D. F. 148, 156–7, 168
MacMunn, G. F. 113
McLean, Donald 164
Madagascar 71, 78
Madras 192
Madurai 51
Maine, Henry Sumner 38, 48, 51–2,
   55
Majeed, Javed 22, 29
Majoribanks, Alexander 61
Malaya 18, 71, 73, 130, 137, 146
Malinowski, Bronislaw 80
Man 124, 135
mana 148, 150, 155, 163, 167
Manu 131
Maori
  as Africans 77–8
  and alienation of land 143, 146,
    158, 161, 163
  and art 131
  as Aryans 11, 62–8
  Christianity 63, 92, 124
  and commercialization of
    knowledge 122
  compared to Tahitians 88–90
  as conservative 68
  depopulation 72–3, 79, 122, 146,
    158
  flag 163
  first encounters with Europeans
    150–1
  and the French 159
  and Ganesh cult 132
  as 'Gangetic' 78–9
  and gender 136, 138
  as Hamites 77
  idols 132
  and Io 123–4
  'irreligious nature' of 116
  Malay connection 60, 62, 67, 73
  material culture 121, 154–5, 169
  meaning of 150–1

  as 'mixed race' 64–6
  and monotheism 123–4
  mythology 120
  'native teachers' 158, 160
  newspapers 148, 153, 154–6
  as 'obstacle' to colonization
    72–3
  oral traditions 58, 67, 91, 123–4,
    147–8, 157
  and 'Oriental despotism' 60
  and pan-tribalism 161, 163
  as 'Peruvians' 73
  political discourse 120
  prophetic movements 151
  religion 63, 118–69
  and social change 157
  'secret cults' 134–5
  sectarianism 158–61
  and Semitic theory 58–65, 77
  and sexuality 135–6, 138
  social organization 149–50
  and textualization of culture
    119–25, 129–30, 133, 142, 145,
    192
  as Tiu/Hurai (Jews) 148, 164–8,
    191
  as Turanians 73–4
marae 88, 143, 156, 158
Marsden, Samuel 59, 94
Marsden, William 34–5, 36, 62
Marshall, William Barrett 61
martial races 49–50, 113
masculinity 50, 53
Massey, Gerald 77–9
matakite 166–7
Mathura 176
Maui 126, 127, 131
Maungapohatu 134, 143
Maunsell, Robert 61, 165
mauri 121–2
Metcalf, Thomas 45
Metcalfe, Sir Charles 52
Methodism 148, 159, 165
'military Orientalism' 113
Mill, James 12, 99, 139
Mill, J. S. 9
millennialism 134–5, 147
miscegnation 80–1, 104

missionary ethnography 58–62, 90–4
Mitcalfe, Barry 157
Mitra, Tarinicharan 25
mleccha 171–2
modernity 9
moko (tattooing) 61, 90
Monier-Williams, Monier 96, 103, 137
Moorehead, Alan 147
Moses 95
Mughals 20, 185
Muir, John 46–7, 50, 66
Müller, F. Max 6, 12, 15, 38, 41–4, 75, 125–7, 140, 173, 176, 180–1, 193
    influence of 52–3, 55, 56, 66, 70
munshi 172
Murihuku (southern South Island) 150
Mussolini, Benito 185

Nadia 23
Nagas 79, 194
Natal 80
nation-state 1, 80–2
    India 49
    New Zealand 63
nationalism
    British 2–3, 40–1, 69–70, 98, 189
    Hindu 169–87
    Maori 161–8
    Pakeha 75, 80–2
    and Sikhism 103
Nazism 33, 185
networks 1–17, 193–6
    Anglo-French 69
    Edward Tregear 75
    Georg Forster 32–3
    Ireland–India 36
    John White 120
    migration 81
    Samuel Peal 78–9
    Sir William Jones 32–3, 36
Newman, Alfred Kingcombe 13, 17, 80–1, 131–2, 135–8, 141–2, 194
New Zealand 12–13, 15–16, 56–7
    Chinese migration 80–1
    colonization of 63, 69, 121, 134
    Exhibition (1865) 67

Gujaratis in 81
Institute 68–9, 75
nationalism 75, 80–2
and the Pacific 16
Parliament 144, 154
Parsis in 80
Sikhs in 80
and South Asian migration 80
Wars 118, 122, 133–4, 160, 165, 193
New Zealand Herald 75
Ngai Tahu 124
Nga Puhi 92, 120, 149, 155
Ngaruawahia 164
Ngati Haua 163
Ngati Kahungunu 164
Ngati Porou 89
Ngati Toa 163
Nigeria 8

Oberoi, Harjot 112, 114
O'Brien, Henry 38
O'Halloran, Slyvester 37
'Oriental renaissance' 76
Orientalism
    authority of 67
    Company 18–55, 97
    classical sensibility of 23, 27, 30–2, 99–100
    critiques of 97–9
    dailogics of 109–11
    empirical turn 100–2
    and military 50, 111–16
    Saidian model 14, 116, 188
origins
    British 41, 190
    Celtic 39–41, 190
    of humanity 28–9, 31, 39, 58, 60–1
    Irish 36–9
    Maori 57–82, 137, 141–2, 167–8, 19
    Polynesian
    South Asians 47, 179–81, 190
Orissa 20, 137
Osborne, W. T. 112
Otago 71, 72
Otaki 161
Oxford 39, 42

Pacific
  'caste' in 60, 140–1
  cross-cultural contact in 87–8
  as extension of India 13, 16, 56–7,
      60, 62, 66–7, 78, 82
  religion in 87–9, 128
Page, Jesse 141
Paihia 152
Pailin, David 125
pandits 23–5, 27, 95–6, 172
Pani 170–1
Panini 31, 48
Panjab Notes and Queries 16, 115
Papatuanuku 126
Paraea, Hone 155
Parihaka 134, 167
pare 132
Parsis 80
Parsons, Lawrence 37
Parsonson, Gordon 147
Patriots 35–6
Parkinson, Sydney 89
Parry, Benita 11
Patna 111
Paxton, Nancy 46
Peal, Samuel E. 13, 17, 78–9, 135–6,
    194
Pere, Wi 144
Persia 136
Peru 73
Peshawar 53
Petrie, George 38
phallus worship 38, 79, 87, 118,
    134–8, 174, 176
Pictet, Adolphe 40
Pocock, J. G. A. 2
Polack, Joel S. 61
Poliakov, Leon, 7
Pollock, Sheldon 33
Polynesian Society, The 16, 79
Pompallier, Bishop 93, 159
Porangahau, 149
Porter, Andrew 14
Potatau, Te Wherowhero 162–3
Poverty Bay 134
Prichard, James Cowles 38–41, 190
  influence 56–7, 66
Priestly, Joseph 95
Prior, Katherine 10

print culture 12–3, 32, 63, 68, 84,
    110, 124, 148, 152–68
Protestantism 83–4, 86, 95, 98, 140,
    144–5
Punjab 49–50, 52–5, 113, 137, 172,
    178, 192
purbia 114
Puranas 100, 108, 183

Queensland 69
Queen Victoria 162, 182

race 4, 39–40
  and aesthetics 37–8, 51–3
  Aryan (*see* Aryan above)
  Aryan-Mongolic 137
  'Barata' 71–4
  and character 113
  Chinese 7
  and climate 47, 49
  Caucasian 129
  and diet 47, 49–50, 113
  Dravidian 50–1, 71, 78, 183, 189
  'Gangetic' 78, 131, 137
  Hamitic 60, 77
  'Himalic' 78
  and hybridization 131
  immutability of 50
  Indo-Pacific 67
  and intermarriage 50–1, 64–5, 67,
    140
  Japhetic 43
  Madagascan 71
  Malay 71, 73, 78, 133, 134
  martial races 113, 114
  Masai 78
  'Mon-Anam' 78, 135
  Mongolic 129, 131, 137
  Native American 88, 130
  'Negroid' 72, 77, 78
  Papuan 67, 78
  and Punjabis 112–13
  and religion 45–6
  Semitic 33, 41, 48, 59, 64–5
  and Sikhism 112
  Tibetan 71
  Turanian 50–1, 53–4, 71, 72,
    73–4, 130–1, 176
rahiras 107

Raffles, Stamford   34
Ragozin, Zenaide   49
*rahit-nama*s   107
Rai, Lala Lajpat   183
Rajasthan   172
Ramlochan, Pandit   23
Ranade, Mahadeva   183
rangatiratanga 162
Ranginui (Rangi)   123, 126
Rashtriya Swayamsevak Singh   185
Rask, Rasmus   38–9
Rawene   155
Raychaudhuri, Tapan   7, 170, 181–2, 185
Rebellion, 1857   44–8
Reilly, M. P. J.   122
religion
  Aboriginal   118
  and degeneration   127–8
  and evolution   125–7, 144
  Heliolatry   127
  and hybridization   131
  'infidel'   93
  meaning of   4, 83–7, 123
  and monotheism   95–7, 102–6, 123–4, 129, 174–5
  'natural'   101, 125, 127, 135
  paganism   88–9
  Polynesian   116, 131, 145
  and polytheism   139, 175
  priesthood   88–9, 94, 97
  'primitive'   116, 125, 135
  and print   83–7
  and race   45–6, 101
  and rebellion   132, 133, 142–4
  scripture   88, 94–5
  'secret cults'   134–5
  and sexuality   135
  solar mythology   126–7
  Sotho-Tswana   118
  'superstition'   91
  as a system   85–7, 90–5, 100–1
  and textualisation of culture   86–7, 119
  Xhosa   118
  Zulu   118
Rendall, Jane   6
Reeves, William Pember   81
Risley, H. H.   54

Roberts, Gwyneth Tyson   114
Robertson, William   34
Rongowhakaata   161
Rousseau, Jean-Jacques   88
round towers   38
Royal Asiatic Society of London   173–4
Royal Irish Academy   37–8
Rua Kenana   134, 143, 151, 167, 191
Ruapehu   133
Russell, W. H.   45

Said, Edward   14, 116, 188
Sakhi Sarvar   109
Salmond, Ann   90
Salsette   64, 66
Sanderson, Kay   161
Sanskrit (*see under* languages)
Sanskritic tradition   49
'Sanskritocentrism'   31–3, 55
Sarasvati, Dayananda   176–9, 184, 190
Sarda, Har Bilas   179, 190
Satan   93–4, 97
Scotland   6, 33–4
Scottish Enlightenment   19, 33–5, 72–3, 190
Schlegel, Frederich von   32, 34
Scrafton, Luke   96
Sen, Keshab Chandra   173
Sen, Krishna Bihari   173
'settler self-fashioning'   35–8, 57, 69–70
sexuality   46, 97–8, 134
Shem   29
Shiva   175
Shortland, Edward   67–8, 120, 121, 156
Shuckford, Samuel   29
Singapore   71
Sikhism   53, 80, 85, 94, 102–17
  and caste   105
  and Christianity   102–3, 117
  Evangelical critiques of   106–9
  and Hinduism   102, 105, 115–17
  historiography of   102
  and Islam   105
  and military recruitment   112, 114
  and militarism   114

and racial determinism 112
as 'Reformation' 102–3, 105, 107,
    109–11
'Singh' 112, 114
Simpson, Jane 123, 124
Sinclair, Keith 151
Singh, Bhai Prem 111
Singh, Bhai Sant 111
Singh, Maharaja Ranjit 112
Singh Sabha 112, 114
Smith, Percy S. 15, 78, 79, 80, 167
Smith, Vincent A. 53
Society for the Promoting Christian
    Knowledge 96
Society for the Propagation of the
    Gospel 45–6
Solvyns, Baltazard 21
Sorrenson, M. P. K. 59, 63, 66
South Africa 118, 120
Southeast Asia 18, 34–5, 71–3, 78–9,
    195–6
Stack, James 93, 159
Stocking, George W. 69
Stubbs, William 41
Subaltern Studies 2
Sutton, Douglas 149
swastika 13, 17, 131

Tahiti 87–9, 149
Tahitians 87–9
Tainui 163
Taitokerau 150
Tamati Waka Nene 120, 156
Tamil revivalism 183
Tane 136
tapu (tabu) 58, 61, 86, 91, 118,
    121–2, 124, 129, 138–42, 164, 194
Taranaki 134, 160, 165
Tarkachudamani, Sasadhar 182
Tarkavagisa, Radhakanta 24
Tat Khalsa 85, 111, 113–17
Taylor, Richard 63–6, 70, 71, 73,
    127–8, 192–3
Te Arawa 120
Te Heuheu, Iwikau 162
Te Kooti Arikirangi 134, 151, 166–7,
    191
Temple, Richard 54
Te Pukuatua, Henare 155

Te Rangikaheke, Wiremu Maihi 120
Te Rauparahau 163
Te Takurua 122
Te Tarapipi, Wiremu Tamihana 163
Te Ua 165–6, 191
Te Whiti-o-Rongomai 134, 151,
    167, 191
Thames-Waikato region 153
Thapar, Romila 171
Theosophy 76
Thomson, A. S. 130
Thomson, J. T. 70–4, 78
Thorpe, Benjamin 6, 40
Tibet 177
Tieck, Ludwig 33
Tikanga Hou 160
tiki 64, 66, 135–6
Tikopia 149
Tilak, Balwantrao Gangadhar
    179–81
tipuna 150
Tod, James 182, 190
Tohu 151
tohunga 119, 123, 130, 139–40, 142–5
Tohunga Suppression Act 119,
    142–4
Tongariro 133
*Transactions and Proceedings of the New
    Zealand Institute* 68–74, 92–3
translation
    and religion 86–7, 106–7
    in South Asia 23, 106–7
    in New Zealand 89
    in the Pacific 89
Trautmann, Thomas 7–8, 19, 29, 47
Tregear, Edward 68, 74–7, 79, 80
'Teutonmania' 40–1
Treaty of Waitangi 63, 148, 156,
    162
Trumpp, Ernest 106–8, 110
Tuhoe 124, 135, 138, 143, 194
tuna 136
Tupaia 58, 89–90
Turner, Nathaniel 153
Tylor, E. B. 16, 78, 127, 193

Uma 131, 136
Uawa (Tolaga Bay) 89–90
Ullathorne, W. B. 159

Upanishads 175
Urewera 134–5
utu 150

Vallancey, Charles 19, 36, 40
Varuna 170
Vedas 5, 27, 32, 52–3, 104, 125,
　　170–87
　as 'Bible' 95
　Brahmans and 95–6
　dating of 181
　and race 171–2
　Rig Veda 5, 42–3, 46, 126, 170–1
　Vedic 'golden age' 31, 43, 97, 100,
　　174, 177, 179–80, 184–5, 189–90
Vidyalankar, Mrtyunjay 25
Vigne, V. T. 112
Virjananda 176
Vishnu 127, 132
Viswanathan, Gauri 16
Von Humboldt, Wilhelm 62

Waiapu 142
waiata 150
Waikato 161
Wai puia (hot springs) 155
Wairoa 165
Waitangi Tribunal 149
waka 149, 163
Wales 6, 41
Walker, Joseph Cooper 32, 36

web as model for empire 14–17, 82,
　145–6, 194–5
Wellington 16
Wellington Philosophical Society 75
Wellesley, Governor-General 20, 22,
　25
Wesleyan Missionary Society 158
whakapapa 149–50, 167, 191
Whakarewarewa 155
whaling 121
whanau 121, 149–50
whare 162
whare wananga 89, 91
White, John 121–3, 128
White New Zealand Defence League
　81
Whitmore, G. S. 80
Wilford, Francis
Wilkins, Charles 96, 102–3, 111
Williams, Henry 160
Williams, William 93, 94, 153, 158,
　161, 165
Wilson, H. H. 22, 100
witchcraft 144
Wolf, Eric 1
Wood, Sir Charles 45
Wright, Harrison 151

Yama 126

Zoroastrianism 48